Business Cycle Economics

Business Cycle Economics

Understanding Recessions and Depressions from Boom to Bust

Todd A. Knoop

 PRAEGER

AN IMPRINT OF ABC-CLIO, LLC
Santa Barbara, California • Denver, Colorado • Oxford, England

Library of Congress Cataloging-in-Publication Data

Knoop, Todd A.
   Business cycle economics : understanding recessions and depressions from boom to bust / Todd A. Knoop.
      pages cm
   Includes bibliographical references and index.
   ISBN 978–1–4408–3174–4 (hardback) — ISBN 978–1–4408–3175–1 (ebook) 1. Business cycles. 2. Economic forecasting. 3. Business cycles—United States. I. Title.
HB3711.K627   2015
338.5'42—dc23   2014039254

ISBN: 978–1–4408–3174–4
EISBN: 978–1–4408–3175–1

19 18 17 16   2 3 4 5

This book is also available on the World Wide Web as an eBook.
Visit www.abc-clio.com for details.

Praeger
An Imprint of ABC-CLIO, LLC

ABC-CLIO, LLC
130 Cremona Drive, P.O. Box 1911
Santa Barbara, California 93116-1911

This book is printed on acid-free paper ∞

Manufactured in the United States of America

To my family:
Deb, Edie, and Daphne.

The long run is a misleading guide to current affairs. In the long run we are all dead. Economists set themselves too easy, too useless a task if in tempestuous seasons they can only tell us that when the storm is past the ocean is flat again.

—John Maynard Keynes, *A Tract on Monetary Reform* (1923)

In the middle of the last century, a great dispute arose among astronomers respecting one of the planets. Some, in their folly, commenced a war of words, and wrote hot books against each other; others, in their wisdom, improved their telescopes and soon settled the question forever. Education should imitate the latter.

—Horace Mann, *Lectures on Education* (1855)

Contents

PART III. FINANCIAL INSTABILITY AND FORECASTING

PART IV. BUSINESS CYCLES IN THE UNITED STATES

PART V. MODERN INTERNATIONAL RECESSIONS AND DEPRESSIONS

List of Figures and Tables

FIGURES

TABLES

Preface

A police officer sees a drunken man walking unevenly down the sidewalk, swerving from one side to the other. He stops the man and decides to conduct a sobriety test. "Walk in a straight line," he demands. The drunk responds, "I'd be happy to, just stop moving the damn line!"

Capitalist economies often behave like this drunk—they have trouble moving in a straight line despite the interventions of economists and policy makers. The real consequences of these economic lurches are often devastating. Not only do recessions and depressions reduce standards of living and increase poverty, but they undermine the public's confidence in the benefits of capitalism and often democracy. As we saw during the global financial crisis that began in 2007 or the Euro-zone debt crisis that began in 2009, economic downturns and their lingering slow-growth aftermaths have the potential to spread fear, encourage xenophobia, and undermine international political and economic systems that have taken decades to develop. Understanding the nature and causes of business cycles in an effort to develop policies to eliminate them is a noble, but difficult, endeavor with potentially enormous implications for human welfare.

The study of business cycles has greatly contributed not only to our understanding of economic contractions but also to our understanding of macroeconomics in general. To the uniformed it might seem that economists are no closer today to understanding business cycles than they were 200 years ago, still fruitlessly demanding the economy to "walk a straight line." However, while our knowledge is still far from complete, when business cycle theory is examined within a historical context it becomes obvious that major advancements have been made. The periodic occurrences of financial crises and dramatic economic slowdowns point both to the validity of much of our knowledge about the nature of business cycles and also to areas that need to be further explored before economists can fully understand economic fluctuations and enact appropriate policies to prevent them.

Studying business cycles is also important because debates over their causes and consequences continue to dominate political discussions and policy debates. These political debates, often directly related to the proper size and role of government, are highly charged. The fact that both John Maynard Keynes's *General Theory* and Friedrich Hayek's *The Road to Serfdom* recently shot to the bestsellers lists decades after their initial publication attest to the interest that politicians and the public have in economic theory. In the words of Keynes, "Practical men, who believe themselves to be quite exempt from any intellectual influence, are usually the slaves of some defunct economist" (Keynes 1936).

This book covers the empirics, the theory, and specific case studies of recessions and depressions. This book is written in a nontechnical narrative aimed at upper-level undergraduate students or general readers with some background and interest in economics. It strikes an appropriate balance between being readable and being rigorous, while at the same time broadly covering the study of business cycles without sacrificing a deeper understanding of the root causes of macroeconomic volatility. As a result, it should have broad interest for use in college courses on Business Cycles, Financial Macroeconomics, Intermediate Macroeconomics, and the History of Macroeconomic Thought, as well as be of interest to a more general audience interested in better understanding the nature of recessions and depressions.

While this book does not necessarily challenge any current thinking in the field of business cycle research, it contributes to the ongoing debate over the nature and causes of recessions and depressions by gathering together the basics of business cycle research and synthesizing it in an understandable and interesting way. This book aims to encourage a deeper understanding of the wide range of issues that surround business cycles. In addition, I hope that this book will generate interest in business cycles so that the next generation of economists will want to investigate questions related to economic contractions.

Given that many of the economic policies related to recessions and depressions—particularly the public policy issues related to the role of government in preventing (or encouraging) them before they begin and ending them once they start—the reader might be curious as to whether I have an ideological viewpoint on the causes and consequences of economic contractions. When it comes to the many economic theories dealing with business cycles, I think that you need to appreciate *all of them* in order to fully understand the causes and consequences of business cycles. The approach here is to take a balanced view of competing theories and then weigh these alternative theories based on empirical evidence. In this book, the evidence will be weighed without placing "a thumb on the scale" and will emphasize pragmatism over ideology.

This book grew out of research that I conducted for an upper-level undergraduate course that I taught at Cornell College entitled Recessions and Depressions. As I was thinking about how to organize this course, I searched for an appropriate textbook. Somewhat surprisingly, I found nothing that was satisfactory for use in an upper-level undergraduate course on business cycles. As a result, I wrote this book to fill this niche. Outside of this book, no other text covers the empirics, the theory, and international case studies of recessions and depressions. In addition, no other book on business cycles is written in a nontechnical narrative aimed at the upper-level undergraduate student or the general reader with some background and interest in economics.

Of course, the seismic economics events that have occurred over the last decade have necessitated new thinking about business cycles in the economics profession, and this book incorporates this new thinking. This new thinking does not make economists flip-floppers—it makes them scientists. As John Maynard Keynes said, when asked if he was being inconsistent when he changed his mind on economic questions over time: "When the facts change, I change my mind. What do you do, sir?" This book includes the newest research and thinking in many fields including new work on the impact of financial crises, behavioral economics, and the causes of the 2008 global financial crisis and 2009 Euro-zone debt crisis. The material and data in every chapter has been updated in order to accurately reflect the dramatic changes in business cycle theory and empirics that have occurred over the last few years.

A number of people were of great help to me in writing both editions of this book, and I am indebted to each of them. Numerous students in my courses provided feedback, including students in my Recessions and Depressions courses. In particular, I would like to thank Linchaun Zhang, who not only provided me with thoughtful insights but also spent many hours putting together (and very carefully improving) the figures used in this book. I would also like to thank Cornell College for awarding me the Campbell R. McConnell Fellowship and Massier Social Science awards which provided many of the resources that were needed to produce this book.

PART I

The Facts of Business Cycles

ONE

Why Study Business Cycles?

INTRODUCTION

Consistent with the popular conception of economics as the "dismal science," economists secretly long for recessions and depressions. Not in any real or concrete sense, for as a general rule economists are not sadists and do not enjoy seeing people suffer through the kinds of hardships experienced by countries that are going through an economic crisis. However, when it comes to the state of economic knowledge, nothing improves economists' understanding of how markets and macroeconomies work more than an economic downturn. The most obvious analogy is to an auto mechanic who learns his craft not by working on cars that are running well but by getting under the hood of autos that have broken down. Much the same can be said of economists. Recessions and depressions are essentially the only substitute that macroeconomists have for an experiment; when markets break down so completely, the underpinnings of what is actually driving the operations of fully functioning economies become more readily apparent. Economic contractions are an opportunity for economists to pop open the hood and take a look inside the engine of modern economic systems.

The best example of the learning opportunities afforded by economic crises is the Great Depression, an unprecedented economic downturn of such a massive scale that it turned the whole discipline of economics on its ear. The Great Depression played a crucial role in the development of macroeconomics as a separate field of study from microeconomics, and also in the development of Keynesian economics, the most fundamental change in the way that economists think about the world since 1776 when Adam Smith published *The Wealth of Nations*. Keynesian economics in turn spawned some of the most radical developments in public policy since the Industrial Revolution and provided the theoretical foundation for the modern welfare state. It also provided the impetus for conservative critiques of the expanded role of government, from Friedrich Hayek to Milton Friedman. Of course, the global financial crisis that occurred in 2008 led many to wonder whether we were going to suffer through a second Great Depression and also whether time-tested policies to combat business cycles need to be rethought.

This book will provide in-depth analyses of the following three questions:

1. Why are economies subject to periods of negative output growth (recessions)?
2. How do you explain severe economic contractions (depressions)?
3. What government policies can be used to moderate and prevent business cycles, or is government policy the cause of, not the solution to, business cycles?

As mentioned above, many of the key developments in macroeconomic theory both before and after Keynes have centered on these questions. The big problem, unfortunately, is that after more than 200 years of debate there is still no general agreement about what causes recessions and depressions. There continue to be multiple competing models of business cycles used among economists. In fact, there is often a disconnect between the models used by academics and those used by private-sector economists. This debate over the root causes of business cycles continues to be a key question in the development of macroeconomic thought. The goal of this book is not to put an end to this debate by providing a definitive answer on why business cycles exist, because there is no single answer at this point and business cycles are complex enough that there never will be. Rather, this book aims to understand all of the competing theories and factors in the debate so that the reader understands the full context in which these debates take place.

For an example of how disagreements persist in macroeconomics, consider the United States' recession of 1990–1991. Some economists have argued that it was caused by an aggregate demand downturn resulting from a reduction in consumer confidence during the Gulf War or by a decrease in the money supply by the Federal Reserve. Others have argued that it was caused by a decrease in aggregate supply brought about by an increase in the price of oil during the war or the delayed effects of tax increases and new government regulations adopted in the late 1980s. To this day, there is no single cause that is generally agreed upon among economists.

Another example of the discord among economists is evident in their handling of the East Asian crisis from 1997 to 1999, at that time the most significant international economic crisis since the Great Depression. Economists did not forecast the East Asian crisis. Most disturbingly, there was no agreement at the time among economists about which policies should be adopted to best deal with the crisis. In fact, the crisis occurred in countries that were previously thought to be model economies that were fundamentally sound.

Then, of course, there is the 2008 global financial crisis. Not only did most economists fail to see it coming, but many refused to believe their eyes as it happened. Once again, economists as a group had no clear and unified set of policies to deal with the downturn, although, in the end, influential policy makers who were well-versed in business cycle theory did piece together solutions (in a somewhat less than timely manner) that did contribute to the recovery. Clearly, there is still much work to be done before economists can come to any sort of consensus about the causes of recessions and depressions and provide clear prescriptions for how to deal with them once they begin.

Given the obvious difficulties inherent in this topic, in the past many people have asked: Why study business cycles if, in the long run, they all average out? This is a question that is only asked by someone who has not lived through a major economic contraction—very few of us today. Business cycles are extremely costly to a society, not just in terms of lost income but in terms of disrupted lives—higher suicide and homicide rates, higher poverty levels, and higher divorce rates amongst other measures of well-being—that have economic, social, and personal consequences that persist for a very long time. During the global financial crisis, the most vulnerable groups in American society—minorities, the poor, the less educated—were disproportionally impacted, worsening economic inequality. Economic uncertainty caused birth rates in the United States to drop to historic lows. Jobs lost during recessions led to a deterioration of labor skills that has had long-lasting effects on productivity and unemployment. Whole communities, from new suburbs in Florida to the entire city of Detroit, were devastated and, in some cases, have disappeared. Keynes's (1923) response to the question posed at the beginning of this paragraph is one of the classic retorts in all of economics. "Now 'in the long run' this is probably true. . . . But this long run is a misleading guide to current affairs. In the long run we are all dead. Economists set themselves too easy, too useless a task if in tempestuous seasons they can only tell us that when the storm is long past the ocean is flat again."

OUTLINE OF THE BOOK

This book is divided into five sections.

Part I: The Facts of Business Cycles. Chapter 2 describes business cycle data both quantitatively and qualitatively. This chapter provides a summary discussion of the duration and depth of business cycles, both in the United States and internationally, with a focus on seven basic facts about business cycles. In addition, the behavior of the components of gross domestic product (GDP) over the business cycle is also described, including a discussion of how economists separate the cyclical components of data from trend. Finally, this chapter summarizes the cyclical behavior of other important macroeconomic time series variables, including whether each variable is a reliably leading, coincident, or lagging indicator of turning points in a business cycle.

Part II: Macroeconomic Theories of Business Cycles. The evolution of thought on the nature of business cycles also traces the evolution of a large part of modern macroeconomic theory. In order to comprehend macroeconomics as it is practiced today and where it is headed in the future, it is crucial to understand the theoretical ground already covered and the economic events that precipitated changes in the way that we view macroeconomic fluctuations.

Part II presents seven primary models: the classical model (Chapter 3), the Keynesian model (Chapter 4), Austrian economics (Chapter 5), the monetarist model (Chapter 6), the rational expectations model (Chapter 7), the real business cycle model (Chapter 8), and new Keynesian models (Chapter 9). For each of these models, the relevant chapter discusses (1) the historical context in which the model was developed, (2) the basic theory behind the model, which includes a description of how the model explains business cycles, (3) a discussion of the policy implications of the model, and (4) a look at whether existing empirical research supports the model's principle implications. Each of these models is discussed in a rigorous but nontechnical narrative with an emphasis on making the discussion accessible to the general reader or undergraduate student.

To briefly preview our discussions from this section: the study of modern business cycles began in the 1930s with Keynesian economics, which focused on the macroeconomic effects of market failure. Before Keynes, early business cycle theories (including the classical model) failed to make a clear distinction between the behavior of individuals and the behavior of economies as a whole. However, these early theories did highlight many important characteristics of economic contractions. After a neoclassical resurgence during the 1970s and 1980s, business cycle research has returned to the study of market failure. However, the newest business cycle models have greatly improved upon the microeconomic explanations of why markets often do not work efficiently and the specific role that various forms of imperfect competition play in output fluctuations. While these new models are more intuitively appealing and are more consistent with the empirical data, they have not yet improved the ability of economists to forecast the future or to preemptively act in order to prevent recessions and depressions.

Every chapter in this book provides suggested readings that can be used to supplement this text. The purpose of these suggested readings is four-fold. First, they offer readers a chance to expose themselves to some of the seminal, but more accessible, research in the business cycle field. Second, they allow readers to explore the insights of groundbreaking economists in their own words in order to better understand the important contributions these authors made. Third, they give readers an idea about how economists talk to each other, as difficult as it may be to interpret these discussions at times. Finally, these readings give readers the benefit of working through a piece of research and all of its difficulties by themselves as opposed to having material presented to them in easily digestible ways. Each of these readings has been chosen because it is written at an appropriate level for an advanced undergraduate student and is either an important article in the business cycle field or is written by significant authors in the field who are providing an overview of an area of research.

Part III: Financial Instability and Forecasting. As evidenced by the 2008 global financial crisis and the ongoing Euro-zone debt crisis, financial crises continue to be one of the defining aspects of modern economics and are associated with the largest recessions and depressions. This part of the book focuses on explanations of business cycles that focus on the financial sector as either the cause or the propagating mechanism for economic volatility. Chapter 10 examines a number of models that emphasize financial market failures, fluctuating financial fundamentals, and changes in the supply of credit as the driving force behind business cycles. This chapter includes a review of the debt-deflation theory of Irving Fisher, the financial instability hypothesis of Hyman Minsky, the financial accelerator model of Bernanke and Gertler, and a model of credit rationing developed by Stiglitz and Weiss.

Next, our attention in Chapter 11 turns to behavioral economics and its role in driving asset bubbles and banking crises. Behavioral economics refers to the use of psychological research to critically examine the economic decision making of individuals in order to determine the extent to which these decisions are "predictably irrational" and the economic implications when this is the case. This chapter weighs alternative theories about whether banking crises and asset bubbles are driven by beliefs or fundamentals. This chapter also examines the costs of banking crises and asset bubbles and the potential role of monetary policy in preemptively preventing, or at least minimizing, their impact.

This part of the book concludes with Chapter 12, which provides an overview of the four primary macroeconomic forecasting techniques— macroeconomic and market-based indicators, econometric models, structural models, and dynamic stochastic general equilibrium models—and their generally poor record in forecasting actual business cycles. Given the emphasis on beliefs and behavior in the discussions on financial crises, it is legitimate to question is whether reliable macroeconomic forecasting is ever possible. This chapter concludes with a discussion of this question, including a discussion of the nature of economic uncertainty and the extent to which macroeconomic behavior is inherently predictable (i.e., characterized by statistical uncertainty) or unpredictable (i.e., characterized by fundamental uncertainty).

Part IV: Business Cycles in the United States. The first chapter in this section, Chapter 13, deals with the Great Depression, primarily from the United States' standpoint but also its international ramifications. While many possible factors will be examined as potential causes of the Great Depression, the primary explanation in this chapter centers on four facts. First, all countries that experienced a depression were on the gold standard and maintained fixed exchange rates. Second, there were severe balance-of-payment inequities in place when the gold standard was restored after World War I. Third, asymmetries in the way the gold standard was administered made it unstable. Finally, a massive international deflation was the result of a strict adherence to the gold standard and naïve macroeconomic policy. This chapter explains in detail the theory behind why deflation is so costly, especially in terms of its effects on financial intermediation. It also compares this explanation with traditional Keynesian, Austrian, and monetarist explanations of the Great Depression.

Chapter 14 deals with postwar business cycles in the United States up through the mid-2000s. After a brief case study of each of these business cycles is a discussion of how postwar business cycles differ from pre–Great Depression business cycles. The basic conclusion of this section is that while there have not been any dramatic changes, postwar business cycles have occurred less frequently and have been slightly shorter than prewar business cycles. Finally, this chapter discusses the reasons for this moderation, including various forms of structural change in the economy as well as the increased role of macroeconomic stabilization policy in mitigating (or magnifying) business cycles.

Part V: Modern International Recessions and Depressions. This section will investigate four recent international economic crises. First, the East Asian crisis is discussed in Chapter 15. After a brief description of other recent currency crises (Mexico in 1994, Latin America in the 1980s, and the European Monetary System in 1992), the East Asian crisis is compared to these previous crises. The critical difference is that the East Asian crisis was actually two distinct crises in that it was a currency crisis that occurred in conjunction with a banking crisis. The large devaluations that resulted from the currency crisis led to complete collapses of fragile banking systems throughout the region, resulting in capital flight, a massive reduction in financial intermediation, and a severe decline in economic activity. Chapter 15 describes this process is in detail. This chapter also investigates the culpability of foreign investors and the International Monetary Fund (IMF) in precipitating the crisis. Finally, recommendations for economic reform in East Asia are discussed and comparisons made between the Great Depression and the East Asian crisis.

Chapter 16 examines the decade-long recession in Japan that began in the early 1990s. The Japanese economy, including the nature of its inefficient markets and fragile banking system, is characterized. This is followed by an examination of the reasons for deflation in Japan and the failure behind macroeconomic stabilization to end this recession. This chapter concludes with a description of economic policy reforms that the Japanese have been reluctant to enact in order to fully recover from this extended recession.

The next chapter, Chapter 17, turns its attention to sovereign debt crisis, in particular the Euro-zone debt crisis. It examines the causes and consequences of sovereign debt crises and looks at the reasons behind their frequent occurrence in history. This is followed by a detailed look at the Euro-zone debt crisis that began in Ireland and Greece in 2009 before spreading through multiple southern European countries. An evaluation of the claims that a similar debt crisis is building in the United States completes the chapter.

The final case study in this section of the book is included in Chapter 18, which examines the 2008 global financial crisis. This crisis became the largest economic crisis to strike developed nations since the

Great Depression. This chapter examines the buildup to the crisis, which was primarily driven by three factors: (1) financial innovation in the form of securitized home mortgages and financial derivatives, (2) the trade and savings imbalances between China and the United States that fueled excessive debt and asset bubbles, and (3) a misunderstanding of the nature of financial risk within our increasingly globalized financial markets. These factors fueled a lending boom in the Unites States that set the stage for housing and bond bubbles and a banking crisis that had unexpectedly large consequences. Next, the timeline of the events precipitating the crisis in the United States are discussed, and the U.S. government's frequently chaotic and experimental policy responses to the crisis are examined. While macroeconomic policy was largely effective, it could not prevent a long-lasting recession and one of the slowest postrecession recoveries in U.S. history; some possible reasons for this will be evaluated. Many other countries outside of the United States were also severely impacted. While Europe was an obvious victim, the tiny economy of Iceland might have been the most severely impacted and is discussed here as an excellent case study of the dangers of modern unregulated global finance. This chapter concludes with some lessons learned and an evaluation of the reforms that have been implemented as a result of the crisis.

The main conclusion that can be gained from these international case studies is that the study of major international contractions is a somewhat different topic than the study of business cycles in general. There are three major distinctions between recessions and major contractions/depressions (apart from just their size). First, major contractions/depressions tend to be international in nature, not primarily isolated to just one country. Second, major contractions/depressions tend to involve the collapse of financial markets in general and the banking industry in particular. Third, major contractions/depressions almost always begin with some sort of macroeconomic policy mistake in the form of runaway monetary and fiscal policy, misaligned exchange rates, deregulation of financial markets, or all of the above. The Great Depression, the East Asian crisis, the Great Recession in Japan, the Euro-zone crisis, and the 2008 global financial crisis each followed this general pattern. Business cycle research has yet to develop a unified model that adequately incorporates each of these factors.

The final chapter, Chapter 19, is a brief conclusion in which the history of economic theory on business cycles is reviewed and the principle insights that have been gained from the study of business cycles are discussed. This is followed by a list of questions which economists are still struggling to provide answers to—questions that serve as signposts to guide future economic research on business cycles.

TWO

Describing Business Cycles

INTRODUCTION

It is important to have a good grasp on the empirical regularities (and irregularities) of key macroeconomic variables that fluctuate as the economy contracts and expands. Understanding the data of business cycles will provide some basic empirical facts that we can then use to evaluate the competing theories that have attempted to provide explanations to the three primary questions posed in this book: (1) Why are economies subject to periods of negative output growth (recessions)? (2) How do you explain severe economic contractions (depressions)? (3) What government policies can be used to moderate and prevent business cycles, or is government policy the cause of, not the solution to, business cycles?

The first purpose of this chapter is to describe the quantitative aspects of business cycles, meaning the depth and duration of both individual and average economic contractions and expansions. The second purpose of this chapter is to describe the qualitative aspects of business cycles, meaning how different macroeconomic variables move in relation to each other during contractions and expansions. While the focus in this discussion is primarily on the United States, international business cycle data will also be examined.

BASIC DEFINITIONS

Economists from the Business Cycle Dating Committee of the National Bureau of Economic Research (NBER), the preeminent economic research organization in the United States, date the beginning and end of

Figure 2.1   Real GDP growth in the United States, recessions noted.

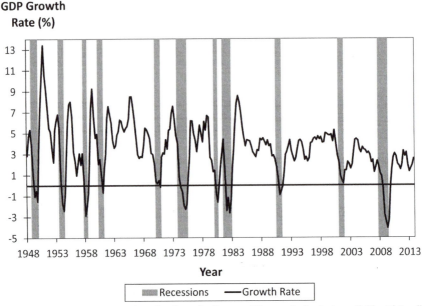

GDP Growth Rate (%)

Source: Author's creation based on data from the Bureau of Economic Analysis available at https://www.bea.gov/national/xls/gdplev.xls, and the National Bureau of Economic Research available at http://www.nber.org/cycles.html.

economic contractions and expansions in the United States. To do this, the NBER needs a working definition of what constitutes a recession and an expansion. The NBER defines a *recession* as when "a significant decline in economic activity spreads across the economy and can last from a few months to more than a year." The *peak of an expansion* is the point in time at which the level of GDP reaches its maximum before it starts to decline. Thus, the peak of an expansion dates the beginning of a recession. Likewise, the *trough of a recession* is the point in time at which GDP falls to its lowest level before it begins to rise again, meaning that a trough dates the beginning of an expansion. Figure 2.1 graphs real GDP growth rates in the United States between 1948 and 2013, where the shaded areas denote the period of time during which the economy was in recession (i.e., the period between the peak and the trough of the business cycle).

Table 2.1 provides a complete list of business cycles (measured from peak to peak) in the United States since dating began in 1854. Looking at recent business cycle episodes, there have been 11 postwar recessions in the United States. The last recession was associated with the global

Table 2.1 Timing and depth of U.S. business cycles.

Trough	Peak	Duration (in months) of Contraction	Duration (in months) of Expansion	Cycle (trough to trough)	Decline in GDP (peak to trough)
	12/1854	—	—	—	—
06/1857	12/1858	18	30	48	—
10/1860	06/1861	8	22	30	—
04/1865	12/1867	32	46	78	—
06/1869	12/1870	18	18	36	—
10/1873	03/1879	65	34	99	—
03/1882	05/1885	38	36	74	—
03/1887	04/1888	13	22	35	—
07/1890	05/1891	10	27	37	—
01/1893	06/1894	17	20	37	—
12/1895	06/1897	18	18	36	—
06/1899	12/1900	18	24	42	—
09/1902	08/1904	23	21	44	—
05/1907	06/1908	13	33	46	—
01/1910	01/1912	24	19	43	—
01/1913	12/1914	23	12	35	—
08/1918	03/1919	7	44	51	—
01/1920	07/1921	18	10	28	—
05/1923	07/1924	14	22	36	—
10/1926	11/1927	13	27	40	—
08/1929	03/1933	43	21	64	−26.7%
05/1937	06/1938	13	50	63	−18.2%
02/1945	10/1945	8	80	88	−12.7%
11/1948	10/1949	11	37	48	−1.7%
07/1953	05/1954	10	45	55	−2.6%
08/1957	04/1958	8	39	47	−3.7%
04/1960	02/1961	10	24	34	−1.6%
12/1969	11/1970	11	106	117	−0.6%
11/1973	03/1975	16	36	52	−3.2%
01/1980	07/1980	6	58	64	−2.2%
07/1981	11/1982	16	12	28	−2.7%
07/1990	03/1991	8	92	100	−1.4%
03/2001	11/2001	8	120	128	−0.3%
12/2007	6/2009	18	73	91	−5.1%

(*continued*)

Table 2.1   (continued)

Trough	Peak	Duration (in months) of			Decline in GDP (peak to trough)
		Contraction	Expansion	Cycle (trough to trough)	
Averages					
1854–2001 (32 cycles)		17	38	55	
1854–1919 (16 cycles)		22	27	48	
1919–1945 (6 cycles)		18	35	53	−19.2%
1945–2009 (11 cycles)		11	58	69	−2.3%

Source: Adapted from National Bureau of Economic Research available at http://www.nber.org/cycles.
html and the Bureau of Economic Analysis available at https://www.bea.gov/national/xls/gdplev.xls.

financial crisis, lasting from December 2007 until June 2009. Before this, the previous recession began in March 2001 and ended in November of that same year, making it one of the shortest recessions in American history. Preceding the 2001 recession, the United States experienced the longest expansion in its history. This expansion lasted more than 10 years, from March 1991 to April 2001.

The NBER's definition of what constitutes a recession has been criticized along a number of lines. One problem with this definition is that a lag exists between getting data and making decisions. Output must be falling for at least "a few months" before the NBER will declare a recession. In practice, the economy has typically been in a recession for at least six months before it has been officially recognized as one by the NBER. For example, the recession that began in the United States in December 2007 was actually not recognized as such by the NBER until December 2008, a full year after it began. This recognition lag might delay a policy response until it is too late to be effective.

Another criticism of this definition is that it ignores *growth recessions*, or periods of positive but below-average growth. The problem here is that a period of growth that is below *trend*, or the long-run average GDP growth rate, is generally regarded as a recession by the public but not technically considered a recession by economists. For example, economists timed the end of the global financial crisis as occurring in June 2009, but the vast majority of the public considered the United States to be in recession until well into 2012 because real GDP growth, while positive, was weaker than trend.

Despite these criticisms, these definitions of recessions, peaks, and troughs are the ones that economists have chosen to work with. Lags in getting and interpreting data are impossible to avoid given the difficulties in collecting economic data. Defining a growth recession is more difficult than defining a recession using the NBER's definition. This is because the definition of a growth recession relies on measuring growth relative to its trend, and measuring trend output growth is imprecise if the trend is not constant over time (as we will discuss in more detail in a moment). As a result, the NBER's definitions of recessions, expansions, troughs, and peaks will be the working definitions used throughout this book.

There is no formal definition of a depression, although an old joke is that a recession is when your neighbor loses their job, a depression is when you lose yours. An informal definition is an economic contraction in which output falls by more than 10 percent. During the era for which we have reliable economic data, the only depression that has occurred in the United States was the Great Depression of the 1930s.

A few additional definitions are extremely useful in characterizing the qualitative relationships between macroeconomic variables over the business cycle. Economists are always looking for macroeconomic variables that can help predict the peaks and troughs of business cycles. A *leading indicator* is a variable that peaks (troughs) before GDP peaks (troughs). For obvious reasons, economists closely watch leading indicators when trying to forecast business cycles. A *lagging indicator* is a variable that peaks (troughs) after GDP peaks (troughs). A *coincident indicator* is one that peaks or troughs at the same time as GDP.

One final set of definitions is extremely useful. A variable is referred to as *procyclical* if its deviations from trend have a positive correlation with deviations in GDP trend; in other words, when GDP is below trend, a procyclical variable is also below trend and vice versa. Some obvious examples of variables that are procyclical are consumption, investment, and employment. A variable is *countercyclical* if deviations in the variable from its trend are negatively correlated with deviations of GDP from trend. Unemployment is an obvious example of a variable that is consistently countercyclical and rises above its trend when GDP falls below its trend. An *acyclical* variable is one that has no consistent correlation with changes in GDP from trend.

DETRENDING: SEPARATING CYCLE FROM TREND

Identifying short-run cyclical movements in macroeconomic variables is problematic because most macroeconomic data is subject to changes along a trend over time. For example, real per-capita GDP growth in the United States has averaged slightly less than 2 percent a year over the last 150 years. As a result, we cannot attribute all changes in GDP to the business cycle. In essence, economists measure short-run behavior as a residual: It is the movements in the actual data that are not related to trend behavior. To calculate the cyclical component of macroeconomic data, the movements consistent with trend behavior must be subtracted out of the data we collect. Doing this is referred to as *detrending* the data. Using detrended data is crucial when trying to identify cyclical behavior, for example when determining whether a variable is procyclical or countercyclical, as discussed above.

Identifying the trend behavior within macroeconomic variables is the first and most important step in detrending and deriving cyclical economic data. Two simple methods of detrending data are commonly used in macroeconomics:

(1) Assuming that trend is constant. By assuming that a variable has a constant trend, we are not assuming that the trend is necessarily linear. For example, consider the following example where the trend in GDP follows an exponential process:

$$\overline{Y}_t = a(1 + \overline{g})^t \tag{2.1}$$

where $\overline{Y}_t$ is the trend level of GDP at time t, $\overline{g}$ is the constant growth rate of GDP, and a is a constant. While trend GDP is growing at a constant rate, notice that the level of trend GDP is growing exponentially over time. Note that while the level of trend GDP is not linear, taking the natural log of trend GDP in this equation is linear. As a result, economists will often refer to the specification in equation (2.1) as being "linear in logs." Equation (2.1) is generally consistent with GDP's actual behavior, as illustrated in Figure 2.2.

After calculating the average periodic growth rate for GDP over time ($\overline{g}$) (which in the United States is equal to .036632, or approximately 3.67 percent), we can then use equation (2.1) to estimate trend GDP, or $\overline{Y}_t$. The cyclical component of GDP is then determined by calculating the difference between actual GDP and trend GDP, that is, $Y_t - \overline{Y}_t$.

(2) Assuming that trend follows a moving average. By assuming a moving average trend, trend is not necessarily restricted to being constant but can vary over time. When using moving averages, economists typically assume that they are centered around the period in question. For example, the centered five-year moving average trend of GDP in 2012 would be calculated as

$$\overline{Y}_{12} = \frac{(Y_{10} + Y_{11} + Y_{12} + Y_{13} + Y_{14})}{5} \tag{2.2}$$

There are two problems with using moving average trends. First, when using a centered moving average you cannot calculate trend for the most recent data because you are missing future observations. For example, you cannot calculate GDP trend in 2014 using the method in equation (2.2) until 2016 because you will not have the data available. Typically, economists will estimate these missing observations for future years, often by using a constant growth rate derived from previous years.

The second problem with using moving averages is that they are sensitive to the number of periods over which the moving average is calculated. Trend measured by a 5-year moving average will be much more variable than trend measured by a 10-year moving average. This will, in turn, make the cyclical movements in GDP less variable for a 5-year moving average. This is a crucial problem because there is often no clear choice for how long moving average calculations should be. One standard assumption when dealing with GDP data is to use a 30-quarter moving average when

Figure 2.2   Real GDP against an exponential trend.

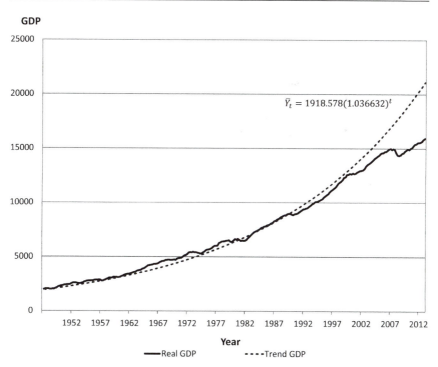

$$\bar{Y}_t = 1918.578(1.036632)^t$$

Year

— Real GDP   ---- Trend GDP

calculating trend GDP because, as can be seen in Table 2.1, 30 quarters is the average length of a business cycle (measured from trough to trough).

It is important to note that putting macroeconomic data measured over time into percentage changes is not a method of detrending the data. Transforming GDP into percentage changes involves subtracting this period's observation from last period's observation, known as *first-differencing* the data, then dividing by the previous value; that is,

$$\%\Delta Y_t = \frac{(Y_t - Y_{t-1})}{Y_{t-1}} \qquad (2.3)$$

Note that when using this method, the percentage change in GDP will not fluctuate around zero; it will fluctuate around the positive trend growth rate of GDP, as in Figure 2.1. As a result, transforming the data into growth rates is a method of making a variable *stationary*, meaning that it will fluctuate around a steady trend. When used by itself, however, it is not a method of detrending data. To calculate the detrended growth rate, one would have to take the current growth rate of GDP and subtract out the trend growth rate of GDP calculated via one of the two methods (constant trend or moving average) discussed above.

SEVEN BASIC BUSINESS CYCLE FACTS

What general properties and relationships can be gathered from studying business cycle data? Seven basic facts are crucial to understanding the fundamental properties of business cycles in the United States and internationally.

1. *Business cycles are not cyclical.* The term *business cycle* is really a misnomer because it implies that recessions and expansions follow a regular, predictable pattern. They do not. In fact, business cycles vary considerably in size and duration over time. Refer to Table 2.1. The shortest recession in United States history was in 1980–1981 (though it was a very sharp recession) and lasted only 6 months. It was followed by the shortest expansion, which lasted only 12 months. The longest modern recession lasted 43 months between 1933 and 1937, while the longest expansion ended in 2001 and lasted 121 months, or more than 10 years. In between these shortest and longest recessions and expansions there is a wide variety of business cycle lengths. Clearly, the length of the previous

business cycle is not a reliable indicator of the length of the next business cycle.

In addition, the size of the decline in GDP associated with post-war business cycles has also varied greatly, from a fall of nearly 27 percent during the Great Depression to a fall of only 0.3 percent during the 2001 recession.

2. *Business cycles are not symmetrical.* In the United States, expansions average 39 months in length while recessions average only 18 months. Thus, expansions are about twice as long as recessions on average. However, output changes tend to be much bigger during recessions than they are during expansions.

These same asymmetries between recessions and expansions hold internationally as well. Figure 2.3 and Figure 2.4 provide some summary data of business cycles across a small subset of developed countries. Looking at Figure 2.3, notice that across all of these countries expansions last considerably longer than recessions. There is a great deal of similarity across these countries in terms of the length of their

Figure 2.3   Average duration of expansions and recessions.

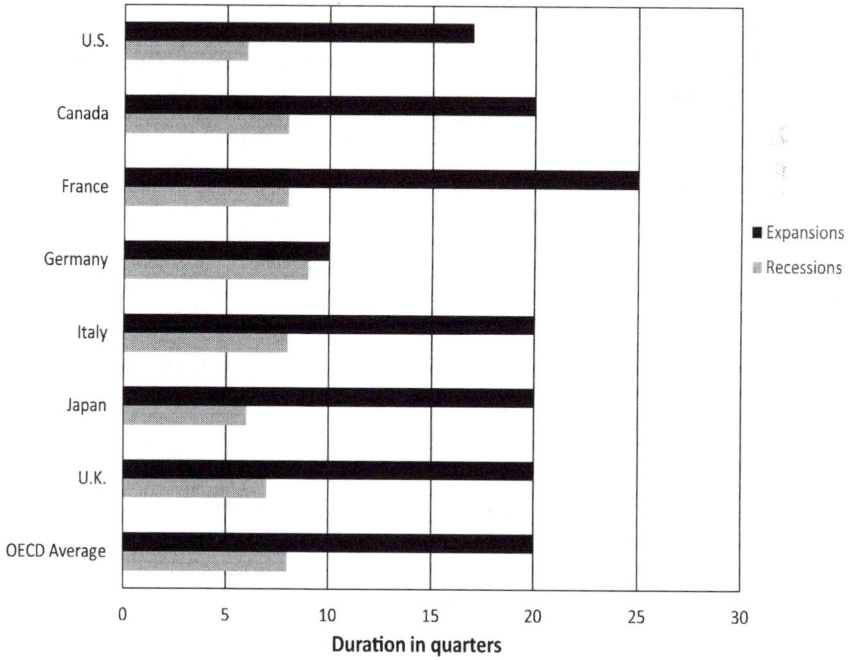

Source: Author's creation based on data available in Chauvet and Yu (2006).

Figure 2.4   Monthly percentage changes in industrial production during business cycles.

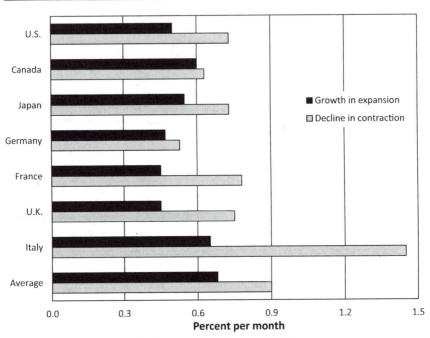

Source: Author's creation based on data available in Artis et al. (1997).

recessions, but slightly more variation in terms of the length of expansions. Figure 2.4 presents percentage increases and decreases in industrial production across countries. Recessions tend to be characterized by larger changes in output than expansions. Thus, as a general rule across countries, recessions tend to be shorter but with sharper changes in GDP, while expansions tend to be longer but with more gradual changes in GDP.

3. *Business cycles have changed over time.* Newer and better historical data has given economists a clearer picture of historical business cycles in the United States, and this better data suggests that postwar recessions have moderated, particularly in regards to their length. A quick glance at the data averages reported at the bottom of Table 2.1 suggests that recessions are about half the length they were in the prewar period, while expansions have gotten significantly longer. This means that recessions have been less frequent than they were in previous eras, although this result has been largely driven by two long expansions in the 1980s and 1990s. In addition, the

declines in output associated with postwar recessions appear to have been smaller. The moderation of business cycles, and an examination of its causes, will be discussed in more detail in Chapter 14 on postwar business cycles in the United States.

4. *The Great Depression and the World War II expansion dominate all other recessions and expansions.* GDP fell by nearly 27 percent in 1929–1933, while unemployment rose to a peak of 25 percent in 1933. The fluctuations of the 1930s and 1940s dwarf the next largest recession, the global financial crisis of 2008, in which GDP declined by 5.1 percent and unemployment rose to 10 percent. Likewise, the expansion that began in 1938 and continued throughout World War II was unparalleled, with GDP rising by 64 percent between 1941 and 1944. The explanation for this large expansion obviously had a lot to do with the huge increases in government purchases and the massive mobilization of resources that took place during the war. The explanation for the Great Depression is less apparent. Obviously, something unprecedented happened during the late 1920s and 1930s that must be explained in order to have a plausible theory of what causes recessions and depressions. The Great Depression will be discussed throughout this book and will be most closely examined in Chapter 13.

5. *The components of GDP exhibit behaviors much different than GDP itself.* The components of GDP are consumption, investment, government purchases, and net exports. Investment, durable consumption, and net exports are highly volatile and change more than output over the business cycle, while nondurable consumption and government purchases are more stable and change less than output over the business cycle.

   Table 2.2 presents the components of GDP and their contribution to both average GDP growth and to changes in GDP during recessions. Consumption includes both nondurables (like food and clothing), durables (like appliances and automobiles), and services. Both nondurables and services contribute less to falls in GDP than they do to the level of GDP, meaning that they are considerably more stable than GDP as a whole and, in fact, are only mildly procyclical. Durables, however, are significantly more volatile than GDP as a whole, strongly procyclical, and a coincident indicator of peaks and troughs in GDP.

   Investment as a whole is consistently procyclical, a leading indicator of changes in GDP, and about 3.5 times more volatile

Table 2.2 Behavior of the components of GDP.

Component of GDP	(%) Average share in GDP	(%) Average share of fall in GDP during recessions
Consumption		
Durables	8.9	14.6
Nondurables	20.6	9.7
Services	35.2	10.9
Investment		
New residential	4.7	10.5
Fixed nonresidential	10.7	21
Changes in inventories	0.6	44.8
Net exports	−1	−12.7
Government purchases	20.2	1.3

Source: Author's creation based on data from the Bureau of Economic Analysis available at https://www.bea.gov/itable/index.cfm.

than GDP. Investment includes new residential construction, fixed nonresidential investment (investments made by firms), and changes in inventories. Looking at Table 2.2, we see that each of the components of investment is considerably more volatile than its share of GDP, together accounting for more than 75 percent of the changes in GDP during recessions. Especially important are inventories, which account for less than 1 percent of GDP but more than 40 percent of the changes in GDP during recessions. Inventories are also a leading indicator of business cycle turning points. Investment clearly plays a crucial role in initiating and propagating business cycles. As a result, investment has also played an integral part in many of the theories of business cycle behavior.

Government purchases include government acquisitions of goods and services but ignore transfer payment programs such as social security and welfare. Government purchases are mildly countercyclical in the United States and not very volatile.

Finally, net exports are the difference between exports and imports. Net exports are actually a negative share of GDP because the United States has consistently run trade deficits since the mid-1980s. Net exports are slightly countercyclical, meaning that net exports tend to rise during recessions and offset some of the falls in output. This is in part because exchange rates tend to fall during a recession, decreasing the price of exports and increasing the price of imports. However, net exports, while volatile, are not a reliable indicator of peaks and troughs in GDP.

6. *Business cycles are associated with big changes in the labor market.* Unemployment is strongly countercyclical, and changes in employment are much larger during recessions than the changes in other inputs into production. Over the long run, increases in the capital stock account for roughly one-third of trend per capita GDP growth while increases in productivity account for the other two-thirds. Changes in employment account for little of the increases in trend per capita GDP (this makes sense if employment and the population grow at roughly the same rate, which they do). However, during business cycles (times when output is growing at a rate different than trend), the story is exactly the opposite. The capital stock changes very little over business cycles because it is largely fixed in the short run, meaning it contributes little to changes in output over the business cycle. Changes in employment, on the other hand, account for two-thirds of the cyclical changes in per capita GDP while changes in productivity account for one-third of cyclical changes. In other words, during recessions and expansions, changes in employment appear to be driving a very large share of the changes in output. This seems to suggest that any plausible theory of business cycles has to give a prominent role to the cyclical behavior of the labor market.

7. *Business cycles are larger and more frequent in poorer countries than richer countries.* The variability of output in poor countries is more than twice what it is in rich countries. According to Uribe (2013), this higher volatility is driven by the fact that consumption and net exports are more volatile in poor countries, but also by the fact that in poor countries government purchases are acyclical. In rich countries, however, government spending is countercyclical because of its use in stabilization policy. The ability to increase government spending during downturns is an option that many poorer countries do not have because they have limited access to debt markets.

Table 2.3 presents business cycle data for 12 countries in the Organization for Economic Co-operation and Development (OECD), which are developed countries, and 12 Latin American countries, which are poorer and emerging-market economies. While the length of recessions between the two groups are similar, notice that

Table 2.3   Business cycles in Latin America and OECD countries.

	Duration of contraction	Duration of expansion	(%) Decline in GDP
Latin America	3.5 quarters	16 quarters	−6.2
OECD	3.6 quarters	23.8 quarters	−2.2

Source: Author's creation based on data available in Calderón and Fuentes (2010).

expansions are roughly eight quarters longer in rich countries. This implies that recessions occur less frequently in rich countries. In addition, as mentioned before, the sizes of the contractions in GDP associated with recessions are nearly three times larger in Latin America than in OECD countries. Overall, these facts indicate that a much more volatile macroeconomic environment exists in poorer countries relative to richer countries.

THE CYCLICAL BEHAVIOR OF OTHER IMPORTANT MACROECONOMIC VARIABLES

As mentioned earlier, economists are always looking for clues to help them forecast the future and to help them evaluate competing models of business cycle behavior. A few of the most closely followed macroeconomic variables are briefly described here. The cyclical behaviors of these variables are summarized in Table 2.4.

Labor Market Variables

A worker is classified as being unemployed in the United States if he or she is currently without work and has been actively looking for work during the previous four weeks. Total unemployment is strongly countercyclical and is a lagging indicator of both peaks and troughs. Total unemployment lags peaks in output because when the economy first slows down, some workers are still finding jobs (even as new layoffs may be increasing) so that unemployment lags peaks. When the economy begins to improve, the last inputs to be re-added by firms are more workers, so unemployment also lags troughs. The lagging nature of unemployment has been particularly pronounced after the last two recessions in the United States, hence the widely recognized phenomena of a "jobless recovery."

Economists also closely follow two other variables related to unemployment. The first is the duration of unemployment, or the average

Table 2.4   Cyclical behaviors of key macroeconomic variables.

Variable	Direction	Timing
Expenditures		
Consumption	Procyclical	Coincident
Investment	Procyclical	Leading
Government purchases	Countercyclical in rich countries; acyclical in poor ones	–
Net exports	Countercyclical	Lagging
Labor market variables		
Total unemployment	Countercyclical	Lagging
Duration of unemployment	Countercyclical	Lagging
Initial unemployment claims	Countercyclical	Leading
Real wages	Inconsistent	Inconsistent
Money supply and inflation		
Money (M1) supply	Procyclical	Leading
GDP deflator inflation	Procyclical	Lagging
Consumer Price Index (CPI) inflation	Procyclical	Coincident
Financial variables		
Short-term interest rates	Procyclical	Lagging
Long-term interest rates	Procyclical	Lagging
Stock prices	Procyclical	Leading
Corporate profits	Procyclical	Leading
Capacity and productivity		
Capacity utilization	Procyclical	Leads peak, lags troughs
Productivity	Procyclical	Leading
Expectations		
Consumer Confidence Index	Procyclical	Leading

period of unemployment for those who are currently unemployed. This is countercyclical and a lagging indicator of peaks and troughs. The second is initial unemployment claims, which are the number of new claims for unemployment insurance. Initial unemployment claims are more sensitive to changes in the business cycle than total unemployment. Unlike total unemployment, which lags peaks and troughs because of lags in the hiring process, initial unemployment claims are a leading indicator because firms anticipate changes in economic conditions and increase layoffs before production falls and decrease layoffs before conditions improve.

Real wages do not behave consistently over business cycles, although changes in the real wage do consistently lag behind peaks and troughs in GDP. During the recessions of the 1970s, real wages were procyclical. During the Great Depression, real wages were countercyclical. If measured over the entire length of United States data that is available, however, real wages are mildly procyclical. Real wages also fail to consistently lag or lead business cycle turning points.

As mentioned in fact (6) earlier in this chapter, the volatility of unemployment indicates that the labor market plays a critical role in business cycles. As a result, the behavior of real wages is an integral component of many of the theories that will be examined in this book. Differences in how each of these models views the labor market provide a useful criterion by which to compare and contrast alternate explanations of business cycles. This puzzle regarding the inconsistent behavior of real wages is one that will be referred to repeatedly throughout our discussions.

Money Supply and Inflation

M1 is the most commonly used definition of the money supply, which includes currency and checkable deposits. M1 is strongly procyclical and a leading indicator of peaks and troughs in the business cycle. Federal Reserve policy largely, but not completely, determines the level of M1. The critical issue is this: Do changes in the money supply lead to changes in output, or do changes in output cause the money supply to change in ways that the Fed cannot control? These questions will be an important topic for later discussion.

There are two commonly used measures of inflation. The GDP deflator measures changes in the price of all goods produced within U.S. borders and included in GDP. Inflation as measured by the GDP deflator is weakly procyclical, only falling during 6 of the 11 postwar recessions. It lags peaks and troughs primarily because it includes investment goods and government purchases, the prices of which are slow to respond to changes in economic conditions.

The consumer price index (CPI) measures changes in the prices of consumer goods. Like the GDP deflator, it is only mildly procyclical, falling during 7 of the 11 postwar recessions. Unlike the GDP deflator, changes in the CPI are roughly coincident with business cycle turning points because consumer prices are more sensitive to changes in prevalent market conditions.

It is important to note that while both measures of inflation have been mildly procyclical on average, they have exhibited periods of countercyclical behavior as well. The variability of the cyclical behavior of inflation is a puzzle that economists need to explain.

Financial Variables

Both short-term and long-term interest rates are procyclical. However, there are a myriad of interest rates that can be tracked, and some are more reliable predictors of business cycles than others. One of the most reliable is the three-month Treasury Bill rate, which has fallen during 10 of the 11 postwar recessions. Even though many long-term interest rates are less reliable indicators of business cycles than short-term rates, they probably have a more direct effect on investment decisions and economic activity. In general, short-term and long-term interest rates are lagging indicators of business cycle turning points because inflation is a key determinant of the level of interest rates, which tends to lag business cycle fluctuations.

Stock prices are one of the most visible and closely followed macro-economic series. Stock prices are procyclical and a leading economic indicator of peaks and troughs. The same holds true for corporate profits. The problem with using the stock market to predict business cycles is that stock prices are much more volatile than GDP. Stock prices cannot be relied on exclusively when forecasting because of the high probability of false signals.

Capacity and Productivity

Capacity utilization is the employment rate of capital. For obvious reasons, capacity utilization is procyclical. Its downturns tend to lead peaks because firms typically purchase large amounts of capital during expansions, and this capital typically comes online before a downturn, reducing capacity utilization. On the other hand, capacity utilization lags troughs because firms first reduce inventories and delay new investment projects for as long as possible during downturns.

Increasing productivity, which is measured as output per worker hour, is the primary way that economies improve the standards of living of their citizens over the long run. However, in the short run, the relationship between GDP and productivity is much less clear. Productivity is procyclical, falling during 10 of the 11 postwar recessions, and it is a leading indicator of peaks and troughs in the business cycle. However, the reasons why this holds remain unclear. Do new technologies drive expansions and technological inefficiencies drive recessions? Or could it simply be that firms ask their employees and their capital to work harder during expansions because firms are pushing their capacity constraints, and then allow their workers and capital some slack during recessions because these same constraints are less pressing?

Expectations

The most popular measure of the public's expectations of future economic conditions is the Consumer Confidence Index, which is based on household survey data collected by the University of Michigan's Survey Research Center. The index is generated based on household responses to questions regarding (1) the family's economic prospects over the next 12 months; (2) the United States' economic prospects over the next 12 months; and (3) the United States' economic prospects over the next five years. This Consumer Confidence Index is strongly procyclical and a leading economic indicator. However, it is much more volatile than GDP, meaning the Consumer Confidence Index often provides false signals of business cycle turning points.

Expectations play a key role in many of the explanations of business cycles discussed later in the book because of their importance in influencing investment and consumption decisions. As a result, measures of consumer confidence are very closely watched by economic forecasters.

CONCLUSIONS

The empirics of business cycles have not been completely covered in this chapter, but in reality, this is impossible to do. New theories often provide economists with new ideas about things to look for in their economic data. Albert Einstein makes this interaction between theory and empirics quite clear in the following quote: "It is quite wrong to try founding a theory on observable magnitudes alone. ... It is the theory which decides what we can observe" (Heisenberg 1971).

The goal for economists interested in why business cycles occur and what can be done about them is straightforward: find a theory that fits the empirical facts of business cycles as they are understood. While this goal is clear, how to achieve this goal has not been. A number of different models have been developed over the past 250 years to explain the nature and causes of recessions and depressions. Many of these models generate predictions that are consistent with much (though never all) of this economic data. How do we evaluate these competing models? Is a model's ability to match economic data the only measure of its worth? Or do things like logical structure and consistency with microeconomic theory matter just as much? These are just some of the many questions that will be dealt with when the macroeconomic theory of business cycles is reviewed in the next part of this book.

SUGGESTED READING

National Economic Trends, International Economic Trends, and *Monetary Trends*: These publications are made available by the St. Louis Federal Reserve. They contain a wide variety of current macroeconomic data as well as economic analysis of the current state of the economy. They are available at http://research.stlouisfed.org/publications/.

PART II

Macroeconomic Theories of Business Cycles

THREE

Early Business Cycle Theories

INTRODUCTION

Before the Great Depression, a number of economic theories existed that elucidated the thinking of early economists about the causes of economic fluctuations. In examining these theories in this chapter, we will take the first step in evaluating just how much progress has been made in our understanding of recessions and depressions. These early theories are simple, to the point that they are somewhat naïve about the way that macroeconomics works. They each focus on a single explanation of what causes business cycles. They also focus on microeconomic phenomena and fail to explain how markets can fail at the aggregate level. However, these simple models are interesting not only for what they cannot explain about business cycles but also because of the things they identify as the key factors that drive recessions and depressions. Many of these early models provided the original insights that were then more fully developed in future, more comprehensive business cycle models.

While many theories are introduced in this chapter, the classical model is the most important of these early theories and is the primary focus of discussion. The classical model attempts to explain macroeconomic business cycles using microeconomic principles. Its clear, simple insights into the causes of business cycles are still the basis of widely held beliefs among many modern economists. However, the classical model of business cycles has also been the focus of generations of critiques and a starting point from which most modern theories have deviated. As a result, the classical model serves as a useful base model for comparing different modern models of business cycles.

EARLY AGRICULTURAL THEORIES

During times when agriculture was a much more important industry than it is today, economists focused on the cyclical nature of agricultural production to explain recessions and expansions. One of the earliest of these models is the sunspot theory developed by W. S. Jevons (1884). His theory proposed that low sunspot activity on the surface of the sun was bad for plant growth and agricultural output (which is questionable botany as well as questionable economics). As a result, Jevons believed that the cyclical behavior of economies closely followed the cyclical behavior of sunspot activity. Jevons presented historical evidence that business cycles lasted approximately 10.43 years from peak to peak, while sunspot cycles lasted 10.45 years. In his mind, this correlation proved his theory. However, new evidence was later presented that sunspot cycles in fact lasted 11 years. Jevons tried to salvage his theory by saying that because his theory was so well known by farmers, if farmers expected sunspot activity to change then they would change their behavior accordingly, breaking the link between actual sunspot activity and economic activity. While the sunspot theory is today discredited, Jevon's hypothesis that expectations can be self-fulfilling, meaning that falling expectations can lead to falling output without any real changes in the economy, anticipates later macroeconomic theories that focus on the importance of expectations and how these expectations might affect behavior.

Another influential agricultural theory was the cobweb theory, first presented by Ezekial (1938). This theory attempted to explain how shocks to supply and demand could lead to cyclical fluctuations in prices and output. There are two critical assumptions in the cobweb theory. First, goods are perishable so that farmers have to accept the current price and cannot store their output until the next period. Second, the amount farmers plant in the spring is based on what the price was last fall. This means that expectations are backward looking, not forward looking.

Figure 3.1 presents the results of a temporary negative supply shock, in which supply falls from S_1 to S_2 in the fall but returns to S_1 before the spring planting. In the spring, farmers make their planting decisions based on the higher price that existed in the previous fall, P_2, continuing until the upcoming fall. However, because supply has returned to its previous level, farmers find that they have planted too much based on their assumption

Figure 3.1   Supply and demand in the cobweb theory after a temporary fall in supply.

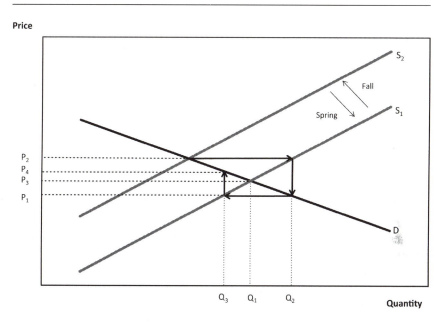

that the price would still be P_2, resulting in excess supply. In order to sell all of the crops that are available in the fall, Q_2, farmers must reduce their price to P_3 in order to clear the market. Next spring, farmers plant based on a price of P_3 and produce an amount equal to Q_3 to sell in the fall. Of course, now there is a shortage of crops because P_3 is below the equilibrium price. As a result, price rises to P_4 in order to clear the market. In the third spring, farmers plant based on the belief that the price will continue to be P_4, and the process continues. Notice that prices and quantities will eventually converge towards the equilibrium price and quantity, but this process takes a long period of time. In addition, this process is very costly because of the instability created as the market cycles between excess supply and excess demand.

The cobweb theory is not a useful explanation of the behavior of modern markets because of the two questionable assumptions on which it is based. First, most goods in modern economies, even agricultural goods, can be stored. If goods can be stored, producers do not necessarily have to accept the current price, which would smooth cyclical movements in prices and quantities. More importantly, producers are not nearly as naïve as the cobweb theory assumes. Do individuals really form their expectations of the future based only on what has happened in the past? Or are they forward looking, attempting to anticipate future market conditions? If producers are forward looking, equilibrium will be restored much more quickly. Once again the cobweb theory underscores the important role of expectations in business cycles, which plays an important role in all modern macroeconomic theories.

Malthus (1798) developed one of the best-known, and most infamous, models of economic cycles. Malthus observed that in an agricultural society such as the one that existed in Great Britain during the late 1700s, capital was primarily land, and land in an island country is fixed in quantity. In addition, given that agricultural production techniques had largely remained the same over the previous century, Malthus assumed that technological knowledge would also be constant in the future. As a result, Malthus believed that as the population in Britain rose, diminishing returns would quickly set in as the capital-to-labor ratio fell. Over time this would lead to chronic underproduction, falling standards of living, and eventually mass poverty and starvation. However, starvation does have its benefits; namely, that the capital-to-labor ratio would rise, increasing per capita income. As income rose, standards of living and general health would improve. Healthy people have more babies, and the whole process would begin again.

Of course, the problem with Malthus's analysis is that capital and technology are not fixed. Malthus never understood that an industrial revolution was taking place at the time he was writing. As a result, he did not anticipate improvements in technology and the invention of new forms of capital that have taken place over the last 200 years. Through this omission, however, Malthus's model highlighted the importance of technological change (or the lack of it) not only in stabilizing economic growth but also in potentially driving business cycles. This later possibility is the basis of real business cycle models, which are discussed in Chapter 8.

EARLY MONETARY THEORIES

Before the Great Depression, most economies in the world were on the gold standard. The gold standard was an international monetary system that required the amount of paper currency in circulation within each country to be backed by a fixed amount of gold. As a result, a country's gold holdings would place an upper limit on the quantity of money supplied within that country. One of the important implications of the gold standard was that the money supply of a country would fluctuate with its trade balance. A country that was running a trade deficit would experience gold outflows, which would eventually necessitate lowering the money supply. On the other hand, a country that was running a trade surplus would see its gold holdings rise and its money supply increase.

Hawtrey (1913) hypothesized that fluctuations in the money supply caused by changes in the trade balance were the cause of business cycles. A country that was running a trade surplus would see its money supply increase. This increased the supply of credit within an economy, increasing investment and output. However, higher output would increase the demand for imports and reduce the trade balance. Eventually, the country would begin to run a trade deficit and see its money supply contract, and the whole cyclical process would take place again in reverse. Hawtrey's model of monetary business cycles is one in which business cycles are *endogenous*, or internally self-generating. Business cycles are not the result of external, or *exogenous*, shocks to the economy. Hawtrey's solution to preventing these cyclical fluctuations was simple: Abandon the gold standard for *fiat money*, or money that is not backed by a commodity so that its supply could be stabilized.

The obvious problem with Hawtrey's theory is that business cycles have not ended since modern economies have adopted fiat money. However, by being one of the first to propose that changes in the money supply and credit drive cyclical fluctuations, Hawtrey laid the groundwork for modern, more fully developed business cycle models in which monetary policy plays a critical role, such as the Keynesian model (Chapter 4), Austrian economics (Chapter 5), and particularly the monetarist model (Chapter 6).

UNDERCONSUMPTION AND MARXIST THEORIES

Underconsumptionist economists such as Hobson (1922) worried that growth in the production of goods within an economy would outpace the growth rate of consumption. Without adequate aggregate demand to absorb these goods, the resulting chronic overproduction would threaten future economic prosperity and create business cycles.

Why would consumption growth be unable to keep pace with production growth? Hobson's underconsumption model focused on the fact that households save a larger share of their income as their income rises. As aggregate income in a country increases over time, the average propensity to consume (consumption divided by income) falls and the gap between aggregate income and total consumption increases. For a while, this gap can be filled with higher levels of investment. However, over time, this increased investment will only aggravate the excess supply of goods and reduce the average propensity to consume even further. Increasingly large excess supplies of goods will eventually necessitate cuts in production and a decrease in aggregate income. This recession leads to a rise in the average propensity to consume, eventually causing the problem of excess supply to disappear—for a while. Ultimately, though, higher aggregate income will lead to a lower average propensity to consume, and the whole process will start all over again. Thus, like early monetary theories, business cycles are endogenous in underconsumption models and not initiated by external shocks.

Marxist theories of business cycles share many similarities with the underconsumptionist viewpoint. Marx theorized that excess capital accumulation over time would reduce the profitability of businesses, leading to periodic business failures and economic contractions. Other Marxists blamed the falling purchasing power of workers that results from the inequality inevitably created by capitalism. As the purchasing power of most of the population falls relative to the size of aggregate output, persistent and destabilizing excess supply will occur.

There were a number of policy solutions offered by the underconsumptionists aimed at preventing the average propensity to consume from falling over time. One was to redistribute income from the rich to the poor who have higher propensities to consume. Another was to increase the amount of government purchases within an economy, which would increase the average propensity to consume for the public and private sectors as a whole. These underconsumption theories were very influential in the development of Keynesian economics (Chapter 4), which also focuses on aggregate demand shortfalls as the primary cause of business cycles. The fiscal policy solutions proposed by underconsumptionists are developed more fully in the Keynesian model, leading to a more complete theory of the proper role of government in stabilizing business cycles.

PROFIT MARGIN THEORIES

A *profit margin* is simply the price minus the average cost of the good. Mitchell (1927) argued that profit margins are strongly procyclical in imperfectly competitive markets because costs fall during expansions. This happens for a number of reasons. First, firms are able to reduce their inventories, reducing costs. Second, input cartels tend to fall apart during recessions, so the beginning of expansions should be characterized by lower input prices. Finally, larger output means that *economies of scale* can be exploited. Economies of scale refer to conditions when the average cost of production falls as the quantity of the good produced rises. Economies of scale tend to exist in industries with large fixed costs because higher production allows these fixed costs to be spread out over more units, reducing average cost.

Procyclical movements in the profit margin feed expansions and magnify contractions. During good times, rising profit margins increase expected profits and encourage firms to undertake investment projects. However, these projects do not immediately increase the capital stock and capacity. In the meantime, as the economy approaches full capacity, costs begin to rise and profit margins begin to fall. Falling profit margins reduce expected profits and reduce a firm's likelihood of undertaking new investment projects, eventually turning an expansion into a contraction. Once again, expectations play an important role in this model, as they do in all modern business cycle theories. In addition, profit margin theories recognize that markets are not perfectly competitive and that imperfect competition plays an important role in explaining business cycles. This later becomes a crucial component of Keynesian (Chapter 4) and new Keynesian (Chapter 9) economics.

EARLY INVESTMENT THEORIES

For as long as economists have known about fluctuations in aggregate economic activity, economists have also intuitively understood that investment is extremely volatile and an important source of economic instability. Investment volatility played an important, but secondary, role in many of the early theories already discussed. In other early theories, investment plays a more central role. Early investment theories of business cycles fall into roughly three categories. Some of these models, such as those of Hawtrey (discussed previously) and Wicksell (1936), focused on unstable fluctuations in the money supply, which creates changes in investment. In Wicksell's model, changes in the money supply push interest rates either above or below the level required for savings to equal investment. As a result, investment and output fluctuate with changes in the supply of money and bank credit.

A second category of early investment theories, also developed by Wicksell, focused on the overinvestment that results from the investment booms and busts that follow the development of new technologies. This theme is later re-examined in more detail by long-wave theories of business cycles, which are discussed in the next section.

Finally, other early investment theories focus on spending multipliers associated with investment, such as that of Clark (1917). Often referred to as accelerator models, these models center on the possibility that higher investment increases aggregate output, which in turn increases spending, which in turn leads to additional increases in investment and output. Thus, small initial changes in investment can lead to large changes in aggregate output. While these models do not explain why investment would initially change, they do explain why changes in investment could be multiplied into very large changes in output. The possibility of spending multipliers associated not only with investment but also with exogenous changes in consumption and government purchases were later to become crucial components of the Keynesian model.

THE CLASSICAL MODEL

The cornerstone concepts of the classical model were laid out in the first book to treat economics as a distinct field of study, Adam Smith's (1776) *The Wealth of Nations*. The model was further refined by many of the founding fathers of economics such as David Ricardo, Jean-Baptiste Say, and John Stuart Mill. The classical model is the most fully developed and influential of the early business cycle theories.

THE ASSUMPTIONS OF THE CLASSICAL MODEL

The classical model is founded upon three crucial assumptions.

1. *Perfect competition exists in all markets.* This means that all firms and consumers are price takers, wages and prices are perfectly flexible, perfect information exists about economic conditions, and markets always clear so that excess demand or excess supply cannot persist.
2. *Real values, not nominal values, are used when making decisions.* In other words, money illusion does not exist, and agents adjust all nominal variables by changes in the price level before they act.
3. *The economy is composed of representative agents, or individuals that all have the same preferences and act alike in every way.* When combined with the assumption of perfect competition, the assumption of representational agents means that macroeconomic behavior becomes a simple summation of average microeconomic behavior. In other words, the classical model does not make any real distinction between macroeconomic and microeconomic behavior.

Output Determination and the Labor Market in the Classical Model

In the classical model, capital and labor are combined using a production function to produce aggregate output. Let Y denote real aggregate output, L denote total labor employed, and K denote the total capital stock. The production function can then be written in the following form:

$$Y = F(L, K) \qquad (3.1)$$

This production function is in *Cobb–Douglas* form. It is easy to show that this production function exhibits both *constant returns to scale*, meaning that doubling both capital and labor will double output. However, each individual input is also subject to *diminishing marginal returns*. Diminishing marginal returns refers to the property that if the quantity of one of the inputs in production is fixed, the additional units of output that are produced by increasing the other input will get smaller as the quantity of that input rises. In other words, the *marginal product of labor*, the change in output from a change in labor, falls as the quantity of labor rises. Diminishing marginal returns is one of the cornerstone concepts in economics because it implies that a firm's ability to increase output is limited unless it can increase all of the inputs to production.

Diminishing marginal returns play an important role in the classical labor market. The equilibrium real wage (denoted as $\frac{W}{P}$) in the classical model is determined by the supply and demand for labor. The demand for labor is determined by firms, who hire labor until the marginal benefit of an additional unit of labor, or the marginal product, is equal to the marginal cost of an additional unit of labor, or the real wage. Diminishing returns imply that the marginal product of labor falls as the quantity of labor rises. As a result, firms will only hire more workers (and accept a lower marginal product) at a lower real wage, meaning that the demand curve for labor must slope downward.

Regarding labor supply, changes in the real wage have two effects. The first is the substitution effect, in which a higher real wage induces more workers to enter the workforce or work longer hours. The second is the wealth effect, in which a higher real wage increases wealth and reduces the incentives to work. The classical model assumes that the substitution effect of an increase in the real wage is larger than the wealth effect so that a higher real wage increases labor supply and the labor supply curve is upward sloping.

In equilibrium, real wages adjust in the classical model so that the quantity demanded of labor equals the quantity supplied. Notice that only the things that affect the quantity of labor, the quantity of capital, or the production function (i.e., things that shift the labor supply or labor demand curves) will affect the level of aggregate output. Thus, changes in output in the classical model must be driven by changes in these three factors, each of which influence the aggregate supply of goods produced within an economy.

Factors that influence the quantity of labor. Immigration and population growth are two obvious determinants of the quantity of labor supplied within an economy. Public policy is also an important influence on labor supply and labor demand because it can play a role in shaping individuals' incentives to work. For example, income taxes on workers reduce the supply of labor, while taxes on payrolls reduce the demand for labor. Likewise, government regulations that place costly restrictions or requirements on firms (such as health and safety requirements) can also reduce labor demand and the quantity of labor.

Factors that influence the quantity of capital. Anything that encourages firms to invest in capital will increase aggregate output, while anything that discourages investment will decrease aggregate output. Once again, tax policy and government regulations play an important role in shaping the incentives to invest. Public policy also plays a critical role in determining how much households save. Tax policies that favor consumption as opposed to saving (such as an income-based tax system instead of a consumption-based tax system) will reduce the total amount of savings and the quantity of funds that are available for investment, reducing the quantity of capital. Finally, the discovery of natural resources will increase aggregate output, while wars or natural disasters that destroy capital will obviously reduce aggregate output.

Factors that influence technology. New technologies change the production function a firm uses, allowing firms to produce more output using the same amount of capital and labor. In addition, new technologies provide firms with incentives to hire more labor and more capital. Anything that improves the incentives to produce and invest in new technologies will eventually increase output growth. For example, the provision of tax incentives and funding for research and development projects, the granting of patent protection, and the provision of educational opportunities are all examples of public policies that can encourage new innovation. However, negative shocks to technology are also possible. For example, during the Organization of Petroleum Exporting Countries (OPEC) oil embargos of the 1970s, higher oil prices made oil-intensive equipment and many oil-intensive technologies too expensive to use, significantly reducing productivity and aggregate output.

Aggregate Demand and Aggregate Supply in the Classical Model

The things that determine real output in the classical model—labor, capital, and technology—are all factors that affect aggregate supply. Nominal variables, such as the price level, have no effect on these inputs and play no role in determining the level of real output, Y. As a result, there is no relationship between the price level and aggregate output on the supply-side of the classical model, meaning that aggregate supply is a vertical line. The position of the aggregate supply curve is determined by a country's stock of labor, capital, and technology.

What about aggregate demand in the classical model? The classical theory of aggregate demand is based on the quantity theory of money demand originally developed by the philosopher David Hume in the mid-1700s. In the quantity theory, people hold money because money is needed in order to conduct transactions. This implies the following quantity theory equation:

$$MV = PY \tag{3.2}$$

P denotes the aggregate price level, so that PY is equal to nominal aggregate expenditure (or nominal aggregate output). M denotes the money supply, and V denotes the velocity of money, or the number of times a unit of money changes hands over a period of time. The intuition behind this equation is straightforward. If money is needed when conducting all trades, then in order for the level of nominal expenditure (PY) to increase either the supply of money (M) or the velocity of money (V) has to increase as well in order to support this higher volume of trade.

The quantity theory is not only a theory of money demand but also a theory of aggregate demand because it states that on the demand side of an economy a negative relationship exists between the price level and the level of real output. The intuition behind this downward sloping aggregate demand curve is as follows: Holding money and velocity constant, a higher price level reduces the real value of money holdings, which in turn reduces real spending and output.

When these aggregate demand and aggregate supply curves are considered together, two important implications of the classical model become evident. First, the role of aggregate demand in the classical model is only to determine the price level. Aggregate demand has no influence on real aggregate output. It is aggregate supply in the classical model that determines aggregate income and, as a result, aggregate expenditure within an economy. This classical principle that supply creates its own demand is often referred to as *Say's Law*.

Second, given that aggregate demand only influences the price level, changes in the money supply, which shift the position of the aggregate demand curve, only affect the price level. The classical principle that changes in the money supply only affect nominal variables (the price level, nominal wages, nominal output) but not real variables (real output, unemployment, labor, capital, technology) is often referred to as *money neutrality*. Thus, changes in the money supply cannot influence the things that really matters in the classical model. The strength of the quantity theory of aggregate demand is that it provides a simple and accurate explanation for the close correlation that exists between average money growth and average inflation across all countries over long periods of time. Sustained money growth, and nothing else, drives sustained inflation.

Business Cycles in the Classical Model

Business cycles do not exist in the classical model, at least not in the traditional sense of temporary deviations of output from a long-term trend. All changes in output in the classical model are permanent and are caused by changes in aggregate supply. As a result, when output falls because of a decrease in aggregate supply, it will not return to its previous level unless something else changes to increase aggregate supply.

So what drives changes in aggregate supply, particularly decreases in aggregate supply that cause economic contractions? Classical economists focused on one primary culprit—government policy, particularly tax policy and government regulation. For example, consider the imposition of a tax on labor income, such as the payroll tax adopted in the United States. Figure 3.2 graphs the effects of this tax, which reduces the labor supply curve, reduces the quantity of labor and increases the real wage. It also shifts the aggregate supply curve to the left, decreasing aggregate output. As another example, Figure 3.3 graphs the effects of a tax on savings (or investment). This tax reduces the capital stock, which lowers the marginal product of labor and shifts the labor demand curve downward. Because of

Figure 3.2   Impact of a tax on labor income on the labor market and aggregate demand and supply.

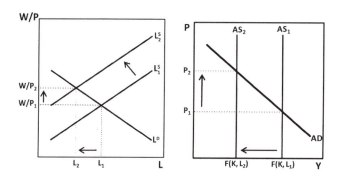

these falls in labor and capital, aggregate supply shifts to the left and aggregate output decreases.

Markets are perfectly competitive in the classical model, and if left alone they will work efficiently and maximize output and welfare. As a result, the role of government in the classical model is essentially a negative one. Anything the government does outside of the basic responsibilities of protecting property rights, providing for national defense, breaking up monopolies, and providing public education will lower efficiency and output. There is no positive role for the government to actively stabilize or manage an economy at the macroeconomic level. Even monetary policy in the classical model is irrelevant to real activity, and its

Figure 3.3   Impact of a tax on savings (or investment) on the labor market and aggregate demand and supply.

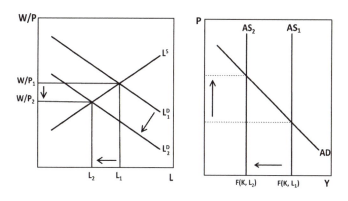

excessive use will only lead to inflation. Hence, the governing philosophy advocated by the proponents of the classical model is one of *laissez faire*, or "hands off." This governing philosophy dominated economic policy debates in the United States and much of Europe during most of the late 1700s and 1800s.

The classical model has framed the debate on business cycles for most of the last 230 years because of its simple and intuitive explanation of the way that the economic world works. Throughout most of its history, however, even when it was the dominant business cycle theory, the classical model has come under heavy criticism for a number of reasons. First, the irrelevance of aggregate demand is troubling to many economists. Is it true that things such as monetary policy or exogenous changes in consumption have no direct effect on real output? Second, the assumption of perfect competition has also been questioned. Are prices and wages really perfectly flexible? Do firms and households really have perfect information about existing conditions in the economy? Another important implication of perfect competition is that financial systems play essentially no role in propagating business cycles; financial systems simply rise and fall in response to changes in the general economy. Finally, the assertion that recessions are driven by falls in aggregate supply seem implausible to many, especially following the events of the Great Depression. It became increasingly difficult to argue during the 1930s that Say's Law was plausible when excess supplies of goods existed throughout the world and unemployment in the United States stood at 25 percent.

CONCLUSIONS

The Great Depression completely changed the study of macroeconomics in general and business cycles in particular. The Great Depression focused the attention of economists on both the costs of output fluctuations and on the inadequacies of their existing theories. However, the more modern business cycle theories that were developed subsequently, such as the Keynesian model that is discussed in the next chapter, looked to these earlier models as a starting point of inquiry. By identifying many of the critical components of business cycles—such as changes in technology, expectations, investment volatility, spending multipliers, the money supply, public policy, the incentives to work and invest, and imperfect competition—these early theories laid the foundation on which much of modern macroeconomic theory has been built.

SUGGESTED READINGS

Grand Pursuit: The Story of Economic Genius, Sylvia Nasar (2011): A narrative account of the historical dramas that surrounded and influenced the thinking of many of the great economists discussed in this chapter as well as in later chapters.

The Worldly Philosophers, Robert Heilbroner (1986): A lively and readable discussion of the lives and ideas of the most influential early economists, with chapters on Smith, Malthus, Mills, Schumpeter, and Keynes.

FOUR

Keynes's and Keynesian Theory

INTRODUCTION

In 1999, 27 prominent economists, historians, educators, political scientists, and philosophers were asked the following questions: (1) What books published this century altered the direction of our society? and (2) Which books will have the most impact on thought and action in the years ahead? The most cited book was John Maynard Keynes's *The General Theory of Employment, Interest, and Money* (1936) because of its broad influence on the study of economics and the rationale it provided for more active government involvement in the economy.

Keynes himself was exceptionally interesting for an economist. He was a classically trained pianist, a philosopher, and a member of the Bloomsbury literary group, which also included Ernest Hemingway and Virginia Woolf among others. During World War I, Keynes served in England's treasury department working on international finance and was hailed by many as the civil servant most responsible for winning World War I. Keynes's (1920) *The Economic Consequences of Peace* was a prescient critique of the peace treaty that ended World War I, which imposed massive reparation payments on the Axis countries and, as Keynes predicted, eventually led to an economic collapse that contributed to Hitler's rise to power in Germany. Keynes also worked on England's war financing during World War II. After World War II, Keynes was the primary architect of the Bretton Woods agreement that governed exchange rates and capital flows throughout the world for more than 20 years. Keynes was also a speculator on the foreign exchange market and became a self-made millionaire (although in the process of making his fortune he nearly went bankrupt twice). He was an accomplished mathematician and wrote a book on probability theory. In his spare time, Keynes studied economics and did groundbreaking research in many areas, including consumption theory, monetary theory, and investment theory. *The General Theory* represents the culmination of his work in economics and was Keynes's attempt to explain his complete theory of macroeconomics and the causes of recessions and depressions. Given its publication during the Great Depression, the timing of this book could not have been more auspicious.

Keynes's model was the first truly aggregate model in economics, meaning it was the first model to make a real distinction between macroeconomics and microeconomics. Keynes's model was also the first quasi-general equilibrium macroeconomic model, meaning that it looked at the interactions among the goods, labor, money, and bonds markets at the same time. In this chapter, Keynes's principal insights into the nature of business cycles will be examined. In addition, Keynesian theory, which is the name given to subsequent versions of Keynes's theory developed by his disciples, will also be discussed with a particular emphasis on Keynesian explanations of the Great Depression.

INVOLUNTARY UNEMPLOYMENT IN KEYNES'S MODEL

Keynes's opinion of the classical theory of business cycles was, to put it politely, not high. Referring to the classical model, Keynes (1936) said "It is astonishing what foolish things one can temporarily believe if one thinks too long alone, particularly in economics (along with the other moral sciences), where it is often impossible to bring one's ideas to a conclusive test either formal or experimental."

Keynes's model of business cycles begins with a critique of the classical labor market. Keynes argued that the classical view of a perfectly competitive labor market was at best naïve, at worst insulting and counterproductive. In the perfectly competitive classical labor market, a representative worker looks for a job in a market where the nominal wage is flexible and instantly adjusts so that the real wage equates labor supply and labor demand. One of the subtle implications of this labor market theory is that only *voluntary unemployment* exists in the classical model, meaning that only those workers who are not willing to work at the current real wage will be unemployed, while everyone else who wants to work at the current wage can find a job. If this is not the case, nominal and real wages will adjust to make it so.

To Keynes, the problem with this classical view of the labor market is that it could not realistically explain two things that are observed in the real world. First, employment is very volatile. Classical economists explained this volatility by appealing to either changes in people's incentives to work or by changes in the marginal product of labor, but this seemed unreasonable to Keynes because these factors do not fluctuate on a month-to-month basis like employment does. Second, the classical model has no explanation for *involuntary unemployment,* or the existence of workers who are willing to work at the current wage but are unable to find a job, even at a slightly lower wage. As a result, classical economists were left to argue that the 25 percent unemployment rate that existed during the Great Depression was simply the result of many workers being unwilling to work for the current wage. Obviously, this was an insulting explanation to those who were standing in bread lines for hours every day.

In contrast, Keynes believed that imperfect competition better describes the way that markets operate. This is particularly true of the labor market, where each worker differs in skill level and, as a result, has to negotiate his or her wage individually. In such a decentralized labor market, workers are not worried about what the economy-wide real wage has to be in order to clear the labor market. Instead, workers worry about their own wages relative to what similar workers are receiving. As a result, there is no guarantee that the aggregate real wage will be at a level where labor demand equals labor supply.

For example, consider a period when the aggregate price level is declining. This will increase real wages because individual workers will be reluctant to reduce their nominal wage and restore labor market equilibrium unless other workers are also reducing their nominal wages as well. If all workers refuse to accept a nominal wage cut without observing others accepting a wage cut first, then wage cuts will take place very slowly. They will only take place after workers observe a significant amount of unemployment, which is the only threat that firms can use to make them amendable to wage cuts. This phenomenon is often called *coordination failure.* Because there is no mechanism for coordinating individual wage negotiations, the end result is nominal wage "stickiness" (as Keynes termed it) that leads to higher real wages and involuntary unemployment during periods of falling prices. This process is illustrated in Figure 4.1. Involuntary unemployment exists because at the current real wage, which is higher than the market-clearing real wage as a result of

Figure 4.1   A decrease in the price level in Keynes's labor market.

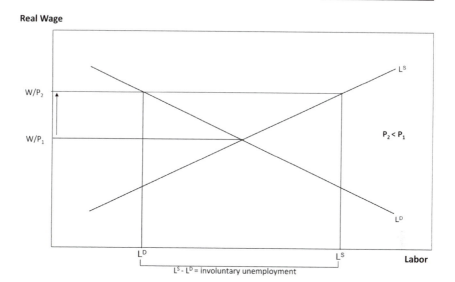

Real Wage

the fall in the price level from P_1 to P_2, there are workers that are willing to work but cannot find employment.

AGGREGATE DEMAND AND AGGREGATE SUPPLY IN KEYNES'S MODEL

In a world with inflexible nominal wages, a decrease in the aggregate price level increases real wages, which forces firms to reduce employment and output. In other words, aggregate supply in the Keynesian model is upward sloping and not vertical like in the classical model. The implication is that if labor markets are not perfectly competitive, aggregate demand can have real effects on output and employment. Consider Figure 4.2, in which there is a decrease in aggregate demand. Lower aggregate demand reduces output below the classical aggregate supply curve—or the long-run aggregate supply (LRAS) curve—consistent with the full employment of capital and labor. As the economy moves along the Keynesian aggregate supply curve (referred to as the short-run aggregate supply [SRAS] curve), the price level moves from p_1 to p_2, which increases real wages from $\frac{w}{P_1}$ to $\frac{w}{P_2}$. A higher real wage leads to an increase in unemployment. Thus, aggregate demand, not just aggregate supply, plays a role in determining the level of real output and unemployment in

Keynes's model. Keynes's model rejects Say's Law, or the principal that aggregate supply determines aggregate demand. This is because nominal wages are not able to fully adjust and balance demand and supply in the labor market.

The simple quantity theory model of aggregate demand was satisfactory to classical economists because aggregate demand only influences the price level in the classical model. However, in a theory where aggregate demand does matter, it requires more attention. Keynes rejected the simple quantity theory and argued that aggregate demand is composed of the demands for the individual components of GDP; in other words,

$$Y^d = C^d + I^d + G^d + (X - M^d) \qquad (4.1)$$

Of these components of GDP, Keynes believed that the demands for consumption, government purchases, and imports are stable. However, Keynes believed investment demand is unstable and the primary source of aggregate demand fluctuations.

The key to understanding investment and aggregate demand volatility is to understand that not only are labor markets imperfectly competitive in Keynes' view, but so are financial markets. The most important market failure in the financial system is the lack of perfect information. Because finance involves trading money across time, uncertainty and risk are defining characteristics of any financial transaction. People have to form

Figure 4.2   A decrease in aggregate demand in Keynes's model.

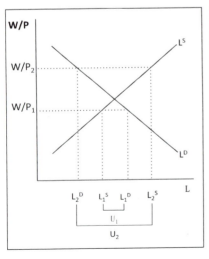
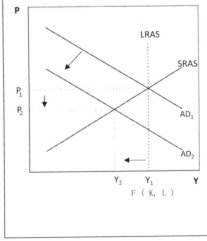

expectations regarding future outcomes under uncertainty. Keynes believed that people's views of the future are highly subjective because they often have little good information upon which to base their expectations. Keynes did not believe in the broad applicability of probabilistic uncertainty, where you do not know the outcome for certain but you have a good idea about the probability of each outcome. In other words, economic forecasting is not like playing "red" or "black" on a roulette wheel where the chances of each outcome are well known. Instead, Keynes believed in true uncertainty, where even the possible range of outcomes is not completely known and no statistical model to forecast the future can be developed. Without any statistical foundation to use in forecasting, small bits of new information will lead to large swings in expectations of the future.

To extend the roulette analogy, imagine if you were playing on a distinctive roulette wheel where you had no idea how many pockets were on the wheel, nor how many of them were red or black. Every new observation from a spin of the wheel would significantly change your calculations about how the wheel was laid out, and each observation would lead to wide swings in your betting behavior between one spin of the wheel and the next. This is how Keynes viewed economic forecasting. In Keynes's words,

> We are merely reminding ourselves that human decisions affecting the future, whether personal or political or economics, cannot depend on strict mathematical expectations, since the basis for making such calculations does not exist; and that it is our innate urge to activity which makes the wheels go round, our rational selves choosing between the alternatives as best we are able, calculating where we can, but often falling back for our motive on whim or sentiment or chance. (Keynes 1936)

Not only are expectations subjective, but Keynes believed that even with good information, decision making and expectations are inherently volatile. There are two primary reasons why Keynes believed expectations are erratic. First, in modern corporations it is the executives of firms who make investment decisions, not the stockholders who are the owners of the firm. Executives are much more likely to focus on creating short-term gains that help their immediate job prospects. This leads executives to overreact to both good and bad news. Second, Keynes believed that most executives' and speculators' returns are correlated with others' returns. This leads them to make economic decisions based on a herd mentality, meaning that if everyone else is buying, they will buy too. People implicitly count on the fact that there is always a "greater fool" to which any asset can be sold, even if that asset is exceptionally overvalued. This obviously leads both individuals and markets to overreact to new information. Keynes referred to the existence of volatile expectations that were in no way related to economic fundamentals as *animal spirits*. The primary repercussion of animal spirits is that asset markets, investment, and aggregate demand will all be extremely unstable and the source of shocks that trigger business cycles.

In this world where expectations are dominant but also uninformed, subjective, and volatile, Keynes rejected the classical notion that higher savings automatically leads to higher investment through lower interest rates. Instead, Keynes believed that the levels of savings and the interest rate only play a small role in determining the attractiveness of investment projects. It is expectations of the future that matter most in investment decisions. This is another important implication of market failures in the financial system: Because interest rates are not the primary factor that determines savings and investment, there is no mechanism to guarantee that investment will be at a sufficient level to keep the economy at its maximum rate of output. Instead, high savings when business confidence is low will not lead to more investment. It will only lead to excess savings, falling aggregate demand, high unemployment, and a recession.

Keynes did agree with classical economists that there is a level of output that is consistent with the full employment of all resources. Keynes referred to this level of output as *potential output*. He also agreed with classical economists that potential output is determined by the total amount of capital, labor, and technology that is available within an economy. However, Keynes's most basic insight is that market failures in labor and financial markets mean that there is no mechanism to ensure that nominal wages, real wages, and expectations will adjust and move an economy towards its potential output. In other words, potential output is more of a theoretically achievable level of output than one that is guaranteed to occur in the long run. Shortfalls in aggregate demand can occur and an economy can get stuck at a point where the current level of production is well below potential output and full employment.

BUSINESS CYCLES IN KEYNES'S MODEL

Business cycles in Keynes's model are triggered by a change in expectations. Recessions begin with a decrease in business and speculator confidence that reduces stock and other asset prices and also investment demand. This creates a *multiplier effect*, where lower investment spending reduces aggregate income, which in turn forces households to reduce their spending, which further decreases aggregate income. This process is similar to the one described by the accelerator model in Chapter 3. As a result, even if there is only a small initial decrease in expectations and investment, the resulting decrease in aggregate demand can be very large. This fall in aggregate demand can also fuel further declines in expectations, further multiplying the decline in demand. As aggregate demand falls, the price level decreases, which increases real wages because of nominal wage stickiness. Higher real wages force firms to lay off workers and reduce production. Aggregate output falls, and the economy contracts. Figure 4.2 graphically illustrates a recession in Keynes's model.

How will this recession end? There are three possibilities. First, it is possible that expectations will rise as people gradually reformulate their expectations as more and better information becomes available. However, there is no guarantee that expectations and financial markets will quickly rebound during a recession because there is no clear market mechanism that will make this happen. In fact, as mentioned above, it is quite possible that a recession will further depress business confidence and further magnify the size of the contraction in output. Second, Keynes believed that wages were not fixed, only sticky. If given enough time, workers will gradually reduce their nominal wage demands as they observe other similar workers taking nominal wage cuts. This will reduce real wages and move the economy back toward full employment. The problem with this approach, however, is that there are no assurances about how long this process will take. Given the difficulties associated with coordination failure, it could take a very long time for wages to fully adjust. In Keynes's opinion, policy makers cannot afford to patiently wait for this process to work itself out in the long run because, in his words, "in the long run we are all dead."

That leaves a third option, which is for the government to attempt to stabilize aggregate demand through the use of monetary or fiscal policy. If falling aggregate demand causes recessions, then enacting a public policy that increases aggregate demand in a timely manner would minimize both the size and the length of contractions. Higher aggregate demand would increase spending, increase the price level, reduce real wages, reduce involuntary unemployment, and possibly restore confidence enough to increase the stock prices and investment.

There are three policy options available to the government that would increase aggregate demand. The first would be for the central bank to increase the money supply. Keynes believed that interest rates are the opportunity cost, or the price, of holding money. Just like any other commodity, a higher supply reduces price so that a higher money supply would decrease interest rates. Lower interest rates would encourage investment directly and might also reduce the cost of borrowing by driving up stock prices. However, there are many reasons which led Keynes to believe that during economic contractions monetary policy would be largely ineffective. First, as mentioned before, Keynes believed that investment is not very sensitive to changes in interest rates. As a result, changes in the money supply might not lead to any change in investment if expectations remain low. Second, households and banks tend to increase their holdings of money as a precautionary measure during bad times. This is especially true when interest rates are low because there is a low opportunity cost to holding money. Low interest rates also make holding bonds unattractive because interest rates are likely to increase, and that will reduce the value of any bonds being held. As a result of these considerations, any change in the money supply during recessions is likely to be hoarded, leading to little change in interest rates, investment, and aggregate demand. Keynes referred to this as a *liquidity trap*. Finally, Keynes was skeptical about the ability of central bankers to manage monetary policy in a timely and proper manner. Given the ineptitude of central bankers during the Great Depression, which will be elaborated on in Chapter 13, it is not hard to understand Keynes's skepticism.

The second option available to the government for increasing aggregate demand during a recession is to cut taxes. However, when households face economic uncertainty, they tend to save the money from any tax cut and not spend it. In this case, tax cuts will not significantly increase spending and will not generate large spending multipliers.

The final option, and the one advocated by Keynes, is for the government to increase the level of its purchases of goods and services. What exactly these purchases are is of less importance than the fact that more government spending will increase aggregate expenditure. Only slightly humorously, Keynes suggested the following:

> If the Treasury were to fill old bottles with bank notes, bury them at suitable depths in disused coal mines which are then filled up to the surface with the town rubbish, and leave it to private enterprise on well-tried principles of *laissez-faire* to dig the notes up again ... there would be no more unemployment and with the help of the repercussions, the real income of the community would probably become a good deal larger than it is. It would, indeed, be more sensible to build houses

and the like; but if there are practical difficulties in the way of doing this, the above would be better than nothing. (Keynes 1936)

In other words, only by increasing purchases, whatever they are, will the government be sure that there will be additional spending within an economy that will initiate the multiplier process and increase aggregate demand enough to return the economy to full employment.

Keynes believed that as a country gets richer, business cycle fluctuations would become larger and take place more frequently. This prediction hinged on the belief that the average propensity to consume of an economy would fall as average income increased. On this point, Keynes shared beliefs similar to those from the underconsumptionist model discussed in Chapter 3. As a country became richer, falling consumption demand would increase the amount of savings within the economy and also increase the level of investment needed to generate full employment. This higher share of investment in output would lead to increased output volatility. Thus, unlike classical economists who worried that economies would not save enough, Keynes was concerned that developing countries would begin to save too much, increasing the frequency of economic cycles. In fact, Keynes believed that any policy effort to increase aggregate savings rates would be largely self-defeating because higher savings would reduce aggregate demand and output, in turn leading to a fall in savings. This concept is referred to as the *paradox of thrift*. The only ways to avoid lower output and the destabilizing effects of higher savings rates is for public policy to encourage consumption by either increasing the percent of GDP devoted to government purchases, redistributing income from the rich to the poor, and/or taxing savings.

KEYNESIAN ECONOMICS

Paul Samuelson (1964) said that "*The General Theory* caught most economists under the age of 35 with the unexpected virulence of a disease first attacking and decimating an isolated tribe of south sea islanders." Publication of *The General Theory* immediately set off an intense period of research surrounding different aspects of Keynes' model. One challenge facing these economists was that *The General Theory* is not an easy read. This is in part because Keynes largely resisted using equations and empirical data in his analysis, believing that economic processes were too complex to be described by simple equations and that empirical data was often unavailable and unreliable. As a result, Keynes was, either unintentionally or intentionally, vague on many of the finer points of his model. Consequently, even before Keynes had put his thoughts down onto paper, other economists had begun the process of trying to interpret exactly what they thought Keynes meant to say and to communicate it in a way that would be more accessible to noneconomists.

The most prominent and influential of these Keynesian models that attempted to place Keynes's theory into a more understandable framework is Hicks's (1937) IS-LM model. In this model, Hicks developed a quasi-general equilibrium model of aggregate demand that explains how changes in the money market (the LM curve) and changes in the goods and capital markets (the IS curve) influence aggregate demand. This Keynesian IS-LM model is consistent with many of the basic principles of Keynes's model, but with a few important differences that generally separate Keynes's theory from Keynesian theory. First, in the Keynesian IS-LM model, both prices and nominal wages are fixed, not just sticky. Thus, the IS-LM model is best thought of as a model of the very short run before prices and nominal wages have had any chance to adjust. Fixed prices and wages imply that the aggregate supply curve is completely horizontal at the current price level and that changes in output are exactly equal to the size of the change in aggregate demand. In other words, the Keynesian IS-LM model is a model of aggregate demand only.

Second, Keynesians believe that changes in aggregate demand can be driven by exogenous changes in consumption and not just by changes in investment. Keynesians recognize that the decisions of households to purchase durable consumption goods are very similar to the decisions made by firms to purchase investment goods. As a result, both investment and durable consumption are sensitive to changes in expectations, making them volatile and an important source of fluctuations in aggregate demand.

By switching the focus away from investment volatility and toward consumption volatility, Keynesians also switched the focus of business cycles away from financial systems. Because finance plays a smaller role in consumption decisions than in investment decisions, Keynesians downplay the macroeconomic effects of volatility in stock and bond markets. In the Keynesian way of thinking, animal spirits have less to do with the inherent nature of financial speculation in stock and bond markets (leading to investment volatility) and more to do with uncertainty regarding future macroeconomic conditions and job security (generating consumption volatility). Thus, the financial system plays only a minor role in transmitting external changes in business confidence to the rest of the economy in the Keynesian model. Financial systems primarily respond to fluctuations; they are not the driving force behind them.

The third important difference between Keynes and Keynesians has to do with the role of monetary policy in stabilizing output. As mentioned previously, Keynes did not advocate the use of monetary policy to stabilize aggregate demand. This was in large part because he did not trust central bankers, who he felt enacted policies that played an important role in magnifying the size of the Great Depression. As a result, Keynes spent relatively little time in *The General Theory* discussing monetary policy. On the other hand, Keynesians are very interested in monetary policy because they believe that postwar central bankers are in the perfect position to freely conduct stabilization policy given their relative independence from political constraints, unlike fiscal policy that has to be formulated within a complicated political process.

Keynesian interest in monetary policy was also spurred by the work of Arthur Phillips (1958). Phillips investigated the relationship between nominal wage inflation and unemployment growth between 1862 and 1957 in the United Kingdom. He found that a very strong negative correlation existed between these two variables. Keynesians immediately modified Phillips's work using U.S. data, but this time focusing on the relationship between price inflation and unemployment. Numerous studies identified a strong negative relationship between inflation and unemployment. To illustrate, Figure 4.3 presents inflation and unemployment data in the United States during the 1960s. Keynesians realized that this negative relationship was very strong evidence in favor of their model of aggregate demand driven business cycles. To understand why, consider Figure 4.4. Higher levels of aggregate demand in a Keynesian model with an upward-sloping SRAS curve drive up both the price level and output. Higher prices and output drive down real wages and unemployment, leading to a negative empirical relationship between inflation and unemployment. Thus, this modified Phillips curve is strong evidence of aggregate demand driven business cycles.

Even more important than the empirical support that the Phillips curve offered, Keynesians viewed the Phillips curve as a practical tool that could be used to help central bankers manage monetary policy. If a stable trade-off between inflation and unemployment exists, then all that a policy maker has to do is change the money supply until inflation is high enough to get the economy to the desired unemployment rate. Thus, the modified Phillips curve implied that the complexity of stabilization policy could be simplified to a simple inflation rate target.

Figure 4.3   Inflation and unemployment in the United States during the 1960s.

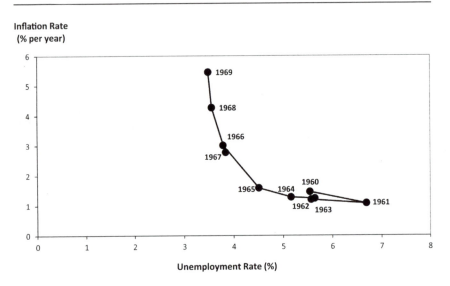

THE KEYNESIAN EXPLANATION OF THE GREAT DEPRESSION

The Keynesian model is closely associated with the Great Depression for obvious reasons. Keynesians attempted to fine-tune Keynes's explanation of the Great Depression in order to completely fit the facts of this period.

Keynesians believe that the most important shocks that reduced aggregate demand during the Great Depression originated in the goods market. The initial negative shock was a large decrease in expectations. Why expectations fell so significantly in 1929 is unclear (just as expectations motivated by animal spirits almost always are), but most Keynesian explanations center on an overreaction to overbuilding, overproduction, and the overvalued stock market that occurred during the 1920s. Falling expectations not only reduced consumption but also reduced investment and precipitated a huge decrease in the stock market. The stock market crash in October of 1929 initiated a chain reaction of other bad events. First, it increased the cost of investment, further reducing investment. Second, it reduced wealth, which reduced spending and consumption. Third, the stock market crash spread pessimism throughout the economy, leading to additional falls in expectations, investment, and consumption.

Figure 4.4   The Keynesian Phillips curve.

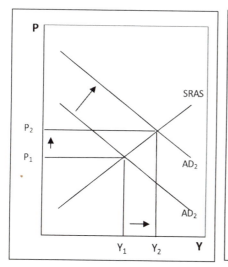
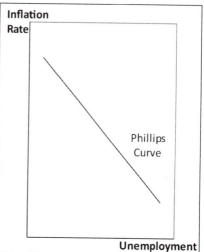

Keynesians believed that falling expectations also played a role in the bank failures that plagued the U.S. economy during the Depression. As the Depression worsened, people began to panic and withdraw their savings from banks throughout the country. These bank runs eventually led to the failure of 20 percent of all banks during the Depression. Those banks that did not fail were forced to severely restrict their lending, effectively halting financial intermediation and further reducing investment and consumption. Note that the resulting financial crisis was a symptom of the depression, however, not the cause of it.

A secondary shock that reduced aggregate demand during the Depression was the refusal of the Federal Reserve and other central banks to stabilize the money supply. As the public and banks began to hoard money as a precautionary measure, bank runs became common, the money multiplier began to shrink, and the money supply began to drop precipitously (this process will be described in more detail in the next chapter). The Federal Reserve, however, stubbornly refused to offset this falling money supply and failed to provide more reserves to banks and more currency to the public. Thus, Keynesians believe that through its neglect the Fed played an important role in reducing aggregate demand, not only by allowing the money supply to fall but also by allowing thousands of banks to fail and financial intermediation to collapse.

Keynesians were, for obvious reasons, highly critical of the *laissez-faire* policies adopted during the first years of the Depression by governments in the United States and Europe. Their attitude towards these classical policy makers could be summed up in a joke. Q: How many classical economists does it take to change a light bulb? A: Zero. When the market conditions are right, the light bulb will change itself.

Keynesian policy proposals to end the Great Depression were aimed at stabilizing the economy through actively attempting to stimulate aggregate demand. Given the ineptitude of the Fed and the high precautionary money holdings and savings rates of the public, Keynesians believed that increasing government spending was the only reliable method of increasing aggregate demand. Not surprisingly, Keynesians were big proponents of the public works programs initiated during the Great Depression in many countries, including the New Deal programs pushed by Roosevelt in the United States. However, given the size of the New Deal programs, which were small relative to the size of the economy, it was not surprising to most Keynesians that the Depression did not immediately end, although the economy did improve somewhat. The Great Depression lingered on throughout the world until governments dramatically increased military spending before World War II. This is entirely consistent with the predictions of Keynesian economists at the time and is influential evidence in support of the Keynesian theory of business cycles and stabilization policy.

The Keynesian explanation of the Great Depression will be reexamined when the Great Depression is considered in more detail in Chapter 13. This Keynesian explanation will be compared and contrasted with alternative views of the causes of the Depression.

EMPIRICAL EVIDENCE ON KEYNESIAN BUSINESS CYCLES

As discussed in Chapter 2, stock prices, consumer durables, and consumer confidence are all leading indicators of changes in aggregate output. Investment as a whole is also a leading indicator of output even though some of the components of investment, such as fixed business investment, lag changes in output because of delays between investment decisions and actual construction. These are very strong pieces of evidence in favor of Keynesian theory. However, some empirical research has raised questions about the validity of other aspects of Keynesian theory.

Are real wages countercyclical? Figure 4.5 presents data on the price level, the nominal wage, and the implied real wage during the Great Depression. Even though nominal wages did fall during the Depression, they did not fall by as much as the price level, leading to an increase in

Figure 4.5   The price level, nominal wage, and real wage during the Great Depression.

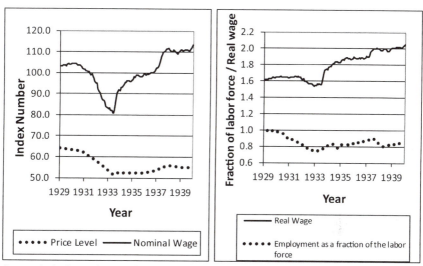

Source: Author's creation based on data from the Federal Reserve Bank of St. Louis Historical database, available at http://research.stlouisfed.org/fred2/downloaddata/

real wages. This is strong evidence that it was increases in real wages that drove the high rates of unemployment that existed during the Great Depression. In other words, unemployment appears to have been largely involuntary, just as Keynes argued.

However, over different time periods and across different countries, it is not at all so clear whether real wages are countercyclical. Table 4.1 presents real wage data across 13 developed countries. Real wages were basically acyclical during the interwar (1919–1939) and gold standard (1870–1914) eras, but slightly procyclical during the Bretton Woods (1945–1971) and the floating exchange rate (1971–present) eras. Thus, looking at a larger subset of countries over a long time horizon, real wages appear to be acyclical to mildly procyclical. This is hard to reconcile with Keynes's sticky wage theory of labor markets.

Is inflation procyclical? Procyclical inflation is consistent with aggregate demand driven business cycles and also with the modified Phillips curve relationship between higher inflation and lower unemployment. However, empirical data on price cyclicality suggest that prices have not been consistently procyclical. Figure 4.6 presents output growth and inflation over two time periods, the interwar period and the floating exchange rate period. Inflation was strongly procyclical in the United States during

Table 4.1   Real wage behavior during different periods.

Gold Standard	Interwar	Bretton	Woods	Float
Standard Deviation	0.038	0.042	0.042	0.033
Comovement with Output	0.025	−0.059	0.162	0.271

Note: The 13 countries included are Argentina, Australia, Canada, Denmark, France, Germany, Italy, Netherlands, Norway, Spain, Sweden, United Kingdom, and the United States.
Source: Author's creation from data by Basu and Taylor (1999).

the interwar period but moderately countercyclical during the recent floating exchange rate period. On average, the correlation between inflation and growth in the United States between 1880 and today is close to zero, or an acyclical relationship. In the next chapter, evidence on the corresponding breakdown of the negative relationship between inflation and unemployment will be discussed. The lack of a consistent cyclical relationship among inflation, real wages, and output raises troubling questions about the Keynesian model; questions that future business cycle models would be forced to address.

Figure 4.6   Output growth and inflation, 1920–1940 and 1970–2008.

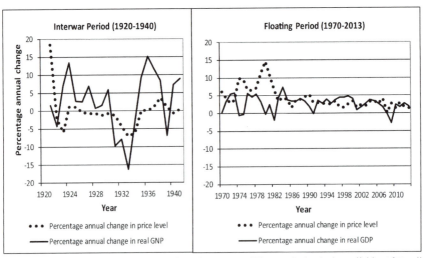

Source: Author's creation based on data from the Bureau of Economic Analysis available at https://www.bea.gov/itable/index.cfm.

CONCLUSIONS

So what makes a Keynesian a Keynesian? Blinder (1988) claims that the following principles generally define Keynesian economics.

1. *Aggregate demand is volatile and is the source of business cycle fluctuations.* This is primarily because of unstable expectations and their effect on investment, consumption, and the stock market. However, erratic fiscal or monetary policy can also contribute to aggregate demand instability.

2. *Output and employment are more volatile than prices and wages in the short run.* Keynesians believe that price and wage inflexibility exists because of imperfectly competitive markets. As a result, changes in aggregate demand can have real effects on output and unemployment.

3. *Following a recession, the return movement of an economy towards its potential output takes place very slowly.* Prices and wages only adjust gradually. Because of this, persistent disequilibria in the goods market (resulting in excess supply) and in the labor market (resulting in involuntary unemployment) can exist and be long-lasting.

4. *Monetary and fiscal policy can be used to stabilize output.* If enacted in a timely manner, increases in the money supply, reductions in taxes, or increases in government spending can be used to offset falls in aggregate demand.

5. *Keynesians are more worried about high unemployment than high inflation.* In the Keynesian model, there is a stable tradeoff between lower unemployment and higher inflation. The inflation that results from using stabilization policy is simply the price that has to be paid for more stable output. Keynesians are much more worried about deflation, as occurred during the Great Depression, than inflation.

In summary, both Keynes and Keynesians believe that capitalist economies are inherently volatile and need macroeconomic management in order to avoid destabilizing business cycles that are extremely costly and persistent. Without government intervention, this instability could eventually weaken the public's conviction in capitalism and lead to its downfall. Keynes and Keynesians believe in capitalism, but not *laissez-faire* capitalism. Consider the following quote by Keynes (1936): "It may well be that the classical theory represents the way in which we should like our economy to behave. But to assume that it actually does so is to assume our difficulties away."

Other economists believe that it is the Keynesians who are the utopians and who are assuming that the world works as they wish it would work. Is stabilization policy in practice as simple as tweaking monetary and fiscal policy until the economy is at full employment? Do economists really understand the economy well enough to properly conduct stabilization policy, or are there reasons to think that they are not so infallible? Is this Keynesian explanation of business cycles consistent with all business cycle episodes, including every aspect of the Great Depression? These are the questions over which the theoretical battle between Keynesians and their critics was joined. However, Keynes so clearly defined the issues relating to the debate that all of the work on business cycles since *The General Theory* can be thought of as a critique of his and his followers' influential models of what causes recessions and depressions.

SUGGESTED READINGS

Essays in Persuasion, John Maynard Keynes (1931): A collection of early essays in which Keynes lays out his basic thoughts on the Great Depression, the use of fiscal policy, and the effects of deflation, among other topics. Also included are brief essays on his thoughts about the state of politics in the 1920s and 1930s.

The General Theory of Employment, Interest, and Money, John Maynard Keynes (1936): The first three chapters summarize Keynes's primary insights and are the most readable chapters of *The General Theory*.

Keynes: The Return of the Master, Robert Skidelsky (2010): A brief introduction to the life and times of Keynes by his preeminent biographer. Skidelsky argues how and why understanding Keynes is still so vital to understanding today's political and policy debates.

"Price Flexibility and Output Stability: An Old Keynesian View," James Tobin (1993): An argument in support of Keynes's continued relevance to modern economics and a critique of classical and neoclassical models.

FIVE

Austrian Economics

INTRODUCTION

The school of macroeconomic thought known as *Austrian economics* was developed in the early 1900s but reached its intellectual zenith in the 1930s at roughly the same time Keynes and his contemporaries were beginning their dominance of the macroeconomics profession. The two biggest names in the Austrian school—Joseph Schumpeter and Friedrich Hayek—were both expatriates from the Austrian empire who left (for the United States and England, respectively) in the early 1930s, never to permanently return to their homelands. The fact that both economists were outsiders, both by nature and experience, contributed to their roles as the most insightful contemporary critics of both Keynes and of classical economics.

This chapter provides a brief introduction to Austrian economics and the ways that its outlook differs from mainstream economics. The principle focus of this chapter will be on Schumpeter and Hayek and their theories on the nature of economic instability. Schumpeter's theory of creative destruction focuses on technology waves that drive longer-run cyclical movements in output. Hayek focuses on unsustainable booms and busts driven by manipulative central banks and breakdowns in the accuracy in the price mechanism. What these theories share is a belief that governments are the cause of—not the solution to—failures in the economic system. They also share a belief that mainstream economic theory took a wrong turn when it began to focus exclusively on formal mathematical modeling. Both of these shared beliefs put Austrians squarely at odds with

Keynesians in the mid-1900s. These two beliefs have also contributed to the resurgence of interest in Austrian economics among modern critics of mainstream economics and of the expanded role of government in modern economies.

THE PRINCIPLES OF AUSTRIAN ECONOMICS

Before examining Austrian views of the causes of recessions and depressions, it is useful to get a broader perspective on what makes Austrian economics different from other schools of economic thought. Although Austrian economists vary widely, there are three basic principles that most proponents of Austrian economics—including Schumpeter and Hayek—agree upon.

1. *The focus should be on individuals, not groups.* Austrians are skeptical about the use of representative agent models where people are lumped together as having the same preferences and perceptions. Austrians believe in what they call *subjectivism*, or the notion that an individual's actions are subject to an individual's perceptions. Because an individual's perceptions are often limited by a lack of knowledge or by their innate abilities, you cannot generalize from individuals to groups because behavioral relationships by their very nature are unstable and always changing.

   For this reason, Austrian economists are strongly resistant to reducing economic questions to mathematical models and econometric testing techniques. They believe that economic questions cannot be couched as simple engineering problems. They disavow generalizing assumptions and what they refer to as "narrow empiricism."

2. *Information, particularly the lack of it, is at the heart of economics.* As Adam Smith noted, there is no one person in the world who knows how to make a pencil. There is simply too much to know—how to harvest and cut the wood, how to make the rubber, how to mine and shape the graphite, and so on. But the beauty of market systems is that no one person has to know all of these things. Through specialization and trade, not only can individuals increase their productivity, but they can also reduce the amount of knowledge needed in order to consume a wide variety of goods. The key to this specialization process working, however, is the price mechanism. Price systems are spontaneous communications networks. When markets are interfered with—particularly by governments—the price mechanism does not create

as much or as accurate information as it should. As a result, bad decisions are made about where resources should be allocated and what goods should be consumed. Over the long run, this will not only make economies more unstable, but it will also reduce their rates of economic growth.

It is the lack of information about monetary policy—caused by secretive central banks—that makes money non-neutral. As a result, Austrians are suspicious of the power and goals of central banks. This lack of information is also the reason why economic problems cannot be reduced to simple computations. Accurately calculating something as simple as an opportunity cost (which is a concept originally developed by Austrian economists) cannot be done in reality because so many costs are subjective and impossible for economists to estimate. According to the Austrians, one of the primary failures of mainstream economics is that it assumes that if something is not calculable, it does not exist.

3. *Capitalist economies evolve according to an evolutionary process.* Optimal economic processes and institutions cannot be designed by policy makers, even if they are enlightened and benevolent, because there is simply too much information needed in order for the proper decisions to be made. Instead, capitalism works best when it is characterized by decentralized decision making that creates a perpetual state of flux. There is no equilibrium, just change. This change is driven by the desire of entrepreneurs to make higher profits and for the firms they create to survive. Consistent with the concept of "survival of the fittest" often associated with Darwinian biological evolution, only the entrepreneurs that can innovate most effectively will be able to survive within competitive markets. Others firms that do not successfully innovate will fail, which is a good thing from an evolutionary perspective because it prevents additional resources from being allocated to firms that are less productive.

SCHUMPETER'S THEORY OF CREATIVE DESTRUCTION

Do economies exhibit extended periods of sustained expansion and contraction that often last one or more decades? The Russian economist Nikolai Kondratiev (1935) argued from an empirical perspective that prices, interest rates, wages, production, investment, and consumption all fluctuated in short waves and in long waves. By focusing solely on these smaller cycles around an assumed constant trend, Kondratiev thought that economists were missing the bigger picture, which was that the long-term trend itself was cyclical. Kondratiev identified three long waves using historical data from the mid-1700s to the early 1900s. The first wave expanded between 1780 and 1815 and contracted between 1815 and 1843. The second wave expanded between 1843 and 1875 and contracted between 1875 and 1887. Finally, the third wave expanded between 1893 and 1920 and contracted from 1920 until 1935, when Kondratiev published his work.

Why might these long waves exist, and what is driving them? This was the question that Joseph Schumpeter (1939), a one-time finance minister for Austria, attempted to address when he emigrated to the United States in 1932. Schumpeter provided the first and most persuasive explanation of these long-wave cycles: technological innovation and creative destruction. Like other Austrian economists, Schumpeter viewed capitalism as an evolutionary process. Economic growth is driven by the desire for entrepreneurs and the firms they build to survive, and to do this they must create new means of business by out-competing their rivals. The primary way they do this is through technological innovation. According to Schumpeter, "The fundamental impulse that sets and keeps the capitalist engine in motion comes from the new consumers, goods, the new methods of production or transportation, the new markets, the new forms of industrial organization that capitalist enterprise creates."

Like biological evolution, technological development generated by this competition does not take place at a constant rate. Instead, innovation is the result of big ideas that are developed sporadically (mutated) within different industries. Initially, these new technologies are not unambiguously good for economic growth because new technologies replace old technologies that have already been fully integrated into an economy. During the adoption phase of a new technology, resources are diverted away from proven production processes to unproven processes that may not yet be as efficient or reliable. In addition, workers may not be trained to efficiently use new technologies when they are first introduced, reducing overall productivity. Finally, new technologies make much of the existing capital stock obsolete, effectively reducing the size of the capital stock. This is the basis of Schumpeter's theory of *creative destruction*, where new technologies initially reduce economic growth and can lead to economic contractions or slowdowns.

As time goes on, innovation begins to take place as firms and workers learn to work with this new technology in more productive ways. In addition, new capital will have had time to be built. At this point, productivity and aggregate output growth begin to increase. However, this adoption phase can take a very long period of time—time usually measured in terms of decades and not just in terms of months.

Unfortunately, the growth booms associated with new technologies do not last forever. Once this new technology is fully integrated into the economy, initial growth will be dramatic. Growth will eventually slow as the productivity benefits of the new technology are exhausted and diminishing returns begin to set in. Without a new technological advance, productivity growth and output growth will eventually decline to zero and the economy will experience an extended slowdown. When another new technology is discovered, this creative destruction process will take place and another long wave will begin once again.

Table 5.1 presents the dates of these long waves and the technological developments that have been hypothesized to be driving these long cycles. Our current wave (the fifth) is believed to be driven by information technology (IT), including things such as better communications technology, the Internet, faster computers, and innovations in software that have broadened the productive use of computers. Notice that each of these waves has gotten progressively shorter over time. The most likely explanation for this is that firms and workers have gotten more adept at adopting new technologies more quickly. While this means that new technologies are more likely to have an immediate positive impact on output growth, the downside of quicker adoption is that the productivity benefits from new technologies are exhausted much more quickly than before. This makes it increasingly important that new technologies are regularly developed in order to sustain high rates of economic growth.

Can government policy serve to mitigate the costs of these long-wave business cycles? According to Schumpeter, the costs of governments

Table 5.1 Schumpeter's long waves.

Wave	Length	Innovations
First Wave	1775–1835 (60 years)	Water power, textiles, iron
Second Wave	1835–1890 (55 years)	Steam, rail, steel
Third Wave	1890–1940 (50 years)	Electricity, chemicals, internal combustion engine
Fourth Wave	1940–1985 (45 years)	Petrochemicals, electronics, aviation
Fifth Wave	1985–2020 (35 years)	Digital networks, software, new media

Source: Author's creation based on data from Kondratiev (1935).

attempting to do so are prohibitive. Trying to prevent economic down-turns by preventing the failure of firms means that the "dead brush" of capitalism will never be cleared. Without failure, resources will continue to be allocated to less productive businesses, leaving fewer resources available for the entrepreneurs that will potentially drive the next great wave to technological innovation. Failure is one of the fundamental aspects of capitalism, and without it the capitalist system cannot thrive.

As a result of his belief in the necessity of failure, Schumpeter was a vehement critic of the bailout of firms and banks that took place during the Great Depression. His approach to dealing with business cycles was *laissez faire*. Consistent with Schumpeter's view, Andrew Mellon, Treasury secretary under U.S. President Herbert Hoover at the beginning of the Great Depression, argued vehemently against bailouts and government stabilization policies while in office. In his words, "liquidate labor, liquidate stocks, liquidate farmers, liquidate real estate ... it will purge the rottenness out of the system. High costs of living and high living will come down. People will work harder, live a more moral life. Values will be adjusted, and enterprising people will pick up from less competent people" (Hoover 1952).

Schumpeter warned in his later books about the dangers to capitalism of the gradual movement toward socialism in democratic nations. Because firms that are nationalized are not allowed to fail, they are a threat to entre-preneurship and economic growth. Likewise, individuals that are pro-tected by the safety nets of the modern welfare state will not adequately develop the entrepreneurial spirit that is at the root of capitalist success.

HAYEK'S THEORY OF BUSINESS CYCLES

Friedrich Hayek was the best-known contemporary critic of Keynes in the 1940s and continued to be influential into the 1980s when he served as an intellectual guru to Margaret Thatcher and Ronald Reagan. Even after his death in 1992, Hayek continues to be one of the most widely read conservative critics of the modern welfare state. Hayek's (1935) theory of the business cycle provides insights into the causes of recession and depressions and also into Hayek's political outlook in general.

The cornerstone of Hayek's business cycle theory is an unsustainable boom fueled by overly expansionary monetary policy. Driven by political demands, Hayek believed that central banks have strong incentives to overstimulate the economy by keeping real interest rates below their long-run, natural rate. By keeping interest rates artificially lower than they should be, central banks effectively encourage too much credit, too much investment, too much consumption, and too little savings than is socially optimal. But most worrisome is not the unsustainably high level of investment but where this investment goes. Because interest rates are kept artificially low, investment projects are financed at rates in which its benefits are likely to be less than the real costs to society. Hayek referred to this as "malinvestment," and it is the primary danger of government manipulation of monetary policy. It is also a danger associated with government spending on public investment, the uses of which are not determined by market signals but by politics. Much of this malinvestment will be unprofitable, and there is too little savings to support these high levels of investment over the long run.

By keeping interest rates artificially low, central banks keep output growth unsustainably high at the cost of creating a great deal of unprofitable investment. Eventually, the fragile fundamentals of this system will reach a tipping point. Many firms will begin to fail as a result of their unprofitable investments. If the government allows this process to go ahead unimpeded, then defaults and liquidation will occur that will eventually free up resources for more profitable firms, but at the cost of higher interest rates, lower output, and higher unemployment in the short run (this is the approach that Andrew Mellon was arguing for). But what if the central bank fights this in the interest of economic stabilization? By providing bailouts and pushing interest rates even lower, policy makers can prevent defaults and liquidation for a period of time. But a central bank does so at the cost of encouraging even more malinvestment and overconsumption, setting the stage for a future, and even more severe, economic contraction.

The best course of action, according to Hayek, is for central banks to follow a *laissez-faire* approach, letting markets determine interest rates and avoiding the calls for it to provide bailouts. Without destruction, there can be no creative destruction. The best approach to dealing with business cycles is to focus on the long run and ignore the short run.

Hayek's (1944) best-known work, *The Road to Serfdom*, has less to do with business cycles *per se*, but everything to do with elucidating his belief in the market system and the dangers of intrusive government intervention into the economy. Here, Hayek focuses on the dangers of central planning. Based on the fact that information is necessarily limited, he argues that markets are preferable to governments because governments can never have sufficient information to efficiently plan an economy. Centrally planned economies are always subject to malinvestment because they lack the knowledge to effectively manage resources and ensure that they are allocated to their most efficient uses. By distorting price mechanisms, activist government policies also distort information and incentives, leading to more bad investment decisions. As a result, they cause economies to be less efficient, grow slower, and become more vulnerable to business cycles.

EVIDENCE ON AUSTRIAN BUSINESS CYCLES

Because of their skepticism regarding economic modeling and narrow empiricism, there is a relative paucity of information formally evaluating the claims of Austrian theories. While claiming that they are trying to avoid a narrowing of their methodology and avoiding mathematical and statistical modeling, Austrian economists have also failed to adopt the scientific method and offer testable hypotheses that can be falsified. There is some observational information that supports Austrian theories, but there is a sizeable amount of empiricism that is inconsistent with their predictions.

Schumpeter's view of creative destruction is consistent with many facts we observe in modern economies. Nearly 10 percent of all firms in the United States fail each year—this number rises to nearly 20 percent during recessions. In addition, over half of all Fortune 500 companies were founded during recessions. There is also evidence that recessions change the allocation of investment. For example, Oray (2008) reports that Stanford MBAs disproportionately shunned the financial sector and moved to other industries during the global financial crisis.

However, many economists are skeptical of Schumpeter's long-wave hypothesis. These long waves are very difficult to identify empirically. How do you distinguish between a long wave and a permanent change in the trend rate of growth within an economy? How do you separate a downward movement on a long wave from a few recessions taking place coincidentally within a short interval of time? And what is causing the short cycles that are taking place within these long waves? These are important questions that Schumpeter and his followers have not adequately answered. However, Schumpeter's ideas continue to provoke a great deal of interest among modern economists. This is particularly true among the advocates of real business cycle models (Chapter 8), which focus on changes in technology and productivity as the primary determinant of business cycle fluctuations.

Despite Hayek's popularity, his theory of business cycles never gained wide acceptance either inside or outside of the economics profession. One problem with this theory is that it resembles early business cycle theories. It is a single-cause model, not a complex and multidimensional model like the Keynesian model. By focusing on monetary policy and interest rates exclusively, Hayek's business cycle theory is easily contradicted by observations regarding the behavior of monetary policy and interest rates that are not consistent with his theory. For example, the fact that interest rates are consistently procyclical is not consistent with Hayek's story that low interest rates generated by the central bank fuel booms and eventually lead to busts.

A second problem stems from the fact that while Hayek places great emphasis on the role of insufficient information and knowledge, he has little to say about the role of expectations and how people form them. In fact, Hayek's theory of business cycles implicitly assumes that people are extraordinarily stupid: Central banks consistently keep interest rates too low, but banks continue to lend and entrepreneurs continue to borrow and invest without any consideration of the impact on risk. For a theory that emphasizes "survival of the fittest," there would seem to be a big survival advantage to those who are forward-thinking in their decision making, but Hayek provides no explanation as to why irrational decision makers continue to act in such self-destructive ways.

A final problem with Hayek's business cycle theory is that it has a unique and implausible explanation of the Great Depression. Blaming a contraction the size of the Great Depression on expansionary monetary policy—particularly when there was little inflation before the Great Depression and deflation during it—does not match the facts of the time. Even conservatives such as Milton Friedman (discussed much more in the next chapter), when asked about Hayek's explanation of the depression, said that he was "an enormous admirer of Hayek, but not for his economics" (Ebenstein 2001).

CONCLUSIONS

In one of the great quotes regarding the study of economics, Hayek (1991) said that "The curious task of economics is to demonstrate to men how little they really know about what they imagine they can design." Despite the fact that Hayek's theory of business cycles has not been widely accepted by economists, the fact that most economists would strongly agree with Hayek's assertion above indicates that he has had significant influence on the profession. While Hayek's theory of business cycles has been marginalized and Schumpeter's creative destruction theory has had more of an impact on the study of technological innovation than business cycles, the Austrian school has made at least three important contributions to modern business cycle theory.

1. *The Austrians raised questions about whether government stabiliza-tion policy can do more harm than good and even be the source of business cycles.* This is to become a dominant theme in neoclassical models of business cycles, including the monetarist (Chapter 6), rational expectations (Chapter 7), and real business cycle (Chapter 8) models that will be discussed subsequently.

2. *The Austrians highlighted the significance of insufficient knowledge and the importance of imperfect information.* Once again, this becomes an important part of all future business cycle models, particularly new Keynesian (Chapter 9) and financial instability (Chapters 10 and 11) models. Maybe most importantly, the Austrian emphasis on the role that prices play in generating information and the resulting critique of central planning was a crucial insight that has impacted many different areas of economic study. It is also an argument that has played an important historical role by undermin-ing confidence in command economy regimes, such as the Soviet and Eastern European communist governments.

3. *By emphasizing the importance of creative destruction and the dan-gers of malinvestment, Austrians highlighted the fact that it is not just the levels of investment and consumption that are important but the deeper issue of where this investment and consumption is allocated.* The dangers of malinvestment have not been lost on many policy makers today, including some in the Chinese government who worry about having investment rates of nearly 50 percent of GDP, some of it going to build public infrastructure projects such as ghost cities and bridges to nowhere. By focusing on how markets can (or cannot) create the proper incentives for resources to be distributed to their most productive uses, Austrians such as Schumpeter and Hayek have spawned a great deal of economic research on the nature of technological innovation and entrepreneurship. This research has played an important role in increasing our understanding of short-run business cycle behavior and also long-run growth.

SUGGESTED READINGS

"Austrian Economics, Neoclassicism, and the Market Test," Leland B. Yaeger (1997): A comment on Austrian economics by a "fellow traveler" of the Austrian school.

"Austrian and Neoclassical Economics: Any Gains from Trade?" Sherwin Rosen (1997): A discussion of the things that mainstream economics can learn, and should not learn, from Austrian economics.

Capitalism, Socialism, and Democracy, Joseph Schumpeter (1942): A thought-provoking book on the impact that democratic socialism has on the future of creative destruction, entrepreneurship, and technological innovation.

The Road to Serfdom, Friedrich Hayek (1944): If you ever wanted to read a modern international bestseller and still learn some economics, this is your book.

SIX

The Monetarist Model

INTRODUCTION

During the 1950s and 1960s, monetary policy rose to the forefront of macroeconomic inquiry and business cycle research. As discussed before, Keynes did not spend much time discussing monetary policy in *The General Theory*. This was in part because he thought monetary policy was largely ineffective during bad times because of the liquidity trap, and also because he was skeptical about the competence of central bankers to engage in timely stabilization policy after their dismal performance during the Great Depression. Keynesians, on the other hand, were very interested in monetary policy for two reasons. First, Keynesians realized that central bankers are relatively independent and have the unique freedom to engage in stabilization policy largely unencumbered by outside political constraints. Second, the Keynesian Phillips curve, which specifies a constant negative relationship between inflation and unemployment, received a great deal of empirical support during the 1950s and 1960s. One important implication of the Phillips curve is that the complexity of stabilization policy could be simplified to a simple inflation rate target that could be achieved through monetary policy.

The 1950s and early 1960s were the pinnacle of Keynesian influence both from a theoretical and a policy perspective. Not only did Keynesian theory dominate macroeconomic theory, but Kennedy's election in 1960 was quickly followed by many of his Keynesian professors from Harvard moving with him to Washington.

While Austrian economists resisted the Keynesian paradigm, they were largely marginalized because of their rejection of methodological orthodoxy in economics, such as the use of mathematical modeling. As a result, one of the few effective voices of dissent during this period was Milton Friedman. Friedman's ideology was influenced by the Austrians, yet his economic methodology was solidly within the mainstream of the profession.

Friedman is probably the second most influential economist of the twentieth century and, like Keynes, a man of many talents. In addition to being a prominent conservative policy guru (Friedman developed many influential public policy ideas, including privatization proposals such as school voucher programs), Friedman did groundbreaking work in the areas of law and economics, consumption theory, and economic history. Friedman was also the father of a unique school of macroeconomic thought referred to as *monetarism*. Monetarists have the following goal: reassert classical principles in new classical, or *neoclassical*, models that better explain business cycles. A critical component of this neoclassical monetarist model is the fact that while it accepts the classical principle of money neutrality, it recognizes that it only holds in the long run. In the short run, monetarists believe (like Keynesians) that fluctuations in aggregate demand can have real effects on output and drive business cycles. However, like Hayek and other Austrian economists, monetarists view the erratic policies followed by misinformed and misguided central banks as the primary source of these shocks to aggregate demand and the cause of business cycles.

In this chapter, the monetarist model and its theory of business cycles are discussed. The focal point of this discussion is the debate regarding the proper role of monetary policy and its potential to both stabilize and destabilize an economy.

MONETARIST THEORY

The Principles of Monetarism

One of the primary objectives of monetarism was to reestablish classical concepts in macroeconomic theory. Monetarists believe in three basic neoclassical principles, each based on a classical principle but with a modification.

1. *Prices and wages are perfectly flexible. However, perfect informa-tion does not exist.* Monetarists believe that perfect competition best

describes the behavior of markets, but with the exception that perfect information about the money supply and the price level is impossible because of the secrecy of central banks. Imperfect information means that expectations of the future can have real effects on an economy if these expectations are wrong.

Monetarists believe that firms and households have *adaptive expectations*. Adaptive expectations mean that individuals are not forward-looking but backward-looking and only change their expectations gradually based on what they have observed in the past. (An example of adaptive expectations at work can be seen on every college campus when the weather suddenly turns cold but many students continue to walk around in shorts and T-shirts.) Adaptive expectations actually hearken back to the cobweb theory, which hypothesized that business cycles were the result of persistent errors in price expectations made by a public that is slow to catch on to any unanticipated change in the economy. In the monetarist model, nominal wages and the price level are slow to adjust to things such as an unforeseen change in the money supply. Disequilibria in labor and financial markets can exist not because of any real market imperfections, as assumed by Keynesians, but because of incorrect expectations of what nominal wages and the price level should be to clear the market.

Like the Austrians before them, monetarists emphasize the role of imperfect information. Unlike the Austrians, monetarists are specific about how expectations of the future are formed.

2. *Changes in aggregate demand do not affect real output in the long run, but they do affect real output in the short run.* Unlike classical economists, monetarists assert that money neutrality only holds in the long run, not in the short run. The reason, once again, has to do with imperfect information and price misperceptions. When the public is surprised by a change in the money supply, firms and workers can be fooled into changing their real behavior, meaning money neutrality will not hold. However, firms and households will eventually recognize their mistakes and gradually adjust their expectations. Wages and prices will then adjust and return the labor and goods markets to their equilibriums.

Consequently, changes in aggregate demand can drive business cycle fluctuations. These fluctuations are not permanent but temporary deviations from the long-run rate of aggregate output, which is determined by the full employment of capital, labor, and technology that is available in the economy. Friedman referred to the long-run level of aggregate output as the *natural rate of output*. This concept of the natural rate of output is similar to Keynes's concept of potential output, but the crucial difference is that Friedman believes that the forces that return the economy to full employment are much stronger because wages and prices are perfectly flexible. As a result, the natural rate of output is not some theoretically achievable level of output (like in the Keynesian view) but a level of output that the economy is typically at in the absence of any unexpected demand shocks.

3. *Fluctuations in the money supply drive fluctuations in aggregate demand and are responsible for business cycles.* Monetarists adhere to the classical quantity theory of money demand and aggregate demand, which asserts that money is needed in order to conduct transactions. This implies that there is a direct relationship between the amount of money in circulation and the level of nominal aggregate spending in an economy:

$$MV = PY \qquad (6.1)$$

Remember that V is velocity and represents the number of times a unit of money changes hands over a period of time. Y is real aggregate expenditure, P is the price level, and M is the money supply. In the quantity theory, any increase in the level of nominal expenditure (PY) has to be matched by either an increase in the supply of money (M) or a higher velocity of money (V) in order to support this higher volume of trade. The quantity theory is a theory of aggregate demand and implies that a negative relationship exists between the price level and real expenditure, holding money and velocity constant (intuition: a higher price level reduces the real supply of money, which leads to a reduction in real expenditure). As a result, changes in this aggregate demand relationship only take place in response to a change in the money supply or a change in velocity. Monetarists believe that the demand for money and velocity are relatively stable if monetary policy is stable so that changes in aggregate demand are almost exclusively the result of changes in the money supply.

Note that, just like in the classical model, financial systems or changes in expectations play no role in initiating aggregate demand volatility; they just respond to it. While deemphasizing financial systems, Monetarists instead view the erratic monetary policies followed by misguided central bankers as the primary source of aggregate demand shocks that cause business cycles.

Output Determination in the Monetarist Model

The quantity theory equation can be rewritten in percent change terms:

$$\%\Delta M + \%\Delta V = \%\Delta P + \%\Delta Y \qquad (6.2)$$

To understand the intuition behind how changes in the money supply affect aggregate output in the quantity theory, consider the following example. Assume that velocity is constant ($\%\Delta V = 0\%$) and that the natural rate of real output growth is 2 percent ($\%\Delta Y = 2\%$). What will be the long-run effects of 5 percent money growth according to the quantity theory? If this 5 percent money growth is completely expected, then output growth will be at its natural rate of 2 percent and inflation will be 3 percent.

Now consider what happens if the central bank increases money growth from 5 percent to 10 percent and this increase is unanticipated by firms and households. The public will suddenly find themselves with excess money holdings because the money supply increased but money demand and velocity did not. The public can get rid of these balances in two ways: They can spend it or they can deposit it in a bank, leading to an increase in bank reserves. Banks get rid of these excess bank reserves by reducing interest rates, which in turn encourages investment and consumption and also stimulates spending. The end result is that if money growth rises by 10 percent then nominal spending growth ($\%\Delta P + \%\Delta Y$) has to rise by 10 percent as well.

However, a key question remains. If nominal expenditure rises by 10 percent, how much of this will be reflected in an increase in inflation ($\%\Delta P$) and how much of this will be an increase in real output ($\%\Delta Y$)? Monetarists contend that inflation will only rise slightly following an unexpected increase in the money supply and that most of the initial change will be in real output growth. Here is where adaptive expectations are important to the monetarist argument. Because firms did not foresee this increase in the money supply, they think that the demand for their specific product has risen, not that aggregate demand has risen. As a result, firms initially respond to any increase in the money supply by increasing production and not prices. At the same time, workers do not observe why firms are hiring more labor and nominal wages are rising. They think that this increase in the nominal wage is also an increase in the real wage and are fooled into working more. Thus, adaptive expectations imply that the aggregate supply curve in the short run is upward sloping and that unanticipated changes in the money supply have real effects on aggregate output. The slower expectations adjust to this unanticipated change in the money

Figure 6.1   The impact of an increase in the money supply in the monetarist model.

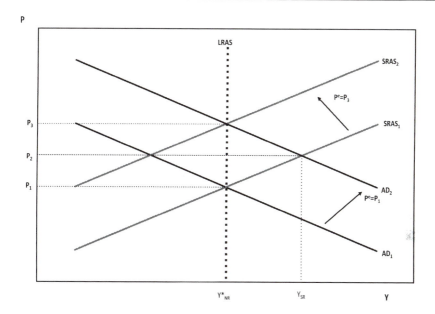

supply, the flatter the short-run aggregate supply curve will be and the larger the real impact of an increase in money growth on aggregate output.

However, the real effects of a change in money growth will not last forever. Figure 6.1 provides an aggregate demand/aggregate supply graph of the short-run effects of an increase in the money supply in the monetarist model and the process by which higher price expectations return the economy to the natural rate of output. Eventually, firms that are increasing their production levels will reach their capacity constraints and become more willing to increase prices. Also, workers will observe that the aggregate price level is rising and that their real wage is falling, causing them to reduce their labor supply, which forces firms to cut back on production. The short-run aggregate supply curve shifts to the left (to $SRAS_2$) as the expected price level increases and the economy gradually returns to its natural rate of output, or the rate of output that is consistent with the full employment of capital, labor, and technology.

Reconsidering the previous example, an unanticipated increase in money growth from 5 percent to 10 percent would lead to at least an 8 percent inflation rate in the long run once the economy returned to its natural rate of 2 percent real output growth (inflation could be higher than this if velocity increases in response to this higher inflation rate). This proposition that in the long run the economy returns to its natural rate of output and that a change in money growth only changes the level of inflation is referred to as the *natural rate hypothesis.*

How long is the long run? In monetarists' minds, the long-run is very long. According to Friedman and his research partner Anna Schwartz, it can take up to 10 years before the real effects of an unexpected change in the money supply disappear and leave only higher prices. This process takes so long because the public never has perfect information about the extent of the change in the money supply. They can only learn about monetary policy by observing past inflation rates. This requires a great deal of time and leads to long response lags.

BUSINESS CYCLES AND MONETARY POLICY

The monetarist model asserts that economic fluctuations are largely the result of unanticipated changes in the money supply that lead to fluctuations in aggregate demand. Expectation stickiness, not price stickiness like in the Keynesian model, means that changes in aggregate demand have real effects on output and unemployment. Recessionary periods in which output growth is below the natural rate are the result of money growth being lower than anticipated. Expansions, where output growth is above the natural rate, are caused by higher-than-anticipated money growth.

This begs an obvious question: If business cycles are largely caused by unstable monetary policy, then why is monetary policy so unstable? This was the topic of Friedman's (1968) address to the American Economic Association entitled "The Role of Monetary Policy." The principle point of this paper, in Friedman's words, is that "we are in danger of assigning to monetary policy a larger role than it can perform, in danger of asking it to accomplish tasks that it cannot achieve, and, as a result, preventing it from making the contribution that it is capable of making" (Friedman 1968). Friedman argues two seemingly contradictory points in this paper: Monetary policy is powerful, and central bankers should rarely, if ever, use it.

Goals That Monetary Policy Cannot Achieve

To understand why monetary policy can be destabilizing, Friedman first argues that there are three things that a central bank cannot do.

Figure 6.2   The impact of targeting an output level above the natural rate.

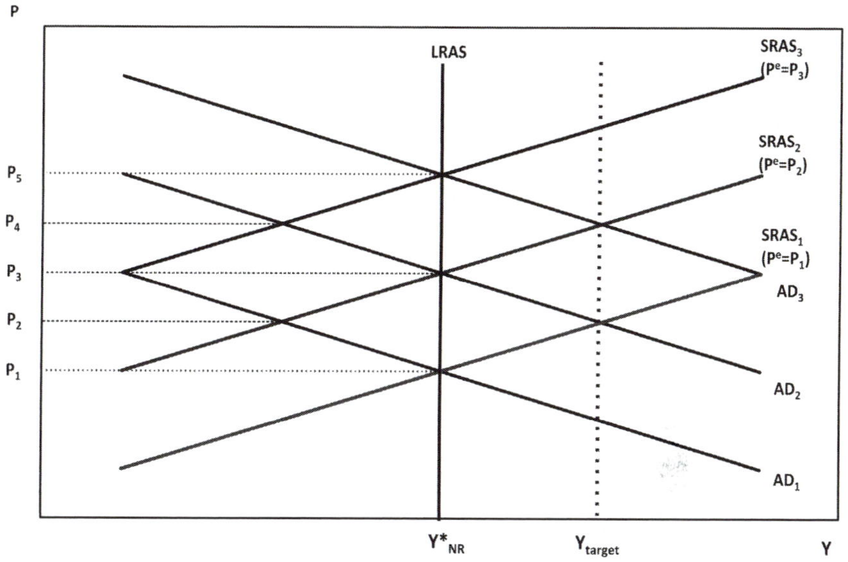

The Central Bank Cannot Control Output in the Long Run

Consider the consequences of a central bank attempting to target a level of aggregate output that is greater than the natural rate of output, such as illustrated in Figure 6.2. If the economy begins at the natural rate of output, the central bank can achieve its target by increasing the money supply and aggregate demand. The problem with this policy is that it will not work forever. Eventually, the public will increase their expected price level, the short-run aggregate supply curve will shift to the left, and the economy will return to its natural rate of output unless the central bank increases the money supply once again. If the central bank is persistent in maintaining this output target, the result will be accelerating inflation rates. Eventually, this high inflation will lead to a public clamor for lower inflation, and the central bank will be forced to accommodate these demands by lowering money growth and aggregate demand, leading to a recession.

The seemingly obvious solution is to make sure that central banks do not target output or employment at levels that are above their natural rates. The problem is that this is easier said than done. The natural rate of an economy is not an observable magnitude. Policy makers always have

Figure 6.3   The unemployment rate and the natural rate of unemployment.

Unemployment Rate (%)

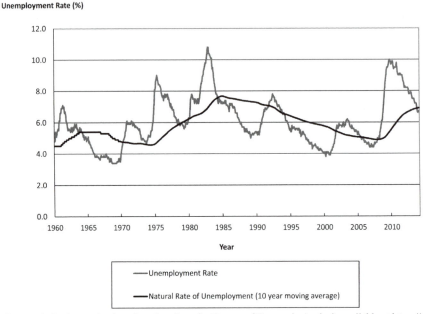

Year

Unemployment Rate

Natural Rate of Unemployment (10 year moving average)

Source: Author's creation based on data from the Bureau of Economic Analysis available at https://www.bea.gov/itable/index.cfm.

imperfect information about what the natural rates of output and employment actually are. In addition, these natural rates are not constant but can move with structural changes in the economy such as changes in demographics, changes in productivity, and changes in public policy. To see this, Figure 6.3 presents the unemployment rate in the United States and a moving-average estimate of the natural rate of unemployment from 1960 to 2013. This simple estimate of the natural rate has fluctuated between 4.5 percent and 7.5 percent over this period, which is a sizeable range. While there are more complex, and likely more accurate, methods of estimating the natural rate, there is no perfect estimate. As a result, targeting the natural rate of output or unemployment can potentially lead to accelerating inflation if the estimate of the natural rate used by policy makers is too high.

Monetarists believe that there is another practical problem associated with using stabilization policy even if you have perfect information about the natural rate of the economy, and that is that there are time lags between when policy makers identify a problem and when an implemented monetary policy has real effects on the economy. For example, there are lags in the information-gathering process, lags in the decision-making process at central banks, lags in the time that it takes the money multiplier to work, and lags in the time that it takes lower interest rates to stimulate aggregate demand and output. As a result, by the time that any policy is implemented and its effects are felt, it may no longer be needed. Friedman referred to this as the "fool in the shower" phenomena, where cold pipes always make the water that first comes out of the shower cold so that the initial reaction is to overreact and turn the hot water way up until the water comes out scalding hot. Likewise, in the case of monetary policy, policy makers that are trying to stabilize output will overact to changes in economic conditions because of lags between when the policy is implemented and when the effects of this policy are felt.

The Central Bank Cannot Control Unemployment in the Long Run

Friedman's natural rate hypothesis also rejects the Phillips curve relationship preached by Keynesian policy makers. Instead, Friedman argues that while a trade-off might exist between higher inflation and lower unemployment, it is temporary and unstable. It is temporary because eventually the public adjusts its price expectations in response to a change in the money supply. Prices and wages then adjust and the economy will return to the natural rate of output. The trade-off is unstable because the rate at which the public adjusts its adaptive expectations is not observable. Consider Figure 6.4, in which the public increases its expected price level in response to higher actual prices. A higher expected price level means that the central bank needs to set money growth and inflation at higher rates than needed before in order to fool firms and workers into increasing employment. In other words, a higher expected price level shifts the Phillips curve trade-off upwards toward higher levels of inflation for every rate of unemployment, and driving unemployment below the natural rate means experiencing even higher rates of inflation. Thus, there are an infinite number of Phillips curves that are possible within an economy, each of them consistent with a different expected price level. Without perfect knowledge of expectations, policy makers can never know exactly what the trade-off between inflation and unemployment is, making monetary policy based on the Phillips curve worthless—or worse, destabilizing.

The Central Bank Cannot Control Nominal Interest Rates in the Long Run

Monetary policy primarily influences output through its effects on interest rates. As a result, traditional operating procedures at most central

Figure 6.4   The Phillips curve tradeoff changes as the expected price level increases.

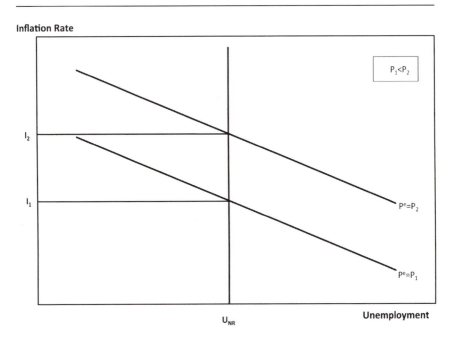

banks, including the U.S. Federal Reserve, are to target nominal interest rates on a day-to-day basis. However, Friedman argues that targeting nominal interest rates can lead to the same destabilizing inflation problems that are associated with targeting output and unemployment levels.

Nominal interest rates have two components, the expected inflation rate (the minimum a lender must receive on a loan in order to break even in real terms) and the real interest rate (the real profit rate a lender is expecting on a loan). The central bank can drive down nominal interest rates in the short run by increasing the money supply. The problem is that if the central bank persists in targeting interest rates at low levels by increasing the money supply, actual inflation will rise. This will eventually lead to a rise in expected inflation as well. When interest rates begin to rise because of higher expected inflation, the central bank will be forced to increase the money supply once again if it is committed to its nominal interest rate target. This process will keep repeating itself and inflation will continue to accelerate until public opinion turns against the central bank. Then the central bank will be forced to reduce the money supply in order to reduce inflation, leading to a fall in aggregate demand and an economic contraction. Thus, rigidly targeting nominal interest rates leads to monetary instability and economic fluctuations. By ignoring this distinction between nominal and real interest rates, Keynesians ignore the destabilizing effects of targeting interest rates just like they ignore the destabilizing effects of targeting output and unemployment.

In addition, targeting interest rates is a bad idea even if Keynesians are right and changes in aggregate demand are driven by exogenous changes in expectations and investment. If changes in investment demand drive business cycles, then interest rates will be procyclical. If the central bank targets interest rates, this would require the central bank to increase the money supply (to lower interest rates) during periods of high aggregate demand and decrease the money supply (to increase interest rates) during periods of low aggregate demand. Thus, rigid interest rate targets force monetary policy to be procyclical and amplify, not dampen, swings in the business cycle.

Goals That Monetary Policy Can Achieve

Monetary policy can prevent changes in the money supply from contributing to aggregate demand fluctuations. Because central bankers insist on using monetary policy to stabilize output, they end up creating a "yo-yo economy" where they let the money supply grow fast in order to increase output but are then forced to cut the money supply and decrease output in an effort to bring down accelerating inflation. Monetarists feel that central banks can avoid these policy swings by changing their goal from economic stabilization to monetary stabilization. Policy makers can do more for economic well-being by doing too little as opposed to trying to do too much.

Monetary policy can be used to achieve price stability. Friedman views inflation as very costly because it distorts the information prices provide and causes markets to operate inefficiently. In addition, unpredictable inflation increases the level of risk in the economy by eating away the real value of goods or assets with a fixed nominal price, such as bonds. According to former Federal Reserve chairman William McChesney Martin, "Inflation is a thief in the night." Friedman believes that sustained inflation is always the result of excess money growth. As a result, monetarists believe that keeping money growth and the inflation rate at low levels will increase economic efficiency and long-run growth.

Monetary policy can be used to offset major economic disturbances. For example, during periods of financial crisis, banking panics, or wars, central banks can provide temporary liquidity to financial markets. However, in the words of Friedman, "In this area particularly the best is likely to be the enemy of the good." In other words, the discretionary use of policy should be used in only the most extreme circumstances in order to avoid its excessive use.

To summarize, monetarists believe that instead of being a source of stabilization, monetary policy has been a destabilizing force that has led to greater inflation. In order to correct this, Friedman argues that central banks should control what they can control and target the money supply, not interest rates, output, unemployment, or any other real variable. By adopting a money growth rule that specifies that the money supply increases at a constant rate—say 5 percent each and every year—central banks will be able to achieve three important goals. First, central banks will be able to avoid sudden swings in policy, which will stabilize economic growth. Central banks will also be able to keep inflation at a low level, reducing the distortions created by inflation and increasing economic efficiency. Finally, central banks will be able to keep inflation steady, eliminating a large source of uncertainty in the economy, which should also increase economic efficiency. This would be a record of success that, in Friedman's opinion, is far superior to the record established by the use of Keynesian stabilization policy. In the words of Friedman:

> By setting itself a steady course and keeping to it, the monetary authority could make a major contribution to promoting economic stability. . . . Other forces would still affect the economy, require change and adjustment, and disturb the even tenor of our ways. But steady monetary growth would provide a monetary climate favorable to the effective operation of those basic forces of enterprise, ingenuity, invention, hard work, and thrift that are the true springs of economic growth. That is the most that we can ask from monetary policy at our present stage of knowledge. But that much—and it is a great deal—is clearly within our reach. (Friedman 1968)

EMPIRICAL EVIDENCE ON MONETARIST BUSINESS CYCLES

Is Money Growth a Leading Indicator of Changes in Aggregate Output?

Monetarists believe that most business cycles are initiated by changes in the money supply. Friedman and Schwartz (1963), in their book

A Monetary History of the United States, 1867–1960, document historical business cycles in the United States. They argue that all recessions over this period were preceded by inflation fears from earlier expansionary monetary policy, which forced the Federal Reserve to purposefully contract the money supply and initiate a recession in order to bring down inflation. This includes the Great Depression, during which the money supply fell by nearly one-third. In Chapter 14, postwar business cycles will be reviewed on a case-by-case basis. This story told by the monetarists appears to be consistent with most postwar recessions after 1960 as well. The most obvious example of this was the 1981–1982 recession, which was the most severe economic contraction in the United States since the Great Depression and was clearly the result of a severe contraction in monetary policy aimed at reducing skyrocketing inflation. Anderson and colleagues (2012) show that contractionary monetary policies have preceded all but the last two postwar recessions (in 2001 and 2007) in the United States.

On the other hand, money growth is not a very reliable indicator of changes in aggregate output. Figure 6.5 presents yearly money growth rates, where recessionary periods are shaded. Money growth is much more variable than output growth, and there are a number of instances where money growth fell quite significantly but the economy did not move into recession. One interesting example of this is the mid-1980s and mid-1990s, when money growth rates declined quite substantially but output growth remained quite strong. On the other hand, there are instances where money growth was quite strong but output growth dropped precipitously, such as during 2007–2009. Thus, there are reasons to question exactly how close a link there is between money growth and output growth.

Are Money Demand and Velocity Stable?

According to the quantity theory, the relationship between the money supply and nominal income is stable assuming velocity is constant. As a result, stable money demand and velocity are critical components of monetarist theory. Friedman argues that the demand for money is very stable because it is primarily determined by the public's wealth. The only factors that lead to fluctuations in wealth over short periods of time are changes in the inflation rate and changes in interest rates. Higher inflation and interest rates reduce money demand and increase velocity by reducing wealth and increasing the opportunity cost of holding money. However, monetary policy largely determines interest rates and inflation rates. If monetary

Figure 6.5   Yearly money growth and recessions in the United States.

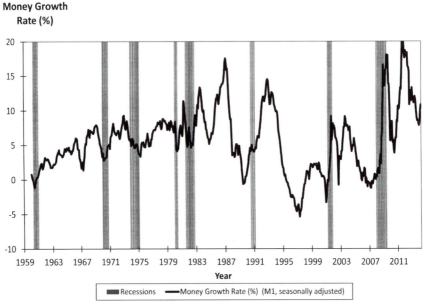

Money Growth
   Rate (%)

Source: Author's creation based on data from St. Louis Federal Reserve FRED database available at
http://research.stlouisfed.org/fred2/categories/25.

growth is stable and low, then interest rates, inflation, and velocity will also be stable and low. Thus, monetarists believe that a constant relationship should exist between money growth and output. If it does not, it is the central bank through its unstable monetary policy that has made it so.

However, there is a great deal of evidence that suggests that money demand and velocity are not stable—so unstable, in fact, that the central bank may not even be able to control the money supply, let alone keep it steady. Consider the M1 definition of the money supply in the United States, which includes the total amount of currency in circulation plus the amount of demand deposits in banks (i.e., bank deposits in which the balance can be withdrawn without condition). The Fed does not control M1 directly; it only controls what is referred to as the *monetary base*, which is currency in circulation plus reserves held by banks. Obviously, if the Fed places more bank reserves into the banking system then M1 will rise. How much it rises depends upon the *money multiplier*, or the ratio of the change in M1 to the change in the monetary base. The size of the money multiplier is based on how much demand deposits change when

Figure 6.6   Currency-to-deposit and excess reserve-to-deposit ratios.

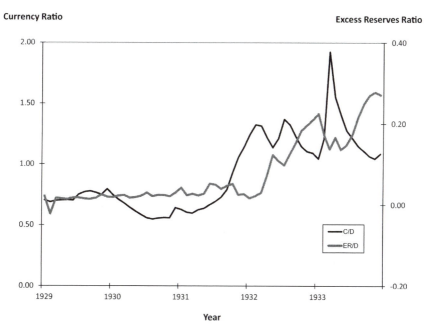

Source: Author's creation based on data from St. Louis Federal Reserve FRED database available at http://research.stlouisfed.org/fred2/categories/25.

there is a change in bank reserves. It is not controlled by the Fed but by the actions of banks, depositors, and borrowers.

To see how changes in money demand can change the money supply, consider two case studies. The first would be a financial crisis, such as what took place during the Great Depression. Figure 6.6 reports data on the ratios of currency-to-deposits (money holdings by the public) and excess reserves-to-deposits (money holdings by banks). The currency-to-deposit ratio rose significantly during the Great Depression, especially during 1931 and 1932 as banking panics occurred throughout the country. The excess reserves-to-deposits ratio rose gradually and did not rise by more because of the significant levels of deposit withdrawals from banks. The effects on the money supply can be seen in Figure 6.7, which presents M1 and the monetary base from 1929 to 1934. The Federal Reserve did little to increase the monetary base during the Depression, but M1 fell by roughly one-third. This was the result of increased precautionary money holdings by banks and the public. As money demand went up,

Figure 6.7   M1 and the monetary base during the Great Depression.

Money Supply
(in billions)

Source: Author's creation based on data from St. Louis Federal Reserve FRED database available at http://research.stlouisfed.org/fred2/categories/25.

bank deposits, lending, and the money multiplier dropped precipitously, significantly reducing M1. Thus, it appears that much of the fall in the money supply was the result of the Great Depression, not necessarily from a change in monetary policy that precipitated the Great Depression.

The problem for the monetarist model is that it argues that financial collapse is a symptom, not a cause, of economic collapse. The fact that this financial collapse was even more severe than the Depression itself and preceded the falls in aggregate output presents a persuasive *prima facie* case in support of the argument that financial systems were the crucial factor in causing this macroeconomic disintegration. Not only did stock values fall by 85 percent from their October 1929 peak, but real estate and other financial assets plummeted as well. In addition, nearly 25 percent of all banks failed—more than 10,000 banks in all. Bankruptcies reached record rates, while investment in new capital dropped to almost nothing. It seems difficult to explain all of these events by arguing that the primary cause was the public's misperception about the rate of growth in the money supply.

The second example of a change in velocity occurred during the 1980s and 1990s when financial deregulation spurred a great number of financial innovations. Some of the financial market changes that took place during the 1980s include ATM systems, interest-paying checking accounts, money market accounts, increased use of credit cards, hedge funds, mortgage backed securities, better information technology, and increased participation in the stock market. Each of these developments significantly changed the public's demand for money and bank deposits. As these variables changed, velocity and the money multiplier fluctuated wildly, and the stable relationship between the money supply and output fell apart. For instance, referring back to Figure 6.5, the money supply fell quite significantly between 1991 and 1995, but the economy experienced fairly strong output growth. The same happened in the mid-2000s. As a result, many economists have lost faith in the idea that maintaining a stable money supply is even possible, let alone the notion that a stable money supply can lead to stable output. In the words of Gerry Bouey, a former governor of the Bank of Canada, "We didn't abandon the monetary aggregates, they abandoned us."

Is There a Stable Trade-Off between Unemployment and Inflation?

Figure 6.8 graphs unemployment and inflation rates in the United States for the period 1961–2013. The breakdown of the Phillips curve during this long period is very strong evidence in favor of the natural rate hypothesis. As Friedman predicted in 1968, any trade-off between unemployment and inflation appears to break down the more that policy makers attempt to take advantage of it. However, Figure 6.8 also raises questions about the monetarist explanation of business cycles. Specifically, the dramatic increases in both inflation and unemployment that took place during 1973–1975 are hard to reconcile with a model in which changes in the money supply and aggregate demand are driving business cycles and in which the public adjusts their expectations slowly due to adaptive expectations. Likewise, how do monetarists explain the 1990s, when both inflation and unemployment fell rather quickly at the same time? It seems that the monetarist model alone cannot do so.

CONCLUSIONS

The monetarist theory of business cycles has been largely discredited by the behavior of the money supply since the 1980s. Likewise, monetarist claims that prices are perfectly flexible, that financial systems only respond passively to changes in output, and that expectations are adaptive

Figure 6.8   Unemployment and inflation rates in the United States, 1961–2013.

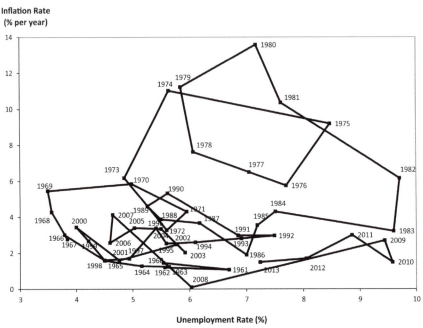

Source: Author's creation based on data from the Bureau of Economic Analysis available at https://www.bea.gov/itable/index.cfm.

have come under severe criticism by many modern macroeconomists. Very few economists today believe that monetary cycles are the primary cause of business cycles and that a stable money growth rule would stabilize output growth. However, that does not mean that Milton Friedman's work and the insights of monetarists have been forgotten. In fact, many aspects of monetarism continue to be very influential and include these five major contributions to modern business cycle theory.

1. *Monetarists raised consciousness about the importance of monetary policy.* Monetarists are largely responsible for the attention that monetary policy receives today from economists. Criticism of the Federal Reserve and other central banks by monetarists has greatly improved the transparency of these institutions by forcing them to be more open about their policies and activities. In addition,

changes in central bank operating procedures, particularly in terms of abandoning inflexible interest rate targets, are largely the result of monetarist criticism.

2. *Monetarists reestablished neoclassical principles such as money neutrality and the natural rate hypothesis.* Friedman's critique of the Phillips curve and his assertion that the trade-off between inflation and unemployment is temporary and unstable was a severe intellectual blow to Keynesian economics.

3. *Monetarists highlighted the importance of price expectations and their role in influencing the impact of government policy.* This is a theme that is adopted and expanded in rational expectations models, which are covered in the next chapter.

4. *Monetarists were the first to clearly make a distinction between the differing responses of real and nominal interest rates to changes in monetary policy.* As a result, they were able to explain differences in the behavior of short-term versus long-term interest. Monetarists explained how expansionary monetary policy might lead to a decrease in short-term interest rates but at the same time increase long-term interest rates by increasing expected inflation rates. Thus, low interest rates may not be indicative of high money growth but of low money growth, something that cannot be explained in Keynesian models.

5. *Monetarists raised real concerns about the destabilizing effects of stabilization policy.* Because of lags in policy and imperfect information about the natural rate of output, monetarists explained how countercyclical monetary policy could actually amplify business cycle fluctuations. Monetarists were not the first to examine Keynesian stabilization policy with a skeptical eye—that was the Austrians. But they were the first to do so in a neoclassical framework and explain their concerns in a way that has convinced most mainstream economists that some limits on the use of active macroeconomic policy aimed at stabilizing output are prudent.

When reviewing each of these contributions, it is clear that while monetarists may have lost the war, they won many of the battles. Monetarism provided an important critique of simple Keynesian theory and set the stage for future business cycle theories that also focused on the role of government policy in destabilizing economic growth. One of these models, the rational expectations model, will be discussed in the next chapter.

SUGGESTED READINGS

"Reflections on the Natural Rate Hypothesis," Joseph Stiglitz (1997): A discussion of the natural rate of unemployment, how and why it has changed over time, and its role in the making of economic policy.

"The Role of Monetary Policy," Milton Friedman (1968): One of the most influential papers in modern macroeconomics, in which Friedman states his vision for monetary policy.

"The Structure of Monetarism," Thomas Mayer (1975): A comprehensive discussion of the differences between Monetarism and Keynesian economics.

"The Triumph of Monetarism," Bradford De Long (2000): A look at the history of monetarism and its contributions to modern macroeconomic thought, including its influence on new Keynesian models, which are discussed in Chapter 9.

SEVEN

The Rational Expectations Model

INTRODUCTION

Economists have always believed that what people think about the future affects what they do today. As a result, expectations have long played a major role in business cycle theory, from early business cycle theories such as the sunspot and the cobweb models to Hayek's Austrian model. However, the debate in the middle of the century over the role of expectations was best exemplified by the different ways that expectations were treated in the Keynesian and monetarist models.

Keynesians focus on the role of expectations in generating investment and consumption volatility. In the Keynesian model, expectations are subject to extreme fluctuations because of uncertainty and animal spirits. These animal spirits are largely irrational, or at least not necessarily based on real economic fundamentals. Keynesians also believe that expectations are herd-driven and self-fulfilling. These volatile expectations drive business cycle fluctuations by influencing the decisions of firms to undertake investment projects and of households to purchase durable consumption goods.

Price expectations play a critical role in generating business cycles in the monetarist model where the public forms their expectations adaptively, or in a backward-looking manner. These adaptive expectations make price expectations slow to adjust to changes in economic conditions. As a result, changes in monetary policy that affect the actual price level can fool firms and workers into thinking that real conditions have changed, leading them to produce more or less than they would if they had perfect information. Thus, monetarists believe that lagging expectations and swings in monetary policy are responsible for business cycles.

There is a major inconsistency that is inherent in the way that both of these models treat expectations. The cornerstone of mainstream economics is the rational choice model, in which individuals make decisions based on weighing the benefits of an activity against its costs. For example, people are assumed to consume a good until the marginal benefit of another unit of the good equals the marginal cost of the next unit. The logical inconsistency in the Keynesian and monetarist models is this: Why do people not apply this same rational choice model to their formulation of expectations? These models assume that individuals are rational and forward looking when making all of their other decisions except when selecting their expectations of the future. As a result, these models are in conflict with a well-established microeconomic theory of utility and profit maximization.

The insight of rational expectations, which was first proposed by Muth (1961), is that this dissonance between how individuals form their expectations and how individuals make their other decisions can be reconciled by simply assuming agents form their expectations based on the rational choice model. In other words, *rational expectations* mean that individuals form their expectations by making an optimal forecast of the future using all currently available information. This implies that while the public can still make errors, they do not make predictable, or systematic, errors. This simple insight revolutionized modern macroeconomics when Robert Lucas developed a model that incorporated rational expectations into Friedman's natural rate model. This rational expectations model raised challenging questions about the causes of business cycles and the benefits of active stabilization policy, both monetary and fiscal policy.

Rational expectations have become an integral component of modern macroeconomics. This chapter discusses both the ways that the concept of rational expectations has revolutionized modern business cycle theory and also the empirical support (or lack thereof) for the rational expectations model and its explanation of recessions and expansions.

WHAT DOES RATIONAL EXPECTATIONS MEAN?

One of the most important misconceptions about rational expectations involves interpreting the phrase "all currently available information" in its definition. All currently available information means that the public knows (1) all data (past and present) that is cost effective to obtain and publicly known that might affect the variable on which expectations are being formed, and (2) the economic model and how different variables interact. It does not mean perfect information because some information may not be publicly available and because some information may be prohibitively costly to obtain (i.e., the marginal cost of such information is greater than its marginal benefit). Knowing the model simply means that individuals understand how, for instance, changes in monetary policy are likely to impact inflation and their nominal wages.

What if some segments of the public are not rational and do not use all available information when setting expectations? In this case, rational expectations are not invalidated. Those who are rational will take advantage of the profit opportunities created by those who are consistently making predictable mistakes. For example, if certain segments of the public consistently underestimate the future inflation rate, firms will take advantage of these workers by consistently paying them a real wage that is too low compared to those who form their expectations rationally and demand larger increases in their nominal wage. Over time, these irrational workers will figure out that their ignorance is costing them real income, and they will change their behavior. By following the lead of other rational workers they can receive higher real wages and higher standards of living at little cost. This notion—that individuals learn and do what is in their own best interest—is at the heart of the discipline of economics. To assert that individuals do not act rationally is to assert that a great deal of our economics is wrong.

Rational expectations imply that the public is both forward- and backward-looking. In other words, they do not just consider past data on things such as government policy when forming their expectations, but they also consider how the government might respond in the future to new information and how this response might affect the economy. Consider another example. Assume that it is widely known that the natural rate of output growth is 2 percent. Assume that the central bank sets the money growth rate at 5 percent. Because people have information about money growth and they (at least intuitively) understand the quantity theory, they will expect a 3 percent inflation rate and adjust their expectations and nominal wage demands accordingly.

Now suppose that the central bank raises money growth to 6 percent in an effort to increase output growth above 2 percent and the public knows what the central bank is attempting to do. Under adaptive expectations, the public would not adjust their expectations until they saw actual inflation begin to rise. As a result, this change in the money supply would have real effects on output growth until inflation expectations caught up with actual inflation. But under rational expectations, the public knows that money growth of 6 percent will eventually lead to inflation of 4 percent. They anticipate this higher inflation and immediately increase their expected inflation rate and their nominal wage demands. Money neutrality is restored very quickly, and real output growth remains at 2 percent. Thus, the central bank's ability to increase output above the natural rate has been greatly reduced. In fact, if the public has good information about monetary policy, then systematic monetary policy cannot affect real output growth, even in the short run. Only by surprising the public through acting unpredictably will monetary policy have real effects.

LUCAS'S RATIONAL EXPECTATIONS MODEL

The idea of rational expectations had floated on the fringes of macroeconomics for most of the 1960s. It was not until Robert Lucas (1972) showed how rational expectations could be integrated into a macroeconomic model that economists began to understand its full ramifications.

Lucas's rational expectations model is based on Friedman's natural rate model, which was discussed in the previous chapter on monetarism. In this model, there are a large number of firms and workers who operate within financial, goods, and labor markets with perfectly flexible prices and wages. The only market imperfection is one of information: Firms and workers cannot observe changes in aggregate demand and the aggregate price level; they can only observe the price of the good that they produce (their *own-price*). The only substantive difference between Friedman's and Lucas's model is that the public has rational expectations and not adaptive expectations.

How do firms and workers respond when they see their own-price increase? There are two extreme scenarios that could be followed. The first is that firms and workers view this as entirely the result of an increase in aggregate demand and inflation. In this case, the public increases its expected price level. Firms will not produce more as their own-price rises because they believe their relative price is staying constant. Likewise, workers will not be willing to work more as their nominal wage increases because they believe that their real wage is constant. In this case, there are no changes in any real variables such as aggregate output or employment.

The second extreme scenario is that firms and workers keep their expected price level constant and treat this increase in their own-price as entirely the result of an increase in their relative price from an increase in the demand for their good. In this case, firms will produce more. As workers see their nominal wage increase, they also believe their real wage is increasing and will work more. As firms produce more and workers work more, aggregate output increases.

Lucas's most important insight was to show that rational individuals who maximize profits and utility will respond to any increase in their own-price as if it was partially the result of an increase in inflation and partially the result of an increase in their relative price. In other words, rational agents will not respond according to either of the extreme scenarios discussed above but instead will make some compromise between these alternatives. As a result, any increase in the aggregate price level will to some extent fool firms and workers into increasing real output and employment, although not by as much as in an economy populated by agents who form their expectations adaptively.

In this rational expectations model, the following *Lucas supply equation* describes how aggregate output is determined:

$$Y_t - Y_{NR} = \alpha(P_t - P_t^e) + u_t \qquad (7.1)$$

Y_{NR} is the natural rate of output, P_t^e is the expected price level, and u_t represents exogenous real supply shocks that can also change the level of output. The intuition behind this equation is straightforward. Assuming no supply shocks ($u_t = 0$), if an increase in aggregate demand and the aggregate price level is completely anticipated ($P_t = P_t^e$), then output will always be at its natural rate ($Y_t = Y_{NR}$). However, an unexpected increase in aggregate demand and the price level ($P_t > P_t^e$) fools firms and workers into producing more and increases aggregate output above its natural rate ($Y_t > Y_{NR}$).

How much aggregate output increases in response to an unexpected increase in aggregate demand (which is based upon the value α of in the Lucas supply equation) is determined by how likely the public is to think that an increase in the aggregate price level is an increase in its relative price. Lucas shows that if people are rational, then the real response to an increase in the own-price becomes a function of how volatile monetary policy and aggregate prices have been in the past and how volatile they are expected to be in the future. In a country that has a history of variable inflation, there may be little real impact from an unexpected change in money growth (i.e., α will be small). On the other hand, in a country with a history of monetary stability, an unexpected change in money growth is more likely to have real effects on output (i.e., α will be large). Of course, if the central bank tries to take advantage of this fact and systematically increases money growth in an effort to increase output growth, the public will adjust its behavior and the central bank will quickly lose its power to influence output (i.e., α falls and the expected price level rises).

BUSINESS CYCLES IN THE RATIONAL EXPECTATIONS MODEL

Business cycles in the rational expectations model are temporary deviations from the natural rate of output caused by unanticipated changes in aggregate demand. For example, consider the effects of an unanticipated decrease in money growth by the central bank. This reduction in the money supply reduces aggregate demand. Firms mistakenly view this fall in aggregate demand, at least in part, as a decrease in the individual demand for their good and respond by cutting production and reducing nominal wages and employment. As workers see their nominal wages fall, they mistakenly believe that this is also a reduction in their real wages and reduce their labor supply. Until firms and workers realize that their own-price fell because aggregate demand fell, output and employment will remain below their natural rates and the economy will be in a recession. However, in a world of rational agents, this should not be a prolonged period of time. People will quickly realize that they have been operating under mistaken expectations. Firms and workers will adjust their production and labor supply accordingly, prices and wages will correct themselves, and the economy will return to its natural rate.

How can changes in aggregate demand be unanticipated if expectations are rational? Once again, remember that rational expectations do not mean perfect expectations. There are three very important reasons why changes in money policy are difficult to observe. First, most information on monetary policy only becomes available after a lag. There is also significant revision in monetary data, with initial estimates often differing significantly from subsequent data. Second, central banks often make temporary adjustments in the money supply to respond to temporary changes in market conditions. For example, the Fed may temporarily increase the money supply during periods of bad weather because the check-clearing process slows down. Even for expert "Fed-watchers," it is often difficult to separate permanent changes in the money supply from temporary changes. Third, the Fed and other central banks have historically been very secretive organizations. Until recently, the Fed never released press statements indicating when they were changing monetary policy. Proponents of the rational expectations model argue that one of the reasons the United States' economy has been more stable recently has been because of the Fed's new openness, which has provided the public better information about monetary policy.

Rational expectations has radical implications for stabilization policy. Systematic, or predictable, policies will always be anticipated by the public, who will adjust their expectations and their actions in anticipation of any change. The only way that a policy maker can influence real variables is if changes in policy are unanticipated by the public. In other words, the only way for policy makers to increase real output is for them to be secretive and unpredictable. Of course, the problem is that stabilization policy by its very nature cannot be unpredictable. Stabilization policy will not be able to stimulate output during recessions if everyone knows exactly how policy makers are going to respond beforehand.

In fact, if taken to its logical conclusions, the rational expectations model implies *policy irrelevance*, or that all government policies that are observable will be completely ineffective. This holds not just for monetary policy but for fiscal policy as well. Consider a deficit-financed tax cut aimed at stimulating aggregate demand. If the public is rational, they will realize that these deficits will have to be paid for in the future with higher taxes (if not by themselves, then by their heirs). As a result, they will likely save this entire tax cut, and aggregate demand will change very little or not at all. Likewise, a deficit-financed increase in government spending will also be matched by an increase in household saving, leading to at most a minimal change in aggregate demand. This notion of deficit irrelevance is often referred to as *Ricardian equivalence*, in reference to the classical economist David Ricardo who first formulated this concept. Unless these changes in fiscal policy are unanticipated, they will not have real effects, but if changes in policy are unanticipated, it cannot be the case that they are serving the goal of stabilizing output, only destabilizing output.

Another important implication of rational expectations is that without an understanding of how people adjust their expectations in response to changes in economic conditions, which in any given circumstance may be impossible to predict, any forecast of the future based on data from the past will be unreliable. This is referred to as the *Lucas critique*, and it raises important questions about stabilization policy because forecasting is an integral part of policy formation for two reasons. First, accurate forecasts of downturns are critical so that policy can be enacted in a timely manner. Second, the eventual impact of changes in policy must be understood in order for these policies to be conducted on the proper scale. If the impact of a policy is different under different sets of expectations, it may be impossible to correctly predict the impact of stabilization policy on the economy. This would result in a level of variability in the timing and effectiveness of policy that would seriously diminish the ability of policy makers to stabilize output.

To summarize, the rational expectations model implies that government policy cannot play a positive role in the economy. In fact, by being a large source of economic uncertainty, changes in government policy destabilize the economy and drive swings in the business cycle. Because of this, rational expectation proponents strongly believe in *laissez-faire* fiscal policies and rules-based monetary policies.

EMPIRICAL EVIDENCE ON RATIONAL EXPECTATIONS

Are Price Expectations Unbiased?

Unbiased expectations mean that, on average, price expectations are correct and errors are not consistently made in one direction or another. Many studies have investigated whether the Michigan Survey of Consumer Sentiment, which includes a question about the public's expected inflation rate, is an unbiased estimator of actual inflation. Other studies have relied on a regular survey of economists' expected inflation rates, called the Livingston survey. There does seem to be some close correlation between these two measures of expected inflation. There is also evidence that both of these estimates are biased in that they make persistent errors: They tend to underestimate inflation during periods of rising inflation and overestimate inflation during periods of falling inflation. See Mankiw and colleagues (2004) for a survey of this literature. Of course, there are problems in these empirical evaluations of rational expectations. The largest is that our estimates of expected inflation are based on survey data, which are very subjective and unreliable and can be biased by only a few individual responses. A second problem is that these are aggregate indices: By adding together everyone's expectations, they do not tell us much about the information differences across people and whether individual expectations might be rational but mistaken because of imperfect information.

How Do People Respond to Extreme Disinflations?

According to the Keynesian and monetarist models, any attempt to reduce inflation by reducing money growth will lead to a significant recession. In the case of *hyperinflation*, which is defined as inflation of greater than 1,000 percent a year, how can a government hope to reduce inflation without causing a complete economic collapse? Sargent (1986) investigated two hyperinflations that took place in Germany and Poland after

Table 7.1   The end of hyperinflations in Germany and Poland.

	Germany	
	Inflation rate	**Index of production**
1921	155%	77
1922	7,488	86
1923	4.2×10^{10}	54
1924	12	77
	Poland	
	Inflation rate	**Number of unemployed**
1921	136%	98,000
1922	819	116,255
1923	44,359	86,003
1924	0.19	127,936

Source: Author's creation based on data from Sargent (1986).

World War I, from which some data are reported in Table 7.1. First consider Germany, where inflation fell from over 42 billion percent in 1923 (that is not a typo) to 12 percent during 1924. At the same time that inflation was plummeting, industrial production actually rose significantly. In Poland, inflation fell from 44,000 percent to less than 1 percent during 1923. While unemployment rose in Poland, it did not rise by nearly as much as any monetarist or Keynesian would predict. The only way to explain these results is to recognize that the public adjusted its price expectations and nominal wages in response to these severe monetary contractions much more quickly than any model of adaptive expectations would predict. This is persuasive evidence in support of rational expectations.

Another economic episode that has received a great deal of attention from economists is the 1981 recession in the United States. This recession was caused by a large decrease in the money supply initiated by the Fed in an effort to reduce inflation, which had risen to nearly 10 percent. Figure 7.1 presents inflation and unemployment rates between 1979 and 1987. Inflation fell from 9.9 percent in 1981 to 3.6 percent in 1983, during which the United States experienced its worst unemployment since the Great Depression. Rational expectations proponents argue that this recession was not as severe as anticipated given the size and steepness of the decline in inflation. In addition, this recession was relatively short, lasting only 16 months. Critics of rational expectations charge that this monetary

Figure 7.1   Unemployment and inflation rates in the United States, 1979–1987.

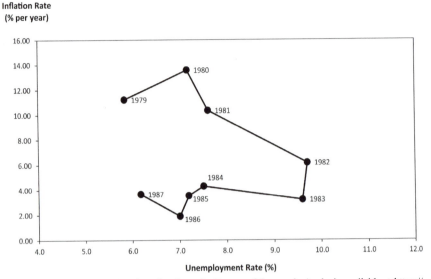

Source: Author's creation based on data from the Bureau of Economic Analysis available at https://www.bea.gov/itable/index.cfm.

contraction was widely announced by the Fed and taken seriously by the public. The fact that a severe recession still took place raises serious questions about the validity of the Lucas's rational expectations model. Instead, Mankiw and colleagues (2004) argue that it is more consistent with a model of rational expectations and "sticky expectations." In this case, information only disseminates gradually throughout the economy because of the high cost (i.e., disinterest) in acquiring it. As a result, inflation expectations are rational in the long run but are lagging and biased in the short run.

Does Output Volatility Differ across Countries?

As discussed earlier, the rational expectations model predicts that changes in aggregate demand and the price level are more likely to lead to large changes in real output within countries with a history of stable inflation. In other words, in terms of the Lucas supply equation (7.1), α should be higher in countries with a reputation for steady inflation. Lucas (1973) tested this hypothesis for 18 countries for the period 1952–1967.

The results for seven of these countries are reported in Table 7.2. Countries with a history of variable inflation, such as Argentina and Paraguay, have low estimated values for α, meaning that changes in aggregate demand had little real effect on output, just as Lucas predicted. Likewise, countries with a history of stable inflation, such as the United States and West Germany, had high estimated values for α. However, the correlation between inflation history and α is not perfect. Note that α is lower in Canada than in West Germany, even though prices were less variable in Canada. Likewise, α is lower in Argentina than in Paraguay even though price variance was considerably higher in Paraguay. However, taken as a whole, Lucas's study is strong evidence in favor of rational expectations and indicates that the reputation established by policy makers plays an important role in shaping the public's response to changes in aggregate demand. Lucas's study has been replicated using more current data and across different countries, with similar results (see Ashraf and Mohabbat 2011, and Holmes 2000).

In one final cross-country empirical study, Ball and colleagues (1988) found that the real effects of aggregate demand shifts both across countries and over time within one country were smaller when average inflation was higher. What is surprising about this study is that it actually raises questions about the rational expectations model. Why should average inflation matter, when it should be the variability of inflation that affects whether a change in aggregate demand is unexpected? This evidence suggests that the real effects from these demand shocks are not the result of the public being fooled but are more likely caused by other forms of market imperfection such as inflexible wages and prices.

Table 7.2 Estimates of the real effects of aggregate demand shocks, 1952–1967.

Country	α	Var(P)
Argentina	0.011	0.01998
Paraguay	0.022	0.03192
Italy	0.622	0.00044
UK	0.665	0.00037
Canada	0.759	0.00018
West Germany	0.820	0.00026
United States	0.910	0.00007

Source: Author's creation based on data from Lucas (1973).

Do Anticipated Changes in Aggregate Demand Have Real Effects?

A number of studies have attempted to classify aggregate demand shocks from fiscal and monetary policy into those that should have been easily predicted by the public and those that were unpredictable. These studies have uniformly found that both predictable and unpredictable shocks have real effects on output (see Mertens and Ravn 2011). In addition, price changes from the predictable demand shocks tend to lag behind changes in output by two to five years. These results are hard to reconcile with a model of rational expectations and perfect competition in which output fluctuations are driven by firms and workers who are temporarily fooled into changing their behavior.

Recently, the Federal Reserve has moved toward more openness in its operations and in its announcements of changes in monetary policy. By any definition, most changes in the money supply today should be anticipated by the public. And yet markets, policy makers, and the public all believe that changes in the money supply have real and long-lasting effects on output and unemployment in the future. The intense debates over expansionary fiscal and monetary policy during the recent global financial crisis attest to this. When are people being irrational—when they form their expectations or when they believe that changes in monetary policy have real effects on the economy?

CONCLUSIONS

Economist Robert Gordon has referred to the rational expectations model as economics "in which theory proceeds with impeccable logic from unrealistic assumptions to conclusions that contradict the historical record" (Gordon 1976). Even the preeminent proponent of rational expectations, Robert Lucas, has acknowledged that some of the implications of the rational expectations model, such as policy irrelevance, are not validated by what we observe in the real world. Few economists today believe that observable changes in policy are irrelevant to real economic activity and that only unexpected changes in policy influence output. Likewise, few people today think that the rational expectations model can adequately explain both the depth and persistence of business cycles. The assertion that the Great Depression as well as other economic and financial crises could be caused by great big misunderstandings takes implausibility to a whole new level.

However, this does not mean that the concept of rational expectations has been abandoned. In fact, rational expectations have become one of the cornerstone concepts in modern macroeconomics along with the natural rate hypothesis. Rational expectations have significantly advanced our understanding of business cycles in three important ways. First, rational expectations have corrected an important contradiction that had existed in macroeconomics by asserting that people do not just act rationally when making a decision about whether or not to buy orange juice, but they also act rationally and use all currently available information when forming their expectations of the future. Research on rational expectations has also focused attention on the importance of information in economics. "What do firms and workers know and when do they know it?" is now a fundamental question that must be addressed in all economic models. Finally, rational expectations have once again raised important questions about the ability of government policy to stabilize the economy and moderate, not amplify, business cycles.

What economists have increasingly come to question is not the idea of rational expectations but the rational expectations model in which individuals form their expectations within near-perfectly competitive labor, goods, and financial markets (the exception being imperfect information) with perfectly flexible prices and wages. Rational expectations in an imperfectly competitive model of the economy can have very different implications. For example, consider a model in which people have rational expectations but firms and households face financial market constraints on the amount of funds that they can borrow regardless of their future ability to pay the money back. In this model, any tax cut may not get saved to pay future taxes (which would lead to policy irrelevance) but instead could be spent in lieu of getting a bank loan. The result would be that tax cuts would increase consumption, investment, and real output growth. This would be a rational response to borrowing constraints. In fact, the initial size of the change in aggregate demand would be larger if expectations are formed rationally than if firms and households were slow to adjust to these tax cuts because of adaptive expectations. In other words, it is not necessarily rational expectations but the rational expectations model of perfectly flexible markets that generates what many economists consider to be implausible results.

Thus, as an idea, rational expectations continue to play an important role in business cycle theory. For example, it is a crucial component of real business cycle models, which are discussed in the next chapter; new Keynesian economics, which will be discussed in Chapter 9; and models of credit and financial instability, which are discussed in Chapters 10 and 11. It is interesting to note that the primary objective of new Keynesian and credit models is to show exactly how models with rational expectations and other microeconomic fundamentals can still exhibit market failure and other Keynesian results. However, the rational expectations model has largely been abandoned as an all-encompassing model of business cycle behavior.

SUGGESTED READINGS

"A Child's Guide to Rational Expectations," Rodney Maddock and Michael Carter (1982): A conversation about rational expectations.

Rational Expectations and Inflation, Thomas Sargent (2013): The 2011 Nobel laureate discusses the importance of rational expectations through historical case studies, beginning with the French Revolution, to the modern day with an analysis of the current financial crises in the United States and Europe.

"Rules, Discretion, and the Role of the Economic Advisor," Robert Lucas (1980): Lucas's arguments in support of Friedman's rules-based monetary policy and how rational expectations reinforce Friedman's skepticism about the effectiveness of stabilization policy.

EIGHT

Real Business Cycle Models

INTRODUCTION

Real business cycle models were developed in the 1980s but really represent the culmination of a movement toward reestablishing classical principles in business cycle theory that began in the 1960s. This process began with the monetarists, who agreed with Keynesians that business cycles were driven by aggregate demand shocks. However, monetarists argued that Keynesians ignored the natural rate of output and that changes in demand were not driven by animal spirits but by unstable monetary policy. As a result, monetarists found themselves arguing for limited government and *laissez-faire* policies, cornerstone beliefs of classical economics.

The rational expectations model took monetarist arguments one step further by asserting that only unexpected changes in policy can drive business cycles. The rational expectations model incorporated a stronger form of the natural rate hypothesis in which only erratic government policy could have real effects on output, eliminating any possibility that stabilization policy can be beneficial. Thus, the belief in rules-based, *laissez-faire* policies was held even more strongly among the advocates of this neoclassical model.

Real business cycle models took this neoclassical movement to its logical, if circular, conclusion by returning to all of the fundamental principles of the classical model. Real business cycle models assert that the natural rate hypothesis holds in the long run and in the short run because markets are perfectly competitive and individuals have perfect information. Aggregate demand is irrelevant to economic fluctuations, as are the workings of financial markets, and money neutrality always holds. Only aggregate supply, which is a function of the amount of labor, the amount of capital, and the aggregate level of productivity in an economy, determines the level of real output in an economy. As a result, in real business cycle models, only changes in aggregate supply generate business cycles. Government policies that create market distortions and reduce the incentives to work, invest, or innovate are the primary culprit in initiating fluctuations in output.

Interest in aggregate supply and its role in business cycles was spurred by two phenomena during the 1970s and 1980s. First, ideology played a role. Not only did real business cycle models build on the neoclassical resurgence of the 1960s and 1970s, but they also dovetailed nicely with a political movement referred to as *supply-side economics*, which is often associated with Ronald Reagan, who became president of the United States in 1981. Supply-side politicians assert that aggregate supply determines output and that the primary focus of policy makers should be on the negative effects of government taxation and regulation. In fact, supply-side politicians believe that taxes are so costly in terms of reducing the incentives to work and invest that cutting taxes will actually increase tax revenue. This is because tax cuts lead to extremely large increases in aggregate output.

Even more importantly, aggregate supply rose to the forefront of business cycle theory during the 1970s because of oil price shocks. OPEC placed an embargo on the United States in 1973, quadrupling the price of oil within a matter of months. Another large increase in the price of oil took place in 1979 after the Iranian revolution. These two oil shocks led to large reductions in aggregate supply. This is, in part, because these increases in the price of oil made much of the existing oil-intensive capital stock too expensive to operate, effectively reducing the level of capital available to firms. In addition, oil is an input into the production of every single good in modern economies (if for no other reason than that oil is needed to transport goods from here to there). As a result, increases in oil prices led to significant increases in the marginal cost of production across every single industry.

The result of these large decreases in aggregate supply was unprecedented *stagflation*, or rising unemployment and inflation at the same time. Stagflation runs exactly opposite of the Phillips curve view of the economy, where inflation and unemployment move in opposite directions. The Keynesian, monetarist, and rational expectations models, which primarily focus on aggregate demand shocks as the cause of recessions, had no plausible explanation for these events. However, the classical model, with its focus on aggregate supply shocks, did.

As a result of these ideological and empirical realities, economists in the 1980s were primed to modernize the classical model in an effort to provide a more plausible explanation of business cycles. How and how well real business cycle models accomplished this goal is the subject of this chapter.

DESCRIBING REAL BUSINESS CYCLE MODELS

The main difference between the classical model and a real business cycle model is in the level of detail that is incorporated into the economic analysis. While both are models of perfect competition in which the economy is always in equilibrium, real business cycle models are much more rigorously specified and explicitly include modern microeconomic principles such as marginal analysis. In other words, real business cycle models are characterized by individuals who maximize their utility and firms which maximize their profits subject to budget constraints. What makes these macroeconomic models and not simply well-specified microeconomic models is the assumption of *representative agents*, or that all individuals have the same preferences and act alike in every way. Likewise, all firms face the same production functions, cost curves, and budget constraints. As a result, macroeconomic behavior becomes a simple summation of microeconomic behavior.

Real business cycle models are actually based on neoclassical growth models, such as the Solow model (1956), which have been used extensively in macroeconomics since the 1950s to investigate issues related to long-run growth across countries. Real business cycle advocates assert that the same models that economists use to investigate the long-run growth behavior of economies can be used to investigate their short-run cyclical behavior as well.

The typical real business cycle production function takes the following form:

$$Y_t = F(K_t, L_t, u_t) \tag{8.1}$$

where

$$u_t = \delta + u_{t-1} + \varepsilon_t \tag{8.2}$$

This is similar to a classical production function but with one important difference: u_t, which represents changes in aggregate productivity. These productivity shocks follow a *random walk process*, given in equation (8.2), where δ is a constant and ε_t is a random variable which captures exogenous shocks to productivity. This random walk process implies that any random change in productivity from ε_t will have permanent effects on productivity and, as a result, on aggregate output. Positive values of ε_t will lead to permanent increases in output, and negative values of ε_t will lead to permanent falls in output. The implication is that business cycles in real business cycle models are not temporary deviations from the natural rate of output; instead, they are changes in the natural rate of output itself. A contraction in output will not end until a series of positive productivity shocks occur to offset previous negative shocks.

Intuitively, where do these productivity shocks come from? Real business cycle proponents argue that they can come from a number of sources.

Changes in the price of important inputs into production, such as the price of oil. Higher input prices can increase the costs of production and also reduce the productivity of capital by making a portion of the capital stock too expensive to operate. Large oil price increases in the United States proceeded recessions in 1973–1975, 1980, and 1990–1991. On the other hand, low oil prices such as those that existed throughout most of the 1980s and 1990s are typically associated with periods of increasing productivity and output. The price of other important raw materials such as steel, food, and coal also contribute to changes in aggregate productivity.

Changes in technology. While we typically think about changes in technology occurring at a constant rate, technology actually increases in fits and starts much like Schumpeter asserted in his theory of creative destruction, which was discussed in Chapter 5. Schumpeter argued that new technologies initially decrease productivity by pulling resources away from existing technologies that are highly productive because firms and workers have learned how to use them efficiently. Eventually, this new technology will increase once workers and firms better learn how to use it, but this process could take a number of years, potentially even generations. Once this happens, however, productivity growth will not remain permanently high because at some point diminishing returns to this new technology will set in. At that point, productivity growth will begin to fall until some other new technology is developed to take its place and begin the cycle all over again. Thus, Schumpeter viewed technology as a random, cyclical process that drives cyclical movements in output. Real business cycle proponents typically agree, although they would emphasize that these fluctuations in technology can explain not only long waves but short-term business cycles as well.

Changes in government taxation and regulation. Taxes lower aggregate productivity by reducing the incentives to work, invest in new capital technologies, and invest in education. For example, consider the effects of highly progressive income taxes. These taxes are most likely to affect those who are more highly educated, reducing the benefits of obtaining an education. Likewise, those who have the largest incomes also tend to save the largest fraction of their income, so progressive income taxation could reduce total savings and also total investment. Through these channels, changes in the tax code have an indirect effect on fluctuations in aggregate productivity.

New government regulations can also be highly distortionary. Worker safety standards, food and drug regulations, regulations on natural resource exploration, and many other government programs are viewed by real business cycle proponents as unnecessary constraints on markets and productivity growth.

Wars and natural disasters. Consider the effects of the terrorist attacks of September 11, 2001. By forcing the U.S. government to increase security requirements on airlines, roads, international travel, and so forth, these terrorist attacks have in all likelihood significantly reduced overall productivity within the economy. Wars often negatively impact the price of oil and other important inputs to production as well as lead to the destruction of both labor and capital.

Natural disasters tend to have their primary impact on the capital stock of an economy, and while their effect on aggregate productivity tends to be initially large, it also tends to be short lived.

Demographics. A worker's most productive years tend to be during middle-age when the worker's experience is at its peak and their physical condition has not deteriorated. As the population of a country gets older—which is happening across most developed countries such as the United States, Europe, and Japan—some impact on aggregate productivity is likely. On the other hand, other demographic factors, such as the continued tendency of women to join the labor market, have undoubtedly increased aggregate productivity because women are increasingly better educated than their male counterparts. However, most demographic changes take place gradually over a period of years, making them an unlikely cause of business cycles.

BUSINESS CYCLES IN REAL BUSINESS CYCLE MODELS

In real business cycle models, recessions and expansions are driven by cyclical changes in aggregate productivity. When a number of negative shocks from various sources occur simultaneously, output is likely to fall to a permanently lower level. The more frequent and the larger these shocks, the bigger the change in output will be.

It might seem strange that random shocks to productivity can create business cycle swings. Won't every negative shock be quickly offset by some positive shock? The answer is no. Economists and statisticians have long known that if you flip a coin 20 times, cyclical patterns will emerge. There will be series of heads that follow each other just as there will be series of tails. If productivity is a random variable, then it is not surprising that economies exhibit cyclical patterns. Persistent business cycles can come about as a result of luck that is inherent in any random process.

Different real business cycle models have highlighted other real reasons for business cycle persistence. One of the most influential real business cycle models is the "time-to-build" model developed by Kydland and Prescott (1982). In this model, lags in the time that it takes to construct capital make changes in output driven by productivity shocks highly persistent. Other real business cycle models have focused on the interplay between industrial sectors in an economy. In a model developed by Long and Plosser (1983), shocks to one industry spread slowly to other industries through changes in the demand for their products. This process takes time and can explain how recessions and expansions gradually build then gradually end.

Real business cycle models have clear prescriptions for how stabilization policy should operate. First, business cycles are efficient in real business cycle models. In other words, they do not represent lost output as suggested by aggregate demand theories of business cycles. Instead, they are an optimal response to real changes in the economy. As a result, stabilization policy is unnecessary. Instead, government policy should focus on supply-side policies aimed at increasing the productive capacity of the economy. The best way to do this is to follow a *laissez-faire* approach to government intervention in the economy.

Unemployment is also efficient in real business cycle models because it is completely voluntary. Involuntary unemployment is not possible because labor markets are perfectly competitive. Voluntary unemployment rises during recessions because real wages fall in response to negative productivity shocks that reduce the demand for labor. While this might strike many as implausible, real business cycle proponents would argue that the concept of involuntary unemployment was developed by economists to justify why some people do not want to take low-paying jobs. Can't a recently laid-off manager always find a job somewhere, even if it means working at a fast-food restaurant? Such a person might be saying that he or she cannot find a job, but what is really happening is that he or she is unwilling to take a large cut in pay.

Even more surprisingly, standard real business cycle models argue that money is neutral and never has real effects on the economy. Central banks control inflation but they cannot influence output because the money supply only influences aggregate demand and not aggregate supply (unless it discourages aggregate supply by increasing inflation). As a result, real business cycle proponents typically ignore monetary policy and argue for rules that will keep money growth and inflation low.

Government can influence output through fiscal policy in real business cycle models, but not in the way envisioned by Keynesians. Keynesians believe that lower taxes and higher government spending stimulate output by increasing aggregate demand. Real business cycle economists believe that lower taxes and higher government spending stimulate output by increasing aggregate supply. Lower taxes increase aggregate supply by increasing the incentives to work and invest in capital, education, and technology. What is not so obvious is why higher government spending would increase aggregate supply. The real business cycle argument is that higher government spending increases government deficits. The public realizes that these higher deficits will have to be paid off in the future with higher taxes, so they begin to work more now in order to accumulate the wealth needed to do this. This increase in labor supply increases aggregate supply and output. Consequently, these supply-side arguments, where everything that affects the economy does so through its effects on aggregate supply, turn traditional views of macroeconomic policy completely upside down.

EMPIRICAL EVIDENCE ON REAL BUSINESS CYCLE MODELS

Do Changes in Productivity Lead to Changes in Output?

Aggregate productivity is a difficult thing to measure. A widely used method of estimating aggregate productivity was developed by Robert Solow (1957) and uses the following production function:

$$Y_t = A_t K_t^{\alpha} L_t^{1-\alpha} \qquad (8.3)$$

This production function is in *Cobb–Douglas* form. Remember that this production function exhibits both *constant returns to scale*, meaning that doubling both capital and labor will double output, and *diminishing marginal returns*, meaning that holding one input constant, the increase in output gotten from increasing the other input falls as the quantity of that input rises.

A_t in this production function represents aggregate productivity. While aggregate productivity is not observable, all the other variables in equation (8.3) can be directly measured. One way to think about A_t is that it is the growth in output that cannot be explained by growth in inputs. As a result, taking output growth and subtracting out capital growth and labor growth, making sure to weight their contributions to output based on the value of α, will leave you with an estimate of A_t. This measure of aggregate productivity is commonly referred to as either the *Solow residual* or *multifactor productivity*.

Figure 8.1 presents the Solow residual and output growth in the United States from 1948 to 2011. Obviously, there is a close correlation between these two variables, with the Solow residual slightly leading changes in output. There is a huge problem, however, with using the Solow residual to measure changes in aggregate productivity. The Solow residual is not a direct but an implied measure of productivity. It is an "everything but the kitchen sink" estimate—everything other than input growth that affects output growth gets lumped together into the Solow residual. Some of the changes in the Solow residual might reflect changes in technology and other advances in productive efficiency, but some of the changes in the Solow residual might be caused by changes in factors that are not accounted for, such as unmeasured changes in the quality of capital or labor. As a result, the Solow residual includes much more than just exogenous changes in aggregate productivity.

For example, changes in worker effort can make the Solow residual respond to changes in aggregate demand even when there has been no change in aggregate supply. To understand why, consider a firm undergoing a decrease in demand during a recession. If this firm thinks that this downturn will be short, it is likely to resist laying off workers because of the costs involved. As a result, the firm's workers will find that they have less to do, and worker effort and productivity will decrease. On the other hand, during periods when business is unusually strong, the firm will ask these same workers to increase their efforts in order to meet higher demand. In other words, firms agree to smooth workers' employment in exchange for workers changing their effort during busy and slack times. This process is often referred to as *labor hoarding*.

A clear example of how labor hoarding and changes in labor effort can affect aggregate productivity occurred during World War II when

Figure 8.1   Solow residuals and real output growth in the United States.

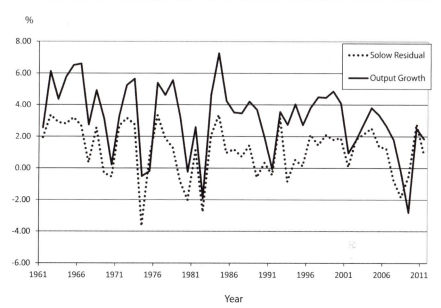

Source: Author's creation based on data from the Bureau of Economic Analysis available at https://www.bea.gov/itable/index.cfm.

productivity growth, as measured by the Solow residual, grew at a remarkable 7.6 percent a year on average. This large increase was not caused by any new technology. Instead, it was caused by large increases in the demand for government purchases and workers working harder because they felt their efforts contributed to the war effort. This suggests that procyclical changes in the Solow residual can be driven by changes in aggregate demand and do not always initiate, but are the result of, fluctuations in output. As a result, critics of real business cycle models would argue that the fact that changes in productivity lead changes in output does not necessarily mean that business cycles are aggregate supply driven.

How Well Do Real Business Cycle Models Mimic Business Cycle Data?

Because real business cycle models are completely specified versions of real economies, they can be used to simulate the real world, and their behavior can be directly compared to actual business cycle data. There are three steps to such a simulation. First, the researcher constructs the model and programs the relevant equations into a computer. Second, the

Table 8.1   Business cycle data for the U.S. economy and a real business cycle model.

	U.S. data	RBC model
Std. deviation of output	1.73	1.48 (0.17)
Std. deviation relative to output:		
Total consumption	0.49	0.55 (0.06)
Hours worked	0.79	0.71 (0.04)
Investment	3.10	3.47 (0.25)
Productivity	0.49	0.44 (0.04)
Correlation with output:		
Total consumption	0.75	0.68 (0.10)
Hours worked	0.87	0.92 (0.02)
Investment	0.89	0.93 (0.02)
Productivity	0.60	0.78 (0.06)
Corr (real wages, hours)	0.10	0.48 (0.11)

Source: Knoop (2013).

model is calibrated, meaning parameter values are chosen so that the model matches certain long-run properties of a given economy. Third, the model is subjected to shocks, such as productivity shocks estimated by the Solow residual or changes in taxes and government spending, and the behavior of key business cycle variables can be observed.

Table 8.1 presents business cycle data for the United States economy in the first column. This data includes the standard deviation of output, the standard deviation of other variables relative to output, and the correlation of these variables with output. In the second column, the same data generated by a standard real business cycle model is presented. This real business cycle model incorporates labor taxes, capital taxes, consumption taxes, Solow residual productivity shocks, and government spending shocks. Each is chosen to be consistent with the United States' cyclical data. Comparing the results, the similarities are striking. While output is not quite variable enough and the correlation between productivity and output is too high, for most variables this real business cycle model mimics the U.S. economy quite well.

Critics would argue that these kinds of results are not persuasive. If you have estimates of productivity shocks that are closely related to changes in output (even if there is no causation), it should not be surprising that putting these shocks into any sort of model will generate results that are close to what are observed in the real world. The key question is this: Where do these productivity shocks come from? Real business cycle proponents would argue that these productivity shocks primarily reflect exogenous changes in technology, government regulation, taxation, and input prices. Critics would argue that it is falling output that causes productivity to fall endogenously and not the other way around.

To better understand why many economists are so skeptical about real business cycle models, consider its explanation of the Great Depression. Real business cycle theorists are forced to argue that the Great Depression was caused by a reduction in aggregate productivity and aggregate supply, even though we know that prices fell during the Great Depression and this is inconsistent with a decrease in aggregate supply. What was the source of this fall in productivity? The most commonly mentioned culprit is the Smoot–Hawley tariff, which was imposed in 1930 and increased tariffs on imports by 40 percent. However, this was during a time when imports were only about 6 percent of GDP. To put it politely, this explanation is a bit of a stretch.

Are Real Wages Procyclical?

This question about the cyclicality of real wages was also raised during the discussion of Keynesian economics in Chapter 4. The evidence presented in Figure 4.5 suggests that real wages were strongly countercyclical during the Great Depression. Table 4.1 presents real wage correlations with output. Real wages have been only slightly procyclical during the postwar era and basically acyclical over the entire period. A large number of other studies have basically supported the conclusion that over long periods of time real wages are mildly procyclical to acyclical within the United States. These results raise red flags because real business cycle models need large procyclical changes in the real wage during business cycles in order to generate large changes in voluntary unemployment.

In addition, quite a bit of empirical evidence suggests that even when real wages do change, labor supply is inelastic and does not change by enough in response to changes in the real wage to explain cyclical movements in employment and the number of hours worked. Referring back to the last row of Table 8.1, the real business cycle model generated a correlation between real wages and hours worked of 0.48, while in the actual data this correlation is much closer to zero at 0.10. Thus, the empirical evidence on acyclical real wages and labor supply inelasticity suggests that it is something other than procyclical changes in real wages that is driving swings in employment. In other words, cyclical changes in employment do not appear to be entirely voluntary.

Do Monetary Policy or Financial Markets Influence Real Output?

The 1981–1982 recession was clearly caused by a large contraction in money growth initiated by the Fed to reduce inflation. How do you explain the 1981–1982 recession in a real business cycle model? The answer is that it is not possible in standard real business cycle models that assert money neutrality.

Any number of empirical studies examining the relationship between money and output could be cited here, but the commonsense answer to this question of whether monetary policy influences real output is yes. Even though it is true that some of the strong positive correlation between the money supply and output results from the money supply responding to changes in output (refer back to the discussion in Chapter 6), it is also clearly true that changes in the money supply have real effects on output, at least in the short run. While the public, policy makers, businesses, and markets all believe this to be the case, it is only the most extreme real business cycle advocates who do not.

The same goes for financial markets and their impact on output. Most observers during the Great Depression placed the primary responsibility for the crash on financial systems. Franklin Roosevelt stated in a 1933 address that "Unrestrained financial exploitations which created fictitious values never justified by earnings have been one of the great causes of our present tragic condition" (Fraser 2005). But in real business cycle models, financial systems only respond to—they do not cause—fluctuations in output. As a result, real business cycle models have no persuasive explanation of why financial volatility was both larger and preceded the collapse in output during the Great Depression and during other financial crises in more recent history.

CONCLUSIONS

Real business cycle theory defined much of the cutting-edge business cycle research during the 1980s, and its influence, though lessened, continues in modern macroeconomic theory. Economists today pay much more attention to supply factors such as productivity, capacity utilization, and input prices when investigating business cycles than they did previously.

While the supply shocks of the 1970s and the resurgence of interest in neoclassical economics played important roles in the popularity of real business cycle models, another extremely important factor in their appeal to economists is that they are based on microeconomic principles—principles such as utility maximization, profit maximization, and market equilibrium. In many economists' eyes, real business cycle models are both elegant and theoretically consistent. The fact that the study of both long-run growth and short-run business cycles could be merged into one unified macroeconomic model is also incredibly appealing to economists.

Gregory Mankiw (1989) argues that any good theory has to be both internally and externally consistent. By internally consistent he means that the theory has to be intuitively plausible and understandable. Because they are explicitly based on microeconomic theory that is widely accepted and has withstood the test of time, neoclassical models such as real business cycle models are internally consistent. However, to be externally consistent a theory has to be able to match the empirical facts. As we have discussed, by asserting that only aggregate supply matters in determining output, that money is neutral, that unemployment is entirely voluntary, and that productivity shocks are the only cause of business cycles, the predictions of real business cycle models do not seem to fit the facts of business cycles as we currently understand them. Keynesian economics, while failing to meet the objective of internal consistency because of its lack of microeconomic rigor, does considerably better at being externally consistent with the empirical data. Can economists develop a model that both is consistent with microeconomic theory and also can explain the facts of recessions and depressions in a plausible manner? New Keynesian models, the subject of Chapter 9, aim to reconcile neoclassical and Keynesian economics in an attempt to provide a unified theory of business cycles.

SUGGESTED READINGS

"Real Business Cycle Models: Past, Present, and Future," Sergio Rebelo (2005): A comprehensive evaluation of the limits and contributions of real business cycle models, including a look at their future in economic research and policy analysis.

"Real Business Cycles: A New Keynesian Perspective," N. Gregory Mankiw (1989): Criticisms of real business cycle models and methodology. Mankiw ends with arguments in support of new Keynesian models, which are the subject of Chapter 9.

"Understanding Real Business Cycles," Charles Plosser (1989): A comprehensive review of real business cycle models and their methodology. In this paper, Plosser works through the details of a basic real business cycle model.

"Unemployment Policy," Robert Lucas (1978): A neoclassical critique of the concepts of involuntary unemployment and full employment. Lucas argues that stabilization policy aimed at eliminating involuntary unemployment is likely to distract policy makers from the more legitimate goal of increasing economic efficiency through maintaining low inflation and reducing government regulation.

NINE

New Keynesian Models

INTRODUCTION

During the 1980s, economists began asking themselves a very important question: Can models be developed that incorporate rational expectations and the natural rate hypothesis but still exhibit Keynesian properties such as market failure, excess supply, and involuntary unemployment? This question was only natural given the decline in the influence of neoclassical models in the late 1980s. Real business cycle and rational expectations models fell out of favor because fewer economists believed their policy conclusions. In addition, new data increasingly challenged the neoclassical assumption of perfect price and wage flexibility. However, economists continued to believe in the concept of rational expectations, and they continued to be attracted to the microeconomic fundamentals incorporated in real business cycle models. At the same time, monetarism declined in popularity among economists for two additional reasons. First, the stagflation of the 1970s was clearly not caused by monetary policy alone, so the belief that changes in the money supply were the sole source of all business cycles seemed increasingly difficult to support. Second, the close relationships between the monetary base, the money supply, and output broke down during the 1980s. It seemed increasingly implausible to argue that policy makers should adhere to simple money growth rules when money demand, M1, and M2 behaved so unpredictably. However, most economists continued to believe, like monetarists, in the natural rate hypothesis and that monetary policy can play an important role in both stabilizing and destabilizing output.

New Keynesian economics is the name given to a new group of models that were developed to fill this void. New Keynesian models borrow the concepts of market failure and price inflexibility from Keynesian economics, the natural rate hypothesis and a focus on monetary policy from monetarist economics, the concept of rational expectations from the rational expectations model, and a belief in the importance of developing models with microeconomic foundations from real business cycle models. New Keynesian researchers have attempted to develop new and widely varied models in which market failure is generated by individuals engaging in optimizing behavior (not just through assumed, or ad hoc, behavioral assumptions). The ultimate goal of new Keynesian models is to better describe both the sources of imperfect competition and the role that market failure plays in business cycles.

WHAT NEW KEYNESIANS DO NOT BELIEVE

It is important to keep in mind that the term *new Keynesian* refers to multiple models with a common theme. In fact, there is no single model that can truly be called representative of this entire school of thought. As a result, it is often unclear exactly what new Keynesians believe in and what separates them from old Keynesians. Mankiw (1992) describes what he believes to be the core new Keynesian beliefs by stressing the six disagreements new Keynesians have with old Keynesians. On each of these points, notice how new Keynesians have adopted principles from previous business cycle theories.

1. *New Keynesians do not believe that reading* The General Theory *is the best way to understand business cycles.* New Keynesians believe that *The General Theory* is ambiguous, and a big reason for this ambiguity is its lack of rigor, especially when it comes to explaining the microeconomic foundations of macroeconomic behavior. For example, Keynes claimed that nominal wages are sticky downward. Why? If the answer is imperfect information and coordination failure, why do people not form their expectations rationally instead of basing their wage demands only on what their wages are relative to other workers? If the answer is wage contracts, then why do workers sign contracts if they lead to costly unemployment? By skipping over a number of the "Why?" questions, Keynes and his followers left many of their conclusions open to criticism. New Keynesians want to answer these questions based on detailed and

specific models in which individuals engage in optimizing behavior (i.e., behavior that is consistent with microeconomic theory).

2. *The lessons of the classical model are helpful* Keynes dismissed the classical model as a special case of his general theory. New Keynesians do not dismiss classical economics so readily. Especially important to new Keynesians is the idea that a natural rate of output and a natural rate of unemployment exist and that these natural rates are determined by capacity (i.e., aggregate supply) in the long run.

3. *Economies are not threatened by saving too much* Keynes's *paradox of thrift*, where economies can stagnate because of saving too much and consuming too little, ignores the fact that there is a positive relationship between higher savings and higher investment across countries in the long-run. New Keynesians place more emphasis on the positive impact of higher savings on long-run capital formation and output growth. As a result, they are more likely to worry about a country that does not save enough as opposed to one that saves too little.

4. *High inflation is not the cost of low unemployment* New Keynesians believe in the natural rate hypothesis and do not believe that there is a long-run tradeoff between inflation and unemployment. In the short run, like Monetarists, they do not believe that the tradeoff is stable enough to serve as a guide for monetary policy. The traditional Phillips curve is not a part of new Keynesian theory, only old Keynesian theory.

5. *Monetary policy can be used as a tool to stabilize output, while fiscal policy is much less useful* Old Keynesians believe in big fiscal policy multipliers. However, new Keynesians are more ambivalent about countercyclical fiscal policy. In part, this is because they recognize the political difficulties of trying to use fiscal policy in a timely manner to stabilize the economy. In addition, they are more worried about the negative impact of budget deficits and lower national savings than old Keynesians. As a result, new Keynesians are much more reluctant to advocate the aggressive use of fiscal policy to offset business cycles. On the other hand, despite Keynes's worry about a liquidity trap, new Keynesians believe that monetary policy can be an effective tool for output stabilization, but only if used correctly by policy makers. New Keynesians have highlighted a number of nontraditional methods of monetary policy which might be effective even if the economy is caught in a liquidity trap.

These new measures focus more on financial risk and the provision of credit than on the actual level of money supply or interest rates.

6. *Policy makers should favor rules over discretion* Keynesian aggregate demand management has an inflationary bias and is also subject to the simultaneous problems of policy lags, a lack of accurate forecasting, and the Lucas critique. Because of this, new Keynesians are generally proponents of policy rules in most circumstances. This is not because they believe that systematic monetary policy cannot influence output (like in the rational expectations and real business cycle models). Instead, they believe that the inherent difficulties in enacting the correct policies at the right time make effective stabilization policy much easier in theory than it is in practice. However, they also recognize the need for designing policy rules that provide policymakers some flexibility to respond to extraordinary economic shocks.

WHAT NEW KEYNESIANS DO BELIEVE

New Keynesian models generally fall into one of three categories: models of price inflexibility, models of nominal and real wage inflexibility, and models of credit and risk. (New Keynesian models of credit and risk will be covered in the next chapter, which discusses business cycle theories that focus on financial systems). Although they vary widely, it is important to understand that each of these new Keynesian models have features in common: in each model imperfect competition leads to some form of market failure and persistent disequilibria that can play a role in generating business cycles.

Models of Price Inflexibility

There is a sizeable amount of empirical data (some of which will be discussed later) which suggests that prices are not perfectly flexible but are slow to adjust to changes in supply and demand. If the prices of goods are rigid, then recessions can originate from disequilibria in the goods market, as opposed to relying on inflexible wages in the labor market as Keynes's general theory does. New Keynesian models focus on five primary sources of price inflexibility.

1. *Delivery and service considerations.* Firms can respond to changes in market conditions in many ways besides changing prices. For example, consider a period of high demand when firms' resources

are stretched. Instead of increasing prices, firms can lengthen delivery lags or cut back on other services associated with the goods they sell. This way, customers do not have to pay a higher price and firms do not have to increase capacity. On the other hand, during periods of low demand when resources are slack, firms can shorten delivery lags and improve services. They can then avoid cutting prices while still providing something of value to their customers. Hence, this group of models recognizes that price is just one margin on which firms can adjust their behavior in response to changes in demand and still satisfy their customers.

2. *Firms incur menu costs when changing listed prices.* Many firms are price setters and not price takers. As a result, prices for many goods are not determined by auctions or negotiation, as assumed in perfectly competitive models, but instead are chosen by firms trying to maximize profits. Often these prices are posted and fixed for a period of time. The primary reason for this is that firms and customers do not want to negotiate every price. Haggling takes time, and as our standards of living have increased, our time has gotten more valuable. Any small amount of money saved by customers through bargaining would likely be outweighed by the wasted time. In addition, higher wages mean that firms are reluctant to pay their workers to spend time negotiating prices. For these reasons, customers and firms alike in developed countries have increasingly preferred to bargain over only the biggest ticket items, such as cars and houses, and list the prices of other goods. (This is one reason why haggling over prices is more common in poorer countries than in richer countries.)

Posted prices mean that there are costs incurred by a firm every time it changes a price. The costs of changing prices are often called *menu costs*, alluding to the costs a restaurant would incur when it changes prices and has to print new menus. However, menu costs apply to a whole range of prices that are publicly posted such as those in department stores, catalogs, the Internet, and other advertisements.

Why do menu costs imply price inflexibility? Because even small menu costs give firms some incentive to resist changing their prices. Until the change in revenue from changing a price is sufficient to offset the menu costs, firms will not change the price. While this might only imply a small amount of price inflexibility at the individual firm level, Mankiw (1985) has shown that it is possible that even small menu costs lead to significant price inflexibility at the aggregate level and can create persistent surpluses or shortages that contribute to fluctuations in aggregate output. The menu costs associated with negotiating changes in prices can also explain why many suppliers and retailers operate under fixed-price contracts with their customers.

3. *Many prices are based on markup-pricing strategies.* For price setting firms with a large number of goods (department or grocery stores for instance), an easy and intuitive pricing method is *markup pricing*. Markup pricing refers to choosing a price that is simply a constant percentage above the good's cost. Markup pricing is simple to understand, straightforward to administer using an unskilled workforce, and easy to justify to customers. For this reason, markup pricing is exceptionally common, especially in the retail industry.

   Firms that follow markup-pricing strategies will only increase prices when their costs rise. They will not look ahead and anticipate changes in the marketplace, nor will they adjust their prices to changes in demand. Because of this, some new Keynesian models have shown that markup-pricing strategies imply a significant amount of price inflexibility.

4. *Firms are concerned about their relative prices.* A firm's optimal price is often dependent upon the pricing strategies of its competitors. As a result, firms may be very reluctant to raise prices unless their competitors raise their prices as well for fear of making their goods relatively more expensive. If firms could coordinate their changes in price, then prices would be perfectly flexible, but without a mechanism to ensure that some firms will not resist price increases in order to reduce their relative price and increase their market share, prices are slow to adjust. This phenomenon is referred to as *coordination failure*, which was highlighted previously in our discussion of the Keynesian model. Remember that Keynes argued that relative wage concerns led to coordination failure and wage inflexibility in the labor market.

   Under what conditions will coordination failure lead to price inflexibility? Obviously, a market has to be imperfectly competitive so that firms are price setters. However, it also has to be the case that the demand curves each individual firm faces in this market must be fairly price-elastic, meaning that consumers have to be responsive to changes in relative prices. If firm demand is highly elastic, then firms will lose a great deal of market share if there is an increase in their relative price. As a result, firms will be reluctant to change their price and there will be more price inflexibility in the industry. New Keynesians often refer to this as *real rigidity*, meaning rigidity in prices that stem from the market fundamentals of supply and demand in which these firms operate. More real rigidity means that prices will be slower to adjust and market disequilibria will be more persistent. However, real rigidity does a better job of explaining why prices are slow to adjust upward than why they are slow to fall.

5. *Firms and the public have sticky information.* Not everyone has the same information on which to base their inflation expectations. In large part this is because information has menu costs associated with collecting and processing it, and for some people these costs are likely to be larger than for other people. Among the public, and even among professional forecasters, quite a bit of disagreement often exists about future inflation rates, and large errors are often made. Mankiw and Reis (2002) develop a model in which information is costly to collect and process. These costs create differences in the speed of expectations adjustment across individuals. In such a model, changes in aggregate demand lead to changes in inflation that are only slowly incorporated into the public's expected inflation rate. The important difference between a model of sticky information and a model of adaptive expectations is that the slow speed of adjustment is consistent with rational behavior. When there are changes in the cost of obtaining information, the speed at which expectations adjust will change.

Models of Nominal and Real Wage Inflexibility

As opposed to models of price inflexibility in which business cycles originate in the goods market, other new Keynesian models have instead focused on Keynes's hypothesis that recessions originate in the labor market and are caused by nominal wage stickiness. These models have attempted to describe the microfoundations of how labor markets operate and explore in detail the reasons behind wage inflexibility.

1. *Explicit wage contracts.* Explicit wage contracts, such as union contracts, are an obvious source of nominal wage inflexibility. One reason for the existence of explicit wage contracts is that in industries with homogenous work forces and collective bargaining, wage renegotiations are very costly for both workers and firms because of the

threat of strike. Explicit contracts are a simple method of reducing the frequency of these negotiations.

Fischer (1977) has shown that an important implication of explicit contracts is that if the timing of contract negotiations is staggered throughout an economy, the time it takes for wages to fully respond to a shock will be much longer than the length of the wage contracts themselves. Consider a simple, if unrealistic, example. Suppose that there exists an economy with two groups of workers. Each group of workers negotiates a two-year labor contract with their employers during alternate years. Now suppose that the money supply and price level doubles in this economy. Can the first group of workers up for renegotiation (call them group 1) afford to demand a doubling of their nominal wage? No, because if they double their wage, all of the workers in group 1 will be twice as expensive as the workers from group 2, meaning that many workers from group 1 will lose their jobs to workers in group 2. Instead, the optimal response is for group 1 to only partially adjust their nominal wages. Likewise, when it comes time for group 2 to negotiate, they will also be reluctant to double their nominal wage and become more expensive than group 1. As a result, each of these groups will see their nominal wages slowly leap-frog over each other until the economy-wide nominal wage doubles. An obvious analogy can be made to a prison chain gain in which each worker has to walk a little slower when shackled to another prisoner than if he was alone. This wage adjustment process is likely to take an extended period of time and lead to persistent disequilibrium in the labor market.

2. *Implicit wage contracts.* When directly monitoring workers within a firm is difficult to do, individual job reviews of workers must be conducted on a regular basis. Because these reviews are costly, they are usually spaced at regular intervals, typically every six months or a year. Wages are usually held constant between reviews and, as a result, this review process implies a certain level of nominal wage inflexibility in labor markets.

3. *Minimum wage laws.* Minimum wage laws are legislated price floors on wages. When minimum wage laws are effective (meaning the legislated wage is above the equilibrium wage that would exist without the law), they create downward wage inflexibility. In the United States, minimum wage laws are only effective in certain subsectors of the labor market, namely the market for unskilled and low-experience workers. As a result, minimum wage laws, like

explicit and implicit contracts, can only provide a partial explanation of nominal wage inflexibility by themselves.

4. *Insider and outsider workers.* The insight of insider–outsider models is that workers who are already working for a firm (insiders) might have interests that differ from those of the firms they work for, which is profit maximization. Specifically, when insiders participate in hiring and training potential new workers (outsiders), insiders want to avoid hiring outsiders that are willing to work for lower real wages and could threaten the insiders' future raises. On the other hand, insiders also do not want to hire outsiders that are going to make considerably more than they are making, which could threaten the insiders' self-esteem. As a result, insider–outsider models show how significant nominal and real wage inflexibility can be inherent in the bargaining process for new workers because of incentive problems in the hiring and training process.

5. *Sticky information.* In the previous section, we discussed how costly information can lead to price inflexibility when these costs differ across different groups of individuals. Using the same intuition, sticky information could also lead to sticky nominal wages. The implications are similar to the explicit contract theories just discussed: Nominal wages are slow to adjust to changes in actual prices, which leads to labor market disequilibria and unemployment.

6. *Efficiency wages.* The foundation of efficiency wage models rests on a seemingly contradictory idea: Firms want to pay workers wages that are higher than equilibrium and are reluctant to cut wages during downturns, even in the presence of an excess supply of workers. The reason is that firms realize that their work force's productivity rises as real wages rise and falls as real wages fall. There are at least three reasons that productivity varies with wages. First, workers are more likely to shirk their responsibilities at lower wages because it is not that costly to be fired from a low-paying job. As a result, higher wages are a way of monitoring worker effort, especially in jobs where direct monitoring of workers is difficult. Second, firms that pay higher wages are more likely to attract and maintain the most productive workers. Third, higher wages reduce worker turnover and reduce the training costs incurred by firms. Therefore, firms with heterogeneous work forces are very reluctant to reduce both nominal and real wages for fear of harming worker productivity and the firm's ability to compete. Notice that, like insider–outsider models, efficiency wage models imply both nominal and real wage rigidity.

These new Keynesian models of price inflexibility and wage inflexibility are not mutually exclusive. In fact, important interactions between these different types of nominal rigidities can exist. Consider the case where both prices and nominal wages are inflexible. In this case, real wages would then be roughly constant and move acyclically over the business cycle. Remember from our discussions in Chapters 4 and 7 that there is quite a bit of empirical evidence that suggests real wages in the United States do not fluctuate very much over the business cycle and are approximately acyclical. Thus, the interaction between price and nominal wage inflexibility might itself be an additional source of real wage inflexibility and play a significant role in explaining the acyclical behavior of real wages. This would mean that a complete model of business cycles could include market failure in both the goods and labor markets simultaneously.

NEW KEYNESIAN BUSINESS CYCLES

An all-encompassing portrayal of business cycles in new Keynesian models is not easy to describe because there are so many different new Keynesian models. There is not one single cause of recessions that all of these models agree upon. Instead, these models highlight a number of market imperfections that, when considered together, explain how market failure and disequilibrium can persist over extended periods of time and create business cycles.

The "typical" new Keynesian recession, which is illustrated in Figure 9.1, begins with a decrease in aggregate demand. This fall in aggregate demand can be caused by a number of potential shocks. Aggregate demand could fall because of a change in expectations or risk perceptions that reduces investment and consumption demand, similar to the old Keynesian model. Aggregate demand could also fall because of a contraction in the money supply, which reduces the supply of credit and investment, as argued by the monetarists. Finally, and original to new Keynesian models, an increase in the default risk perceptions could reduce the supply of credit, leading to falls in consumption and investment (more on this in the next chapter).

New Keynesians also differ from previous theories in the propagation of recessions. New Keynesians provide a much more detailed analysis of the specifics of market failure and how market failure can magnify falls in output. First, inflexible prices can lead to persistent excess supply in the goods market, prompting firms to make additional cuts in production. Second, inflexible nominal and real wages can create excess supply in the labor market, leading to unemployment. Third, increases in risk

Figure 9.1   Recession initiated by a decrease in aggregate demand.

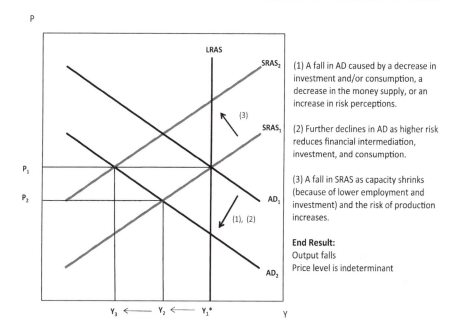

(1) A fall in AD caused by a decrease in investment and/or consumption, a decrease in the money supply, or an increase in risk perceptions.

(2) Further declines in AD as higher risk reduces financial intermediation, investment, and consumption.

(3) A fall in SRAS as capacity shrinks (because of lower employment and investment) and the risk of production increases.

End Result:
Output falls
Price level is indeterminant

perceptions can discourage production and also reduces the incentives to expand capacity. Note that each of these three factors not only magnifies the initial fall in aggregate demand but can also lead to decreases in aggregate supply. This means that a recession that starts with a decrease in aggregate demand can sustain itself through subsequent decreases in both aggregate demand and aggregate supply. Thus, new Keynesian business cycles recognize that contractions propagate themselves through many sectors of the economy simultaneously and typically involve declines in both aggregate demand and aggregate supply through failures in labor, goods, and financial markets.

Demand-initiated recessions can be self-correcting, but only after a number of things have happened. First, investment and consumption will recover as firms and households replace capital and consumer durables that have depreciated or become obsolete, increasing aggregate demand. In addition, prices and wages will fully adjust to the initial fall in aggregate demand and the price level, which will return the goods and labor markets to equilibrium and the aggregate economy back to its natural rate of output. Finally, as markets begin to clear, individuals will reassess their risk perceptions and be willing to engage in riskier spending and lending behavior. It is unclear how long it will take for all of these adjustments to take place; it could take a considerable length of time.

New Keynesians also accept the proposition that recessions can be initiated by changes in aggregate supply, such as during the 1970s oil price shocks, which reduce long-run aggregate supply and the natural rate of output. However, once again, the propagation of a supply-initiated recession is different from previous business cycles. An increase in input prices would also lead to involuntary unemployment in the labor market (because of inflexible wages) and higher risk perceptions. This would, in turn, lead to a decrease in aggregate demand and also a decrease in short-run aggregate supply that is larger than the decline in long-run aggregate supply. As a result, output in the short run would actually fall below the new, lower natural rate of output. Figure 9.2 illustrates a recession initiated by a decrease in aggregate supply. After initially dropping significantly (to Y_3), output will eventually rise to the new, but lower, natural rate of output (Y_2^*) as wages and prices adjust and as firms and financial institutions reduce their risk appraisals.

Figure 9.2   Recession initiated by a decrease in aggregate supply.

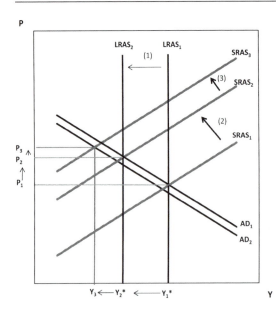

1) An increase in input prices (e.g. oil) reduces LRAS and the natural rate of output.

2) This increase in input prices also reduces SRAS.

3) AD falls and SRAS continues to fall as capacity falls and the risk of production increases.

End Result:
Output falls
Price level rises

NEW KEYNESIAN STABILIZATION POLICY
AND INFLATION TARGETING

What should be the role of monetary and fiscal policy in offsetting contractions to stabilize the economy? New Keynesians have a much more complicated view of discretionary stabilization policy than old Keynesians. On one hand, new Keynesians believe that monetary policy can be an effective tool for stabilization, while Keynes did not. New Keynesians are not as skeptical about the abilities and intelligence of central bankers as Keynes was. In addition, they do not view the liquidity trap as a dead end for monetary policy. New Keynesians believe that monetary policy can still be effective when interest rates are close to zero by serving to reduce financial risk and also by stabilizing asset prices (more details on these arguments in the next chapter).

On the other hand, new Keynesians are more reluctant than old Keynesians to believe that stabilization policy is unambiguously good. First, new Keynesians believe that fiscal policy is a very unreliable tool given the long policy lags created by the political realities of changing government spending and tax policies. New Keynesians also believe in rational expectations and the Lucas critique, meaning that they believe that policy changes can often have unpredictable effects on an economy depending upon how the public's expectations respond to any changes in policy. New Keynesians are also skeptical about the effectiveness of traditional monetary policy when risk perceptions are high because increasing the money supply will not necessarily lead to more lending being provided for investment and consumption (more on this in the next chapter as well). Finally, New Keynesians believe that recessions usually take place because of market failures that lead to declines in both aggregate demand and aggregate supply. The use of monetary policy, which works primarily through aggregate demand, may not be powerful enough to offset all business cycles.

Given the multiple complications that new Keynesians see in conducting monetary policy, most economists who call themselves new Keynesians (but not all) believe that policy makers should adopt some sort of policy rule. However, these rules tend to be broader and more flexible than the simple and rigid money growth rules proposed by monetarists like Friedman. The rules proposed by many new Keynesians adopt some combination of inflation and/or output targets. For example, Mankiw (1992) suggests that the Federal Reserve adopt a nominal GDP growth goal of 5 percent. If nominal GDP growth falls below 5 percent, either because of lower inflation or lower real output growth, the Fed would then increase the money supply until either inflation or real output growth rises.

Another policy rule that is increasingly popular among new Keynesians is an explicit inflation target. Under an inflation target, the central bank is required (through a law or a change in the constitution) to make the primary goal of monetary policy to be achieving a publically announced numerical target for the inflation rate. If this target is not achieved, then consequences must be imposed on policy makers in the central bank so that the inflation target is credible. (In democratic countries, publically announcing the inflation goal will create some market and political pressures that can serve to punish central bankers.)

According to its proponents, inflation targeting allows central banks to achieve the best of all possible worlds. A credible inflation target will stabilize inflation expectations and lead to more stable inflation and interest rates, also helping to create output stability. In addition, inflation targeting gives a central bank some flexibility to respond to short-run shocks, particularly if the central bank is judged on inflation averaged over a longer period of time (one to two years).

However, inflation targeting does come with potential limitations. One is that it is often difficult to sufficiently punish policy makers; without consequences, central bankers may fail to achieve their targets, reducing the credibility of the whole system. An even bigger problem with inflation targeting is that while inflation is primarily a function of monetary policy in the long run, central banks do not perfectly control the inflation rate in the short run. Many types of shocks can influence short-run inflation. As a result, many question how a central bank can achieve an inflation goal and create credibility when it does not perfectly control inflation.

One final problem with inflation targeting is that it can force central banks to engage in destabilizing monetary policy in the face of real supply shocks. To understand why this is, consider a negative supply shock. Under an inflexible inflation target, a central bank would be forced cut the money supply and reduce inflation at the cost of magnifying the fall in output.

Despite these concerns, inflation targeting is becoming increasingly popular among central banks. The early returns are quite positive. Empirical studies (for one review, see Woodford, 2007) have generally found that countries that adopt inflation targets have lower and more stable inflation without any increase in the volatility of output. This said, inflation targeting is a relatively new monetary strategy and has not been tested by a major economic crisis in many of countries where one has been adopted. Also, there are large differences in the credibility (and benefits) of inflation targeting within different countries depending upon the political and fiscal institutions that are in place. As a result, inflation targeting is unlikely to be a panacea under all circumstances at all times. But it is a potentially useful synthesis of rules-based and discretion-based monetary policy.

EMPIRICAL EVIDENCE ON NEW KEYNESIAN MODELS

A few of the most important empirical studies evaluating new Keynesian models of price and wage inflexibility are briefly reviewed here.

Are Nominal and Real Wages Inflexible?

Many studies have focused on microeconomic wage data, which indicates that nominal wages in the United States change only periodically and at irregular frequencies (see Barattieri et al. 2014). In a review of U.S. industry-level data from the large contractions of 1893, 1929, and 1981, Hanes (2000) found that nominal wages were more rigid in industries with higher earnings, higher capital intensity, and higher market concentration. Each of these characteristics is highly correlated with heterogeneous work forces. Because heterogeneous work forces are more difficult for firms to monitor, the insider–outsider, implicit contracts, and efficiency wage models of wage determination are each plausible explanations of this nominal wage rigidity.

In previous discussions, numerous references have been made to studies which suggest that real wages have been mildly procyclical to acyclical across countries (see Table 4.1). However, over shorter periods real wages have exhibited countercyclical (the 1930s) and procyclical (the 1970s and 1980s) behavior. One way to interpret this evidence is to say that a good business cycle model must be able to exhibit acyclical, procyclical, and countercyclical wage behavior depending upon different conditions. As discussed earlier, if both nominal wages and prices are inflexible, real wages will be acyclical in new Keynesian models. However, if prices are more rigid than nominal wages then real wages will be slightly procyclical, and if nominal wages are more rigid than prices then real wages will be slightly countercyclical. In other words, under different conditions, new Keynesian models can exhibit a wide range of real wage behavior just like that observed in the data. Consistent with this, Messina and colleagues (2009) find that real wages are more countercyclical in countries with stronger unions (less flexible nominal wages) and more open economies (with more flexible prices). Within the United States, the general consensus of the literature is that wages are not clearly countercyclical or procyclical (see Woitek 2004).

In addition, new Keynesian models can exhibit different real wage behavior depending upon whether shocks to aggregate demand or aggregate supply are driving business cycles. Sumner and Silver (1989) and

Kandil (2010) find that real wages tend to be countercyclical when prices are procyclical (which indicates that aggregate demand is moving) and real wages are procyclical when prices are countercyclical (which indicates aggregate supply is moving). Because new Keynesian models incorporate both aggregate demand and aggregate supply shocks in addition to nominal wage inflexibility, they are consistent with these different combinations of real wage and price cyclicality as well.

Are Prices Inflexible?

In a broad survey of studies investigating the microeconomic evidence on the price-setting behavior of firms, Klenow and Malin (2010) find that a great deal of variability exists among different goods regarding the frequency at which prices change. Their primary conclusions are that half of all prices change only a few times a year, but the changes are large when they do occur. These facts are consistent with menu costs, real rigidity, and sticky information explanations of price inflexibility. Also, they find that fundamentals do play a role in the frequency of price changes. Goods have fewer price changes when average inflation is low, the good is a service, or when the good is subject to few input cost shocks. These facts are consistent with markup-pricing behavior.

In a broad survey of business executives, Blinder (1991) reported that 55 percent of the 72 companies surveyed changed their price no more than once a year and that the average lags between a shock and a change in price was three to four months. Blinder found that delivery and service considerations, coordination failure, markup pricing, implicit and explicit contracts, and menu costs were all rated as moderately important reasons for price inflexibility by more than 40 percent of business executives surveyed.

Levy and colleagues (1997) looked at the cost of changing prices at supermarkets, which includes the costs of posting tags and signs or entering price information into computer systems. They find that these menu costs range between 0.5 percent and 1 percent of total revenues, which is large relative to the low profit margins in these stores. This suggests that menu costs might be a significant reason behind the reluctance of retailers to change prices.

Regarding the macroeconomic effects of this price inflexibility, Kiley (2000) found that countries with higher mean inflation changed prices more often. For example, the United States averaged 4 percent inflation between 1948 and 1996, during which the average price changed every 3.5 years. On the other hand, Argentina averaged 58 percent inflation and the average price changed every year (which is still a remarkably low rate of change). These results make sense given that firms have more incentive to change prices more often when inflation is higher. Kiley also found that countries with higher mean inflation had less persistent deviations of output from their natural rate, presumably because they changed their prices more often. Likewise, Ball and colleagues (1988) found that the real effects of demand shifts were smaller both across countries and over time within a single country when average inflation is higher, not just when it is more variable. This suggests that these real effects are not simply the result of the public being fooled by unexpected demand shocks but are caused by price and wage inflexibility. In addition, numerous other studies have found that both expected (i.e., easily predicable) and unexpected changes in aggregate demand have real effects on output, with price changes lagging behind changes in output by two to five years. All of this research supports the proposition that price inflexibility exists and that it plays a central role in creating persistent fluctuations in aggregate output.

CONCLUSIONS

Business cycles are different in subtle ways. A complete model of business cycles has to incorporate both aggregate demand and aggregate supply driven business cycles. A complete model of business cycles has to be able to account for multiple shocks from different sectors of the economy, whether from goods markets, labor markets, or financial markets. A complete model of business cycles also has to be able to exhibit a wide variety of behaviors in certain key variables. For example, consider real wages. As discussed in this chapter, over the long run real wages have been roughly acyclical. However, over shorter periods of time real wages have exhibited both countercyclical movements and procyclical movements.

Although the new Keynesian models discussed here are not yet a single, unified model of business cycles, taken as a whole they can explain this variety in behavior. By focusing on the microfoundations of market imperfections in goods markets (through price inflexibility), in labor markets (through wage inflexibility), and in financial markets (through imperfect information and risk discussed in the next chapter), new Keynesian models are consistent with both demand and supply driven contractions. New Keynesian models can also generate a wide variety of behavior in key variables. For example, once again consider the behavior of real wages in new Keynesian models. If both prices and nominal wages are inflexible, real wages will be acyclical. In the face of aggregate demand shocks, if nominal wages are more rigid than prices, then the real wage will be countercyclical; if prices are more rigid than nominal wages (or if aggregate supply is shifting), then the real wage will be procyclical.

However, what is considered a strength by some is considered a weakness by others. Critics of new Keynesian models charge that new Keynesian economics is not really a coherent school of thought but rather a hodge-podge of reasons for this or that market failure. To these critics, the fact that new Keynesian models can be consistent with any behavior in the real wage is an indictment of new Keynesian economics. How can you consider something a good model when it is always consistent with anything and everything you observe? A good model has to have empirically testable implications, and many economists feel that new Keynesian models fall short by this standard on many measures.

New Keynesian economics cannot yet provide a simple, specific, and complete model of business cycles. But by carefully focusing on the microfoundations of imperfect competition and market failure, they have advanced the discipline of economics considerably towards this goal. This is especially true regarding new Keynesian research on the role of financial markets, a topic that we turn to now as we examine macroeconomic models of risk and financial instability.

SUGGESTED READINGS

"The Fall and Rise of Keynesian Economics," Alan Blinder (1988): A discussion of why Keynesian thought has been so persuasive and persistent in macroeconomic theory. Included is a discussion of why Keynesian theory fell out of favor in the 1970s and 1980s and the reasons for its recent resurrection in the form of New Keynesian economics.

"New and Old Keynesians," Bruce Greenwald and Joseph Stiglitz (1993): This paper describes the primary differences between old and new Keynesians. It also provides an excellent discussion of new Keynesian models of risk and imperfect information.

"The New Keynesian Synthesis," David Romer (1993): A broad overview of the past and future directions of New Keynesian research.

"Price Flexibility and Output Stability: An Old Keynesian View," James Tobin (1993): A defense of old Keynesian economics against New Keynesian economics.

"The Reincarnation of Keynesian Economics," N. Gregory Mankiw (1992): This paper, which was briefly summarized at the beginning of this chapter, presents an interesting and understandable discussion of the differences between new and old Keynesians.

PART III

Financial Instability and Forecasting

TEN

Models of Credit and Financial Instability

INTRODUCTION

The study of financial markets within macroeconomics has undergone its own periods of boom and bust, but for a long time following Keynes financial explanations of business cycles were primarily bust. Keynes placed market failure in financial markets at the forefront of his general theory. According to Keynes, financial intermediation was synonymous with risk, and risk necessitated expectations based on limited information, which in turn created the animal spirits that drive business cycles. However, for the nearly 50 years following *The General Theory*, macroeconomic theory deemphasized the role that financial systems play in macroeconomic performance. First, Keynesians moved their focus away from investment volatility and toward consumption volatility, while the IS-LM model emphasized financial market flexibility. Then monetarists, followed by neoclassical theories such as the rational expectations model and real business cycle models, emphasized perfectly competitive financial markets with perfectly flexible prices. In these models, financial volatility was not the cause, only the symptom, of overall movements in the economy. As a result, in the opinion of many neoclassical economists, studying financial systems had little to contribute to the study of business cycles.

What is so surprising about these developments is that macroeconomic theory was ignoring financial markets at the same time that the importance of finance in the economy was growing. For example, the financial sector's share of GDP in the United States rose from 5 percent in 1980 to nearly 9 percent in 2013. The same holds in, and between, other developed countries as well. When people today talk about globalization, they are in large part talking about "financialization," or the increasing size and interconnectedness of capital markets (bond, equity, foreign exchange, and financial derivatives) and financial intermediaries (banks, investment banks, investment funds, insurance, and pension companies) within countries and across the world.

It is doubly surprising that finance was largely ignored in business cycle research because since 1900 every major economic crisis across the world has been associated with a financial crisis. When people think about the causes of major economic crises such as the Great Depression, the East Asian crisis, or the 2008 global financial crisis, financial markets are the first thing that comes to most people's minds. For example, "the stock market crash" and "bank failures" are the most commonly cited reasons for the Great Depression by the average person on the street.

A branch of new Keynesian theory slowly began to develop in the mid-1980s that aimed to end this neglect by focusing attention squarely on financial systems as the key source of macroeconomic volatility. Many of these newer theories owe much to older theories that were marginalized in mainstream macroeconomic research in the postwar era. This chapter begins by introducing two of these early theories, Fisher's debt-deflation theory and Minsky's financial instability hypothesis. We then move to new Keynesian theories of credit, particularly focusing on the financial accelerator model of Bernanke and Gertler and a model of credit rationing developed by Stiglitz and Weiss. After describing these models, the discussion turns to some of the implications of these models of credit for stabilization policy, specifically monetary policy. Finally, this chapter examines the empirical support for these models of credit and financial instability.

THE DEBT-DEFLATION THEORY

Irving Fisher, a prominent Princeton economist and the wealthy inventor of the Rolodex, pronounced that stocks had reached a permanently high level from which they would never retreat—two days before the October stock market crash. In a week, Fisher lost most of his fortune. Fischer subsequently tried to repay himself by figuring out what went wrong and why. Fischer's (1933) explanation became known as the debt-deflation theory.

The debt-deflation theory is broadly consistent with Keynes's general theory in a number of ways and eventually became a significant precursor to new Keynesian models of credit. The debt-deflation theory emphasizes what Fischer sees as the inherently volatile lending and borrowing behavior of banks and speculators. In Fisher's model, recessions actually begin during economic expansions. As an economic expansion sustains itself over time, households and firms gradually begin to build up debt. As debt levels grow, higher *leverage* (the ratio of debt to assets) raises concerns that many borrowers are growing increasingly close to being unable to meet their debt payments. At this point, a negative external shock, such as a drop in profits or a decrease in the money supply that puts upward pressure on interest rates, can tip the scales and push many borrowers into insolvency. Once a few defaults occur, panicked asset selling begins to quickly take place, particularly among those who are the most highly indebted. As others in the market observe increased selling, they begin to dump their assets as well and the broad-based panic selling of assets begins in earnest.

The larger the drop in asset prices, the larger the losses incurred by firms and households. This is primarily because the nominal value of the debt accumulated during the expansion is fixed and does not adjust with changes in the value of the asset. Most debt contracts are not *indexed*, meaning that the nominal value of debt owed does not adjust as the aggregate price level or the value of other assets drop. As a result, when the panic selling of assets puts downward pressure on prices, the real value of debt begins to increase. This puts additional strain on indebted firms and households, further exacerbating the panic selling and the speed of financial collapse. As bankruptcy becomes widespread, the financial positions of lenders deteriorate even more. In order to avoid collapse, lenders stop lending money, potentially to the point of a complete halt in financial intermediation. Without lending and borrowing, investment and consumption collapse, firms are forced to cut output, and a recession or even a depression occurs.

Recessions will eventually end, but only after a long period of retrenchment. After some time has passed, market observers will realize that there has likely been some overreaction and asset prices will begin to partially recover. As this happens, financial positions will gradually solidify, bankruptcies will decline, and lending will gradually resume. However, instead of waiting for a protracted recession to play itself out, Fisher argued that the better solution is to prevent full-scale financial collapse from occurring in the first place. His preferred remedy was the preemptive and aggressive use of monetary policy and emergency loans by the central bank aimed at stabilizing asset prices and credit before things spin out of control.

Two implications of Fisher's debt-deflation theory deserve emphasizing. First, Fisher believed that markets overreact to both good and bad news. Lenders provide loans too easily and borrowers tend to take on too much debt during booms, while lenders tend to pull back too much and borrowers begin panic selling too quickly during recessions. The question then, which is a fundamental one in financial theory, is just how rational, or irrational, is the decision making and expectations formation of individuals.

The other important feature of the debt-deflation theory is its recognition of the devastating effects of deflation. Asset and price level deflation is exceptionally costly because nominal debt contracts are fixed. Fischer's theory was the first theory to explain why deflation has been such a regular component of most major economic contractions in United States and European history, such as the Great Depression. Just how costly deflation is to an economy depends upon exactly how indebted a country is.

Economists have also observed other costs of deflation. For example, deflation can lead to *disintermediation*, or the withdraw of deposits from banks, by reducing interest rates to zero and eliminating the incentive people have to save their money in banks or in financial markets. Zero interest rates also reduce the power of monetary policy to stimulate consumption and investment by cutting interest rates any further. Thus, deflation can also be an integral component of Keynes's liquidity trap (more on this later).

THE FINANCIAL INSTABILITY HYPOTHESIS

During the 1960s, Keynesian theory was the prism through which economists viewed business cycles. However, many believed that Keynes's insights were perverted by the Keynesian IS-LM model, particularly in regards to its complete exclusion of market failure in the financial system. One group of rebels confusingly known as *post-Keynesian* economists (to be distinguished from Keynesians in general) attempted to reassert the role of financial systems as the primary driving force behind business cycles.

The most influential of these post-Keynesian economists was Hyman Minsky (1982), whose thinking owes a get deal not just to Keynes but to Irving Fischer as well. In his financial instability hypothesis model, Minsky argues that capitalist economies are inherently unstable because financial systems are inherently unstable. To understand finance, you first have to understand the decisions managers make. Specifically, Minsky believed that managers of firms engage in one of three types of financial strategies. *Hedged finance* refers to situations where firms have cash flows that are greater than the service payments they have to make on their debt, which includes both interest and principle payments. Hedged finance is obviously a safe situation for a firm to find itself in, but also less profitable because of a lack of leverage. *Speculative finance* refers to situations where firms have cash flows greater than interest payments that they are required to make, but not enough to significantly reduce the principle they owe. When engaging in speculative finance, firms find themselves in a more leveraged and risky financial position. *Ponzi finance* is the most risky of all and takes place when cash flows are insufficient to meet interest payments. As a result, these firms have to accumulate additional debt over time just to stay in operation. (The term *Ponzi* refers to the swindler Charles Ponzi and his "pyramid strategy" of paying off existing investors through attracting new investors without ever actually making profits.) Ponzi finance allows a firm to avoid bankruptcy in the near term but obviously cannot be pursued indefinitely without default.

Minsky believed that the financial strategies followed by firms change over time, sometimes as a result of conscious decisions made by managers to increase leverage and profitability, but many times because of macroeconomic changes associated with boom/bust cycles. During periods of strong growth and rising profits, firms find it easier to repay debt, so they have incentives to borrow more. This leads to increases in investment and further increases in growth. But continued borrowing also leads the firm past hedge financing and into speculative financing, possibly even into Ponzi financing. At some point, excessive optimism associated with the boom begins to dissipate. A negative shock occurs, possibly a large default or series of defaults. Business confidence disappears, leading to a contraction in credit, investment, profits, and output. Almost immediately, firms intending to engage in hedge or speculative financing find themselves engaging in Ponzi finance. As defaults begin to escalate, panic selling of assets starts and a process of financial and economic collapse similar to that described in the debt-deflation theory takes place. Thus, psychology and leverage, reflected in the fragile financial fundamentals of firms, play the primary roles in driving business cycles.

The psychology of markets is important in Minksy's opinion, and Minsky views the assumption of rational expectations as naïve. Instead, Minsky believes that rationality is more of a "long-run hypothesis," not an accurate portrayal of how market participants with limited information and subjective biases make decisions in the short run.

According to Minsky, there are no simple rules to combat financial crises. While central banks have the responsibility to serve as a lender of last resort in order to minimize financial collapse, they also have to worry about encouraging future speculation by always bailing lenders out (this is referred to as *moral hazard*). In addition, central banks have to worry about the inflationary pressures that will build over time if central banks are constantly issuing money to stabilize financial systems.

The most important thing that governments can do to promote economic stability is to engage in *prudential regulation* aimed at reducing speculative and Ponzi finance in the financial system. That said, Minsky was skeptical that regulation would ever be completely successful because of financial innovation. Any type of financial regulation implemented by governments aimed at limiting speculative and Ponzi financing will be circumvented over time because of the power of the profit motive. Governments must be constantly watchful and ready to adapt their practices and policies in anticipation of changes in market conditions. Most importantly, regulators have to closely monitor the financial conditions of firms and banks, being ever vigilant for signs of Ponzi financing and financial fragility. Proactive creation of new policies and effective enforcement of financial regulation requires a degree of competence that Minsky believed was quite uncommon in most regulatory agencies.

NEW KEYNESIAN MODELS OF CREDIT

By focusing on the importance of psychology and leverage, both the debt-deflation theory and the financial instability hypothesis model highlighted the role that the financial position of borrowers and lenders play in driving business cycles. New Keynesian models of credit build upon many of these same insights, but within more rigorous models that emphasize the microeconomic foundations of financial fragility.

The Four Fundamental Assertions of New Keynesian Models of Credit

1. *Understanding the macroeconomic implications of financial systems means first understanding the microeconomic fundamentals of borrowers and lenders and their impact on risk.* What defines a financial transaction from any other economic transaction is that finance takes place over time; as a result, there is an element of uncertainty and risk associated with any financial trade. Because all borrowers and lenders are unique, there is a great deal of heterogeneity in finance and not every transaction will involve the same amount of default risk. To understand the unique default risk associated with each loan, you must understand the microeconomic financial

fundamentals of both borrowers and lenders. The term *financial fundamentals* refers to net worth (assets minus liabilities), cash flows (cash receipts minus cash payments), leverage, and profits. It is these factors that determine the financial stability and risk of a borrower or lender. If these fundamentals are volatile, so too will be perceptions about default risk.

Although risk perceptions in new Keynesian models of credit are subjective, they are also formed on the basis of rational expectations. Changes in risk perceptions in new Keynesian models are rational responses to changes in the financial fundamentals of firms and banks. This separates new Keynesian theory from the Keynesian model as well as Fischer and Minsky's models. In these older models, expectations are governed by animal spirits and changes in expectations are highly speculative and not necessarily rational reactions to changes in the fundamentals of an economy.

2. *Credit is not the same thing as the money supply.* Changes in the money supply affect the amount of liquidity in the financial system, which is the total supply of funds available to be lent. However, a change in the money supply does not mean that there will be a change in the amount of credit actually provided to borrowers. The reason is risk. If perceived default risk is high, lenders will restrict credit regardless of the amount of liquidity in the financial system. Vice versa, if perceived risk is low, lenders will expand credit by increasing leverage regardless of the level of the money supply. As a result, the levels of lending and borrowing that are taking place within an economy reflect perceived levels of risk, not just the level of the money supply as often assumed in neoclassical models.

3. *Financial markets are imperfectly competitive because information is imperfect.* Going back to Adam Smith and *The Wealth of Nations*, it has long been recognized that financial systems are subject to market failures because of a lack of perfect information. Most government involvement in financial systems is aimed at improving the information available to participants so that they can make informed and efficient decisions. In fact, information is the most important input into any financial transaction. In the words of Walter Baghot (1873), credit is "the disposition of one man to trust another." Without information, there is no trust and there will not be credit.

The fundamental problem in finance is that *asymmetric information* is endemic, as borrowers always have better information about their ability (or intent) to repay a loan. This creates two problems. The first is *adverse selection*, which stems from the fact that the people who apply for loans are also more likely to default on a loan. For example, a gambler is more likely to apply for a loan than a tightwad. Lenders know this, and as a result are likely to restrict credit to all borrowers because they cannot always separate the good credit risks from the bad credit risks.

The second information problem comes after a loan has been made. Once someone has a loan, they get to keep all of the profits that result from this loan, but they share the losses with the lender in the case of default. If someone takes out a loan and plays roulette with the proceeds, they keep all of the winnings. If they lose it all, they default and the lender is stuck with the losses. This creates perverse incentives that encourage borrowers to engage in riskier behavior once they have a loan than they would if they were using their own money. This problem is referred to as *moral hazard*. Once again, lenders know that this is a problem, and as a result restrict credit because they cannot separate those who are most susceptible to adverse selection and moral hazard behavior from those who are not.

4. *Asymmetric information creates market failure, and as a result financial markets will not clear and persistent disequilibrium will exist.* In a financial market without risk, interest rates and prices would adjust to equate supply and demand. But in a world with asymmetric information, there is no reason to think that markets will clear. When risk perceptions are high, the demand for credit could be much greater than the amount of credit lenders are willing to provide. This disequilibrium not only means that financial intermediation is less than perfectly efficient, but it also has important implications for the volatility of credit during business cycles.

The Financial Accelerator Model

There are two principle new Keynesian models of credit. The first was developed in a series of papers by Ben Bernanke (the recent chairman of the U.S. Federal Reserve) and Mark Gertler (1987, 1989, 1990, 1995) and is referred to as the financial accelerator model. In this model, changes in the financial fundamentals of borrowers and lenders lead to changes in the *costs of credit intermediation*. These costs include the interest rate, but they also include information-gathering costs. In the case of a bank loan this would include *monitoring costs*, or the costs of periodically gathering and reporting information; *collateral costs*, or the costs of pledging collateral to back a loan; and *compensating balances*, or deposits made by the borrower to be held by the lender. In the case of stocks or bonds, this could also include things such as *underwriting costs*, or the costs of issuing these assets and selling them to the public.

Bernanke and Gertler's principle insight is that these costs of credit intermediation can be significant, and they fluctuate with the financial fundamentals of borrowers and lenders. Assume that a recession occurs that reduces profits, cash flows, and the net worth of firms. As financial fundamentals decline, the bankruptcy risk of these firms will rise. Lenders will now only provide financing to these firms under a much stricter set of conditions. Lenders will demand a higher interest rate to compensate for risk. Lenders are also likely to demand more information and more monitoring that will increase the costs of credit intermediation. All of these costs together will effectively price many firms out of the credit market at a time when, because of the recession, they need credit the most. This increase in the costs of credit will reduce the quantity demanded of investment and consumption, ultimately serving to magnify the severity of the recession.

The same thing can occur when the financial fundamentals of lenders deteriorate. As their own default risk rises, lenders become less willing to accept risk and will demand higher financing costs from potential borrowers. This also serves to restrict credit, investment, and consumption.

This simple model has four important implications for business cycles. The first is that the financial system does not initiate business cycles, but it does amplify them. Recessions begin with an exogenous shock to either aggregate demand or to aggregate supply that reduces the financial fundamentals of borrowers and lenders. From there, financial systems magnify the impact of this initial shock, making its effect on aggregate income much bigger than it would be without the resulting decline in credit.

Second, the financial accelerator mechanism creates changes in both aggregate demand and aggregate supply that propagate business cycles. Refer back to Figure 9.1 in Chapter 9, which describes a typical new Keynesian recession. This recession began with a negative shock to aggregate demand, such as a decline in expectations. Once aggregate demand falls, the financial fundamentals of borrowers and lenders also begin to decline. This drives up the costs of credit intermediation. As credit becomes more expensive, the demand for investment and consumption falls, which reduces aggregate demand even further. In addition, costly credit also increases default risk, increases the cost of holding inventories, and increases the risk for firms of producing more output. Each of these factors causes firms to cut back on their production, reducing aggregate supply as well. In essence, the increase in risk becomes a negative aggregate supply shock (as modeled by Christiano et al., 2014). This process of increasing risk leads to a downward spiral of simultaneous falls in aggregate demand and aggregate supply that generates a significant and lengthy economic contraction.

This recession will not end until a few things happen. First, consumption and investment demand will eventually stabilize once firms and households begin to replace capital and consumer durables that have depreciated over time. Second, real wages will gradually adjust to restore equilibrium in the labor market. Finally, as the financial fundamentals of lenders and firms stabilize, risk assessments will be reevaluated and risk perceptions are likely to fall, reducing the costs of credit intermediation and stimulating credit once again. How long these transitions back to equilibrium take, however, depends upon the flexibility of wages and prices. It also depends upon the flexibility of financial market participants in evaluating their risk perceptions. However, because financial fundamentals are slow to recover once they have fallen and because many borrowers will have to reestablish credit histories after a recession, the recovery is likely to take an extended period of time, leading to long-lasting recessions.

Third, the impact of the financial accelerator mechanism is nonlinear and asymmetric. It is nonlinear because the impact of the financial accelerator gets stronger the further financial fundamentals decline: A small fall in net worths may have no impact, a larger fall in net worths might lead to a large rise in the costs of credit intermediation and a disproportionately large fall in credit. It is asymmetric because the financial accelerator is one-sided. During good times when financial fundamentals are strong, risk perceptions are low, and profit opportunities are high, firms are unlikely to be sensitive to changes in their costs of credit intermediation. It is only during downturns when default risk is rising and profits are falling that firms will be sensitive to any change in their costs of credit.

The fourth implication is that changes in the costs of credit intermediation do not affect all borrowers the same. They disproportionally impact borrowers with smaller net worths and shorter credit histories. This means that households with lower income as well as smaller and newer firms are most likely to find their credit costs rise the most during recessions. Likewise, smaller lenders with lower net worths, such as regional banks, are most likely to find themselves increasing their costs of credit during a recession. This heterogeneity means that economic downturns disproportionally impact the weakest within an economy.

Models of Credit Rationing

A potential weakness of the financial accelerator model is that it relies on changes in the quantity demanded for credit, caused by changes in the costs of credit, to explain why financial intermediation declines during recessions. The problem with this explanation is that credit actually fluctuates a great deal more than interest rates and other costs of credit intermediation. In addition, during any recession there are voluminous reports of firms and households who are willing to pay higher prices for credit but still are not able to get access to it. In other words, it is likely that changes in the supply of credit, not changes in the quantity demanded for credit, are the driving factors behind credit fluctuations.

This is the principle insight of the seminal model of credit rationing developed by Joseph Stiglitz and Andrew Weiss (1981), which is one of the most influential models in modern macroeconomics. Like the financial accelerator model, this model of credit rationing emphasizes the importance of financial fundamentals and default risk. However, models of credit rationing assert that credit is not price-rationed but quantity-rationed. During periods when financial fundamentals are deteriorating and risk perceptions are rising, lenders may stop lending regardless of the price a borrower is willing to pay because if the lender does not think they are going to get their money back, lending at even the highest interest rates with the strictest information standards will not be profitable. As net worths fluctuate over the business cycle, so too will the credit limits that lenders impose on borrowers, leading to procyclical changes in the supply of credit that amplify business cycles.

In Stiglitz and Weiss's model, lenders prefer credit rationing over price rationing because of the problems of asymmetric information and moral hazard. The authors argue that the return a lender receives on a loan is a function of the interest rate paid on the loan but also of the probability the loan will be repaid. If a lender tries to increase the interest rate on a borrower during a recession, it might actually reduce the lender's expected return because higher interest rates will encourage borrowers to engage in riskier behavior than they previously would; this is what we referred to earlier as moral hazard. As a result, increasing the costs of credit during downturns might actually reduce the profits of lenders. The only way lenders can increase their profitability is by reducing their risk exposure, specifically by cutting back on lending to the riskiest borrowers (those with the weakest financial fundamentals). They do this through the imposition of credit limits. These credit limits can be specific quantity amounts, they could be a percentage of any borrowing requested, or they could be imposed by requiring more collateral to back loans. Regardless of the exact form, these credit limits mean that persistent disequilibrium will exist in financial markets and many borrowers will be willing to pay higher rates to get credit but still cannot find access to it.

In a similar model of credit rationing developed by Kiyotaki and Moore (1997), lenders require all of the loans they provide to be fully backed by collateral, imposing a credit limit on borrowers that is equal to the total value of their assets. Under these conditions, it is not changes in cash flows or net worth that change the credit constraints borrowers face, but it is changes in the price of the borrower's assets that tighten or loosen these constraints. As a result, when borrowers see the value of their assets fall, they also see the value of their collateral drop, tightening their credit limits. This forces reductions in investment and consumption that create a feedback loop in which reductions in aggregate output lead to continued reductions in asset prices and credit, which in turn leads to additional falls in aggregate demand. If a firm's primary collateral is its stock value, Liu and Wang (2014) show that business cycles can be self-fulfilling: An increase in the perceived risk of a recession leads to falls in stock prices, which tightens credit constraints and causes a recession.

Models of credit rationing have many similar implications to the financial accelerator model discussed earlier. First, credit rationing does not cause business cycles, it only amplifies them. Second, credit rationing not only reduces aggregate demand by causing falls in investment and consumption, but it also reduces aggregate supply by increasing the risk of production and the costs of holding inventories. Third, the impact of credit rationing is asymmetric and nonlinear, only amplifying contractions and only impacting the macroeconomy when borrowers reach their credit limits, but not before. Fourth, credit rationing disproportionally affects those with the weakest financial fundamentals: poor households, small and newer firms, and smaller lenders.

However, there are two important differences between the financial accelerator and credit rationing models. The first is that under credit rationing, interest rates and the demand for credit are not good indicators of the actual amount of credit available to borrowers. In fact, lenders are reluctant to increase interest rates during downturns because of the moral hazard problems that higher interest rates create. Instead, it is the supply of credit that drives credit cycles in models of credit rationing. In this sense, models of credit rationing are more similar to the debt-deflation and financial instability hypothesis models that also emphasized fluctuations in the supply of credit, not only the demand for credit. The fact that credit is not driven by the demand for borrowing also has important implications for monetary policy, which we will talk about in the next section.

Second, credit rationing also implies that credit chains can be broken. Most firms are simultaneously consumers and producers, lenders and borrowers. Firms consume inputs from suppliers and produce output for their customers. Likewise, firms borrow money from their suppliers and lend money to their customers, often in the form of accounts receivable. This is a very important, and often ignored, source of finance that creates "credit chains." These credit chains ease the flow of funds and increase efficiency across the economy. In the presence of credit rationing, however, when one firm gets cut off it is forced to cut off its customers, breaking a link in these credit chains that can magnify the impact of credit rationing across the economy. Thus, credit rationing creates a potentially powerful amplifying mechanism for economic contractions.

MONETARY POLICY IN NEW KEYNESIAN MODELS OF CREDIT

New Keynesian models of credit have not only changed how macroeconomists think about business cycles, but they have changed how they think about stabilization policy, particularly in regards to monetary policy. In traditional views of monetary policy, an increase in the money supply stimulates output through three channels: the *interest rate channel* (lower interest rates spur lending, consumption, and investment), the *wealth channel* (lower interest rates increase stock prices and other assets, increasing wealth, consumption, and investment), and the *exchange rate channel* (lower interest rates and higher inflation reduce the exchange rate, increasing exports). According to each of these channels, monetary policy impacts aggregate output only by changing aggregate demand.

The key to each of these channels is this assertion: Monetary policy primarily works through interest rates. The question, however, is why should interest rates be so important? In the financial accelerator model, interest rates are only a part of the costs of credit intermediation and do not tell the whole story about how costly credit actually is. In credit rationing models, interest rates are no indication of the supply of credit actually available. As a result, these new Keynesian models of credit raise real questions about how monetary policy works outside of its impact on interest rates.

New Keynesians point to alternative avenues through which monetary policy has the power to affect the net worths of banks and firms and as a result can affect credit and output regardless of the level of interest rates.

These alternative mechanisms are referred to as *balance sheet channels* because they work through the financial fundamentals of borrowers and lenders. For example, when the central bank increases the money supply and lowers interest rates, the profits and cash flows of borrowers typically improve. Also, stock prices and other assets are likely to rise, increasing liquidity, cash flows, and net worths. These improvements in financial fundamentals can stimulate credit and output in a number of ways. Improved financial fundamentals reduce the costs of credit intermediation, as emphasized by the financial accelerator model. They also lead to looser credit limits, either directly or by increasing the value of collateral, as emphasized by models of credit rationing. As highlighted in Stiglitz and Weiss's model, lower interest rates can also reduce moral hazard behavior, reducing risk and increasing the supply of credit. Finally, increases in the money supply can reduce the default risk of financially vulnerable lenders, allowing them to loosen the credit limits they are imposing. Note that these potential balance sheet channels are not mutually exclusive and may all be working at the same time in conjunction with traditional monetary policy channels.

The key implications of these new monetary policy channels are fourfold. First, monetary policy works through financial fundamentals, not just interest rates. As a result, interest rates are not necessarily a sign of loose or tight monetary policy. Even when interest rates are close to zero, central banks may not find themselves in a liquidity trap and powerless to stimulate output. Instead, monetary policy can still affect financial fundamentals, risk, and the supply of credit available.

Second, monetary policy works through the supply of credit as well as the demand for credit by changing risk. It also works through aggregate demand and also through aggregate supply by reducing the risk of production. In this view, monetary policy is actually a form of production insurance that ensures producers that liquidity will be made available during recessions.

Third, the impact of monetary policy is asymmetric and nonlinear, just like the impact of credit market imperfections in general. It is most likely to have an impact when credit limits are binding. It is least likely to have an impact if perceptions of default risk are exceptionally high or exceptionally low.

Fourth, monetary policy is most likely to impact the financially vulnerable: poorer households as well as smaller and newer firms. This creates an equity concern for monetary policy makers. It also raises questions about the best tools for implementing monetary policy. For example, would targeting direct lending to the most vulnerable firms be more effective than traditional monetary policy tools such as broadly increasing bank reserves through buying government bonds? Or maybe during extreme circumstances, central banks could directly buy the assets of vulnerable firms in an effort to improve their financial fundamentals and ability to attract credit? Or maybe central banks could change risk and the supply of credit by changing the regulations that banks face, such as the amount of capital they are required to hold for each loan they make?

These questions, and many like them, are not just abstract queries thrown out among theoretical economists. During the 2008 global financial crisis, short-term interest rates approached zero and policy makers across the globe were forced to face the fact that the traditional tools and channels of monetary policy had largely become ineffective. As one of the founders of the new Keynesian movement, Federal Reserve chairman Ben Bernanke put many of these new ways of thinking about monetary policy into practice. Chapter 18 on the global financial crisis of 2008 examines the policies the Fed and other central banks implemented during this crisis and evaluates the effectiveness of these policies.

EMPIRICAL EVIDENCE ON NEW KEYNESIAN MODELS OF CREDIT

Do Financially Vulnerable Firms Also Have the Most Volatile Credit?

A great deal of empirical evidence suggests that smaller and newer firms play a disproportionally large role in business cycles. For example, Bernanke and colleagues (1996) find that one-third of the changes in the aggregate output of manufacturing firms in the United States can be explained by differences in the financial fundamentals of small firms relative to large firms. This same result holds true firms for firms that rely more heavily on bank finance relative to those that do not. Looking at 5,000 firms, Perez (1998) finds that all firms of all sizes faced persistent shortages of credit, but the constraints were most significant for smaller firms. Finally, Nilsen (2002) finds that while accounts payable loans account for only 13 percent of total finance in manufacturing industries, they account for nearly 60 percent of the financing available to small firms, indicating that small firms are the most credit constrained through traditional channels and the most likely to be harmed by breaks in credit chains.

Similar results are consistently found looking across countries. For example, Beck and colleagues (2008) finds that smaller firms and poorer households are most likely to be credit constrained across a wide variety of countries. For these poorer households and firms, investment levels consistently track income because of their inability to gain access to credit.

Focusing on monetary policy, Gertler and Gilchrist (1993) find evidence that changes in the money supply have differing effects on large and small firms. They find that during periods of contractionary monetary policy, bank loans to small firms fall relative to loans to large firms. Similar results have been found for new bond and stock issues of small firms relative to large firms. Focusing on the fundamentals of lenders, Kashyap and Stein (2000) and Jiménez and colleagues (2012) find that the credit provided by less liquid banks responded more to changes in the money supply than that of more liquid banks. In addition, fluctuations in the supply of credit are much more important than changes in the demand for credit when it comes to the impact of changes in monetary policy.

Do Financial Fundamentals Affect Macroeconomic Performance?

Numerous studies find that changes in aggregate financial activity affect the behavior of investment, consumption, employment, and aggregate output. For example, Stanca (2002) finds that asset-to-debt and interest-payments-to-cash-flow ratios are strongly procyclical over the business cycle and drive changes in macroeconomic performance. Asea and Blomberg (1998) find evidence that various measures of the cost of credit intermediation are countercyclical, with the interest rate risk premiums attached to loans and collateral requirements rising during recessions and falling during expansions. Similarly, Lown and Morgan (2006) find that loan standards tighten during downturns and lead to significant reductions in lending and output during depressions, particularly for higher-risk borrowers, just as predicted by new Keynesian models of credit.

Evidence on the importance of the costs of credit intermediation over the business cycle can also be found in data on interest rate spreads. Figure 10.1 presents the interest rate spread between Baa bonds (highest risk investment grade bonds) and U.S. 10-year Treasury bonds (with zero default risk). This interest rate spread is an aggregate measure of perceived risk. As seen from this figure, when this market measure of risk rises, commercial lending growth strongly declines. Gilchrist and Zakrajsek (2012) find that similar interest rate spreads are countercyclical and significant predictors of real economic activity. They also find that changes in the supply of commercial credit are a significant predictor of economic activity, suggesting the credit rationing is also playing a role in driving output fluctuations.

Figure 10.1   Interest rate spread and commercial lending in the United States.

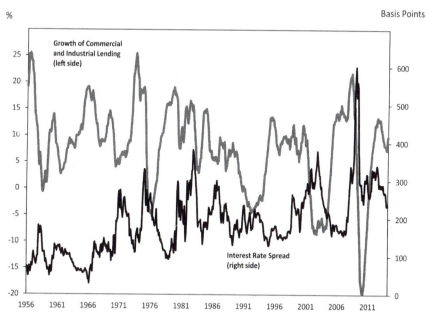

Source: Author's creation. Data on interest rate spread from the Federal Reserve Board of Governors available at http://www.federalreserve.gov/releases/h15/data.htm. Data on commercial lending from the St. Louis Federal Reserve FRED database available at https://research.stlouisfed.org/fred.

Finally, a great deal of empirical evidence suggests that financial systems play a huge role in specific economic crises episodes, such as the Great Depression and the 2008 global financial crisis. Evidence from these crises will be examined later in Chapters 13 and 18.

CONCLUSIONS

New Keynesian models of credit, building upon the seminal work of pioneer models such as the debt-deflation theory and the financial instability hypothesis, have gradually begun to move the study of financial systems to the forefront of business cycle research. Given that credit cycles have been important factors in all of the major economic crises over the last 100 years, this is where it should rightfully belong.

New Keynesian theories of credit have also squarely placed the focus on understanding the microfundamentals of finance as being the key to understanding macroeconomic behavior. Without understanding what is happening on the balance sheets of households, firms, and governments and how net worth impacts perceived default risk and credit, it is impossible to predict future behavior. It was the focus on macroeconomic data and ignoring the microfinancial fundamentals that may have led many to be so surprised by the 2008 global financial crisis. Seemingly out of nowhere, borrowers found their costs of credit rising (as emphasized by the financial accelerator model) and their credit limits tightening (as emphasized by models of credit rationing). As credit disappeared, the general economy collapsed. A more complete discussion will be presented in Chapter 18.

Financial fundamentals also appear to play an important role in two of the most spectacular and feared features of credit contractions: asset bubbles and banking crises. However, there are good reasons to think that psychology and expectations also play a role in in both the existence and the size of asset bubbles and banking crises as well. This is where the discussion of the role of financial systems in business cycles moves to in the next chapter.

SUGGESTED READINGS

Can "It" Happen Again? Essays on Instability and Finance, Hyman Minsky (1982): This book lays out the basics of the financial instability hypothesis, as well as walks the reader through Minsky's take on various financial crises in history.

"Deciphering the Liquidity and Credit Crunch 2007–2008," Markus K. Brunnermeier (2009): An investigation into the reasons why the financial fundamentals of lenders and borrowers deteriorated so quickly beginning in 2007, as well as the impact of weakened fundamentals on credit and aggregate output during the global financial crisis.

"Financial Fragility and Economic Performance," Ben Bernanke and Mark Gertler (1990): An excellent overview of the ways that monetary policy actually works in the real world, written by the recent and influential chairman of the Federal Reserve.

ELEVEN

Beliefs, Behavior, Bubbles, and Banking Crises

INTRODUCTION

Much of the most recent research on the interaction between financial systems and business cycles has focused on two phenomena: asset bubbles and banking crises. An *asset bubble* is best defined by Joseph Stiglitz (1990): "If the reason that the price is high today is only because the investors believe that the selling price is high tomorrow—when 'fundamental' factors do not seem to justify such a price—then a bubble exists." As Stiglitz's definition indicates, asset bubbles exist when market psychology is more important than the real, measurable characteristics of an asset.

Asset bubbles have been occurring for as long as markets have existed. Table 11.1 presents a few of the more famous examples of asset bubbles in world history. The world's first stock market in Amsterdam was also the site of the first recorded asset bubble. This bubble occurred in tulips, whose prices rose by nearly 6,000 percent before the eventual collapse. In modern economies, asset bubbles have primarily arisen in stock and real estate markets. When bubbles burst, the fall in prices dramatically reduces wealth, increases perceived risk, and can lead to huge contractions in credit and output.

Banking crises are defined as a situation in which numerous banks fail simultaneously because of an inability to roll over their short-term debt. Banks by their very nature are illiquid; they borrow short-term and lend long-term. As a result, banks must continually attract new debt as old debt expires, leaving them vulnerable to failure if their deposits or other

Table 11.1   Famous asset bubbles in history.

	% Rise bull phase	Length of up phase (months)	% Decline peak to trough	Length of down phase (months)
Tulips Holland (1634–1637)	5900	36	−93	10
Mississippi shares France (1719–1721)	6200	13	−99	13
South Sea shares Great Britain (1719–1720)	1000	18	−84	6
U.S. stocks United States (1921–1932)	497	95	−87	33
Mexican stocks Mexico (1978–1981)	785	30	−73	18
Silver United States (1979–1982)	710	12	−88	24
Hong Kong stocks Hong Kong (1970–1974)	1200	28	−92	20
Taiwan stocks Taiwan (1986–1990)	1168	40	−80	12
Dot.com stocks United States (1997–2000)	733	60	−78	32
Japanese stocks Japan (1985–1989)	225	48	−40	25
Housing bubble United States (1996–2006)	139	121	−34	62

Source: Adapted from Cecchetti (2006) using data from the S&P Case-Shiller Housing Price dataset available at http://research.stlouisfed.org/fred2/release?rid=199.

sources of short-term financing dissipate. This is what happens during a *bank run*, when depositors fear that a bank will fail. This causes depositors to attempt to withdraw all of their money at once, forcing the bank to, in fact, fail.

Banking crises have been around as long as banking has taken place. Laeven and Valencia (2013) identify 147 banking crises in 74 countries that took place between 1970 and 2011 (25 banking crises occurred between 2008 and 2011 alone). Only 34 of 117 countries did not experience a banking crisis between 1970 and 2010. However, banking crises that involve the complete failure of the banking system and losses to depositors are considerably less common than they were in the early twentieth century because of the provision of deposit insurance by governments and the strengthening of the role of central banks as a lender

Figure 11.1   Costliest banking crises since 1970.

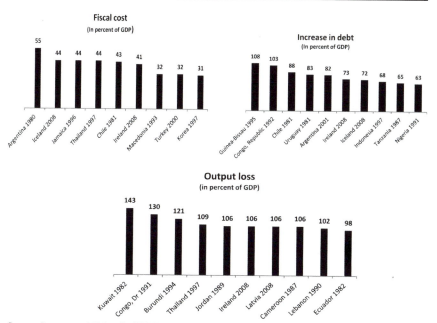

Source: Laeven and Valencia (2013). Reprinted with permission.

of last resort. However, increasing government involvement in mitigating the economic impact of banking crises through bailouts has come at a cost: Government bailouts can be very expensive to taxpayers. Figure 11.1 presents data on the 10 costliest banking crises in history in terms of the fiscal cost of the bailout, the increase in debt to pay for this bailout, and the lost output from the economic contraction associated the banking crises. While these are extreme cases, clearly banking crises are often associated with large fiscal costs and recessions, sometime depressions.

There are three good reasons to study asset bubbles and banking crises together. The first reason is that they often—although not always—occur at the same time. Both have occurred during the Great Depression, the East Asian crisis, and the 2008 global financial crisis to name a few major financial crises. There are important feedback effects between asset bubbles and banking crises, the most important of these being the provision of credit. During a boom, a large part of what fuels asset bubbles is easy credit from banks that is funneled into asset markets, driving up prices; a large part of what drives excessive banking lending is the easy profits to be made when asset prices are rising rapidly. During a bust, banking crises are driven by defaults on loans that do not get repaid when asset bubbles pop and prices tumble; often these bubbles pop when easy credit begins to dry up because of rising fears of higher defaults in the banking system.

A second reason to study asset bubbles and banking crises together is that they are costly for the same reasons. Both asset bubbles and banking crises reduce wealth and weaken financial fundamentals, leading to a collapse in credit that, in turn, impacts the rest of the economy through the mechanisms laid out in the new Keynesian models of credit discussed in the previous chapter.

Finally, asset bubbles and banking crises are closely related to the concepts of expectations, beliefs, and behavior. Because of their extraordinary nature, asset bubbles and banking crises have always been associated with the notion that they are driven by irrational behavior. Recently, a new field of economics known as *behavioral economics* has attempted to study the psychological underpinnings of humans in an attempt to better understand economic decision-making. While still a new and developing field, behavioral economics has played an important role in forcing economists to rethink how people make financial decisions, particularly when it comes to understanding the booms and busts associated with asset bubbles and banking crises.

This chapter begins with a brief introduction to behavioral economics. It then examines the causes of asset bubbles and banking crises and the extent to which they are based on beliefs (or expectations about the future), or the extent to which they are based on economic fundamentals. This chapter then looks at stabilization policies aimed at preventing asset bubbles and banking crises before they begin and mitigating their effects once they occur. This includes a discussion of whether central banks should attempt to "pop" asset bubbles in their early stages to limit their damage before they grow larger and burst to greater effect. Finally, the empirical evidence on their causes and costs are examined here.

BEHAVIORAL ECONOMICS

Expectations and beliefs about the future have played a recurrent role in almost all of the business cycle theories that we have talked about in this book. In most modern neoclassical and new Keynesian theories, the assumption that expectations are rational and that people do not make predictable mistakes has come to dominate the profession's thinking regarding expectations. This is much different than in earlier business cycle theories, where expectations were generally assumed to be biased in some way. In monetarist models, expectations could only be formed by looking backwards, not forwards, leading people to make predictable mistakes. Keynes, Keynesians, Austrians, and Minsky believed that expectations were irrational. The most famous characterization of irrational expectations was Keynes's use of the term "animal spirits." By using this phrase, Keynes was trying to convey the characteristics that he believed to be true about how people form their expectations. First, that there is fundamental uncertainty regarding the future, including ignorance about how the economy works and little conception of what outcomes are even possible. In Keynes's (1936) words, "About these matters, there is no scientific basis on which to form any calculable probability whatsoever. We simply do not know."

The second idea captured in Keynes's term "animal spirits" is the importance of psychology when it comes to forming beliefs about the future. While rationality might be descriptive as a long-run concept, in the short run our decision-making is often distorted by emotions, prejudices, and short-cuts. As a result, expectations formed in the "heat of the moment" are likely to be wrong, and predictably so.

Over the last decade, psychologists, neurologists, and economists have gotten more interested in trying to deconstruct the decision-making process that goes on within people's minds in order to identify just how closely people behave like the mythical "rational economic actor" in everyday life. The goal of this research has not been to determine whether people are rational but to identify under what conditions people exhibit biased decision-making and the impact of these biases on economic outcomes. Two of the leaders in this movement are the psychologists Amos Tversky and Daniel Kahneman. Kahneman (2011) differentiates between two different forms of decision processing: intuitive (system 1), which is fast and automatic decision-making, and reasoning (system 2), which is slower and more deliberative decision-making. Kahneman argues that system 1 decisions have the advantages of being quick and less costly in terms of spent energy but are also subject to many systematic biases. Experimental subject research has identified many cognitive traps that people regularly fall into. According to Kahneman, these traps include the following:

1. *Risk (loss) aversion bias:* People weigh losses more heavily than gains.

2. *Availability bias:* Information that is easy to obtain is weighted more heavily in decision-making than more useful information.

3. *Hindsight bias:* People assign higher probability to something occurring after it happens than before it happens.

4. *Induction bias:* Humans tend to overgeneralize from small amounts of information.

5. *Conjunction bias:* People overestimate the probability of independent events occurring at the same time but underestimate the probability of a single independent event occurring.

6. *Confirmation bias:* The tendency to look for evidence that confirms an initial hypothesis over evidence that would invalidate this hypothesis.

7. *Contamination bias:* Irrelevant but contemporaneous events and experiences often influence decision-making.

8. *Scope bias:* The difficulty of accurately assessing two different events in which the costs and benefits differ dramatically in scale.

9. *Overconfidence bias:* Forecasters tend to overstate the accuracy of their forecasts and minimize the probability of outcomes that fall outside of their forecasts.

10. *Bystander bias:* The tendency for individuals to ignore their own responsibilities when part of a crowd.

For each of these biases—and the many more identified by behavioral psychologists—there is a rational basis to the bias. Biases are shortcuts; they allow people to make quicker decisions based on less information and expend less mental energy. Given the innumerable decisions each of us is forced to make each and every day, intuitive decisions based on system 1 thinking are absolutely critical to our survival as a species. The problem, however, is that while such decision-making may be rational at the individual level, the aggregated decisions of large groups of people look irrational. For example, *herding behavior* occurs when individuals try to follow market leaders because they think they are better informed or because many people overreact to new information in all the same way. Herding behavior can fuel booms and busts and make them self-fulfilling: If everyone thinks that prices will rise, they rise, and vice versa. Cipriani and Guarino (2014) find empirical evidence that herding behavior driven by asymmetric information explains a significant amount of trading behavior and price movements on the New York Stock Exchange.

Another individually rational behavior that is irrational in the aggregate is the "greater fool" theory of investing. Here, people continue to buy assets that are appreciating under the assumption that fundamentals do not matter in pricing the asset as long as there a greater fool to sell the asset to in the future. This sort of market psychology is often associated with asset bubbles but appears to be irrational in hindsight when the market runs out of fools. The greater fool theory also plays into asset bubbles because, using an analogy offered by Keynes, speculation on asset prices is similar to picking winners in a beauty contest: You are not picking whom you think is most beautiful, you are picking whom you think the public thinks is most beautiful. Basing private expectations on public expectations which are in turn based on subjective opinions and limited information can lead to many different forms of seemingly irrational behavior.

One final form of "rational irrationality" also discussed by Keynes is the paradox of thrift. During economic downturns, it is individually rational to take precautions and increase savings at the expense of consumption. But in the aggregate, if everyone attempts to save more and consume less, aggregate demand will fall, reducing aggregate income and precluding total savings from rising.

BELIEF-BASED THEORIES OF ASSET BUBBLES AND BANKING CRISES

Taken together, many of the biases identified by behavioral economics point to reasons why the most accurate models of decision-making may not involve individuals simply balancing costs and benefits. In a world with limited information and biased individuals, many decisions are made that are not clearly rational. This is particularly true when it comes to decisions pertaining to financial assets for three reasons. First, financial transactions take place over time, and as a result they are inherently subject to a great deal of uncertainty and risk. Second, many financial assets—such as real estate, raw materials, stocks, and long-term bonds—are long-lived. As a result, there is a very long horizon over which their returns must be valued. For assets such as stocks and real estate with no maturity, speculation is particularly important (and likely the reason why these types of assets are most susceptible to asset bubbles). Third, financial markets are highly competitive, demanding many decisions to be made quickly, often in the absence of complete information. As a result of all of these factors, beliefs and expectations play an important role in any explanation of financial markets behavior, particularly for the existence of asset bubbles and banking crises.

There are two broad categories of theories pertaining to the causes of asset bubbles and banking crises. The first category is *belief-based models*.

In these models, bubbles and banking crises are driven by expectations not linked to financial fundamentals. Charles Kindleberger (1978) has been one of the leading proponents of this view, arguing that a careful study of economic history shows us that financial decisions are inherently unstable. He sees four important reasons for this. First, speculation is a necessary and efficient part of the financial market process. Without it, markets would not work. However, speculation can also lead to excessive manias or panics, which is the second important reason that finance is unstable. In Kindleberger's view, a great deal of financial behavior is irrational and cannot be justified by any real changes in economic fundamentals. Actions by irrational individuals then get magnified because investors are linked by intertwined beliefs (Keynes's beauty contest), herding behavior, and incentives to invest in the hope for the greater fool. These behaviors (consistent with many of the biases that behavioral economics has identified) make asset bubbles self-fulfilling in the sense that when everyone thinks asset prices will rise, they rise, and when everyone thinks asset prices are going to fall, they fall.

This same self-fulfilling behavior occurs during bank runs as well: If everyone thinks their money is safe in a bank, then it probably is. However, if people lose confidence in its safety for whatever reason (or believe that others have lost confidence in the safety of their money), then their money is not safe and people will withdraw their deposits all at once, triggering a banking crisis. In the words of Walter Baghot (1873), "Credit—the disposition of one man to trust another—is singularly varying."

Third, Kindleberger argued that financial manias and panics are fed and spread throughout the financial system by the fact that much of this speculation is debt-financed. During manias, investors and banks see profits to be made, causing credit to flow easily and fueling asset price bubbles that are associated with huge increases in leverage and risk throughout the financial system. However, when the mania turns to panic, huge losses are suffered across the financial system, leading to busts that bring down banks and other asset markets not even involved in the bubble. It is for this reason that asset bubbles and banking crises are correlated across boom/bust cycles.

Fourth, and finally, Kindleberger identified financial innovation as the trigger for the booms that precede asset busts and banking crises. New financial technology encourages investors to believe what, according to the well-known adage, are the most expensive words in finance: "This time it's different." New financial developments and products, coupled with a lack of regulation to limit speculative behaviors and credit growth, provide a narrative and justification for manias and panics that would otherwise seem irrational to participants.

While Kindleberger thinks that a great deal of financial behavior is irrational, others have shown that self-fulfilling banking crises and asset bubbles can be consistent with rational expectations. Diamond and Dybvig (1983) develop a model of banking crises where the rational fear of being "last in line" causes depositors to flee a bank whenever they think there is a sufficient probability that others might flee. Regarding asset bubbles, Allen and Gale (1999, 2000) show how moral hazard lending and greater fool lending incentives increase the attractiveness of risky assets to such an extent that asset bubbles are rational investment strategies—at least until they pop. Thus, the key insight of belief-based theories is that even when people are rational, but particularly if they are not, as long as people's optimal behavior is a function of what they believe other people believe, asset bubbles and banking crises are likely.

FUNDAMENTALS-BASED THEORIES OF ASSET BUBBLES AND BANKING CRISES

The second broad category of theories is referred to as *fundamentals-based models*. In these models, asset bubbles and banking crises are a function of the real financial fundamentals of banks and markets. Regarding banking crises, any negative shocks to the profitability of banks or to the ability of borrowers to make their payments can potentially spark a fundamentals-based banking crisis. Such negative shocks could come from the following sources:

1. *Recessions:* As described in new Keynesian models of credit, any recession can reduce the financial fundamentals of borrowers and lenders, leading to restrictions in credit that further exacerbate the recession and declines in financial fundamentals, which creates a vicious cycle that can trigger a banking crisis.

2. *Asset bubble collapses:* When asset bubbles are debt-financed, a collapse in the bubble will increase bankruptcies and losses among banks large enough to threaten a banking crisis.

3. *Unexpected inflation:* Unanticipated inflation reduces real interest rates and the real value of a bank's assets, potentially reducing bank net worth enough to trigger a banking crisis.

4. *Unexpected deflation:* As discussed in Fischer's debt-deflation model, unanticipated deflation increases the real value of debt,

initiating defaults among borrowers that could also start a banking crisis among lenders.

5. *Higher interest rates:* Given that banks lend long-term and borrow short-term, their liabilities are more interest-rate sensitive than their assets, and any increase in interest rates will increase their costs of funds more than their revenues, potentially reducing profitability enough to cause a banking crisis.

6. *Exchange rate depreciation:* Many banks in smaller or emerging market economies are forced to borrow in foreign-denominated debt, and any depreciation of the local currency will reduce the value of their assets relative to their liabilities, threatening a banking crisis.

7. *Sovereign debt crises:* Banks are typically large holders of government bonds, and any default by the government on these bonds can reduce bank capital enough to trigger a banking crisis.

With so many potential dangers threatening banks, it might appear that no bank could ever avoid experiencing a banking crisis. The fact of the matter is that well-run banks mitigate and insure against these risks by screening borrowers, rationing credit, diversifying their assets and liabilities, and requiring collateral. Just as importantly, *prudential bank regulations* imposed by governments place limits on the amount of risk banks, depositors, and the government can be exposed to. These prudential regulations include capital adequacy requirements, limits on certain types of asset holdings, restrictions on credit growth, limits on lending to individual borrowers, controls on international financial flows, and ceilings on foreign-denominated debt. When it works properly (easier said than done), prudential regulation limits the moral hazard lending that fuels the growth of asset bubbles and weakens the financial fundamentals of banks. However, prudential regulation is often not properly enacted or enforced. When this is the case, banks are free to engage in risky lending behavior, often driven by moral hazard incentives, that initiates asset bubbles and banking crises.

THE PREVENTION OF ASSET BUBBLES AND BANKING CRISES

Regardless of whether asset bubbles and banking crises are belief-based or fundamentals-based, the prescriptions for preventing them are quiet similar, although difficult to accomplish. The most important protective measure is to enact prudent financial regulation that allows for sensible credit growth but that prevents reckless booms in credit and ballooning asset prices that fuel short-term economic surges but eventually lead to financial busts and prolonged recessions.

As carefully described by Charles Calomiris and Stephen Haber (2014) in their book *Fragile by Design*, systems for prudential regulation are not created in a vacuum: They are a function of the political environment in which they are shaped. Based on their analysis of the history of banking crises, the authors argue that effective prudential regulation and stable banking systems are created in political systems that are neither authoritarian nor excessively democratic. In authoritarian systems, banking regulation becomes a means to enhance government expropriation of resources and increase its access to credit, not a means of expanding overall credit and maintaining stability. In democratic systems that are more populist and vulnerable to special interest lobbying, regulation focuses too much on expanding credit and providing generous banking safety nets without sufficient emphasis on limiting long-run risk to the banking system and to taxpayers. Only in liberal democracies with checks on the rent-seeking behaviors of politicians, bankers, and special interests do stable banking systems consistently exist that provide abundant credit. The authors point to any number of countries in Latin America and Africa that have suffered from banking crises driven by authoritarian regulation. Regarding excessively populist regulation, the authors point to the United States as an example of a country that has consistently incentivized credit expansion over limiting risk exposure (as seen during the buildup to the global financial crisis, to be discussed in Chapter 18), making it vulnerable to the periodic banking crises that it has experienced throughout its history.

Another important policy to prevent bank runs and asset bubbles from spilling into the rest of the economy is for the government to provide deposit insurance and have a strong central bank that is willing and able to serve as lender of last resort. These actions will prevent belief-based bank runs, but they will not prevent bank failures if the banks' financial fundamentals are weak. In the postwar era, deposit insurance and strong central banking have become more prevalent across countries. As a result, the number of banking crises has dropped dramatically despite the fact that asset bubbles are not occurring less frequently. In some recent instances, the popping of an asset bubble did not weaken the overall financial stability of the economy and impact credit and aggregate output. An example of this was during the 1987 stock market crash in the United States, which was the largest one-day stock price decline in U.S. history. This crash did not lead to a recession because of aggressive lending by the Federal Reserve and the U.S. Treasury to provide temporary financial support to firms and banks. This quick action calmed markets before panic set in.

Another important way that governments can prevent asset bubbles and banking crises is by preventing excessive credit creation by adopting tight monetary policies. Many central banks have fallen into the trap of allowing fires to start, then finding out that these fires are too large to put out (such as, arguably, the Federal Reserve during the 2008 global financial crisis). When money is too easy and interest rates are low, credit is often lent for uses that are not as productive and cannot be justified under normal credit conditions.

An important ongoing debate among economists is the extent to which monetary policy should be used to "pop" bubbles before they become too large. Traditionally, monetary policy focuses on the aggregate price level, with asset prices factoring into these calculations only to the extent that they impact the price of everyday goods and services. However, in the aftermath of the global financial crisis and the worldwide housing bubble, many central banks appear to be placing more weight (informally, if not explicitly) on asset prices in their decision-making process.

In order to understand a central banker's perspective on these questions, we have the writings of Ben Bernanke (2002) before he became chair of the Federal Reserve. In Bernanke's opinion, monetary policy is most effective at controlling macroeconomic variables such as inflation and aggregate output. It is not effective at controlling prices and quantities in individual markets. According to Bernanke, there are two problems with preemptively popping an asset bubble by cutting the money supply and raising interest rates. The first is that there is no reason to think that the central bank can do a better job at identifying asset bubbles than investors. When bubbles are building, there is often great disagreement about whether the price buildup is a bubble or whether it can be justified by fundamentals. According to the rational expectations hypothesis, the only way that a central bank could identify bubbles is if they had better information than the public, which is unlikely to be true over the long term. Without better information, a central banker is as likely to make a mistake and unnecessarily contract the economy to prevent a bubble that is not occurring as it is to pop a bubble that is building.

Bernanke's second problem with pricking bubbles is that it is not possibly to do safely. In the words of Bernanke (2002), using monetary policy to prevent a bubble is like trying "to perform brain surgery with a sledgehammer." Monetary policy tools, such as interest rates, are blunt instruments that will traumatize the entire economy at the same time that it is squeezing the asset bubble.

Bernanke's alternative for dealing with bubbles is to tighten prudential financial regulation to limit the credit that fuels bubbles during their growth phase. By requiring banks to be better capitalized, more diversified, tightly regulated in their risky lending, and transparent in their activities, central banks can limit the speculation and moral hazard that builds up within financial systems to devastating effects when asset bubbles occur. Such approaches are becoming more common among central banks. For example, the Bank of China aggressively imposed regulations in 2011 to limit mortgage lending in response to a perceived housing bubble that has been building in major metropolitan areas, to some good effect.

Once a banking crisis has begun, the only way to prevent a collapse in credit is to restore the financial fundamentals of the banking system. This happens when the central bank serves as a lender of last resort in the short term and the government finances a bailout of the banking system that restores financial stability in the long-term. Governments are going to be responsible for losses in their role as deposit insurer and lender of last resort, regardless. History shows us that those countries that "take their lumps" and quickly and fully recapitalize their banks are the countries that avoid the worst of the economic collapse. Those countries that do not (see Japan's Great Recession in Chapter 16) suffer the worst recessions and eventually have to pay the largest bailouts.

Of course, there is a cost to deposit insurance and government lending over and above the costs of bailouts; this is the dangerous moral hazard incentives governments are creating over the long term. By failing to allow banks to incur penalties for their actions, governments risk encouraging riskier behavior, more asset bubbles, and more banking crises in the future. This is a real concern. However, this long-term concern is typically outweighed by the far more pressing concerns that most governments have of avoiding short-term financial and economic collapse. Whether it should be or not is subject to serious debate.

EMPIRICAL STUDIES ON ASSET BUBBLES AND BANKING CRISES

Over the last two decades many countries have liberalized their highly regulated financial systems in an effort to spur growth and satisfy the appetite for lending among their credit-constrained populations. However, too often this financial liberalization has been conducted indiscriminately, facilitating moral hazard lending and a reckless expansion of credit in many countries. Much of this credit expansion has been funneled into asset markets, setting the stage for the asset bubbles and banking crises. Many studies have identified a strong empirical relationship among liberalization, credit booms, asset bubbles, and banking crises. For example, Kaminsky and Reinhart (1999) estimate that real estate and stock prices rise by an average of 40 percent following financial deregulation. They also find that in 26 banking crises episodes they studied, 18 of them occurred within five years of significant financial liberalization. Likewise, Eichengreen and Arteta (2002) conclude that countries that have recently liberalized had high precrisis levels of credit growth and low levels of bank capital were significantly more likely to experience a banking crisis. These results correspond with the argument that a lack of appropriate prudential regulation fuels lending booms that, in turn, increases risk and weaken financial fundamentals in the banking system.

Other studies have shown that banking crises and asset bubbles have consistently occurred where debt-to-asset ratios are high, financial market regulation is lax, deposit insurance is not provided by the government, and no strong lender of last resort is available. For example, Reinhart and Rogoff (2009, 2011) identify 40 examples of stock price collapses associated with a banking crisis since 1920 and seven housing price collapses associated with a banking crisis since 1997 alone. Their empirical results indicate that credit growth, sovereign debt, and other measures of the financial fundamentals of banks are significant predictors of both asset bubbles and banking crises.

Regarding the costs of asset bubbles and banking crises, Figure 11.1 illustrates that the costs of the bailouts incurred by governments to recapitalize banks and restore their solvency are huge. The costs of these 10 costliest bailouts were over 30 percent of GDP in each country, and in the worst cases over 50 percent of GDP. As a result, debt rose between 60 and 110 percent in every country. Laeven and Valencia (2013) estimate that the median financial system bailout costs approximately 7 percent of GDP, increases debt by 12 percent, results in lost output of 23 percent of GDP, and causes a financial crisis that lasts two years.

The costs of banking crises reported above only factor in the recapitalization costs of banks and ignore the cost of the recession itself. In regards to lost output, Boyd and colleagues (2005) find that in 30 percent of banking crises, no aggregate output losses occurred. However, for those countries that did contract, the output losses were huge: between 60 and 300 percent of precrisis GDP. Laeven and Valencia (2013) estimate that the median level of lost output from a banking crisis is 23 percent of GDP, which is staggeringly large when added to the fiscal costs of crises.

Regarding the costs of asset bubbles alone, Carroll and colleagues (2010) find that a $100 decline in stock wealth reduces consumption by $4, while a $100 decline in housing wealth reduces consumption by more than $9. Reinhart and Rogoff (2009) find that average bust of an asset bubble reduces housing prices by 35 percent and stock prices by 56 percent. They find also find that asset busts are typically associated with recessions that average 3.5 years in duration.

CONCLUSIONS

In the words of Charles Kindleberger (1978), asset bubbles and banking crises are a "hardy perennial." Why are these phenomena, which have such significant indirect costs (from the lost output associated with the corresponding recession) and such large direct costs (associated with the government bailouts of failed financial institutions) so stubbornly common? Modern economic research points to two reasons. First, because of the very nature of financial intermediation, financial institutions are risky and vulnerable to negative economic shocks. While prudential regulation in theory can help minimize these risks, policy makers and the policies they enact are fallible, lawmakers often face intense political pressure to liberalize financial markets and expand access to credit, and bankers have many incentives to find ways around the rules that do exist.

In addition, new research in behavioral economics indicates that rationality, particularly when it comes to financial decision-making, may be best thought of as a long-run concept. In the short run, individuals are saddled with incomplete information and numerous biases that favor prejudices over cost/benefit analysis. In addition, in finance the best reaction of one investor is a function of other investors' beliefs, making it optimal for people to do what they think other people are going to do. It is this combination of biases, incomplete information, and intertwined incentives that make manias, panics, greater fool investing, herding, and self-fulfilling behavior so common. As long as people are people, it appears that bubbles and crises are a fact of economic life.

These problems of biases, incomplete information, and intertwined incentives not only make behavior and beliefs volatile, they also greatly add to our difficulties as economists in macroeconomic forecasting. This is the topic we turn to in the next chapter.

SUGGESTED READINGS

Mania, Panics, and Crashes: A History of Financial Crises, Charles Kindleberger (1978): Very readable case studies of various financial panics and crises throughout history and across countries.

Misunderstanding Financial Crises: Why We Don't See Them Coming, Gary Gorton (2012): A broad and historical look at why asset bubbles and banking crises are endemic to finance and also why prudential regulation has failed to prevent them.

Thinking, Fast and Slow, Daniel Kahneman (2011): The most comprehensive, and readable, summary of behavioral economics from the psychologist who won the Nobel Prize in Economics.

This Time Is Different: Eight Centuries of Financial Folly, Carmen Reinhart and Kenneth Rogoff (2009): An empirical look at financial crises across 66 countries on five continents over three centuries in which the authors collect the definitive statistical account of the regularity of financial crises.

TWELVE

Macroeconomic Forecasting

INTRODUCTION

The jokes are almost as old as the profession itself. Q: Why did God create economists? A: To make weathermen look good. Did you hear that economists have forecasted eight of the last two recessions? Or how about the one-handed economist, who was popular because of his inability to say "On one hand, but on the other hand. . ."?

Economists themselves have been no less critical of their profession's ability to forecast the future. The economist John Kenneth Galbraith (*Wall Street Journal*, January 22, 1993) claimed, "There are two kinds of forecasters: those who don't know and those who don't know they don't know."

Because of the poor historical performance of economic forecasting, many firms have reassessed their need for extensive and personalized economic forecasts. In the 1950s and 1960s, many firms hired in-house economists to do their forecasting. Today, almost none of the Fortune 500 companies directly employ economists. For example, IBM had 26 economists on their staff in the early 1970s, but today they have zero. Instead, they avoid relying on forecasts altogether, or at the very least, they rely on one of a small number of commercial economic forecasting firms to provide general macroeconomic forecasts at a relatively minimal price.

Why has *macroeconomic forecasting*, or the methods of quantifying macroeconomic uncertainty, fallen upon such hard times? One important reason is that economic history has always been filled with large, unanticipated shocks. Forecasters rely on the past as the basis for both their theories and their data. When shocks occur that have never occurred before and were not anticipated, the result is large forecasting errors.

A quick walk through business cycles in the United States over the last 30 years illustrates the importance of the unknowable shock. In the 1970s, higher oil prices increased the costs of production and decreased aggregate supply. This led to high levels of inflation and unemployment at the same time, an unprecedented event that forecasters could not have anticipated before the existence of OPEC. The 1981–1982 recession was caused by a large decrease in the money supply initiated by the Federal Reserve aimed at reducing historically high inflation rates. This destabilizing action by the Fed was unparalleled in U.S. history and was largely unanticipated by forecasters. The remarkably long and resilient expansion of the 1990s, driven by strong productivity growth and a booming stock market (two of the most perplexing and unpredictable variables in modern economies) was also largely unforeseen by forecasters. Because of this, consensus forecasts of economic growth were an average of 1.4 percent too low for five years straight between 1995 and 1999. Even the East Asian crisis, which many predicted would depress the U.S. economy as well, failed to noticeably slow the surprisingly rapid rate of growth during this period. Finally, the 2008 global financial crisis was largely unforeseen by forecasters. The buildup to the crises was fueled by numerous new financial developments, the consequences of which were not understood by many until after the crisis had started. The result was that many seasoned economic observers were surprised by the size of the contraction and the speed at which it spread through financial markets and the real economy.

Unique and unanticipated shocks, however, cannot fully explain the decline in economic forecasting. Economists' disagreements about what model to use in economic forecasting have played an important role as well. Economists disagree about whether models of market failure (such as Keynesian or new Keynesian models) or models of perfect competition (such as classical, monetarist, or real business cycle models) are best to use as the basis of developing forecasts. In addition, a large and influential body of research on rational expectations suggests that without an understanding of how people adjust their expectations (which in any given circumstance may be impossible to accurately predict), any forecast of the future based on data from the past will be unreliable. This is the basis of the Lucas critique, which by itself has done more to shake economists' faith in their ability to foresee the future than any series of forecasting mistakes. Because of this loss of faith in forecasting by the profession, few top-notch academic researchers are currently engaged in work related to economic forecasting. Instead, the practice and advancement of forecasting has been largely left to a few commercial forecasting firms, leaving a sizeable disconnect between academia and the commercial world.

Finally, there are some economists who, like Austrians, Keynes, and post-Keynesians, believe that the unknown is fundamentally unknowable and therefore forecasting is always a science destined for failure. Rational expectations incorporate the fundamental assumption that the future behaves according to some known probability function; in other words, the behavior of the unknown is known, just like I know that if I flip a coin a million times, there is a good chance I will get close to 500,000 heads and 500,000 tails. But Keynes, Austrians, and post-Keynesians believe in fundamental uncertainty, or unknown unknowns. In a world in which you do not know the range of possible outcomes and where large outliers are possible, how can you ever accurately forecast the future? The past will be no predictor of the future.

This chapter will review the four primary forecasting techniques used to predict future economic performance: macroeconomic and market-based indicators, econometric methods, structural modeling, and dynamic stochastic general equilibrium modeling. The advantages and disadvantages of each forecasting method will be discussed with an eye towards understanding what each of these techniques can add to our understanding of business cycles, both in the past and in the future.

MACROECONOMIC AND MARKET-BASED INDICATORS

The Index of Leading Indicators

The oldest, and also the simplest, way to forecast business cycles is to identify a group of variables that are leading indicators of aggregate output and use these to predict turning points in the business cycle. Beginning in 1937, the Commerce Department began to report the Composite Index of Leading Indicators. Since that time, this index has undergone substantial revision, and many variables have been added or removed over the years.

Table 12.1 reports the current variables that comprise the Index of Leading Indicators. Notice that there are variables included in this index for proponents of every business cycle theory. Classical or real business cycle economists who focus on fluctuations in aggregate supply get average weekly hours and vender delivery speed (slower speeds indicate that capacity constraints are becoming binding). Keynesians get consumer expectations, the stock market, new housing starts (a volatile component of investment), manufacturer orders, and unemployment claims. Monetarists and Austrians get M2. Proponents of credit and financial theories get the interest rate spread between long-term T-bonds and the short-term federal funds rate (which is the overnight interest rate on interbank loans). A larger interest rate gap is a rough indicator of the risk of lending money long-term relative to lending money short-term. Thus, decisions regarding which macroeconomic variables to include in this index are not based upon one specific theory. Instead, the Index of Leading Indicators focuses on what works, meaning the variables that are the most reliable leading indicators of output.

Figure 12.1 presents data on both GDP growth and the Index of Leading Indicators. This figure illustrates that while the index is a simple and intuitive way to forecast business cycles, there are two significant problems with its use in practice. First and foremost is the problem of false signals. Between 1959 and 2012, the index correctly forecasted all eight recessions but also five recessions that did not occur. For example, in 1977 and again in 1987 the index fell and output growth did not. In addition, even when changes in the index correspond with changes in output, the index is much more volatile than GDP growth. There have been a number of times when the indicator has changed dramatically without any

Table 12.1   The components of the Index of Leading Indicators.

1. Average weekly hours of manufacturing production workers *(Average weekly hours)*
2. Average weekly initial claims for unemployment insurance, state programs—inverted scale *(Initial unemployment claims)*
3. Manufacturers' new orders for consumer goods and materials, in constant dollars *(Manufacturers' orders)*
4. Vendor performance *(Percentage of companies receiving slower deliveries)*
5. Manufacturers' new orders for nondefense capital goods industries, in constant dollars *(Manufacturers' capital orders)*
6. New private-housing units authorized by local building permits *(Housing starts)*
7. Prices of 500 common stocks, index *(Stock market price indexes and dividend yields)*
8. Money supply (M2), in constant dollars *(Money supply)*
9. Interest rate spread, 10-year Treasury bonds less federal funds *(Interest rates)*
10. Consumer expectations, index *(Consumer attitude indexes)*

Figure 12.1   Real GDP growth and the Index of Leading Indicators.

% change

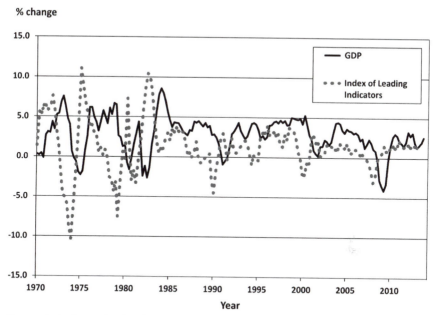

Source: Author's creation based on GDP data from the Bureau of Economic Analysis available at https://www.bea.gov/national/xls/gdplev.xls and the Index of Leading Indicators available at http://www.conference-board.org/data/bcicountry.cfm?cid=1.

(or at least very much) change in output growth. Also, some of the largest declines in the index, such as between 1975 and 1980, were associated with only very short recessions. However, there was only a relatively small decline in the index before the severe recession of 1981–1982 and in 2007.

The second major problem with the Index of Leading Indicators is that it does not lead GDP growth by very much—one quarter at most. This is in part because there is a two-month lag in collecting the data that comprises the Index of Leading Indicators. As a result, the index does not provide enough time to make the index very useful when formulating monetary and fiscal policy. Given the lags in monetary and especially fiscal policy, policy makers need much more than one quarter lead time in order to take the appropriate actions to stabilize output. During the global financial crisis that began in December 2007, the index peaked five months earlier in July 2007 but did not significantly decline until June 2008, well past the point when the recession was underway.

Numerous empirical studies have been conducted investigating the forecasting effectiveness of the Index of Leading Indicators. Diebold and

Rudebusch (1999) review many of these studies and reach the general conclusion that the index is not a reliable indicator of business cycle turning points. Even when used in conjunction with other forecasting methods, the Index of Leading Indicators does little to improve the accuracy of macroeconomic forecasts, especially in terms of identifying the peaks and troughs of business cycles with a sufficient lead time. Guerard and Schwartz (2007) find that the Index of Leading Indicators is a significant predictor of GDP, but only with a three-quarter lag, limiting its effectiveness in forecasting.

Other economists and forecasters have attempted to put together different indexes comprised of different variables that are reportedly more reliable indicators than those used in the Index of Leading Economic Indicators. The problems with these alternative indexes are many. First, many may work for a short period of time but fail to stand the test of time. In addition, putting together an index based only on its predictive power opens up the potential of *overfitting*, or forecasting from past data more closely than can be justified by the underlying uncertainty that exists in the real-world. Overfitting makes a forecasting model look good when compared to historical data because it is fitted to explain as much variability in the data as is statistically possible. However, when used to forecast the future, it fails because it is confidently forecasting randomness in the data that is not forecastable. Overfitting is an important reason why statistical forecasting techniques based on historical data perform so poorly in real time.

Market-Based Indicators

Instead of relying on a composite of various macroeconomic indicators, many economists believe that market-based indicators of turning points in the business cycle are more reliable because they more accurately reflect the prevailing perceptions of those actively playing a role in future economic performance. The stock market is one such indicator, but as can be seen in Figure 12.2, stock market variability dwarfs the variability of output growth and is so filled with false signals that it cannot be a reliable indicator by itself.

Another more reliable market-based indicator is the yield curve. A *yield* is a measure of the yearly return on holding an asset, typically a bond. It is calculated by determining the interest rate that equates the present value of future payments received from the bond with the current price that the bond is selling at. One of the important determinants of the yield on various bonds is the risk of that bond. In order to assume higher risk, a

Figure 12.2   Real GDP growth and stock prices in the United States.

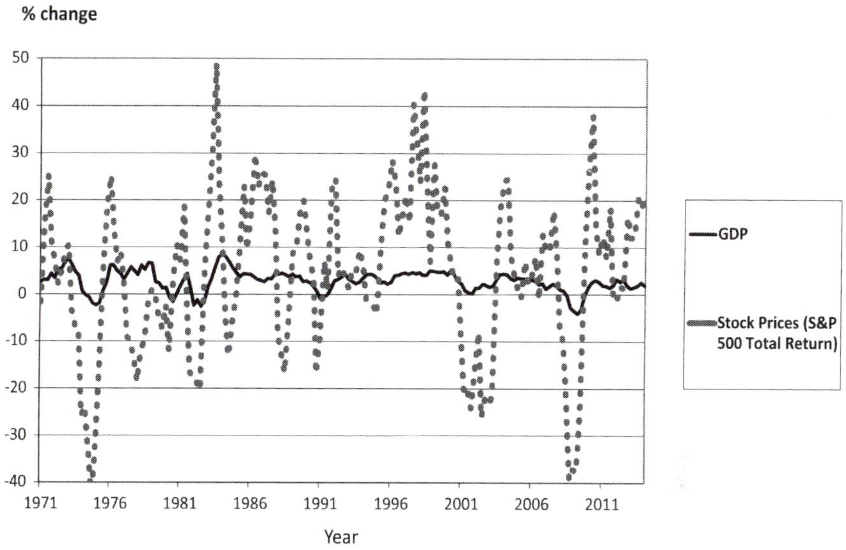

% change

Year

Source: Author's creation based on GDP data from the Bureau of Economic Analysis available at https://www.bea.gov/national/xls/gdplev.xls and S&P 500 data from Yahoo Finance available at http://finance.yahoo.com/q/hp?s=%5EGSPC+Historical+Prices.

purchaser will demand a higher yield. The risk of a bond rises with the default risk of the firm issuing the bond. The risk of a bond also rises with increases in the bond's *maturity*, or the time at which the bond's principal is repaid. Longer maturities mean more risk, both because the probability of default is larger over longer periods of time and also because the owner is exposed to more risk from large changes in market interest rates that could reduce the attractiveness of the bond on the secondary, or resale, market.

A widely accepted theory about how maturity affects the yields on bonds is the *expectations hypothesis*. This theory asserts the following relationship between long-term and short-term yields: The yield on a bond with *n* years to maturity should be equal to the average return from holding *n* number of one-year bonds plus a premium to compensate the investor for the fact that the longer maturity bond is riskier. Thus, the yield on a five-year bond should be the average of the yields from holding five one-year bonds plus an extra return to encourage the investor to accept the higher risk of holding a five-year bond.

A *yield curve* is a representation of how the yields on comparable bonds change as their maturity changes. Yield curves are usually calculated using government bond yields (in the United States this means T-Bonds and T-Bills). According to the expectations hypothesis, the slope of the yield curve provides a clear indication about what the market expects to happen to short term interest rates in the future. If short-term interest rates are expected to remain constant in the future, the yield curve should have a gradual upward slope because of the risk premium. If short-term interest rates are expected to rise in the future, then the yield curve should slope upwards very steeply. If short-term interest rates are expected to fall in the future, then the yield curve should be flat or downward sloping.

What role can yield curves play in economic forecasting? There is a strong rationale for thinking that an inverted (or possibly flat) yield curve is a market-based signal of a future recession. The reason is that short-term interest rates are strongly procyclical in the empirical data. This is in part because investment demand and inflation are procyclical and in part because countercyclical monetary policy makes short-term interest rates procyclical. As a result, if an accurate measure of future short-term interest rates can be obtained, then a good indicator of future output growth has also been found. An expected decline in short-term interest rates in the future—as evidenced by an inverted or flat yield curve—likely indicates that markets are also expecting a decline in output growth.

Over the last 30 years, yield curves in the United States have been a reliable indicator of recessions. One good example is the 1981–1982 recession. By the end of 1980, short-term interest rates reached roughly 18 percent and the yield curve in the United States became significantly inverted. It became more so in 1981 when the Fed began cutting the money supply in order to reduce inflation, initiating a severe recession. Yield curves in the United States also became inverted in mid-1979 (before the 1980 recession) and mildly inverted in both mid-1989 and mid-2000 (before the relatively mild recessions of 1990–1991 and 2001–2002) and in 2007. Most importantly, yield curves have not provided false signals, meaning that there has not been a time when the yield curve became inverted but the economy did not soon slip into a recession.

Figure 12.3 presents Treasury yield curves for the United States in the period leading up to the global financial crisis that officially began in December of 2007. In February 2005, the yield curve looked fairly typical, with a slight but gradual upward slope. However, by March 2007, the yield curve had become slightly inverted, signaling that the market expected a significant slowdown over the next two years, if not a recession. In February 2008, the recession had started. While this fact was not widely accepted at the time, it appears the Treasury markets believed that a recession was underway. The yield curve is actually slightly inverted for maturities up to two years, then strongly upward sloping after that.

Figure 12.3   Yield curves for the United States.

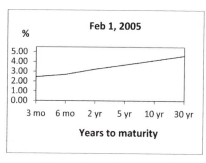

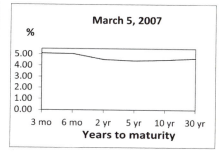

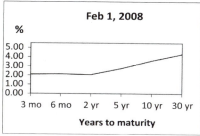

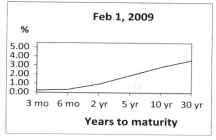

Source: Author's creation based on data from the U.S. Department of Treasury available at http://www.treasury.gov/resource-center/data-chart-center/interest-rates/Pages/TextView.aspx?data=yield.

This could be an indication that at the time the market expected that the next two years (2008–2010) would be slow, with the economy picking up strongly after that. Finally, the February 2009 yield curve paints a somewhat less rosy picture than the yield curve from the year before. While yields start to rise at maturities greater than a year, indicating an expected pickup in economic activity sometime in early 2010, the entire curve has shifted down significantly from where it was in 2008. This is an indication of how bad the economy was in early 2009, driving down interest rates to 30-year lows, and how bad the markets expected the economy to be for the rest of the year. It is also an indication of how aggressively monetary policy moved in late 2008 to cut both short-term and long-term interest rates in an effort to minimize the economic collapse.

From an economist's point of view, yield curves are certainly a more reliable measure of expectations than survey data, such as the Consumer Confidence Index, because they are market driven. However, one big drawback of yield curves is that interpreting them is somewhat subjective. How flat does a yield curve have to be before it is clearly indicating a future recession? How steep does a yield curve have to be before it clearly signals an expansion? These are important questions that have not yet been fully addressed empirically.

A few studies have been conducted evaluating the forecasting power of yield curves. For example, Haubrich and Dombrosky (1996) measured the slope of the yield curve by calculating the interest rate spread between the 10-year T-Bond and the three-month T-Bill. They found that during the previous 30 years there had been a strong correlation between this interest rate spread and GDP growth one year in the future. In fact, yield-curve-based forecasts do better than other more complex forecasting methods. Estrella and Mishkin (1998) also found evidence that the slope of the yield curve outperforms a wide variety of other market and nonmarket-based macroeconomic indicators such as the stock market, monetary aggregates, and the Index of Leading Indicators. However, Schrimpf and Wang (2010) find that during the last 10 years the slope of the yield curve has not performed as well, raising questions about whether a longer period of time is needed to accurately assess its forecasting effectiveness.

One additional problem that the yield curve, or any widely used economic indicator, can suffer from is the *observer effect*. According to the observer effect, once any indicator is measured and followed, its behavior will start to change. This is because closely watched indices begin to influence, and not just reflect, behavior. For example, as more market participants watch the yield curve, they may significantly increase risk perceptions and change their behavior based only on changes in the yield curve—not on any other information or observed changes in the economy. This will change the relationship between the yield curve and the rest of the economy in unpredictable ways. As the yield curve has become more closely followed, it is possible that it is less of an independent indicator of recessions and more of part of the mechanism through which recessions work.

Recently, new market-based indicators have been developed through the creation of prediction markets. In these prediction markets, agents can "bet" on future macroeconomic data by signing financial contracts that pay off (or fail to pay off) when this data is released. These prediction markets can be used for *hedging*, or reducing, risk as well as for speculation. By following the trades in these markets, it is possible to glean information about what market participants that are willing to risk their own money think will happen in the future. While still in their infancy, these prediction markets have been shown in studies (Snowberg et al., 2012) to provide unbiased forecasts that outperform surveys of economic forecasters, particularly during business cycle turning points. While prediction markets have the potential to provide a significant tool to forecasters as these markets develop and more people participate in them, they also will become more vulnerable to the observer effect, potentially reducing their effectiveness at the same time.

ECONOMETRIC TECHNIQUES

Econometrics refers to the use of statistical methods to address economic questions. Most econometric forecasting techniques are not based upon a specific macroeconomic theory. Instead, the objective is to examine a broad variety of macroeconomic data in order to determine reliable historical relationships and then extend these historical relationships into the future in order to generate a forecast.

The most common econometric technique used in forecasting is *ordinary least squares (OLS) regression*. While the purpose of this discussion is not to examine the technical details of OLS regression, intuitively it works in the following manner. Assume that real GDP growth next period is a linear function of time t, multiple current explanatory variables X_{it}, and their marginal effect on GDP growth β_{it}, as represented by the following equation:

$$GDP_{t+1} = \alpha_0 + \alpha_1 t + \beta_{1t} X_{1t} + \beta_{2t} X_{2t} .... + \beta_{kt} X_{kt} + \varepsilon_t \qquad (12.1)$$

Some of these explanatory variables are likely to be lagged variables, meaning that they may be from one or more periods in the past. The variable ε_t represents error in the hypothesized model that cannot be controlled for or is inherent in the determination of GDP growth. The objective of OLS is to choose the "best" values of each α_i and β_{it} using historical macroeconomic data, where best is defined as the values for each α_i and β_{it} that minimize the sum of the squared differences between the predicted and actual values of GDP. These errors are squared because it makes all of the errors positive and because it more heavily weighs large errors than small errors when choosing the best parameters.

OLS regression is surprisingly flexible. While it only works well under fairly strict conditions, economists have developed a number of techniques that allow them to manipulate macroeconomic data so that these conditions are met. This includes circumstances when an explanatory variable has a nonlinear relationship with GDP growth.

Once an econometric model has been built, forecasting becomes straightforward. Forecasts of future values of GDP growth are generated by combining the current values of explanatory variables with the α_i and

β_{it} coefficients that were estimated using historical data, adjusting for past variability in the model's errors.

The advantages of econometric techniques are twofold. First, econometric methods are a relatively cheap and simple way of making economic forecasts given the remarkable increases in computing power that have taken place recently. Some of the most popular econometric models are the Massachusetts Institute of Technology–Federal Reserve Board (MIT-FRB) model, the NBER model, and the commercial Data Resources, Inc. (DRI) model. Each of these models has more than 1,200 variables and more than 100 equations that are estimated simultaneously. Second, econometric methods generally do not rely on a single macroeconomic theory of output determination, which is appealing given that there is no agreement among economists on which model should be used. While theory does inform forecasters on which explanatory variables should and should not be included in the regression, it does not specify a specific structural relationship between each explanatory variable and GDP. Instead, that relationship is determined empirically using historical data.

The things that make econometric models attractive, however, are the same things that limit their ability to accurately forecast business cycles, particularly the turning points of business cycles. The fact that econometric forecasting relies little on economic theory is a big disadvantage in many economists' view because theory tells you what should and should not be determining business cycles and, by implication, which variables should be included in the econometric model and exactly how they should impact growth. Without theory, econometric forecasting can turn into "data mining," where all sorts of data is entered into a computer in an attempt to find some correlation that can be used to predict GDP growth, even if there is no causation involved. An extreme example of this would be to use the length of ladies' hemlines to forecast stock market prices because there is a reported correlation between the two, even though there are no serious theories (only humorous ones) as to why there should be any relationship between them. The atheoretical nature of econometric forecasts also leaves it vulnerable to overfitting the data and finding statistical explanatory power where no real explanatory power actually exists.

An additional problem with econometric techniques is that they are based on historical data, which means that the accuracy of their predictions is reliant on past conditions continuing to exist into the future. Many economists would ask how can forecasters believe that each α_i and β_{it} will remain constant in the future when different conditions that cannot be controlled for may not be the same. This is the basis of the Lucas critique, which was originally discussed in Chapter 7. Basically, the Lucas critique says that when policy changes, peoples' behaviors change as well. This changes the relationships that have historically existed between variables. Consider the following example. During World War II, the Federal Reserve and the U.S. Treasury reached an agreement that the Fed would peg interest rates at a low level during the war in order to aid the Treasury's financing of the war. Under this policy, people did not change their expected nominal interest rate when government spending increased because they knew interest rates would remain unchanged. As a result, savings, investment, bond prices, and other variables sensitive to future interest rates would also remain unchanged. If you included data from this period in a forecast of future GDP growth, you would get much different values for each α_i and β_{it} related to interest rate or monetary variables than you would get if you only used data from the postwar or prewar periods alone. Thus, changes in policy change expectations, which then change behavior. The Lucas critique raised real questions in many economists' minds about the validity of using econometric techniques to forecast the future in a world where monetary policy, fiscal policy, and government regulations are constantly changing.

Another problem with using historical data is the possibility that many events simply can never be forecasted based on the past alone. This was Keynes's, as well as the Austrians', critique of forecasting. They believed in unknown unknowns, where many future possible outcomes can never be anticipated based only on past experience. These unknown unknowns could be evolutionary changes in technology, structural changes in the economy, or events that have no precedent in history. Keynes thought that many economic shocks were inconceivable before they happened, and forecasters who do not accept this are underestimating the large amounts of potential error that exists within their forecasts.

An example of how dynamic the economy is, and how what is true today may not be true tomorrow, was observed recently during the "jobless recovery" in the aftermath of the global financial crisis. Typically, the U.S. economy has closely followed *Okun's Law*: A 1 percent increase in GDP growth reduces the unemployment rate by 0.5 percent. But in 2009, GDP growth rose, but so did the unemployment rate. Economists formed many hypotheses about why this was the case, the increasingly globalized nature of the U.S. economy and increased competitiveness in domestic labor markets being two of the most common. But the fact of the matter is that it would have been almost impossible to predict this outcome using past macroeconomic data alone.

One final problem with econometric modeling is that it relies on empirical economic data which, unfortunately, has inherent limitations. Data on variables such as GDP, inflation, and unemployment are costly and time-consuming to obtain. In an effort to improve the timeliness of this data, the government often issues preliminary reports that can be significantly different from the final revisions of the data publicized months later. Silver (2012) found that between 1965 and 2009 the average revision to the initial estimates of quarterly GDP was plus/minus 1.7 percent, which is very large given that GDP growth averages less than 3 percent. This means that if the government's initial estimate of GDP growth was anything less than 2 percent, the economy could very well be in a recession but the initial estimates would not show it.

There have been numerous studies that have evaluated the performance of the most popular econometric models in forecasting business cycles. Almost all of these studies conclude that econometric forecasting techniques perform adequately during stable periods but perform poorly during turning points in the business cycle. Clements (2002) examines the Survey of Professional Forecasters, which is a consensus forecast created by pooling individual professional forecasts. He found that actual GDP fell outside the 90 percent confidence interval of the forecast half of the time (not 10 percent of the time as it should if these forecasts were unbiased). However, Silver (2012) found that this consensus forecast is 20 percent more accurate than individual forecasts at predicting GDP growth. This still does not mean it is accurate. Based on the actual performance of the Survey of Professional Forecasters, the 90 percent confidence interval for their forecasts is a staggeringly high plus/minus 3.2 percent of GDP. In other words, with a forecast of 2 percent, actual GDP growth has a 90 percent chance of falling between –1.2 percent and 5.2 percent. That is quite a large range and does not provide a very valuable forecast.

Interestingly, the Survey of Professional Forecasters, where the participants provide information unanimously, outperforms another consensus forecast called the Blue Chip Economic Survey, where the participants provide their names. This seemingly counterintuitive result may be explained by McNees (1990), who found that making adjustments to econometric forecasts based on the judgment of the forecaster actually increased the accuracy of forecasts by 15 percent. Why? It is possible that forecasters have less fear of being an outlier and more willing to use their judgment when they are providing forecasts anonymously, as opposed to when they are forecasting publically and their reputations are at stake. Regardless of why, these results are damning critiques of standard econometric forecasting.

Given the limitations of purely historical forecasting, an alternative approach is *Bayesian forecasting*. Under the Bayesian approach, the forecaster begins with a prior belief about which variables should be included in the model and the values of the model's parameters based on economy theory. It then updates the values of these parameters as new information becomes available. The most important difference between Bayesian forecasting and standard econometrics forecasting is that here the focus is on producing the model that most accurately forecasts future outcomes, not the model that best fits the historical data. In theory, by weighing the most recent outcomes more heavily, Bayesian forecasting more accurately responds to structural changes in the economy and also avoids some of the problems associated with data mining and overfitting in many standard econometric models. Of course, this improved accuracy comes at the price of being much more complicated to estimate. It also places a great deal of importance on the accuracy of the forecaster's prior beliefs—that is, the theory that the forecaster is using to pick which variables to include in their model and the initial parameter values. (This problem can be somewhat mitigated using a technique called Bayesian model averaging, where many different models are estimated and the best model is obtained by using the variables that were most often found to be relevant.) As a result, Bayesian forecasting can have limitations that are similar to forecasting using structural models, which are discussed in the next section.

STRUCTURAL MODELS

Structural models are based on using a specific macroeconomic theory—and the relationships between variables that this theory implies—to forecast future economic performance. For example, Keynesian structural forecasts would involve using econometric techniques to estimate the parameters of the IS and LM equations in an economy. Given these equations, the expected values of policy variables such as government spending, taxes, and the money supply could then be used to determine the future value of aggregate output. Thus, structural modeling is really a synthesis between macroeconomic theory and the use of econometric techniques to match data to this theory.

Even more than econometric forecasting or macroeconomic indicators, structural modeling has almost completely fallen out of favor with most professional forecasters. The reasons are fairly obvious. First, structural forecasts are really conditional forecasts—conditional upon a specific theory. This is problematic given that there is currently no generally accepted theory of business cycle determination. During the 1950s and 1960s, when Keynesian economics was generally accepted, Keynesian structural modeling was the most widely used forecasting method. However, the stagflation of the 1970s raised serious questions in most economists' minds about the simple Keynesian model of aggregate demand-driven business cycles. Keynesian structural modeling in the 1970s was plagued by huge and persistent forecasting errors and also played an important role in justifying the inflationary monetary policies of the Fed during this time. In addition, the development of rational expectations and the Lucas critique raised questions about the reliability of the estimated parameters in a structural model because these parameters can change as policy and expectations change. Finally, the fact that Keynesian structural models were not based on microeconomic foundations, or the optimizing behavior of individuals, raised serious questions in many minds. Many of the structural relationships between variables were simply assumed to exist, as opposed to being derived from a detailed microeconomic theory.

Some structural forecasting still does take place, but it is largely used in academic research and not in the business community where the large commercial forecasting models primarily rely on pure econometric methods.

DYNAMIC STOCHASTIC GENERAL EQUILIBRIUM MODELS

Dynamic general equilibrium (DSGE) models are based on the assumption that microeconomic models of individual households, firms, and markets can be used to understand macroeconomic behavior. To do this and still allow these models to be manageable, DSGE models typically assume *representational agents*, or individuals who all have the same preferences and act alike in every way. When combined with the assumption of perfect competition, macroeconomic behavior becomes a simple summation of average microeconomic behavior. Real business cycle models, which were discussed in Chapter 8, were the first example of DSGE models. In real business cycle models, representational agents operate in perfectly competitive markets where business cycle fluctuations are driven by random (stochastic) productivity shocks to production.

While DSGE modeling began by focusing on models of perfect competition, many newer DSGE models incorporate different forms of market failure and price rigidities, such as sticky nominal wages, price inflexibility, credit rationing, and changes in financial risk. Some newer DSGE models have also began to loosen the assumption of representative agents and explore how heterogeneity among individuals can impact macroeconomic behavior. Thus, DSGE models no longer only take a neo-classical approach, and new Keynesian DSGE models that incorporate one or more forms of market failure are increasingly used in academic research. However, all DSGE models share two characteristics. The first is that all economic choices, such as the choices to work versus enjoy leisure or to save versus consume, must be consistent with microeconomic behavior where individuals make decisions based on optimizing their welfare. Second, one or more random shocks exist in some sector of the economy that complicates this optimization and creates economic uncertainty.

DSGE models can be used in simulation experiments to forecast the future path of an economy. Changes in exogenous variables such as technology or monetary or fiscal policy can be incorporated within a DSGE model, and the behavior of the model economy when these exogenous variables change can be observed. The critical idea behind the use of DSGE modeling is that these models will more accurately predict changes in the real economy because only macroeconomic theory that is consistent with microfoundations can avoid the Lucas critique and fully incorporate the fact that peoples' behaviors change as policy changes.

Like all forecasting methods, DSGE modeling is fraught with difficulties. The biggest problem is that these models are extremely complex. They are so complex, in fact, that commercial researchers have largely ignored them, relegating their use to academic research. In addition, because of their complexity, the parameters in DSGE models cannot be easily estimated. Instead, forecasters often go through a process called *calibration* in which they choose values for the parameters of the model so that it behaves in a way that is consistent with the long-run properties of the economy. Of course, once fixed parameters are chosen that govern key macroeconomic relationships, the Lucas critique is once again applicable. This is a big problem given that one of the principal rationales for DSGE modeling is to avoid problems associated with the Lucas critique.

As discussed in Chapter 8, DSGE models such as real business cycle models have difficulty in matching many of the facts of business cycles, particularly in regards to the behavior of many labor market variables. The same holds regarding the ability of these models to forecast future macroeconomic behavior. As demonstrated by Rotemberg and Woodford (1996), real business cycle DSGE models cannot match the performance of econometric models in forecasting the behavior of GDP, consumption, and unemployment. Del Negro and Schorfheide (2012) find that a new Keynesian DSGE with a variety of market rigidities does not perform as well at near-term forecasting compared to professional Blue Chip consensus forecasts but does perform almost as well at forecasting key macroeconomic variables over the long term.

In academic research, DSGE models are often used in policy analysis. The implications of changes in various public policies, such as the economic implications of tax reform or financial regulation, can be interestingly investigated within these models. However, the standard assumption of representative agents severely limits their use in policy discussions with distributional implications because the study of distributional issues requires that not everyone is exactly the same. DSGE models also allow forecasters to simulate a wide variety of future paths for the economy under alternative scenarios and attach probabilities to these future outcomes. These are valuable features that can allow forecasters to better quantify the likelihood of different outcomes compared to traditional econometric forecasts. But when it comes to straight forecasting of future output and inflation levels, econometric models continue to generate better results and are less complex. Hence, DSGE models have, to this point, captured little of the commercial forecasting market.

CONCLUSIONS

The profession of macroeconomic forecasting is currently stuck in a long, protracted recession with no trough in sight. A few large commercial forecasters still exist, but the days when every Fortune 500 company had its own in-house forecasters are over. Maybe more importantly, interest in forecasting among the best academic research economists has waned, meaning future improvement will be slow.

Much of this decline in the use of forecasting has been the result of its unreliable past performance. While econometric models and leading indicators do a good job predicting growth during stable economic periods, they are very poor predictors of turning points in the business cycle and generate large and persistent errors when there are major economic shocks such as the oil price shocks of the 1970s, the strong productivity growth of the 1990s, or the housing price bubble of the later 2000s. Yield curves might be more reliable indicators of business cycle turning points, but at this point interpreting yield curves is still more of an art than a science. The use of other market indicators such as prediction markets also show some promise but as yet are relatively undeveloped and untested. The same holds for DSGE models, which are attractive from a theoretical standpoint and widely used in academic research but have generated little excitement among commercial forecasters because of their complexity and uneven forecasting performance.

It is important to note that forecasting is difficult, not just in economics but in most areas of study. It is not just economists but also weathermen, scientists, political commentators, sports pundits, and public officials that have a sketchy history in predicting the future. Prediction is a difficult business because of many of the biases behavioral economists have identified, specifically confirmation bias (the tendency to prioritize information that confirms preconceived ideas) and overconfidence bias (the tendency to place too much confidence in your own beliefs). But economic forecasting is particularly difficult because of these problems: the complexity of economic systems, the difficulties of fundamental uncertainty, the Lucas critique, our lack of reliable and timely data, the possibility of evolutionary structure change, and the difficulty of separating cause and effect. It is reasonable to conclude that economic forecasting will always be an exercise much like hitting a baseball: To get it right only a small percentage of the time is to be successful at it.

However, it is possible that this view of forecasting as an inherently flawed endeavor is too pessimistic. Consider the following parable offered by Gregory Mankiw (1990). When scientists first tried to explain and predict the positioning of planets and stars in order to aid naval navigation, they developed a simple but mistaken theory referred to as the Ptolemaic system. Developed by the Egyptians, this theory assumed that the sun and planets revolved around the Earth and that these bodies followed circular (not elliptical) paths. When the Copernican system was first introduced in the 1500s with its assumption that the Earth revolved around the sun in an elliptical orbit, it was widely rejected by ship captains, largely because its astrological forecasts were not as accurate as those made using the old system. However, over time academics refined the more complex Copernican system, and it eventually provided very accurate predictions. With work, getting the theory right eventually can lead to getting the forecasting right. The hope for economists is that as we continue to improve, refine, and deepen our understanding of economic theory and the nature of business cycles, our abilities to predict the future will advance as well. Maybe the study of macroeconomics will one day reach a similar harmony between theory and practice.

SUGGESTED READINGS

"After Keynesian Economics," Robert Lucas and Thomas Sargent (1978):
    A criticism of both econometric forecasting and Keynesian

structural models of forecasting. The Lucas critique and its role in the decline of macroeconomic forecasting is discussed in detail.

"The Past, Present, and Future of Macroeconomic Forecasting," Francis Diebold (1998): A nontechnical discussion of the historical evolution of macroeconomic forecasting and its track record. Included is the author's suggestions for future areas of research that are needed to improve the state of forecasting.

The Signal and the Noise: Why So Many Predictions Fail—but Some Don't, Nate Silver (2012): A look at the reasons why predictions and forecasts fail to live up to expectations in many fields of study. Silver makes an argument for Bayesian forecasting, or conditioning forecasts based on prior beliefs but updating these beliefs dynamically as new information becomes available. Chapter 6 of this book, entitled "How to Drown in Three Feet of Water," discusses the shortcomings of economic forecasting.

PART IV

Business Cycles in the United States

THIRTEEN

The Great Depression

INTRODUCTION

The Great Depression is the most analyzed economic event of all time. Even so, the sheer magnitude of it is still difficult to comprehend for those who did not live through it. Looking at figures and tables of data is a very poor substitute for experience, but the data still paints a sobering picture of an economic world that went horribly wrong. Table 13.1 reports macroeconomic data from the United States during the Great Depression. Real income fell by nearly one-third, which is nearly four times greater than any other postwar contraction in output. Unemployment almost reached 25 percent, stock prices fell 85 percent, and 25 percent of all banks failed.

One of the most important aspects of the Great Depression was that it was a world-wide phenomenon. Figure 13.1 reports industrial production in the four major economies of the time (the United States, Germany, United Kingdom, and France). Table 13.2 reports unemployment rates in these same countries. While the Great Depression adversely affected every major economy, the United States experienced the steepest declines in production and the largest increases in unemployment. Another important aspect of the Great Depression is that it was associated with international deflation. Figure 13.2 reports wholesale prices for these four countries during of the Great Depression. Between 1929 and 1932, prices fell by roughly 40 percent in the United States and by similar levels in Germany and Britain.

Table 13.1   Key macroeconomic variables during the Great Depression.

	Real GNP ($ billions)	Unemployment rate (%)	Stock prices ($)	Bank failures	Consumer Price Index
1928	98.2	4.2	153	498	100.0
1929	104.4	3.2	201	659	100.0
1930	95.1	8.7	161	1,350	97.4
1931	89.5	15.9	100	2,293	88.7
1932	76.4	23.6	36	1,453	79.7
1933	74.2	24.9	79	4,000	75.4
1934	80.8	21.7	78	57	78.0
1935	91.4	20.1	80	34	80.1
1936	100.9	16.9	112	44	80.9
1937	109.1	14.3	120	59	83.8
1938	103.2	19.0	80	54	82.3

Source: NBER Macrohistory Database available at http://research.stlouisfed.org/fred2/categories/33061.

Many theories of business cycle behavior have been developed around providing a plausible explanation of the Great Depression. The most well-known is the Keynesian model. Although many of Keynes's theories had been developed prior to the Great Depression, Keynes and his followers were quick to assert that their model not only explained the causes

Figure 13.1   Industrial production in four countries.

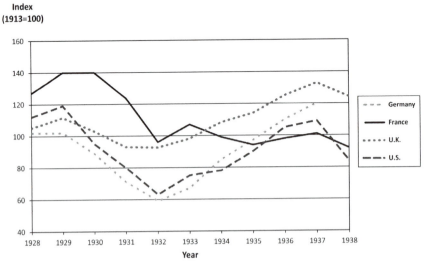

Source: Author's creation based on data from Romer (1993).

Table 13.2 Unemployment rates in four countries before and during the Great Depression.

Country	1921–1929 (%)	1930–1938 (%)	Average rate (%)	Difference (%)	Ratio of difference to average
United States	7.9	26.1	17.0	18.0	1.07
United Kingdom	12.0	15.4	13.7	3.4	0.25
France	3.8	10.2	7.0	6.4	0.91
Germany	9.2	21.8	15.5	13.0	0.81

Source: Author's creation based on data from Temin (1989).

of the Great Depression but also provided clear policy prescriptions for how to best deal with it. As discussed in Chapter 4, the Keynesian explanation of the Great Depression centered on a major decline in aggregate demand caused by sharp falls in investment and consumption. These falls in investment and consumption were the result of a huge decline in expectations. The fall in aggregate demand had real effects on the economy because of wage inflexibility in the labor market. Keynes's policy solution for ending the Great Depression was to increase government spending in order to stimulate aggregate demand and move the economy back toward its potential level of output and full employment.

The monetarist theory of business cycles was also, in large part, developed around a hypothesis about what caused the Great Depression.

Figure 13.2 Wholesale prices in four countries.

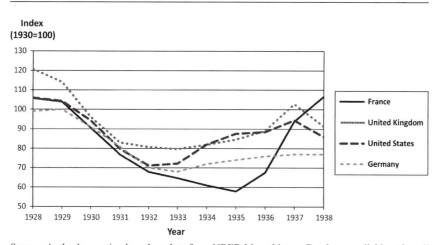

Source: Author's creation based on data from NBER Macrohistory Database available at http://www.nber.org/databases/macrohistory/contents/chapter04.html.

Monetarists argued that the Great Depression was caused by a large decrease in the money supply that occurred because of the Federal Reserve's ignorance and incompetence. This decline in the money supply reduced aggregate demand for two reasons. First, a lower money supply reduced aggregate spending in accordance with the quantity theory. Second, a decrease in the money supply reduced liquidity in the banking system, leading to banking failures and high real interest rates. The decline in financial intermediation that resulted from contractionary monetary policy led to further reductions in spending, investment, and aggregate demand. While this theory was developed well after the Great Depression, its policy recommendations for dealing with future contractions were simple: Constrain monetary policy and stabilize the money supply by mandating a simple money growth rule that central banks must follow.

Many financial-based theories, such as Fischer's debt-deflation model and Minsky's financial instability hypothesis, were also founded upon observations made during the banking, asset, and financial market crashes that occurred during the Great Depression. For these theories, the Great Depression was evidence of the mania and panic that is an endemic aspect of finance. However, despite the obvious importance of the financial system in the overall collapse, the influence of these models on business cycle theory and in research on the Great Depression was minimal during most of the postwar era.

Other business cycle theories have fallen out of favor with many economists because of their inability to provide a plausible explanation of the Great Depression. The Austrian emphasis on the role of expansionary monetary policy was not consistent with the remarkable deflation that occurred. Real business cycle models, with their emphasis on supply-driven business cycles, are viewed with skepticism by many economists because their explanation of the Depression is unconvincing. What was the source of the large decrease in aggregate supply that caused the Great Depression? If the Great Depression was caused by a fall in aggregate supply, why did prices fall instead of rise? Likewise, a big problem with the rational expectations model is that in this model business cycles are caused by imperfect information and misperceptions about the state of the economy. What kind of mistaken expectations could cause output to fall by one-third and remain below its peak level for nearly eight years?

During the 1980s, economists once again began to reevaluate their hypotheses about what caused the Great Depression. Much of the new research that took place examined the Great Depression from a different perspective, one which viewed the Great Depression as not just an economic contraction but as an international financial crisis. This distinction is important because it refocused macroeconomic research on financial markets as playing the crucial role in propagating the Depression. This new focus was inspired by the development of new Keynesian economics, specifically, the development of new Keynesian models of credit that emphasized the role of risk and fragile financial fundamentals.

This chapter will discuss this new approach to explaining the events of the Great Depression. Two economists in particular, Peter Temin (1989) and Ben Bernanke (1983, 1995), contributed to this research that focuses (though not exclusively) on the international financial aspects of the crash. Specifically, the role of the gold standard, which was reinstated after World War I, is closely examined and identified as a major culprit in setting the stage for a major international deflation. This deflation had important microeconomic implications for both labor markets and financial fundamentals, ultimately leading to a financial and macroeconomic collapse of unprecedented proportions.

THE GOLD STANDARD AFTER WORLD WAR I

Most countries dropped off the gold standard during World War I because of the constraints it imposed on monetary and fiscal policies—constraints that were superseded by the need to finance war efforts. However, most of the major economies reinstated the gold standard between 1925 and 1929. The main rationale for returning to the gold standard was a simple one: Policy makers at the time had not thought through any feasible alternatives. Until that point in history, countries had backed their currencies with gold and had maintained fixed exchange rates in order to facilitate international trade. The times when countries were not on the gold standard (primarily when they were engaged in war) were also periods when almost all international trade came to a halt. Most policy makers had not even considered a peacetime option to the gold standard and assumed that abandoning the gold standard meant contracting international trade.

Temin (1989) asserts that the gold standard system that was reconstituted after World War I had four principal characteristics.

1. Countries fixed their currencies to gold and, as a result, fixed their exchange rates to each other.
2. Gold movements across countries were unconstrained. Gold flowed into countries with trade surpluses and flowed out of countries with trade deficits.

3. Asymmetries in the effects of running trade surpluses versus trade deficits were inherent in the system. A country experiencing a trade surplus could accumulate gold reserves without increasing the money supply, which is referred to as *sterilization*. On the other hand, trade deficit countries were forced to reduce their money supplies as their gold reserves fell in order to avoid *devaluation*, or reducing its exchange rate. This meant that trade deficits led to deflation and a contraction in economic activity. As a result, countries had significant incentives to bias their economic policies toward hoarding gold through running trade surpluses in order to avoid the negative effects of running trade deficits.

4. No organization or structure was in place to encourage international economic cooperation, to enforce international agreements, or to provide temporary financing to countries that were short of gold reserves.

It is important to understand how different the gold standard system is from a floating exchange rate system. When a country floats and let markets determine its exchange rate, it has the freedom to control its domestic money supply and use monetary policy to stabilize domestic output. Under a gold standard system, a country fixes its exchange rate at the cost of giving up control of the money supply. Because there was no way for a gold standard country to adjust its exchange rate in the face of a large trade imbalance, any country experiencing a trade deficit was forced to contract its money supply. This would lead to a fall in aggregate demand and output, but in the long run falling prices would make exports cheaper and improve the trade balance of the country.

An important difference between our era and the interwar period is that today there are multiple layers of international organizations that provide help in financing and coordinating economic policies, such as the IMF, the World Bank, the G7, and the World Trade Organization. Before World War II, none of this international infrastructure existed. Many countries felt free to act as if they operated in a vacuum and not within an interconnected international economy. The result was that most countries attempted to run large trade surpluses at the expense of their trading partners. In addition, there was no safety net of emergency financing for countries that were running unsustainable trade deficits and losing gold reserves. Instead, they were forced to cut their money supplies and fend for themselves.

THE EVENTS OF THE GREAT DEPRESSION

1929–1931: The First Wave

In the aftermath of World War I, most countries returned to the gold standard. The problem with this quick resurrection of the system was that extreme economic inequities existed after the war was over. The British and Germany economies were much weaker after the war and immediately suffered from large trade deficits and gold outflows. On the other hand, the economies of the United States and France had suffered much less during the war and were relatively much stronger. Upon resumption of the gold standard, the United States and France began running trade surpluses and acquiring large gold stocks.

These trade imbalances led to falling money supplies and deflation worldwide because of the asymmetries inherent in the gold standard. The British and Germans were forced to reduce their money supplies as gold flowed out of their countries. On the other hand, both the Americans and the French chose to sterilize their large gold inflows and not increase their money supplies because of worries about inflation. In fact, the United States actually reduced its money supply beginning in 1928 because of worries within the Federal Reserve about an inflated stock market. The end result was that by 1929, the United States and France had 60 percent of the world's gold but were still decreasing their money supplies. Coupled with the falling money supplies in much of the rest of Europe, the world economy began to experience significant deflation starting in 1929, before the Depression began (see Figure 13.2).

The obvious question is this: Couldn't the U.S. Federal Reserve understand what was going on with worldwide deflation and, as a result, act to increase the money supply in order to avoid a worldwide recession? As Friedman and Schwartz (1963) make clear in their book *A Monetary History of the United States, 1867–1960*, Fed officials (and other central bankers at this time) were considerably less sophisticated than they are today. Their obsession with controlling inflation and maintaining the gold standard dominated all their thinking. The appropriate monetary policy under the gold standard was always to hoard gold by sustaining trade surpluses regardless of the worldwide economic situation. This policy of attempting to run trade surpluses at the expense of other countries is often referred to as a *beggar-thy-neighbor* policy. The problem with beggar-thy-neighbor policies is that every country in the world cannot run a trade surplus at the same time. The attempt to do so can lead to exactly what happened during the Great Depression: a contraction of world money supplies, world trade, and world incomes. Without any mechanism for coordinating international economic policy, other countries could not force the United States or any other country to reevaluate its deflationary policies and increase its money supply even though the United States was quickly accumulating much of the world's gold and forcing the rest of the world to reduce their money supplies as well. As a result, America largely drove the world economy into deflation and depression by itself because of its unyielding commitment to protecting the gold standard, low inflation, and trade surpluses.

Although the decline in the U.S. money supply that occurred between 1928 and 1929 was partially responsible for the October 1929 stock market crash, the Federal Reserve continued to reduce the money supply after the crash in order to protect against gold outflows and inflation during 1930 and into 1931. The stock market crash reduced consumption and investment by increasing uncertainty and reducing wealth. The Hoover administration's fiscal policies made things even worse. Hoover enacted reductions in government spending in order to balance the federal budget and higher import tariffs to protect the U.S. trade surplus. These policies only magnified the decline in aggregate demand, and prices continued to fall precipitously. However, this process was seen by many in the Fed and the federal government as a "cleansing" of economic excesses. For example, in a quote consistent with the Austrian view that recessions represent an opportunity for creative destruction, Hoover's Secretary of the Treasury Andrew Mellon urged markets to "liquidate labor, liquidate stocks, liquidate the farmers, and liquidate real estate. ... It will purge the rottenness out of the system. High costs of living and high living will come down. People will work harder, live a more moral life. Values will be adjusted, and enterprising people will pick up from less competent people" (Hoover, 1952). This statement is akin to arguing that the outbreak of a disease was not such a bad thing because it primarily affected the infirmed and the elderly. Altogether, contractionary macroeconomic policy played a crucial role in fueling the Great Depression—so great, in fact, that Peter Temin (1993) has referred to the Fed's monetary policy between 1929 and 1931 as "one of the most memorable acts of misguided monetary policy in history."

1931–1933: The Second Wave

The second, and most severe, phase of the Great Depression in the United States was characterized by banking panics and failures that effectively halted all financial intermediation and investment. Roughly 25 percent of all banks failed or suspended operations during this period. Bank depositors and stockholders lost an amount equal to 2.4 percent of GDP, which was a much larger loss than what occurred during the stock market crash in October of 1929. As banks began to fail, the economy contracted rapidly. Industrial production fell by 43 percent between April 1931 and June 1932, and unemployment rose to over 24 percent.

The monetary base was roughly constant between July 1929 and July 1931. But then M1 fell by 28 percent as fear set in and banks and the public began to hoard money, leading to a precipitous drop in the money multiplier. Finally, beginning in late 1931, the Fed reversed course (under threat from Congress) and began to rapidly increase the monetary base. By this time, however, it was too late. Despite a large increase in the monetary base, the money supply did not increase because money hoarding continued to be rampant. The currency-to-deposits ratio rose by 29 percent and the excess reserves-to-deposits ratio rose by 47 percent between June 1930 and February 1933. Together, these reduced the M1 multiplier by 35 percent, or roughly the amount of the fall in the level of M1. The contraction in the money supply only accelerated when the United States began to experience huge gold outflows in 1931 because of speculation that it would abandon the gold standard. The United Kingdom abandoned the gold standard in 1931 (and, not coincidentally, rapidly recovered as gold flows, their money supply, and their trade balance immediately increased), leading many speculators to sell their dollars for gold in anticipation of the United States doing the same in the near future.

1933–1941: Recovery

The United States resisted abandoning the gold standard until 1933, at which point Roosevelt was elected president and immediately devalued the dollar. France and other European countries held onto the gold standard until 1936, while Germany held on throughout the decade (Germany is a special case because of the economic constraints placed on it by the Allies after World War I—constraints that severely damaged the German economy and set the stage for Hitler's rise to power). Referring once again to Figure 13.1, no countries other than Germany recovered from the Great Depression until they dropped off of the gold standard. Once they did, the economic recoveries were often quite strong. This is especially true in the United Kingdom, which was the first to abandon the gold standard. Spain is also an interesting case study because it was not on the gold standard to begin with. As a result, it suffered no banking panics and no depression.

Bernanke (1995) found that beginning in 1931, non-gold-standard countries had higher production, prices, money supplies, employment, interest rates, exports, imports, and stock prices than their counterparts that remained on the gold standard.

In the United States, the New Deal policies initiated by Roosevelt also helped to stabilize the economy. Increases in government spending and reductions in taxes stimulated aggregate demand and raised consumer confidence by creating the impression that the government was doing something to improve the economic situation. Bank holidays imposed by Roosevelt also slowed the bank runs and calmed the rampant speculation that was plaguing the financial system. However, none of these New Deal policies were sufficient to end the Depression by themselves. These initiatives were simply much too small and too delayed relative to the size of the contraction in output.

While the trough in American GDP occurred in 1933, recovery from the Great Depression was painfully slow. This was partially because output had fallen so far below the natural rate that it would necessarily take a long time for it to recover. The recovery was also slowed by the large decline in the capital stock and the lost job skills and training that accompanied lost job opportunities. Output rose very gradually from 1933 to 1937, followed by a short recession from 1937 to 1938 (which was once again initiated by the Fed cutting the money supply in response to inflation fears). By 1940, unemployment was still at 14.6 percent. In fact, the United States did not return to the natural rate of output until 1941, when huge increases in defense spending (a 59 percent increase in government spending between 1940 and 1941) were triggered by Germany's invasion of France in May 1940. American GDP increased by 17 percent between 1940 and 1941 while unemployment dropped below 10 percent for the first time since 1930.

WHY IS DEFLATION SO COSTLY?

There remains one missing piece to the puzzle explaining what caused the Great Depression. Why was it that deflation, which was caused by falling money supplies and aggregate demands throughout the world, had such a huge impact on the real economy? In other words, why didn't the classical principle of money neutrality hold, where under the assumption of perfectly flexible prices a nominal shock such as deflation would not matter for real economy activity? New Keynesian research has pointed out two primary costs of deflation, both of them the result of imperfectly competitive markets.

1. *Deflation increases the real value of debt relative to the value of assets because the prices of nominal debt contracts are fixed.* Irving Fischer, in his debt-deflation theory, first highlighted the importance of the fact that nominal debt contracts are not *indexed*, meaning that they do not have contractual clauses that adjust the value of payments for changes in the price level. Because the prices (or the principal to be repaid) of debt contracts are fixed, unexpected changes in the price level change the real value of debt. An unexpected decrease in the price level increases the real value of debt if the nominal value of this debt is fixed. This is a severe financial hardship on firms and households who tend to be borrowers, and while it might seem to be a good thing for banks to see the real value of their loan assets rise, the probability that these loans will be repaid will also fall significantly.

In the same way, consider how unexpected deflation impacts the value of assets. The market prices of assets are not fixed, and a decrease in the price level decreases the prices of these assets. This includes decreases in the value of assets a bank uses to generate income, such as stocks or bonds, and it also decreases the value of the assets firms and households use as collateral to back their bank loans, such as the prices of homes or land. Thus, firms and households will see the value of their assets fall and the real value of their debts rise as a result of a large and unexpected deflation. This means that many of these same firms and households will become bankrupt, leading to higher rates of default on loan payments and deterioration in the soundness of banks' financial fundamentals.

Keynes recognized that nominal debt prices were fixed and that deflation weakened the financial position of banks, reducing the amount of credit supplied to firms. However, both Keynes and the Keynesians focused on the demand for credit, believing that low expectations were primarily responsible for low investment regardless of how much credit was available. As a result, the role of debt and financial stability receives little attention in *The General Theory* and from Keynesians.

Monetarists, on the other hand, agree with the debt-deflation theory that changes in the supply of credit drive business cycles. However, they believe that credit cycles are the result of vacillating monetary policy, not the result of changes in risk and the willingness of banks to lend.

The debt-deflation theory appears to be an accurate description of what happened in the U.S. financial system during the

Great Depression. American banks, particularly a large number of rural banks, had been weakened during the 1920s because of deflation in agricultural prices, which had dramatically increased farm foreclosures. During the generally prosperous 1920s, nearly 6,000 banks failed. When economy-wide deflation occurred in the 1930s, the debt-to-income ratio in the United States jumped from 9 percent in 1929 to 19.8 percent in 1932, and 45 percent of farms became delinquent in their loan payments. As a result, the typical American bank, which was small and undiversified, was left facing historic levels of defaults. Coupled with the difficulty of borrowing funds elsewhere because of the tight money supply, these loan defaults led to an unprecedented number of bank failures. In addition, the initial failure of a small number of banks led to a loss of confidence among depositors, leading to regional bank runs that further weakened banks' balance sheets. Consequently, between 1930 and 1933, roughly one-fourth of all banks in the United States failed or suspended payments.

While this debt-deflation theory of financial crises has been around since the Great Depression, new Keynesian economists such as Ben Bernanke gave it new life with their work on the macroeconomic effects of imperfect information and risk. Chapter 9 on new Keynesian models of credit discussed two mechanisms by which changes in financial fundamentals impact lending: through changes in the costs of credit intermediation (the financial accelerator model) and through the imposition of credit limits (the credit rationing model). During economic contractions, the risk of bankruptcy by firms and households rises because of increases in the real value of debt and also because of decreases in the value of collateral that reduce net worth. Those banks that do not fail will be willing to engage in new lending only under the strictest conditions. They might increase their costs of credit intermediation by increasing interest rates, imposing stricter monitoring requirements, or demanding more compensating balances. Or they might ration credit by imposing credit limits, either directly by limiting loan amounts or indirectly by requiring more collateral. Under either alternative, credit intermediation will decline, reducing aggregate demand, aggregate supply, and aggregate output.

Bernanke (1983) found a great deal of evidence that suggests that the costs of credit intermediation dramatically increased during the Great Depression, while credit limits significantly tightened; these changes were the result of higher levels of debt, lower values of collateral, lower levels of bank deposits, and higher bankruptcy risk.

For example, Figure 13.3 presents the interest rate spread between Baa bonds (corporate bonds of moderate risk) and T-Bills. This spread is a measure of perceived default risk and of changes in the costs of credit intermediation. Not only did this spread rise dramatically during the Depression, but it tracked the number of banking failures in the economy. Bernanke also presents evidence from surveys conducted during the Depression that indicate that credit rationing was prevalent, particularly among smaller and newer firms. Almost 75 percent of firms in one survey reported that they could not get sufficient credit between 1933 and 1938, which is even after the worst of the Depression had passed. Bernanke found that bank failures, credit rationing, and increases in the costs of credit intermediation all preceded steep declines in investment and industrial production during the Depression.

Figure 13.3   Interest rate spread and bank failures in the United States.

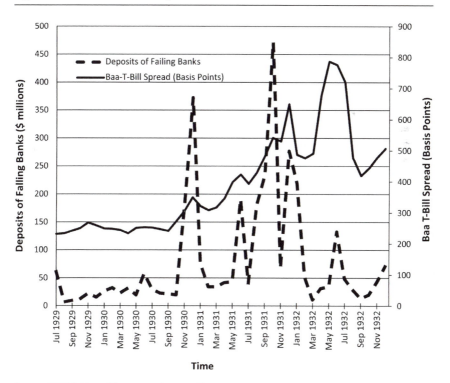

Source: NBER Macrohistory Database available at http://research.stlouisfed.org/fred2/categories/ 33061.

The Great Depression was also an international phenomenon. Because deflation took place across the globe, financial crisis and economic collapse also took place across the globe. Bernanke and James (1991) present quantitative evidence that those countries that had the most fragile financial fundamentals in their banking systems even before the Depression began were the countries that were most likely to experience banking crises. Across countries, banking crises were triggered by deflation caused by adherence to the gold standard. In every country that suffered an economic crisis, financial collapse proceeded economic collapse and ended only when the country abandoned the gold standard, which then allowed prices, financial fundamentals, and the financial system to stabilize.

2. *Deflation increases real wages because of nominal wage inflexibility.* One of the key tenets of Keynesian economics is that nominal wages are inflexible, particularly downward, so that a decrease in the price level increases real wages and generates unemployment in the labor market. One of the important contributions of new Keynesian economics has been to explain the microeconomic foundations behind this nominal wage inflexibility. In Chapter 9, a number of theories of why nominal wages are rigid were examined: implicit and explicit contracts, minimum wage laws, insider–outsider theories, sticky information, and efficiency wage theories. Each of these models explains how wage rigidity and disequilibrium can persist within imperfectly competitive labor markets.

Bernanke (1995) investigated real wage behavior across countries during the Great Depression and reported that in gold standard countries such as the United States, real wages rose by an average of 11 percent in 1931 and 6.4 percent in 1932. This is in spite of the fact that nominal wages were falling in these countries—they were just not falling fast enough to restore equilibrium in the labor market. In the United States, real wages rose by roughly 3 percent during 1931, even though nominal wages fell nearly 13 percent and unemployment was over 20 percent. On the other hand, real wages in non-gold-standard countries were either stagnant or falling, particularly from 1934 on. This is primarily because prices in these non-gold-standard countries began to rise as they were freed to increase their money supplies and stimulate aggregate demand.

OTHER EXPLANATIONS OF THE GREAT DEPRESSION

The primary explanation of the Great Depression presented in this chapter focuses on deflation that resulted from naïve adherence to the gold standard and its impact on financial fundamentals, credit, and real wages. However, this is not the only explanation of the Great Depression that has been proposed by economists. In fact, many other alternative explanations have been offered. Most of these alternatives are not mutually exclusive, however, meaning that an economic contraction the size of the Great Depression did not just have one single cause. Multiple theories make sense if there are multiple causes. On the other hand, most other explanations appear to be of secondary importance to the primary cause focused on in this chapter.

Keynesians believe that the Great Depression was caused by a decrease in expectations that reduced investment and consumption, which in turn reduced aggregate demand and output because of wage inflexibility. While low expectations obviously played a role in the Depression, it is hard to see how a 50 percent fall in GDP could be initiated only by pessimistic expectations. If this were the case, why have we not seen depressions comparable to the Great Depression since the 1930s? And what exactly occurred in 1929 that could explain such a large decline in confidence across countries? In addition, while Keynesians identified the role of inflexible nominal wages in driving involuntary unemployment in the labor market, they largely ignored other important factors that had a real impact on economic activity, such as the effects of nominal debt contracts and the role deflation played in weakening the financial system. Thus, the Keynesian explanation only appears to be a partial explanation of a much bigger crisis.

The Austrians and monetarists focus on the role of the Federal Reserve's monetary policies during the Great Depression. The Austrian emphasis on the role of expansionary monetary policy in encouraging overbuilding and malinvestment was not consistent with the contractionary monetary policy that actually occurred before the Great Depression (once again, driven by the gold standard) and the remarkable deflation that transpired once it started. Friedman and other monetarists more plausibly suggest that it was the Fed's contractionary monetary policies that drove the Depression. Monetarists believe that decreases in the money supply affect output by reducing the supply of credit, driving up real interest rates, and reducing spending. In their theory, bank failures were a symptom of the Depression, not a cause. These failures occurred only because of a shortage of liquidity that prohibited banks from meeting their deposit withdrawal demands.

Two problems exist with this monetarist explanation. First, relying on the 250-year-old quantity theory, which assumes a direct relationship between the money supply and spending, is implausible to many. Does monetary policy, through its ability to influence bank credit and spending, really have the power to reduce output by 50 percent by itself? Second, interest rates did not rise during the Great Depression as predicted by the monetarists, but instead fell. This indicates that it may not have been tight monetary policy that was the cause of falling investment. More likely, it was credit rationing that restricted the supply of credit. This credit rationing was the eventual result of deflation precipitated by following the gold standard. Deflation in turn led to higher real wages, higher loan default rates, and an increase in the risks of financial intermediation, triggering credit rationing as well as bank failures and falling output. Thus, proponents of the explanation laid out in this chapter would say that the monetarists were right that monetary policy started the Great Depression but not about why monetary policy had such a large impact on the economy.

The explanation of the Great Depression most often mentioned by laymen is that it was caused by the stock market crash or the decline in real estate prices. In other words, it was caused by asset bubbles, which in turn led to a banking crisis. While the stock market and real estate crashes undoubtedly played a contributing role in the Great Depression by increasing uncertainty and decreasing wealth, it is implausible to think that these were large enough, by themselves, to explain an economic contraction the size of the Great Depression. The stock market has fluctuated wildly since the Great Depression (e.g., the crash of 1987 was actually larger than the 1929 crash) but never with anywhere near such dire economic consequences. Likewise, declines in the prices of rental space, raw materials, and food all occurred, but most of these price declines were no greater than the overall deflation that occurred within the economy. Thus, asset bubbles were not the primary culprit in triggering the banking crisis that played a large role in making a recession into the Great Depression. Instead, it was overall deflation and the role it played in weakening the financial fundamentals of borrowers and lenders that was primarily responsible for the banking crisis.

Finally, many classical, neoclassical, or supply-side economists intent on finding some supply-driven cause of the Great Depression have focused on the effects of the Smoot–Hawley export tariffs imposed at the beginning of the Great Depression. At the time, however, exports were only 7 percent of American GDP, making it unlikely that these higher tariffs explain more than a small fraction of the large contraction in output.

CONCLUSIONS

The main conclusion of the modern research on the Great Depression reviewed here is that the Great Depression was primarily the result of macroeconomic policy failure of unparalleled proportions. An unflinching commitment to a flawed gold standard, where there were penalties for experiencing trade deficits and gold outflows but not for experiencing trade surpluses and gold inflows, provided the rationale for naïve policy makers to reduce money supplies, reduce aggregate demands, and reduce prices throughout the world's economies. This deflation had two devastating effects. First, in financial markets, deflation increased the real value of debt relative to the value of assets, increasing the bankruptcy risk of firms, households, and banks while also increasing the costs of credit intermediation within the banking industry. This placed a stranglehold on financial intermediation and investment as lenders rationed credit. Second, in the labor market, deflation led to an increase in real wages because of nominal wage inflexibility. This led to unprecedented levels of involuntary unemployment. The end result was a historic economic contraction driven by labor and financial market imperfections. This same basic story holds throughout the world's economies that suffered from the Depression. However, it is especially applicable to the United States, which held much of the world's gold in 1929 but still stubbornly reduced its money supply until deflation, banking failures, and the Depression were so rampant that when the reversal in monetary policy came, it was largely ineffective.

Discussions of the Great Depression typically end by asking the following question: Could it happen again? Within developed countries such as the United States and Europe, it seems that a crisis of the same size and with the same causes is unlikely to occur again. Macroeconomic policy knowledge and responsiveness are much greater than they were during the Depression. Today it would be hard to imagine Federal Reserve policy makers decreasing the money supply during a recession in order to maintain a fixed exchange rate. At the same time, technological advances have made financial and labor markets much more flexible and efficient than they were during the Depression. Finally, the American economy as a whole, but particularly its financial markets, is much more diversified and is better able to withstand shocks than it was during the 1930s. For example, consider how well the U.S. economy withstood the September 11 terrorist attacks and the financial and stock market losses associated with it.

The argument that the Great Depression is unlikely to occur again in the United States may strike many readers as bizarre given the events that occurred during the 2008 global financial crisis. Clearly, the global financial crisis illustrated that the United States is not immune from macroeconomic volatility. As the crisis spiraled downward at an alarming rate, the word *depression* was increasingly used to describe it. Things certainly became worse than the vast majority of economists predicted before the crisis began. However, as we will discuss in much more detail in Chapter 18, macroeconomic policy clearly served to moderate the 2008 crisis, not make it worse as during the Great Depression. While monetary and fiscal policy was not perfect, it prevented the 2008 crisis from being worse than it was and becoming another depression. In other words, the recent global financial crisis is evidence that we have learned something, but not everything, from past mistakes.

Maybe, in the words of Mark Twain, history does not repeat itself, but it rhymes. While the Great Depression has not repeated itself in the United States, there are strong similarities between the Great Depression and the East Asian crisis (Chapter 15), the Great Recession in Japan (Chapter 16), and the 2008 global financial crisis (Chapter 18). This rhyming of history is why continued research and investigation into the nature and causes of the Great Depression is so valuable.

SUGGESTED READINGS

Lessons from the Great Depression, Peter Temin (1989): A nontechnical review of the Great Depression on which much of the discussion in this chapter is based. This book's particular focus is on the international aspects of the Great Depression, and it contains interesting insight into cross-country differences in macroeconomic policy. Chapter 1 is particularly recommended.

"The Macroeconomics of the Great Depression: A Comparative Approach," Ben Bernanke (1995): A review of the empirical regularities and differences between countries during the Great Depression, with an emphasis on the effects of the gold standard and deflation on the financial industry.

A Monetary History of the United States, 1867–1960, Milton Friedman and Anna Schwartz (1963): Chapter 7 of this book covers the Great Depression and is a very interesting look into Federal Reserve policy and its ineptitude during the crash.

"The Nation in Depression," Christina Romer (1993): A comprehensive review of the Great Depression in the United States by Obama's first Chair of the Council of Economic Advisors and one of the chief architects of the administration's initial response to the 2008 global financial crisis.

FOURTEEN

Postwar Business Cycles

INTRODUCTION

When discussing the empirical facts of business cycles in Chapter 2, one of the principal observations was that business cycles are not cyclical—meaning that they do not exhibit a regular pattern. To some extent, each business cycle is different. As a result, case studies of specific business cycle episodes in the United States are a potentially useful way to determine whether there are certain characteristics that modern recessions and expansions share. A detailed review of postwar business cycles in the United States before 2007 and a discussion of the regularities that can be found is the first objective of this chapter.

One of the questions typically raised when discussing postwar business cycles in the United States is whether there has been any moderation in output fluctuations during the postwar era compared to earlier periods in history. Most economists would hope this to be the case because this would be a strong piece of circumstantial evidence that advances in business cycle theory are leading to more effective macroeconomic policies and are having a beneficial impact on the economy. The second objective of this chapter is to examine the empirical evidence on whether postwar business cycles are in fact more moderate than they were in the prewar era and why this might be the case.

POSTWAR BUSINESS CYCLE EPISODES

1945–1961: Not Waves But Ripples

Most economists and the public were worried about a return to Depression-era conditions once World War II was over, in part because of large anticipated decreases in government spending and in part because of the huge increase in the labor force that would occur when soldiers returned from the war to find a large number of women now working outside of the home. While there was, in fact, a large and sharp decrease in GDP after the war's conclusion, it was not nearly as severe as what had been feared. GDP fell by 19 percent in 1946 but only by 2.8 percent in 1947, leaving the economy at output levels that were still above the natural rate. Output did not fall by more because decreases in government spending were largely offset by huge increases in durable goods consumption (automobiles and appliances) and new housing, both of which were financed by household savings accumulated during the war. Unemployment also remained stable as many women left the labor force and many soldiers went to college under the GI Bill.

The 1946–1961 period was characterized by small, regular business cycles. The 1948–1949, 1953–1954, 1957–1958, and 1960–1961 recessions were each short and mild. A variety of factors contributed to each of these recessions, such as the increase and decrease in government spending before and after the American involvement in the Korean War (1950–1953) and a U.S. steel strike in 1959. Each of these recessions was also preceded by sharp but temporary decreases in the money supply that were the result of inflationary fears within the Federal Reserve (many of these fears at the beginning of the period were driven by the gradual expiration of wage and price controls imposed during the war). Overall, each of these recessions (and the following expansions) appears to have been aggregate demand–driven. In fact, the stability of the negative relationship between unemployment and inflation during the 1950s fueled the popularity of the Phillips curve. In addition, the close relationship between aggregate output and money growth over this period later played a role in the development of monetarist thought during the 1960s.

While this was a relatively stable period economically, it was also a period of relatively slow economic growth. Real GDP growth during the 1950s averaged only 2.1 percent, which was lower than pre-Depression levels. Lower growth was coupled with a slow but steady rise in unemployment, from an average of 3 percent in the early 1950s to an average of 4 percent in the late 1950s. At the same time, inflation was high by historical standards during the 1950s and greater than 2 percent many years.

This suggests that, if anything, changes in aggregate supply during this period tended to be negative and might have been the consequence of increases in the minimum wage and labor unionization.

While monetary policy played a role in initiating each of the four recessions during this period, it does appear that the Federal Reserve was beginning to learn from the mistakes it made during the Great Depression. In each case, the Fed quickly reversed itself when it became clear that it had overreacted, which is the primary reason why the recessions during this period were short. Other changes in the economy also helped to moderate business cycles. Primarily, Roosevelt's New Deal program created welfare insurance, unemployment insurance, social security insurance, and more progressive federal income taxation, each of which served as an automatic stabilizer of consumption and aggregate demand during contractions. As a result, by the end of this period there was a feeling among economists, particularly among Keynesians, that they were figuring out business cycles and could possibly eliminate them in the future if the proper policy makers were in power.

1961–1970: The Rise and Fall of Keynesian Economics

The 1961–1969 expansion lasted 106 months and was the longest in American history until the 1990s expansion. Real output growth averaged 4.5 percent a year over this period. Once again, this expansion appeared to be largely aggregate demand–driven, with investment and consumption growing at 8 percent and 9 percent a year, respectively, on average. Strong increases in the money supply, increases in government spending on the Vietnam War and Johnson's Great Society programs, and reductions in taxes on investment and income spurred aggregate demand growth over this period.

The 1960s represented the pinnacle of Keynesian influence. When Kennedy became president in 1961, he brought to Washington many of his Keynesian associates from Harvard. Once in power, they began to actively engage in Keynesian stabilization policy. Because government spending was largely constrained by military spending on the Vietnam War, these Keynesians relied on tax policy to manipulate aggregate demand. For example, tax cuts on investment were enacted in 1962 and income tax cuts were enacted in 1964 during periods when the economy appeared to be slowing.

In 1968, the Johnson administration enacted a temporary tax increase in an effort to slow down the economy at a time when output growth was clearly above its natural rate and inflation was rising. This temporary tax increase was a failure and shook economists' faith in the Keynesian model. The failure of this temporary tax increase to slow aggregate demand growth rested on the fact that it was only temporary. As a result, this tax increase did not really change households' incentives to spend. Instead, households anticipated future tax reductions and just paid for this tax increase out of their savings, leading to continued growth in aggregate demand. This temporary tax cut is an important episode in economic history because it clearly contradicted the predictions of the Keynesian model. For that reason, it is often referred to by neoclassical economists as evidence in support of the Lucas critique of stabilization policy.

By 1969, another unanticipated consequence of Keynesian stabilization policy was becoming evident: accelerating inflation. Inflation gradually rose throughout the 1960s, from 1.5 percent in 1964 to 3.6 percent in 1966 to 5 percent in 1969. Keynesian fiscal policy solutions aimed at reducing inflation failed as government spending continued to rise throughout the period and the temporary tax increase in 1968 failed to reduce aggregate demand. Consequently, the Federal Reserve was forced to cut money growth. The Fed first cut money growth in 1965, which could have driven the economy into a recession at that time if it had not been for the strong growth of government spending. The Fed once again reduced money growth in 1969, and the economy slipped into a mild recession from 1969 to 1970. During this recession, unemployment increased to 5.8 percent. However, the reduction in the money supply was not large or sustained enough to rein in inflation and inflationary expectations. In fact, inflation actually rose slightly in 1970 to 5.5 percent. This was the beginning of *stagflation*, or a period of simultaneous increases in inflation and unemployment, which had never before been experienced in the United States.

1970–1980: Sustained Stagflation

The expansion that began in late 1970 was actually initiated by a negative shock—the collapse of the Penn Central Railroad. This bankruptcy shook financial markets, and the Fed responded by increasing the money supply in order to increase liquidity and stabilize the system. This monetary loosening also spurred economic activity. The resulting expansion, which lasted until 1973, was accompanied by rising inflation in spite of misguided attempts by the Nixon administration to place wage and price controls on the economy. These wage and price controls primarily created market distortions but did not halt the overall rate of inflation. Meanwhile, the Fed continued to increase the money supply at a robust pace throughout this period. While it is not clear exactly why the Fed continued to increase the money supply in the face of significant inflationary momentum, it appears that political pressures from the Nixon administration associated with the 1972 election played some role. One piece of evidence supporting this conclusion is the fact that the Fed immediately began reducing money growth after the election.

Another important event that occurred during this period was the abandonment of the Bretton Woods system of fixed exchange rates. Under Bretton Woods, it was impossible for the United States to devalue the dollar because every other currency was fixing its exchange rate to the dollar. As inflation rose in the United States, the dollar became overvalued and the United States began to experience significant gold outflows. In 1971, the United States suspended gold convertibility of the dollar, and by 1973 the dollar was allowed to float, removing another constraint on monetary policy and allowing further money growth.

By 1973, inflation had risen to 5.9 percent and real GDP growth had risen to 5.3 percent. In the fall of that year, however, the economy began to slow. This was partially because of slower money growth (postelection). The main shock, though, was the OPEC oil embargo that was imposed in October 1973. This embargo increased the price of a barrel of oil from $3 to $12 and had a number of negative effects on the economy. It increased the aggregate price level and reduced real incomes, which decreased aggregate demand. More importantly, it reduced aggregate supply through two channels. First, it immediately made a large fraction of the existing technology and capital stock prohibitively expensive to use. Second, it also increased the marginal cost of production across most industries because oil is a significant input into the production of almost every good produced in modern economies.

The 1973–1975 recession was the worst recession in the United States since the 1930s. Unemployment, from trough to peak, rose from 4.8 percent to 8.9 percent. At the same time, inflation rose from 7 percent to an unprecedented 12.1 percent in 1975. Stagflation put an end to many economists' fascination with the Phillips curve and also left them more skeptical of Keynesian economics in general. In addition, monetarism was also discredited by the fact that this recession was largely driven by supply factors and not by monetary factors. In fact, this period is best characterized as one in which any consensus of thought on business cycles among economists broke down. Economists were left searching for alternative business cycle theories that were logically consistent and which could explain stagflation.

In 1975, the oil embargo was loosened. Immediately, both the price of oil and inflation fell sharply. Aiding in the economic recovery, the Fed began to increase money growth. The expansion that followed, which lasted until 1979, saw another buildup of inflation from its trough of 6.4 percent in 1976 to 8.9 percent in 1979.

In hindsight, an obvious question can be raised about monetary policy throughout the 1970s: Why did the Federal Reserve persist in increasing the money supply and inflation, even during times of relatively healthy output growth? While it is difficult to go back and read the minds of policy makers, especially because the Federal Reserve was a much less transparent institution at that time, the most plausible explanation of this prolonged policy mistake was that the Federal Reserve was wrong about the true level of the natural rate of unemployment. The Fed's actions are consistent with a belief that the natural rate of unemployment was considerably lower than what it actually was, leading it to persistently increase the money supply even in the face of higher and higher inflation. This is exactly what Friedman (1968) predicted would happen to imperfectly informed policy makers in his address to the American Economic Association (see Chapter 6). Unbeknownst to the Fed at the time, in hindsight it is clear that the natural rate of unemployment rose during the 1970s for a number of reasons. First, higher oil prices had reduced capacity and productivity. Second, government policies in the form of minimum wage laws, wage and price controls, and tax increases also reduced productivity and increased the costs of hiring labor. Third, a significant amount of structural unemployment was created by the struggling automobile and steel industries. Finally, a large increase in the labor supply took place as more women and baby boomers entered the labor force. As a result, while the Fed was consistently aiming for an unemployment rate of around 5 percent, actual unemployment never fell below 6 percent throughout the entire decade. The result was increasing levels of inflation.

The 1970s ended on another negative note. In the spring of 1979, the Iranian revolution led to another large jump in oil prices from $14 to $29 a barrel. Coupled with slower money growth and credit controls imposed by the Carter administration (both aimed at slowing inflation), a recession occurred during 1980. However, both monetary policy and credit restrictions were quickly relaxed, and the 1980 recession ended up being the shortest in American history, lasting only six months. Output fell 2.3 percent while unemployment only rose from 6 percent to 7.3 percent. Of course, the downside of experiencing such a small recession was that, once again, the Fed had failed to rein in accelerating inflation. Inflation rose from 7.3 percent in 1979 to 8.5 percent in 1980. Frustration began to grow inside the Federal Reserve over its inability to reduce inflation. With the election of Ronald Reagan in 1980, who campaigned against the "misery index" of high inflation and high unemployment that had existed during the Carter administration, the stage was set for a major policy correction.

1981–1991: A Policy Correction Followed by an Expansion

The shortest recession in American history was quickly followed by one of the most severe recessions in American history. The 1981–1982 recession was the deepest since the Depression, with unemployment peaking at 10.8 percent in 1982. The cause of this recession is well understood. Aided by political cover from the Reagan administration, the Federal Reserve, led by Chairman Paul Volker, made a concerted effort to drive down inflation by decreasing money growth, even at the cost of postwar highs in unemployment. The Fed characterized its monetary policy during this period as a "monetarist experiment," where it claimed to be reasserting control over the money supply in an effort to reduce inflation. While monetarists were upset by this characterization, primarily because money growth remained very volatile over this period, the decline in average money growth was large enough to drive inflation down from 9.9 percent to 3.6 percent in just under two years. The costs of such a dramatic reduction in inflation were rising real interest rates and significant declines in investment and consumer durables spending.

The benefits of the Fed's policy correction were soon obvious. Inflation expectations and wages adjusted downward very rapidly in response to the credible commitment made by the Fed to lower inflation (a point not lost on rational expectations proponents). In fact, the Fed's disinflation was so successful that the Fed ended its monetarist experiment and loosened monetary policy in late 1982. Faster money growth and lower expected inflation provided the foundation for a protracted expansion that lasted for eight years until 1990. The 1982–1990 expansion was driven by a number of positive factors. On the demand side, Reagan fiscal policy that pushed large increases in defense spending, income tax reductions, and large budget deficits stimulated aggregate demand. In addition, investment and consumer durables demand were quite strong over this period. On the supply side, the collapse of the OPEC oil cartel in 1986 dropped oil prices from $27 to $14, more than offsetting the price increase that occurred in 1979. Together, all of these factors lead to strong output growth (of roughly 3 percent), falling unemployment rates (below 5 percent by the end of the decade), and steady inflation (of roughly 3 percent) throughout the rest of the 1980s.

One interesting event that took place during this period was the 1987 stock market crash. This crash was larger than the one that occurred in

1929, erasing roughly $1 trillion of wealth in 1987 dollars, or 20 percent of yearly GDP. However, a recession was avoided in large part because of the Fed's adept handling of the crash. The Federal Reserve's aggressive response, which was to immediately increase liquidity in the financial system but quickly remove it when it became apparent that there would be no major macroeconomic consequences from the crash, stabilized consumer expectations, investment, and consumer demand.

The expansion that began in 1982 lasted until 1990. At that time, a number of factors affecting both aggregate demand and aggregate supply turned negative. The major supply shock associated with the 1990–1991 recession was the Gulf War, which led to a brief but significant increase in the price of oil. In addition, a tax increase enacted in 1990 and new financial regulations that were imposed on banks may also have played some role in decreasing aggregate supply. In regards to aggregate demand, Iraq war worries and new financial regulations also reduced investment and durables consumption. At the same time, the Fed began to tighten money growth in early 1990 in response to inflation fears, possibly overreacting to a modest increase in the inflation rate at precisely the wrong moment. Finally, the world economy had also slipped into recession, decreasing American exports and increasing the trade deficit.

1991–2001: A "New Economy"?

Following the Gulf War, consumer expectations and money growth rebounded strongly. Even though the 1991–2001 expansion, which is the longest in recorded American history, was initiated by strong aggregate demand growth, it was the remarkable increases in aggregate supply throughout this period that drove this unprecedented expansion. Table 14.1 presents real GDP growth, unemployment rates, and inflation rates for the decades of the 1990s, 1980s, 1970s, and 1960s. Compared to the 1970s and 1980s, both unemployment and inflation were significantly lower in the 1990s, and real output growth was just as strong. In fact, unemployment fell throughout this period, while inflation remained low and steady, once again violating the Phillips curve relationship. Not only was macroeconomic performance strong in the 1990s, but it actually got stronger as the expansion went on. During the second half of the 1990s, there was a significant improvement in all three macroeconomic indicators compared to the two previous decades. In fact, the unemployment rate reached a 40-year low by 2000. Economic growth was so robust and inflation was so low throughout this period that economists began to question whether the U.S. economy was entering a new economic era—one with permanently

Table 14.1   Macroeconomic statistics by decade.

	1990s (%)	Second half (1995–1999) (%)	1980s (%)	1970s (%)	1960s (%)
Real GDP growth	3.2	4.0	3.0	3.3	4.4
Unemployment rate	5.8	5.0	7.3	6.2	4.8
Inflation rate	2.9	2.4	5.1	7.4	2.5

Source: Author's creation from the St. Louis Federal Reserve FRED database available at http://research.stlouisfed.org/fred2/.

higher productivity growth and faster improvements in standards of living without the threat of inflation.

Other measures of economic prosperity also indicate that the 1990s were a remarkable decade. Real wages grew 1.3 percent a year between 1991 and 2001 (trough to trough), which is the highest real wage growth since the 1950s and compares favorably to the 0.2 percent average real wage growth between 1982 and 1991. Home buying and home ownership boomed. Between 1991 and 2001, home ownership among American families rose from 64 percent to 68 percent, the highest level in history. There was also an education boom. The percent of the workforce with some college education rose dramatically from 40 percent in 1991 to 57 percent in 2001. The stock market grew strongly at 11.1 percent a year (although, as measured by the S&P 500 index, stock market returns were actually slightly lower than returns during the 1982–1991 period of 12.8 percent), primarily fueled by spectacular increases in the stock prices of IT firms. One final measure of the strength of the American economy was the size of capital inflows. Between 1991 and 2001, the United States attracted $2.3 trillion dollars of net foreign investment, far and away more than any country in the world.

The macroeconomic evidence—rising output growth coupled with falling inflation, historic growth in real wages, and postwar lows in unemployment—suggests that the "new economy" of the 1990s was driven by large increases in aggregate supply. A number of hypotheses have been offered as to why aggregate supply increased much more rapidly during the 1990s. Many pointed to *globalization*, or the increased cultural and economic integration among individuals, markets, and nations. The argument is that globalization resulted in increases in the volume of international trade, increases in international capital flows between countries, and increased competition that has spurred world-wide productivity (and, in fact, the 1990s outside of East Asia was a decade of strong growth for the world as a whole). Some pointed to deregulation in the United States, particularly deregulation of financial markets, as having increased economic efficiency and encouraged greater capital flows. Others argued that advances in management systems, such as better inventory control and better information systems, allowed firms to more effectively respond to changing market conditions, increasing productivity and also reducing uncertainty and output volatility.

Still others argued that monetary and fiscal policy played an important role by providing a remarkably stable macroeconomic environment during the 1990s in which to do business. Macroeconomic policy during the 1990s could be generally characterized as tight fiscal policy and loose monetary policy. The Clinton administration placed a high priority on reducing the federal government's deficit, which stood at $260 billion (almost 5 percent of GDP) in 1992. A tax increase in 1993, low growth in government spending throughout the decade (partially as a result of reductions in military spending made possible by the end of the Cold War), and remarkable increases in tax receipts generated by strong economic growth led to budget surpluses of upwards of $250 billion (or roughly 2 percent of GDP) by the end of the decade. Lower government borrowing helped drive down long-term interest rates and reduce the cost of financing investment, housing purchases, and consumer durables.

On the other hand, expansive monetary policy served to keep short-term interest rates low. The Fed's refusal to "lean against the wind" and slow the economy during the 1990s expansion, even though there were significant worries among many economists that its refusal to do so would eventually lead to inflation, provided enough short-term stimulus to offset any contractionary effects of tighter fiscal policy. Federal Reserve Chairman Alan Greenspan was one of the first to identify that the 1990s expansion was largely aggregate supply–driven, meaning that the natural rate of output growth had risen and that the Fed could allow faster growth without worrying about inflation. This one-two punch of fiscal discipline and accommodative monetary policy kept interest rates low and provided high levels of cheap credit that fueled growth.

However, the most commonly mentioned explanation for this extraordinary decade, and the justification for the moniker "New Economy," is the remarkable advances in IT that occurred during the 1990s. This "IT revolution," as it has been called, led to extraordinary economic change. De Long and Summers (2001) estimate that the calculation speed of computers increased by 56 percent a year between 1960 and 2000, leading to a 4 billion-fold increase in computational power over that same time. The primary result of all of this new computational power was a dramatic decline in the price of sharing and obtaining information. The real cost of information processing and communication is estimated to have fallen by roughly 10–20 percent a year during the 1990s.

As evidence of the importance of IT in increasing productivity, Bailey (2002) reports industry-level data that indicates that IT-intensive industries increased their productivity by more during the 1990s than less IT-intensive industries. In case studies of eight major industries, the McKinsey Global Institute (2001) concluded that the primary cause of higher productivity growth was increased competition that directly resulted from better IT. This is especially true in the retail sector, which Walmart came to dominate because of its size and high productivity, both of which owe a great deal to new management systems that rely heavily on new IT.

Others attempted to measure the productivity benefits of IT directly using the Solow residual method (see Chapter 8 for a more detailed description), which involves taking output growth and subtracting out capital and labor growth (weighted by their share of aggregate income). What is left over is the growth in output that cannot be explained by growth in inputs. This measure of the change in total productivity is referred to as the Solow residual or *multifactor productivity*. Table 14.2 presents results from a study by Oliner and Sichel (2000). They focus on three periods: 1974–1990, 1991–1995, and 1996–1999. According to their calculations, IT played two important roles during the 1990s in increasing output growth compared to earlier periods. First, the amounts that firms have invested in IT and communications capital increased quite dramatically. Second, better computer and semiconductor technologies increased the efficiency of computer production. These efficiency benefits show up in the data as higher multifactor productivity growth. Together, when the effects of both higher capital growth and higher multifactor productivity growth are considered, Oliner and Sichel's results indicate that changes in IT directly accounted for roughly 60 percent of the increase in growth during the New Economy period. This ignores many of the indirect productivity benefits of IT that are more difficult to measure, such as increased market size and competition.

These results, and others like them, can be criticized on a number of levels. The most common criticism has to do with the nature of growth accounting itself. Multifactor productivity is not a direct but an implied measure of productivity. Everything other than input growth that contributes to output growth, including things economists do not well understand or cannot easily measure, is lumped together under the name *multifactor productivity*. This includes things such as unmeasured changes in the

Table 14.2   Contributions to growth in the U.S. economy.

	1974–1990 (%)	1991–1995 (%)	1996–1999 (%)
Output growth	3.06	2.75	4.82
Total capital	1.35	1.01	1.85
IT capital	0.49	0.57	1.10
Total labor	1.38	1.26	1.81
Multifactor productivity	0.33	0.48	1.16
Computer and semiconductor sector	0.20	0.28	0.65

Source: Adapted from Oliner and Sichel (2000).

quality of labor or capital, errors in data collection, changes in worker effort, changes in government policy, and other structural changes in the economy. As a result, many would argue that the fact that IT expenditure was highly correlated with multifactor productivity and output growth does not in any way prove that IT is the cause of these changes in economic performance.

Robert Gordon (2000) argues that the impact of the IT revolution was much more limited than past technological revolutions for three reasons. First, according to Gordon, most of the increases in productivity that took place during the 1990s were in computer hardware, which is only 12 percent of the economy. In the other 88 percent of the economy, productivity growth actually decelerated. Gordon argues that this is because jobs that could be automated by computers were automated very early on. As a result, advances in productivity from IT were limited after the first few years within most industries.

Second, because computer hardware is a relatively minor part of any production process, diminishing returns to new computer technologies set in very quickly. As a result, doubling the megahertz of a computer does not make that computer twice as productive. For example, consider the time spent by a student writing a paper. Faster computer speeds and the invention of word processing software reduced the amount of time spent writing papers quite dramatically at first. Very soon afterwards, however, faster computers and new software led to little reduction in the time spent on writing a paper. The primary constraints are human ones: how fast a student can think and type. Better computer hardware cannot eliminate these restrictions.

Finally, Gordon argues that many of the technologies that are most closely associated with the IT revolution, such as the Internet and cellular phones, have not significantly altered production. Instead, they are better thought of as entertainment mediums, more akin to the television than the combustible engine. Many of the markets created by the Internet are duplicative, meaning they exist in similar forms elsewhere, such as the Web services provided by previously existing retailers. Their main advantage is not one of productive efficiency but of convenience for the consumer. This does not mean that these communication technologies are worthless; it only means that most of the benefits come in the form of utility to consumers and not higher productivity of firms. As a result, compared to other technological revolutions such as electricity, the combustible engine, chemicals and plastics, and plumbing sanitation, IT did not change things as much as those who are myopic to the history of technology might think.

Maybe the best reason to be skeptical of the New Economy argument is that many previous booms were followed by busts. While the 1990s was a period of strong growth, it was not an unprecedented period of strong growth. Refer once again to Table 14.1, which reports macroeconomic data by decade. Noticeably absent from our previous discussion of this table was a comparison between the 1990s and the 1960s. The New Economy of the last half of the 1990s looks a lot like the old economy of the 1960s. The 1960s were a period of remarkable advances in petrochemicals, electronics, aviation, and pharmaceuticals. However, the boom times of the 1960s were followed by the volatile 1970s, a decade characterized by painful periods of stagflation. Similarly, the 1990s were followed by the volatile and slow-growth decade of the 2000s.

The 2001 Recession

The best way to characterize the 2001 recession is to note just how difficult it was for the NBER to determine exactly when this recession began and when this recession ended. The movements into and out of recession were so gradual as to be almost imperceptible. What is more obvious, however, is that the 2001–2003 period was one of persistent below average growth, followed by a period of simply average growth. As seen in Figure 14.1, growth was roughly 2 percent or below for most quarters during this period.

The NBER dates the beginning of this recession to March 2001, which is actually before the September 11 terrorist attacks. Even though GDP growth was positive (but low) since the fourth quarter of 2001, it was not until July 2003 that the NBER chose November 2001 as the ending date of the recession. In other words, the NBER did not recognize that this recession began until it ended, and it took 20 months for the NBER to officially recognize it as being over because the recovery was so weak.

Figure 14.1   Real GDP growth in the United States, quarter to quarter.

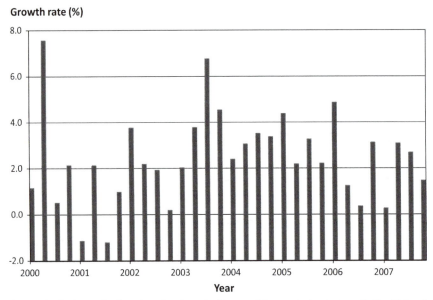

Growth rate (%)

Source: Author's creation based on data from the Bureau of Economic Analysis available at https://www.bea.gov/national/xls/gdplev.xls.

Six basic facts describe the 2001 recession and its slow-growth aftermath.

1. *The size of the recession was exceptionally small and its length very short.* Output fell by only one-half of a percent during this recession as compared to the 2 percent output usually falls during an average recession. The recession lasted only eight months.

2. *A significant decline in stock prices preceded this recession.* Stock prices peaked during early 2000 and fell consistently until their trough in early 2003. As measured by the S&P 500 index, stock prices fell by roughly 40 percent from their highs. Most severely hit was the technology sector, which played a big role in the bull market of the 1990s. Technology stocks are most heavily represented in the NASDAQ stock index, which fell from its high point by 80 percent.

3. *Fixed business investment experienced a sharp decline.* Fixed business investment fell by an average of –5.6 percent a year during 2001 and 2002, with quarterly growth rates as low as –14.5 percent in the second quarter of 2001. The largest factor in this decline was

sharp reductions in IT equipment investment, which played a major role in the strong rates of overall investment growth during the 1990s.

4. *There was a "jobless recovery."* It is very unusual for unemployment and output to be moving in the same direction, but this is what happened after 2001. Many economists characterized the 2002–2003 period as the weakest postrecession job market in postwar history. Figure 14.2 presents the unemployment rate between 2001 and 2003. Unemployment stood at a 25-year low in 2000 and only increased from 4 percent to 5.6 percent by the end of 2001. However, between 2001 and mid-2003, unemployment actually crept upward slightly. By mid-2003, the American economy had lost nearly 2.5 million jobs from its peak employment levels, and unemployment only fell very slowly after that.

5. *International political turmoil and corporate scandals affected the business environment.* The September 11 terrorist attacks, wars in Iraq and Afghanistan, and shocking corporate scandals involving Enron, WorldCom, Arthur Anderson accounting, and numerous major stockbrokers all increased uncertainty, increased perceived financial risk, and reduced consumer confidence. These destabilizing events played

Figure 14.2   Unemployment rate in the United States, 2000–2004.

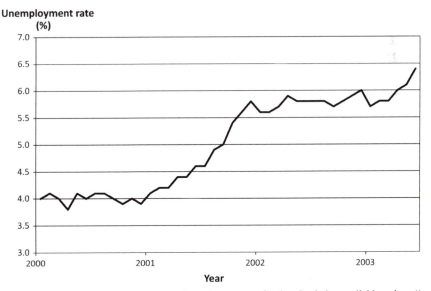

Source: Author's creation based on data from the Bureau of Labor Statistics available at http://data.bls.gov/timeseries/LNS14000000.

a large role in the 30 percent fall in the Consumer Confidence Index from its high in 2000. Economic uncertainty is likely one important reason behind the slow postrecession growth of investment and employment, as many firms seemed unwilling to expand their capacity in the midst of this turbulence.

6. *Things would have been worse without timely and aggressive monetary and fiscal policy.* Federal tax reductions were passed soon after George W. Bush took office in 2001. Coupled with increased government spending, particularly military spending on wars in Iraq and Afghanistan and higher spending on domestic security, fiscal policy was quite expansionary during the early 2000s. A $250 billion surplus in 1999 turned into a $300 billion deficit by 2003.

At the same time, the Federal Reserve was very aggressive, allowing the money supply to grow at an average annual rate of roughly 12 percent and reducing the federal funds rate (the interest rates on overnight loans between banks) dramatically from 6.5 percent in late 2000 to 1 percent by mid-2003. Expansionary monetary policy, coupled with continued low inflation of between 1 and 2 percent, reduced nominal interest rates to 40-year lows. The interest rate on the three-month T-Bill fell to nearly 1 percent, and the 10-year T-Bonds fell below 4 percent in 2003. Low interest rates spurred the housing market and consumer spending. In addition, in an important simulative impact largely unforeseen by the Fed, low interest rates encouraged an unprecedented amount of mortgage refinancing, which increased the disposable income of households and further stabilized consumer spending. Roughly 40 percent of all home mortgages ($2.4 trillion) were refinanced between 2001 and 2003. Lower home mortgage rates allowed people to not only afford larger homes but also to increase their disposable income and even cash out some of their equity.

One thing that should be clear after considering these six basic facts: The 2001 recession and the following growth recession were driven by weak aggregate demand. This recession appears to be consistent with a Keynesian-style recession, in which falling expectations and a falling stock market reduced wealth and investment, dampening aggregate demand. In response, the federal government aggressively enacted expansionary fiscal and monetary policy that largely offset these falls in aggregate demand from creating a recession, but not enough to keep growth and unemployment at their natural rates.

2003–2007: Buildup to a Crisis

While the aggressive use of stabilization policy may have moderated the 2001 recession, it was not enough by itself to generate a strong recovery. While the economy performed close to average during the 2003–2007 period according to many measures, there were also disturbing underlying trends building. Most importantly, debt levels continued to rise as the federal government continued to run budget deficits and most new household consumption was financed by borrowing, much of it from abroad. Also, the United States ran historically large trade deficits, the flip side of all of the borrowing from abroad. In addition, real wage growth was stagnant, even declining slightly for those in the lowest income brackets. Finally, a large portion of the wealth created during this period came from unprecedented appreciations in the housing market and financial markets. These were fueled by new and complicated financial instruments and low interest rates sustained by expansionary monetary policy. In hindsight, it is clear that the aggressive fiscal and monetary policy of the early-to-mid-2000s papered over structural problems in the U.S. economy that were ignored for too long, eventually creating the financial conditions that contributed to the 2008 global financial crisis, which will be covered in detail in Chapter 18.

ARE POSTWAR BUSINESS CYCLES DIFFERENT FROM THEIR PREWAR PREDECESSORS?

Quite a bit of circumstantial evidence exists which suggests that modern business cycles have been less severe than those before World War II. For example, no contraction nearly as severe as the Great Depression has occurred during the postwar era. Does a closer examination of business cycle data support the fact that business cycles have moderated? And if so, why has this occurred?

Comparing Postwar Business Cycles to Earlier Periods

Economists interested in comparing postwar fluctuations to those from earlier periods have faced a large hurdle in their investigations: the lack of reliable historical macroeconomic data. Until the 1920s, almost no macroeconomic data was collected. In a series of papers, Christina Romer (surveyed in Romer, 1999) re-examined historical business cycles using new and improved historical macroeconomic data. Using Romer's data, Keating and Valcarcel (2012) estimate the standard deviation of output

growth and inflation between 1902 and 2009 and draw two important conclusions. First, the interwar period (1920–1940) was extremely volatile. In
fact, changes in output were roughly 2.5 times more volatile during the
interwar period than during the prewar (1902–1916) or postwar (1948–
2009) periods. Even if the Great Depression had not occurred, the interwar
period still would have been the most volatile economic period in
American history. Second, the postwar period has, until the last decade,
generally been a period of declining volatility in both output growth and
inflation (although there was a spike in inflation volatility in the 1970s).
This period of declining macroeconomic volatility in the postwar era is
often referred to as the "Great Moderation." During this period, output
volatility has been between one-third and one-half of what it was before
World War II, while inflation volatility has fallen by roughly 80 percent.

In addition to the reduction in the size of fluctuations in output, the frequency of business cycles has also changed dramatically. Referring back
to Table 2.1, note that the postwar period has had shorter recessions and
longer expansions. Recessions have been seven months shorter and
expansions nearly two years longer than compared to the interwar period.
Diebold and Rudebusch (1999) have referred to this phenomenon as *duration stabilization*. They report evidence that only 20 percent of postwar
time has been spent in recession, as compared to 40 percent of the time
spent in recession during the prewar period. Thus, postwar business cycles
have moderated both in terms of the size of output fluctuations and in the
reduced frequency of recessions.

This moderation in business cycles has not just occurred in the United
States but internationally as well. Summers (2005) and Keating and Valcarcel (2012) look at other developed countries and find that output has
varied considerably less since the 1980s in these countries as well: about
50 percent less variation than before the Great Moderation. However,
the exact timing and pace of this moderation has varied across countries.

The Causes of the Great Moderation

Most of the Great Moderation has taken place during two particular sub-
periods: the 1960s and the New Economy era of 1985–1997. Figure 14.3
presents quarterly GDP growth rates in the United States over the postwar
period, where the declines in volatility during the 1960s and particularly
the New Economy period are clearly evident.

Because such a great proportion of the decline in macroeconomic volatility took place during the New Economy era, explanations of the Great
Moderation have tended to focus on this period of time. Some have

Figure 14.3   GDP growth variability in the United States.

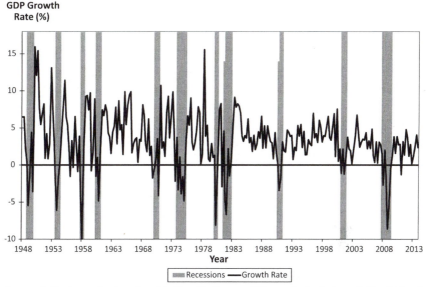

Source: Author's creation based on data from the Bureau of Economic Analysis available at https://www.bea.gov/national/xls/gdplev.xls.

suggested that as the United States has gotten richer, it has become a more diverse economy in terms of the number of goods it produces. Diversification better protects an economy from negative shocks that might affect a small number of industries. American financial markets and banks have also benefited from this economic development and diversification, making them more stable, which in turn made investment and durable consumption demand less volatile. Dynan and colleagues (2006) find that both financial innovation and financial deregulation that started during the 1980s played an important role in explaining the improved stabilization of output (or at least until the 2008 global financial crisis—more on this in Chapter 18).

Also suggested as a cause of the Great Moderation is the switch in developed countries toward consuming more services and nondurables, as evidenced by the fact that services have risen from 39 percent of GDP in 1960 to nearly 80 percent of GDP in 2011. Because the demand for nondurables and services is less volatile than the demand for durable manufactured goods, aggregate output is likely to be more stable as a result (see Black and Dowd, 2009).

There have also been structural changes in the economy driven by energy-saving technological development, which may stabilize GDP by reducing the reliance on nonrenewable energy sources and their volatile prices. Nakov and Pescatori (2010) find that reduced oil supply shocks during the New Economy period coupled with less intensive oil usage may explain up to one-half of the decline in output volatility during the Great Moderation.

Davis and Kahn (2008) present evidence that changes in the management of inventories during the 1990s have substantially contributed to output stability by reducing variation in the most volatile components of GDP. These changes in inventory management include better supply-chain management practices, just-in-time procedures, lower shipping costs, and increased production-to-order.

Other economists have looked at demographic changes in the United States. For example, Lugauer (2012) finds that the aging of the American labor force has actually reduced output volatility because older workers are more productive and have less volatile labor force participation.

In another attempt to explain the moderation, some economists have argued that advances in communications and IT have improved the quality of information and have stabilized business and consumer confidence, reducing its role in destabilizing aggregate demand.

However, the most often mentioned, and most examined, explanation for output and duration stabilization has been the aggressive and effective use of macroeconomic stabilization policy in many countries during the postwar era. In the prewar period, macroeconomic policy did not really exist. In the United States, there was no federal income tax, and government spending averaged only about 2 percent of GDP. Financial crises and banking failures were a regular fact of economic life during the prewar period.

During the interwar period, the role of the federal government in the economy expanded greatly. A federal income tax was adopted and government spending rose significantly as a percent of GDP. The Federal Reserve was created in 1914, although at first it was very weak with a decentralized structure and little understanding of monetary policy and how to facilitate financial stability.

The Great Depression and World War II set the stage for an even greater role for macroeconomic stabilization policy during the postwar period. As military expenditures began to shrink after the war, they were largely replaced by domestic spending programs aimed at providing an economic safety net. A number of automatic economic stabilizers were introduced into the U.S. economy immediately following World War II, such as unemployment insurance, bank deposit insurance, and welfare assistance. In terms of discretionary policy, the Federal Reserve was strengthened and power centralized within the Board of Governors in an effort to allow the Fed to better serve as a lender of last resort in order to provide financial stability and also to allow better management of monetary policy in order to facilitate macroeconomic stability. The Employment Act of 1946 was also passed, which legislated a role for the federal government in actively promoting growth and full employment. The final, and maybe most important, factor in the postwar rise of macroeconomic policy was the ascension of Keynesian economics. Keynes provided a coherent and persuasive argument for the use of discretionary macroeconomic policy to stabilize the economy.

Many empirical studies have found evidence in support of the important role of improved macroeconomic policy—particularly monetary policy—in explaining the Great Moderation (see Clarida et al. [2000] for a more complete review of this literature). For example, Romer and Romer (1994) attempted to quantify the costs and benefits of macroeconomic policy in the postwar era. First, they identified indicators of changes in monetary policy, fiscal policy, and automatic stabilization programs. They then used these policy indicators to predict how much output would have changed without any changes in macroeconomic policy. Their results indicate that monetary policy was the most important factor in explaining the Great Moderation. In fact, they report that a change in monetary policy towards faster money growth preceded the trough in output during every postwar recession. Their results also indicate that fiscal automatic stabilizers have played a significant role in business cycle stabilization, with discretionary fiscal policy playing only a small role. Enders and Ma (2011) find that the Fed's improved performance in stabilizing inflation and nominal interest rates played an important role in stabilizing sectors of the economy that are the most interest rate sensitive, contributing to aggregate stability in the economy. In Figure 14.4, we see that over the same time that output volatility has declined, inflation volatility has somewhat declined. This is evidence that improved monetary policy has played some role in stabilizing output. Finally, Stock and Watson (2003) find similar empirical evidence that suggests that monetary policy has been responsible for 25 percent of the decline in postwar output volatility. However, these authors also find that the other 75 percent of the improvement is due to fewer temporary external shocks (in particular, less volatile oil prices)—in other words, good luck. It is better to be lucky than good, and the Fed appears to have been both during the 1990s.

The argument that the increasingly effective use of monetary policy has played an important role in the Great Moderation is entirely consistent with the discussions of specific business cycle episodes conducted in the

Figure 14.4   Inflation variability in the United States.

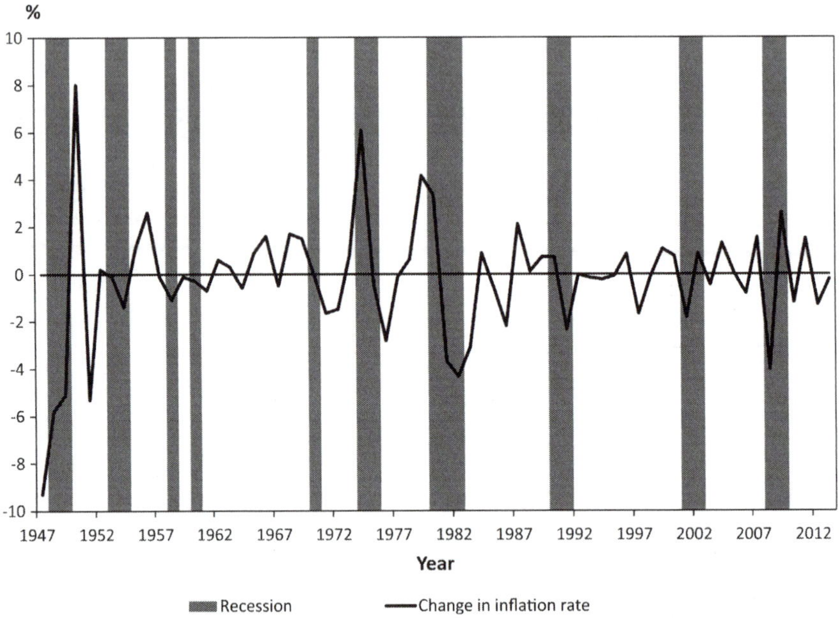

Recession   ——Change in inflation rate

Source: Author's creation based on data from the Bureau of Labor Statistics available at http://www.bls.gov/cpi/data.htm.

first part of this chapter, which also suggested that the Fed has been important in preventing and moderating recessions. Other research on specific business cycle case studies has found similar results. For example, Bernanke (2002) argues that the Fed's aggressive move to increase the money supply and liquidity following the 1987 stock market crash prevented a financial crisis and a contraction in output.

Of course, while macroeconomic policy has prevented some postwar recessions, it has also clearly been the cause of other ones. In the words of MIT economist Rudiger Dornbusch (1997), "None of the United States expansions of the past 40 years died in bed of old age; every one was murdered by the Federal Reserve." The 1981–1982 recession is a clear case in point. In 1981, the Fed was forced to severely contract the money supply in order to reduce the accelerating inflation rates it helped create during the 1970s. This sharp decline in money growth led to the most severe economic contraction in the United States since the Great Depression. In fact, sharp declines in money growth have proceeded six of the eight postwar recessions in the United States. Romer and Romer (1994) argue that output growth would not have been negative during the recessions of

1948–1949, 1969–1970, 1980, 1981–1982, and 1990–1991 if the Fed had not reduced money growth. Their results indicate that over the 11 years of these recessions, industrial production would have been constant if monetary policy had remained unchanged. Instead, industrial production fell during these recessions by an average of 4 percent a year.

In every one of these cases where contractionary monetary policy preceded a recession, worries about inflation were the primary cause of the Fed's tightening. Consistent with this, Blanchard and Simon (2001) find that a strong relationship exists between higher output volatility and higher inflation volatility during the postwar era (as we see in Figure 14.4). Thus, while macroeconomic policy has stabilized business cycles and inflation volatility, an excessive focus on stimulating output has had the unintended consequence of occasionally putting upward pressure on inflation rates. This in turn has led to policy corrections that have at times destabilized output, offsetting some of the potential benefits of improved stabilization policy during the postwar era.

Regarding the reduced output volatility in countries outside of the United States, Summers (2005) argues that similar changes in monetary policy occurred in the G7 countries and Australia as occurred in the United States. In all of these countries, output became less variable as inflation became less variable, and this correlation is much stronger than the correlation between reduced output variability and other suggested causes of output moderation such as financial development.

CONCLUSIONS

How do we characterize postwar business cycles in the United States? Postwar business cycles have been smaller and less frequent. It is clear that the rising importance of macroeconomic policy has played a crucial role in both moderating and preventing many recessions, but also in creating others.

A brief review of postwar business cycle episodes reveals that expansions and recessions have largely been policy-driven. The 1940s and 1950s were periods when growing concerns about a return to the Great Depression were followed by growing concerns about rising inflation, leading to unstable money growth and aggregate demand. The 1960s saw the rise of a confident group of Keynesian policy makers using macroeconomic policy to "fine-tune" the economy, but at the cost of ignoring the rising inflation that accompanied their overly expansionary policies. Macroeconomic policy makers faced their most crucial test during the stagflation of the 1970s; unfortunately, it was a test that they failed. In hindsight, it is clear that during the 1970s the Fed underestimated the natural rate of unemployment, which had risen because of negative shocks to aggregate supply, primarily in the form of higher oil prices. Coupled with its misguided belief in the Phillips curve, political pressures, and higher levels of government spending that accompanied new social policies and the Vietnam War, the Fed repeatedly made the mistake of allowing money growth to expand too rapidly and inflation to grow. Unprecedented inflation rates eventually forced the Fed to reduce aggregate demand and initiate economic contractions in order to reduce inflation, the most obvious example of this being the 1981–1982 recession. Although "policy correction" recessions tend to be short, they are costly in terms of lost output. Thus, higher inflation has been the reason why the rise of macroeconomic policy in the postwar era has not led to greater moderation in postwar business cycles. Instead, stabilization policy has often given rise to policy-driven business cycles.

Only two minor recessions marred growth for the more than two decades between 1983 and 2007. Some would argue that the relative stability of the American economy in the 1980s, 1990s, and 2000s indicates that policy makers have learned from past mistakes and are figuring out how to more effectively manage stabilization policy, better balancing the tradeoff between output stabilization and inflation. It does appear that Federal Reserve policy makers have been more cautious in their policy actions. For instance, the Federal Reserve only changed its monetary stance one time between 1994 and 1998. Discretion is not just the better part of valor; it is also the better part of macroeconomic stabilization policy. Greenspan's term as Federal Reserve chairman, which was generally regarded as exceptionally successful when he left office in 2006 (although significantly less so now following the events of the global financial crisis), seems to support this.

Certainly, many would argue that economists have been too fallible in the past to become arrogant about their ability to perfectly control business cycles and continue to believe that while stabilization policy might work great in theory, it often works poorly in practice. These critics advocate policy rules because of the many difficulties associated with enacting stabilization policy: policy lags, imperfect information about the natural rate of the economy, forecasting errors, rational expectations and the Lucas critique, and political constraints. Also, many economists—particularly those of the Austrian and classical schools—see a danger in policy makers obsessing about eliminating small recessions because it will only allow speculative pressure to build towards an eventual large contraction, even depression. Even many of the Keynesian persuasion worry about this. In the words of Hyman Minsky (1982), "stability breeds instability." Did our effective stabilization policy of the 1980s, 1990s, and early 2000s set the stage for the 2008 global financial crisis?

In summary, during good economic times—times where productivity and aggregate supply are expanding—it is a lot easier to make good macroeconomic policy decisions than during bad times. Part of the Great Moderation may have been the absence of large negative shocks—luck, in other words. There is good evidence that structural changes in the economy from demographic changes, the movement toward a service economy, new inventory management, energy-efficient technologies, and IT have also played important roles in the Great Moderation. Unfortunately, there currently is no consensus about which of these many factors contributed the most to the Great Moderation. While these factors do not have to be mutually exclusive, it would be useful to know which is most important in order to ascertain whether the moderation in output volatility is a permanent or temporary phenomenon. Can we expect business cycles to be rarer and more moderate in the future because they are caused by long-lasting changes in the structure of our economy? Or are they only a function of better policy and subject to the uncertain ability of future policy makers to forecast and correctly respond to shocks? Or is the Great Moderation simply a function of good luck, which unfortunately ran out in 2008? These are only a few of the questions that economists continue to wrestle with. We will continue to grapple with them as well as our discussion turns to international recessions and depressions, including the 2008 global financial crisis that shook many people's belief in the sustainability of the Great Moderation.

SUGGESTED READINGS

The Age of Turbulence: Adventures in a New World, Alan Greenspan (2008): The memoirs of the man who served for 20 years as chairman of the Federal Reserve. Greenspan's time at the helm included the 1987 stock market crash, the 1991 recession, the 2001 recession, the New Economy period, and the buildup to the 2008 global financial crisis.

A History of the Federal Reserve, Volume 2, Book 2, 1970–1986, Alan Meltzer (2010): The definitive history of the Federal Reserve. In this volume, Meltzer covers the disastrous policy mistakes of the early 1970s and the Volker Fed's triumph over inflation during the turbulent early 1980s.

"Rules, Discretion, and the Role of the Economic Advisor," Robert Lucas (1980): A discussion by the Nobel laureate regarding why he favors economic policy rules over discretion.

"The 2001 Recession: How Was It Different and What Developments May Have Caused It?" Kevin L. Klieser (2003): A review of the causes of the 2001 recession and a discussion of why it was different from previous recessions. There is also an interesting discussion of the mixed record of forecasters in predicting the recession and its aftermath.

PART V

Modern International Recessions and Depressions

FIFTEEN

The East Asian Crisis and the IMF

INTRODUCTION

Between 1997 and 1999, an exceptionally large and virulent economic crisis swept through a large number of East Asian economies, economies that for the previous 35 years had experienced sustained growth at unprecedented levels. Table 15.1 reports GDP growth rates for East Asian economies from 1991 to 1999. Between 1991 and 1996, with the exception of the Philippines, all of these countries averaged more than 5 percent growth a year, with 10 percent growth common for Singapore and China. Growth rates in the 1970s and 1980s were even higher than this throughout East Asia, commonly reaching 10 percent. Even in 1996, when output growth had noticeably slowed across most of these countries, growth appeared to be fundamentally sound. In fact, in May 1996, just months before the onset of the economic crisis, the International Monetary Fund (IMF) reported in the *World Economic Outlook* that "(East Asia's) sound fundamentals bode well for sustained growth . . . (the IMF's endorsement) was rooted in the region's strong macroeconomic fundamentals; in (East Asia's) tradition of, and commitment to, efficient allocation of investment; and in the widespread belief that the external environment will continue to be supportive" (IMF, 1996).

Unfortunately, many of these East Asian countries saw real wages fall by a third, unemployment triple, and aggregate income fall by more than 10 percent between 1997 and 1999. This East Asian crisis was the largest and most significant economic crisis to strike the world since the Great Depression. Hardest hit during this crisis were those that were the

Table 15.1 GDP growth in East Asia.

	1991 (%)	1992 (%)	1993 (%)	1994 (%)	1995 (%)	1996 (%)	1997 (%)	1998 (%)	1999 (%)
Thailand	8.2	8.1	8.4	8.9	8.8	5.5	−0.4	−10.4	4.2
Indonesia	7.0	6.5	6.5	15.9	8.2	8.0	4.6	−13.2	0.2
Malaysia	8.5	7.8	8.4	9.2	9.5	8.6	7.8	−7.5	5.4
Korea	9.1	5.1	5.8	8.6	8.9	7.1	5.4	−6.7	10.7
Philippines	−0.6	0.3	2.1	4.4	4.8	5.8	9.6	−0.5	3.2
Singapore	7.3	6.3	10.4	10.1	8.8	7.3	8.4	0.4	5.4
Hong Kong	5.0	6.2	6.2	5.5	3.9	5.0	5.0	−5.1	2.9
Taiwan	7.6	6.8	6.3	6.5	6.0	5.7	6.8	4.7	5.5
China	9.2	14.2	12.1	12.7	10.6	9.5	8.8	7.8	7.1

Source: Author's creation based on data from International Financial Statistics of the IMF available at http://elibrary-data.imf.org/finddatareports.aspx?d=33061&e=169393.

most vulnerable: the poor, the young, and women. For example, one-fourth of the South Korean population fell into poverty during the crisis.

What shocked economic observers was not so much the size of the crisis but the fact that it happened in East Asia. How could a depression strike countries that had so long been held up as examples for other less developed countries? The East Asian crisis highlighted a very important fact that prior to the crisis had not received much attention from economists in their closed-economy models of business cycles: Globalization has the power to change macroeconomic volatility, both for the better and for the worse. *Globalization* is the term often used to refer to the increasing cultural and economic integration among individuals, markets, and nation states. Globalization has been driven by advances in IT and falling communication and transportation costs. Economically, it has resulted not only in increased international trade of goods and services but also in large increases in international finance and capital flows across countries. The fact that these East Asian countries were some of the most globally integrated economies in the world plays a major role in explaining why these countries grew so fast and steadily during the 1980s and 1990s and also why they crashed so hard in 1997. The primary goal of this chapter is to explain what economists have learned from the East Asian crisis and how globalization affects both the propagation of business cycles and the public policies governments should follow to prevent future crises. Also, the controversial role the IMF played during the East Asian crisis, and the role it should play in future international crises, and will be discussed.

INTERNATIONAL CURRENCY CRISES IN RECENT HISTORY

In order to put the East Asian crisis in some perspective, it is important to understand a few basic facts about some of the other major international financial crises that have occurred in the postwar era.

Throughout the 1960–1980 period, a series of currency crises occurred under the Bretton Woods and subsequent Smithsonian international financial agreements. The objectives of the Bretton Woods agreement were twofold. Its primary goal was to coordinate international economic policy in order to avoid potential recurrences of the Great Depression when countries followed "beggar-thy-neighbor" policies that raised tariffs and contracted money supplies in an effort to create large trade surpluses at the expense of their trading partners. These policies contracted aggregate demands worldwide and initiated the Depression. In order to achieve this goal, Bretton Woods established a system of fixed but adjustable exchange rates throughout the world. The IMF was given the responsibility of evaluating and approving applications for devaluation by a member country that was experiencing an unsustainable disequilibrium in its balance of payment account. This process of evaluation was aimed at preventing competitive devaluations by which a country might manipulate its exchange rate in an attempt to make its exports cheaper. Second, Bretton Woods encouraged liberalization and deregulation of world trading institutions, which had suffered a complete breakdown during World War II. The IMF was also available to provide temporary financing to countries experiencing balance of payment problems in return for promises of economic reform.

Most of the crises that occurred under Bretton Woods and in its immediate aftermath occurred when countries *overvalued* their exchange rate. This occurs when a country attempts to maintain a fixed exchange rate that, because of high domestic inflation or other domestic fiscal policies, was higher than would have existed if the exchange rate were allowed to float. Overvalued exchange rates helped these countries attract foreign investment and also reduced the price of imports. To maintain an overvalued exchange rate, countries are forced to sell their foreign-denominated reserves and buy their own currency in an attempt to support the currency's value. The danger in doing this is that if an overvalued exchange rate is pursued long enough, investors and speculators will observe declining foreign reserves and, at some point, make the calculation that the government will not be able to defend this overvalued exchange rate much longer. At this point, speculators begin to flee, selling their assets denominated in the domestic currency. This puts further downward pressure on the exchange rate until (1) the country devalues (usually by an amount significantly larger than would have been necessary to pacify markets before the crisis occurred), and/or (2) the country receives a loan from the IMF of sufficient size to convince markets that the country can defend its existing exchange rate and that no future devaluation would be necessary. During a typical currency crisis, both of these events would occur.

What are the root causes of this type of currency crisis? To use terminology we used when discussing banking crises and asset bubbles in Chapter 11, this type of currency crisis is *fundamentals-based*. Crisis governments adopted poor macroeconomic policies that made the fixed exchange rate they were trying to maintain overvalued and indefensible over the long-run. Thus, currency crises happened because of real, fundamental factors. For example, the currency crises that struck Latin America in the early 1980s were all the result of governments fixing their exchange rates while concurrently running large budget deficits and accumulating large levels of international debt. Eventually, international credit dried up and these countries suffered sovereign debt crises (see Chapter 17). As a result, many countries were eventually forced to finance their deficits by increasing their money supplies. This led to high rates of inflation (in some cases, such as Argentina, larger than 5,000 percent a year) and significant downward pressure on exchange rates throughout the region, eventually culminating in capital flight and currency crises. Another example of a crisis that followed this same basic script was the Mexican peso crisis of 1994.

The role of psychology, animal spirits, herding behavior, and self-fulfilling expectations also cannot be ruled out as a contributing factor of many currency crises. These *belief-based* causes of currency crises are similar to the conditions that drive bank runs: Investors become worried about not being able to withdraw their funds before the currency depreciation; when they begin to expect that other investors are going to flee, they will do so as well, triggering a currency crisis.

As mentioned above, many currency crises ended with an intervention by the IMF and the provision of a bailout package. These bailouts, known as *structural adjustment loans*, come with strings attached. These bailouts require the crisis country to agree to devalue then defend its new exchange rate and also to reform the poor macroeconomic policies that got the country into the crisis in the first place. In most cases, these reforms consist of *austerity conditions*, or the imposition of severe budget cuts and new taxes aimed at reducing large budget deficits in order to reduce future pressures to increase the money supply and inflation. These austerity conditions are essentially aimed at restoring the financial fundamentals of the economy and encouraging the confidence of foreign investors. Typically, after accepting these bailout conditions and adopting reforms, the worst impact of these currency crises was over. Thus, intervention by the IMF usually signaled the trough of the crisis, although it often took years for crisis countries to return to their natural rates of output.

THE FUNDAMENTALS OF THE EAST ASIAN CRISIS

How did the East Asian crisis differ from the currency crises just described? There are two critical differences. First, the East Asian crisis was not the result of bad monetary and fiscal policy, at least not in the traditional sense of high budget deficits and inflation. None of the East Asian countries that experienced a crisis were running sizeable budget deficits (in fact, some were running budget surpluses prior to the crisis) and none were experiencing high levels of inflation. The solid macroeconomic fundamentals of these East Asian countries were in direct contrast with those of the Latin American crises during the 1980s and 1990s.

Second, previous currency crises were over when the country gave up its exchange rate peg and devalued, with or without the help of the IMF. In almost every case, domestic growth and unemployment began to immediately, if slowly, rebound. However, devaluations in East Asia did not end the crisis, and the first devaluation essentially signaled the beginning of the spread of the crisis throughout East Asia. As a result, the East Asian crisis was more than just a currency crisis primarily centered in international financial markets but instead was a full-blown economic crisis that had persistent effects on all markets within these economies. It is the magnitude and persistence of the East Asian crisis, coupled with the fact that typical policy prescriptions did not work, that makes the East Asian crisis so important to understand.

Why these two differences from previous crises? The East Asian crisis is really better thought of as two distinct crises that occurred simultaneously. The first crisis that these countries were experiencing was a currency crisis. These currency crises were caused by maintaining exchange rates that were pegged to the dollar and became overvalued. The results were large current account deficits and, beginning in early 1997, a fundamentals-based speculative attack on pegged exchange rates throughout East Asia. Thailand was the first to devalue in July 1997, followed by Malaysia, Indonesia, and the Philippines. Korea suffered only mild depreciations until October 1997.

In each case, however, the currency crisis and eventual devaluation only signaled the beginning of the economic crisis within each country, not the end. This is because at the same time that currency crises were breaking out in these countries, a second, and less immediately obvious, series of crises was erupting. This second crisis was a banking crisis. Banks throughout the region were heavily leveraged in short-term debt denominated in foreign currencies and heavily invested in highly speculative assets. As a result, even before the events of 1997, the financial fundamentals in many East Asian banking systems were on the brink of collapse. The devaluations that alleviated the currency crisis made the financial fundamentals in the banking system even worse, leading to a contraction in credit and a downward spiral that spread to all sectors of the economy. This is the primary plot line of the East Asian crisis: The countries in East Asia that experienced "twin crises," that is, both a currency crisis and a banking crisis, tumbled into a full-blown depression. On the other hand, countries that had more sound banks experienced only a currency crisis and were able to avoid the worst of the economic crisis.

To understand this crisis more fully, it is important to describe in more detail the situation that existed in early 1997 in East Asia regarding each of these twin crises.

The Currency Crisis in East Asia

In early 1997, a large number of East Asian countries were maintaining pegged (or floating within a small range) exchange rates with the U.S. dollar in order to attract foreign investment. Because of the appreciation of the dollar versus the yen in 1995, these pegged exchange rates became overvalued relative to Japan and the rest of the world. This appreciation of the dollar against the yen was due in large part to the strong American economy and weak Japanese economy (although fundamentals were probably not sufficient alone to explain the size of this appreciation). In April 1995, the dollar was trading at 100 yen, but it rose precipitously to 150 yen per dollar by early 1997. Because of this large appreciation, each of these East Asian countries began to run significant current account deficits. Other contributing factors to these deficits were the weak demand for imports in Japan and Europe, gluts in the computer chips and electronics markets, and high domestic interest rates. Those countries that experienced the largest increase in their current account deficits were those countries whose currencies were pegged most rigidly to the appreciating dollar: Thailand, Malaysia, and the Philippines. The end result was that each of these countries was poised to experience a good, old-fashioned, fundamentals-based currency crisis. However, none of these countries' exchange rates were so overvalued that a speculative attack seemed imminent to most observers, at least not until right before the first series of speculative attacks on Thailand during July 1997.

Table 15.2 reports the current account deficits for selected East Asian countries. Other than Taiwan and Singapore, these countries were running significant current account deficits. A common rule of thumb is that any country that has a current account deficit of more than 5 percent of its GDP is in danger of having a rapid capital flow reversal. By this standard, Korea, Indonesia, Malaysia, the Philippines, and Thailand were all in danger of suffering a currency crisis during either 1995 or 1996, with Thailand, the Philippines, and Malaysia experiencing sizeable current account deficits for more than a decade. These large deficits were sustainable only as long as these economies continued to grow at high rates, but at the lower rates of growth that began in 1996 these deficits were no longer manageable. Those countries with smaller current account deficits or surpluses, such as China, Hong Kong, Singapore, and Taiwan, did not suffer large depreciations as the crisis spread throughout the region.

Therefore, at least on the surface, the East Asian countries that slipped into crisis during 1997 appeared to be suffering from currency crises akin to the currency crises suffered in Latin America in the early 1980s.

Table 15.2   Current account balance as a percentage of GDP.

	1991 (%)	1992 (%)	1993 (%)	1994 (%)	1995 (%)	1996 (%)	1997 (%)
Thailand	−8.01	−6.23	−5.68	−6.38	−8.35	−8.51	−2.35
Indonesia	−4.40	−2.46	−0.82	−1.54	−4.27	−3.30	−3.62
Malaysia	−14.01	−3.39	−10.11	−6.60	−8.85	−3.73	−3.50
Korea	−3.16	−1.70	−0.16	−1.45	−1.91	−4.82	−1.90
Philippines	−2.46	−3.17	−6.69	−3.74	−5.06	−4.67	−6.07
Singapore	12.36	12.38	8.48	18.12	17.93	16.26	13.90
Hong Kong	6.58	5.26	8.14	1.98	−2.97	−2.43	−3.75
Taiwan	6.97	4.03	3.52	3.12	3.05	4.67	3.23
China	3.07	1.09	−2.19	1.16	0.03	0.52	3.61

Source: Author's creation based on data from International Financial Statistics of the IMF available at http://elibrary-data.imf.org/finddatareports.aspx?d=33061&e=169393.

However, a key difference between the East Asian and Latin American crises is that the Latin American crises were clearly the result of bad macroeconomic policy. This is not the case in East Asia, where all countries were maintaining fairly stable or declining rates of inflation and roughly balanced budgets. The problem here was a naïve adherence throughout the region to maintaining fixed exchange rates to the dollar, even when this caused their exchange rates to be unsustainably overvalued.

Even though the source of this currency crisis in East Asia was different, the conventional solution to a currency crisis remains the same: Devalue your currency enough to restore a sustainable equilibrium to your balance of payments. In addition, countries typically adopt austerity conditions and tighten fiscal policies (higher taxes and lower government spending to reduce the budget deficit) and monetary policy in order to increase domestic interest rates and reduce the outflow of foreign investment. However, another hidden crisis was also occurring simultaneously within these economies that made the implementation of these conventional policies economically disastrous.

The Banking Crisis in East Asia

East Asian economies have traditionally relied on banks as the primary source of financial intermediation within their economies. For example, banks provided two-thirds of corporate finance in Indonesia before the crisis (Corsetti et al., 1998). In Thailand, this number was 75 percent. In Korea, 50 percent of corporate financing was done directly through banks, 87 percent of corporate bonds were guaranteed by banks, and only

7 percent of corporate financing was in equity. These statistics on corporate finance are very different from those found in other developed countries. For example, in the United States less than one-third of corporate finance comes from banks.

Beginning in the mid-1980s, East Asian countries, as well as other countries throughout the world, began a process of rapid bank liberalization and deregulation. This financial liberalization included (1) abolishing credit controls, (2) deregulating interest rates, (3) opening entry into banking markets, (4) reducing banking regulations, (5) allowing for the private ownership of banks, and (6) allowing the free movement of funds across international borders. A survey by Williamson and Mahar (1998) of 34 rich and poor countries indicated that in 1973, 24 of these countries were classified as having repressed capital flows while only 2 had liberal capital markets. In 1996, zero countries were classified as having repressed capital flows while 18 were classified as having liberal capital markets.

Recent history has illustrated that financial deregulation can potentially be both good and bad. As we discussed in Chapter 11, financial liberalization has often been associated with asset bubbles and banking crises. For example, while rapid deregulation in the early 1980s and 1990s increased the efficiency of the U.S. financial system as a whole, it also led to an increase in speculative behavior by financial institutions that weakened financial fundamentals and contributed to a crisis among savings and loan banks in the early 1990s and the global financial crisis in 2008. Deregulation in East Asia, especially in Thailand, Korea, Malaysia, and Indonesia, was far more rapid and greatly exceeded anything that has gone on in the United States.

In addition, a great deal of financial innovation took place throughout Asia in the 1980s, much of it driven by new information technologies and globalization. Better information communication greatly increased the potential size of financial markets by allowing banks easier access to international capital, which in turn allowed banks to take advantage of economies of scale in their operations. *Securitization*, or the transformation of nonmarketable assets (such as mortgages) into marketable assets (such as bonds), played a critical role in the development of better secondary, or resale, financial markets throughout the region. Finally, the development of *offshore banking* (international banking conglomerates that are chartered in countries with little or no financial regulation) and *hedge funds* (discussed later in this chapter) greatly increased the volume of foreign investment that was available to Asian economies.

Four key factors stemming from financial liberalization and financial development in East Asia contributed to an increase in bank riskiness and eventually to the banking crises in East Asian economies. The interaction between these factors eventually served to magnify the effects of currency crises into full-blown economic crises.

1. *The flip side of running large current account deficits is that these same East Asian countries were also running large capital account surpluses.* In other words, before the crisis these countries were attracting large levels of foreign investment in order to fund their current account deficits. Much of this was foreign-denominated debt, meaning that it was debt that had to be paid back in a foreign currency, usually dollars. The primary reason why Asian countries chose to peg their exchange rates to the dollar in the first place was to attract foreign investment. Foreign investment in East Asian countries ranged between 5 percent and 14 percent of GDP before the crisis (Corsetti et al., 1998). Speculative asset bubbles in many financial markets, including a real estate bubble in Malaysia, fueled (and were fueled by) some of these inflows of foreign capital. Most of this foreign investment was filtered through East Asian banks, but also through Asian corporations that were borrowing heavily from abroad.

2. *Much of the foreign debt that these banks accumulated was short-term, meaning that these banks relied heavily on periodic rollovers of their debt in order to finance their lending activities.* Short-term, dollar-denominated debt is often referred to as "hot money" because of the ease with which it can be moved between countries. Table 15.3 presents the ratio of short-term debt to foreign reserves of the central bank. If this ratio is small it implies that the central bank of a country could cover the short-term financing needs of its banks in the event that foreign creditors become unwilling to roll over their short-term debt. Not surprisingly, three of the four countries that were hit the hardest during the crisis were countries in which this ratio was the largest, namely Thailand, Indonesia, and Korea. To put these numbers in perspective, consider these facts: (1) Indonesia alone had more than $200 billion worth of short-term borrowing; (2) short-term borrowing in 1996 alone was $93 billion in Indonesia, Malaysia, Korea and Thailand, up from $41 billion in 1994 (these short-term inflows turned into a $12 billion outflow in these countries in 1997); and (3) in Korea, 56 percent of their foreign-denominated debt (which was 37 percent of their total debt) was in short-term liabilities (Krueger, 2003). The implication of all of this hot money was that when the speculative crisis hit, large

Table 15.3   Short-term debt as a percentage of foreign reserves.

	1991 (%)	1992 (%)	1993 (%)	1994 (%)	1995 (%)	1996 (%)
Thailand	71.31	72.34	92.49	99.48	114.21	99.69
Indonesia	154.62	172.81	159.70	160.36	189.42	176.59
Malaysia	19.05	21.12	25.51	24.34	30.60	40.98
Korea	81.75	69.62	60.31	54.06	171.45	203.23
Philippines	152.31	119.37	107.68	95.00	82.85	79.45
Singapore	2.67	2.35	2.04	1.75	1.78	2.60
Hong Kong	21.78	18.38	17.09	16.49	14.16	22.35
Taiwan	20.21	21.00	23.64	21.76	21.64	21.31
China	24.68	66.76	68.33	33.04	29.62	23.74

Source: Author's creation based on data from International Financial Statistics of the IMF available at http://elibrary-data.imf.org/finddatareports.aspx?d=33061&e=169393.

amounts of foreign capital was able to quickly leave these highly leveraged banks, devastating their balance sheets.

3. *In addition to a foreign borrowing boom, a domestic lending boom was also taking place within these countries.* Domestic lending by banks grew between 17 percent and 30 percent a year between 1991 and 1996 in East Asian countries (Corsetti et al., 1998). Because a large source of the funds that banks used for these loans was from foreign creditors, banks in the region found themselves holding large amounts of debt denominated in foreign currencies but primarily holding assets denominated in domestic currencies. Table 15.4 reports the ratio of foreign liabilities to foreign assets for banks and nonbank financial institutions, where the largest ratios existed in the crisis countries of Thailand, Indonesia, and Korea.

Much of these funds went into stock and real estate bubbles throughout the region. The end result of these binges of lending and borrowing was that banks in the region were left with fragile financial fundamentals and huge exposures to exchange rate risk. A depreciation of their domestic currency (and an appreciation of the dollar) would reduce the value of their domestic-denominated assets and increase the value of their foreign-denominated liabilities, devastating their balance sheets.

4. *The fourth and final piece of the banking systems crisis was the poor quality and riskiness of the investment projects that the lending boom financed.* Well before the crisis of 1997, there was a great deal

Table 15.4   Ratio of foreign liabilities to foreign assets.

	1993	1994	1995	1996	1997
Thailand	6.93	7.73	7.81	11.03	8.12
Indonesia	2.95	4.01	4.26	4.24	5.43
Malaysia	0.83	1.40	1.44	1.48	2.22
Korea	2.98	2.97	3.31	3.75	2.51
Philippines	1.14	0.97	1.10	1.72	1.71
Singapore	1.51	1.62	1.66	1.62	1.38
Hong Kong	1.42	1.43	1.56	1.65	1.59
Taiwan	n/a	n/a	0.61	0.61	0.62
China	0.99	0.94	1.17	1.20	1.36

Source: Author's creation from data from the Bank of International Settlements, as reported by Corsetti et al. (1998).

of worry about not only the quantity but the quality of the loans that were being made within East Asian banking systems. As discussed in Chapter 10, new Keynesian models of credit have focused on the macroeconomic effects of imperfect information and risk. Especially important is the effect of risk on financial intermediation, particularly in regards to *moral hazard*. To reiterate, moral hazard exists when individuals are able to allocate some of the downside risk of a project to others while keeping all of its upside benefits for themselves, thus encouraging individuals to participate in riskier projects than they otherwise would. High levels of moral hazard existed in three areas of Asian economies well before the crises of 1997 for three reasons.

First, moral hazard was rampant within the operations of East Asian banks. Because of financial deregulation in many of these countries, banks found themselves subjected to little or no prudential regulation regarding the types of loans they could make or the types of debt they could acquire. Because of low capital adequacy requirements, undercapitalized banks had little to lose by gambling on riskier and riskier assets such as overvalued stock and real estate markets that were inflated by asset bubbles.

One way to measure the riskiness of bank lending is to look at the number of nonperforming loans (NPLs) as a percentage of total lending, which is reported in Table 15.5. NPLs refer to loans that are not being paid and are either in default or in the process of being defaulted on. With the exception of China, the countries with the highest percentage of NPLs in 1996 suffered the worst

Table 15.5   Nonperforming loans as a percentage of total lending.

	End of 1996 (%)	End of 1997 (%)
Thailand	13	36
Indonesia	13	15
Malaysia	10	15
Korea	8	30
Philippines	14	7
Singapore	4	4
Hong Kong	3	1
Taiwan	4	n/a
China	14	n/a

Source: Author's creation based on data from the Bank of International Settlements Annual Report, as reported by Corsetti et al. (1998). Data in column 2 is from Peregrine (1997).

crises: Thailand (13 percent), Korea (8 percent), Indonesia (13 percent), and Malaysia (10 percent). To put these numbers in some perspective, the average rate of NPLs in developed-country banking systems is typically less than 1 percent of total loans. Default rates on bank loans in East Asia had been rising well before the speculative crises of 1997, and, in fact, a large number of Korean and Thai banks were technically bankrupt even before the currency crisis began.

Second, moral hazard also existed at the national and international level. Many banks, particularly in Thailand, Indonesia, and Korea, engaged in excessive borrowing of foreign funds and excessive domestic lending based on the belief that their governments would bail them out in the event of an economic downturn. This was a plausible assumption given the extent of government involvement and subsidization in these financial industries. Even though explicit deposit insurance did not exist, the governments of Korea, Thailand, Taiwan, and Malaysia effectively guaranteed all deposits given that none of their domestic banks had ever been allowed to fail. If things became exceptionally bad, banks could also reasonably believe that they would be indirectly bailed out by the IMF when their government appealed for a loan. Hence, many banks felt protected from the exchange rate risk they exposed themselves to when they borrowed short in foreign currencies and lent long in their domestic currency.

Finally, moral hazard was also evident at the corporate level. Corporations are much more highly subsidized and market power is much more concentrated in East Asian economies than in other developed economies. Many outsiders have referred to the domination of most sectors of East Asian economies by a few large and interrelated conglomerates as "crony capitalism." The end result has been little competition in many markets and low returns on capital for these conglomerates. The best example of this is South Korea, a country with an exceptionally high degree of industrial concentration, primarily within 30 large conglomerates referred to as *chaebols*. In 1997, as many as 7 of the 30 largest chaebols were insolvent (meaning their debt was greater than their assets), and the return on invested capital was less than the cost of capital in 20 of these chaebols (Krueger, 2003).

As an indication of just how shaky the financial fundamentals in these countries were, by 1998 31 percent of Korean, 45 percent of Indonesian, and 18 percent of Malaysian and Filipino corporations were insolvent, up from their 1994 levels of 16 percent in Korea and 8 percent in Indonesia, Malaysia, and the Philippines (Pomerleano, 1998). This suggests that despite many of these East Asian countries' excessively high rates of investment, much of this money was not being channeled into productive projects. Together, little competition, easy capital, and the belief that many of these conglomerates were too big for governments to allow them to fail created incentives for these corporations to adopt exceptionally risky projects in the absence of government regulation. Financial fundamentals deteriorated and the stage was set for a wave of bankruptcies and banking crises.

The Interaction between the Twin Crises and the Role of IMF Policies

How did these currency crises and financial crises interact to create the massive and far-reaching economic crisis that swept through East Asia between 1997 and 1999? Consider the typical policy response of a country that is experiencing a large capital outflow because of an overvalued exchange rate, which is to devalue its currency. As discussed earlier, in the event of a currency crisis alone this depreciation usually ends the crisis as long as the country follows appropriate fiscal and monetary policies so that no future devaluations become necessary. However, in those East Asian countries that were also experiencing a banking crisis, a devaluation of their exchange rates was only the beginning of their troubles because this devaluation adversely affected the balance sheets of highly leveraged banks and corporations. East Asian banks and corporations saw the real value of their foreign-denominated debt rise and the real value of their domestic-denominated assets fall as their exchange rates fell. For example, in Indonesia the exchange rate depreciated by 75 percent. As a result, foreign-denominated debt quadrupled in value at the same time that their domestic-denominated assets fell by three-fourths. Few banks and corporations could withstand such a shock, and most very quickly became insolvent. The crisis in Thailand began in July 1997, and by December 8 of that year the government had announced the closing of 56 of the 58 largest banks in the country. This insolvency led many banks to sell off as many assets as they could, further depressing asset prices in financial markets worldwide and reducing the amount of collateral for any future loans.

In this regard, the similarities between the East Asian crisis and the Great Depression are obvious. According to Fischer's debt-deflation theory (Chapter 10), the falling price of assets caused by deflation (as during the Great Depression) or depreciation (as during the East Asian crisis) reduced the value of assets but increased the real value of debt because debt prices are fixed at the time of the loan (in the case of depreciation, these changes in the value of debt and assets are in terms of dollars). As a result, firms saw their assets fall in value and the real value of their debt rise, leading to declines in financial fundamentals. As bankruptcy rates rose, the financial fundamentals of banks also fell. The result was either bank failure or, at best, credit rationing and increases in the cost of credit intermediation. These declines in credit then impacted the real economy in the ways described by new Keynesian models of credit. Thus, deflation and currency depreciation work in similar ways within countries that were as exposed to international capital flows and exchange rate risk as the banks in East Asia.

Depreciation also led to unprecedented capital flight, further reducing financial fundamentals, because depreciation significantly reduced the return on East Asian assets and raised concerns about the stability of East Asian financial systems. Capital outflows averaged 11 percent of GDP for Indonesia, Malaysia, Korea, the Philippines, and Thailand. Precipitous drops in investment and growth followed, which in many investors' eyes validated the initial foreign exchange speculation that started this whole process. Thus, the crisis spread from currency markets to the rest of the economy through a highly leveraged banking system.

The twin banking and currency crises that many of these East Asian crisis countries were facing simultaneously put them in an unenviable bind, a bind in which any policies they could enact to deal with one crisis would make the other crisis worse, and vice versa. Many domestic governments in these countries seemed to understand the conundrum they were in from the beginning of the crisis, as evidenced by their reluctance to follow the conventional policy reaction to a currency crisis, which is to devalue in conjunction with tightening monetary and fiscal policy. The purpose of such austerity is to increase domestic interest rates and re-attract foreign investment. Not only did these governments initially attempt to resist devaluation by trading large amounts of their foreign reserves at unfavorable terms, but they also resisted tightening monetary and fiscal policy because they realized that higher interest rates would only further weaken their already fragile banking systems by making it more costly for banks in need of resources to borrow. Of course, to take the opposite policy and loosen monetary and fiscal policy in an attempt to reduce domestic interest rates, stabilize bank portfolios, and spur economic growth would only have led to more capital flight and further exacerbated the currency crisis.

Unfortunately, it is not clear that the IMF completely understood that there were two distinct crises occurring in East Asia. The IMF structural adjustment bailout programs negotiated throughout Asia typically focused on three general reforms as a condition for short-term financing. First, countries were asked to close insolvent banks and recapitalize other domestic banks, with those funds at least partially coming from an IMF loan and partially through reductions in government spending. Unfortunately, without the protection of deposit insurance, these IMF-orchestrated closures frightened depositors throughout East Asia and initiated large bank runs that compounded the banking crisis. Second, countries were asked to reduce their reliance on short-term debt, mainly through bankruptcy reform and "sunshine" regulations that required better dissemination and measurement of banking information. While this is a laudable long-term goal, it did little to help an already devastated banking system that was desperate for credit of any maturity. Third, the IMF asked these countries that already had low inflation and balanced budgets to further tighten monetary and fiscal policies. The thinking, which appears to have taken place almost reflexively, was that the standard policy solutions to a currency crisis—devaluation (which these countries had already experienced) and higher domestic interest rates—should be followed in East Asia as well, ignoring the financial fundamentals of East Asian banking systems. This is the reason that the IMF's involvement in the crisis triggered a worsening of banking conditions throughout the region.

Explaining Variations in the Magnitude of the Crisis across Countries

While there was quite a bit of variation in terms of the size of the contractions in each of these East Asian economies, one simple observation explains most of this variation: The countries with the most financially fragile banking systems were also the countries that experienced the largest falls in output growth. The countries with the weakest financial fundamentals in their banking system were those that were the most severely affected by the currency crisis: Thailand, Indonesia, Korea, and to a lesser extent Malaysia. Additional factors, however, played a role as well. Many of these countries were also suffering through a variety of political problems, including elections and labor unrest in Korea, the collapse of a government in Thailand, the revocation of an election and the eventual removal of President Suharto in Indonesia, and the rantings of Prime Minister Mahathir in Malaysia (which will be discussed later).

The best example of the importance of banking system stability is the Philippines. By almost every measure, the Philippines had the worst macroeconomic fundamentals in the region, with the lowest growth rates, the highest inflation and unemployment rates, and the largest current account and budget deficits. However, GDP growth rose strongly in 1997 to 9.6 percent, slowed to −0.5 percent in 1998, and then rose again to 3.2 percent in 1999. As can be seen in Table 15.5, the Philippines was the only country that actually lowered the level of NPLs between 1996 and 1997 and, in fact, had been steadily improving in this category since the mid-1990s. Likewise, Singapore, Taiwan, and Hong Kong had relatively low levels of NPLs and also avoided the worst of the crisis. The reason is that, relative to the rest of the region, these countries had the most stringent financial regulations and the most solid financial fundamentals in their banking systems.

The one notable exception to this relationship between banking stability and the size of the economic crisis is China, which was able to avoid much of the economic crisis despite a banking system with very weak financial fundamentals because of a stringent series of capital controls (including a nonconvertible currency) that placed restrictions on the amount of capital that could leave and enter the country. These capital controls also limited the amount of foreign investment that flowed into the country before the crisis occurred and the kinds of lending that took place.

WERE FOREIGN INVESTORS TO BLAME?

Many feel that someone has to receive the blame for what happened in East Asia. Was it international financiers, who attempted to use their wealth to make billions more at the expense of poor nations? This hypothesis that the investment managers of large foreign investment funds were responsible for the East Asian crisis dates to the very beginning of the crisis. After his country was forced to devalue in the face of a speculative attack that his central bank did not have enough foreign reserves to prevent, Malaysian Prime Minister Mahathir Mohamad immediately blamed the crisis on foreign financiers such as George Soros (the fact that he also blamed the crisis on Jewish speculators and claimed that IMF policies were part of a Western conspiracy to recolonize Asia did not lend his claims any credibility). Large international hedge funds, like the Quantum Fund managed by Soros, became easily identifiable symbols of what many claim is wrong with the financial liberalization and globalization that has taken place within world financial markets since the 1980s.

In brief, *hedge funds* are large investment funds financed by very large investors or banks, typically requiring minimum deposits of $100 million or more. Hedge funds engage in highly risky behavior and attempt to make large returns by speculating on changes in asset prices, either positive or negative. Often these assets are currencies. Because hedge funds can move large amounts of capital within very short periods of time, hedge funds have often been accused of trying to influence markets to their advantage.

Hedge funds, however, are just a small part of the big picture, which is the incredible amount of liberalization in the laws that govern capital movements between countries. One implication of more open and highly developed financial markets is that large amounts of investment now flow more freely into all regions of the world, both rich and poor. Earlier in this chapter we discussed the unprecedented flow of foreign funds into East Asia and, as a result, the unprecedented investment rates that these countries were able to maintain until 1997. Of course, the problem with financial liberalization is that while it improves the flow of funds to regions of the world that need them the most, it also, in the words of Alan Greenspan, improves "the transmission of financial disturbances far more effectively than ever before" (Greenspan, 1998). While it is easier for capital to flow in, it is also easier for capital to flow out. As discussed earlier, this is exactly what happened in East Asia during the crisis.

However, an outflow of capital does not necessarily mean that foreign investors are causing the crisis. Since the mid-1980s, Argentina, Venezuela, South Africa, and Sri Lanka were all closed to short-term capital flows at the time they suffered economic crises. Foreign investors who left East Asia were in large part responding to poor fundamentals in these economies, particularly in regards to overvalued exchange rates and unstable banking systems. Consistent with this view, Froot,

O'Connell, and Seasholes (1999) found that foreign investors did not begin to pull large amounts of capital out of Asia before the crisis, only during and after. Their study suggests that the correlation between what different foreign investors do is now higher than ever before because of the better dissemination of information. Likewise, Kaminsky and colleagues (2003) examined different capital flight episodes and found that fundamentals-based causes such as financial linkages, high levels of debt, and hot money are significant contributors to the spread of capital outflows across countries. We also know from behavioral economics research that the combination of biases, incomplete information, and intertwined incentives leads to belief-based reasons for herding among fund managers and increases the chances of panic and capital flight. The East Asian crisis showed that these mass exoduses can be exceptionally costly.

Thus, while foreign investment and globalization might make the symptoms worse, they almost certainly are not the cause of the disease. To significantly reduce foreign investment and to deliberalize financial markets in a haphazard way would almost assuredly be a situation in which the cure is worse than the disease. Remember the case of South Korea: Even after the crisis, Korean GDP was still 50 percent higher in 1999 than 1990. Much of this sizeable growth was fed by capital inflows. Capital inflows also contributed significantly to the economic recovery that occurred in the region after the crisis. However, these new capital inflows were most beneficial for those countries that reformed their approach to financial liberalization and development and maintained appropriate prudential regulation of their banking systems.

WAS THE IMF TO BLAME FOR THESE CRISES?

Probably no other institution was more widely criticized as a result of the East Asian crisis than the IMF. Its impotence in quickly ending these crises has attracted a great deal of blame from many sources.

The IMF was created as part of the postwar Bretton Woods agreement to serve as a lender of last resort for governments suffering from financial crises. The IMF has at its disposal a lending fund (which currently stands at roughly $750 billion) comprised of *subscriptions*, or contributions each country must make (and which earns interest from the IMF) to become a member. Under the IMF's quota system, each member country's subscription to the fund's loan portfolio also determines its proportional voting rights. The United States contributes roughly 17 percent of the IMF's total subscription, Europe 32 percent, and China only 4 percent.

The IMF then lends directly to governments that are experiencing crises, who can then hold these funds as foreign reserves to support their currency or distribute these funds in bailouts.

The IMF has been harshly criticized for the loans it has made and the structural adjustment conditions that it attaches to these loans, from the right, from the left, and from the center of the political spectrum.

Criticisms from the Right

The primary criticism from those on the right of the political spectrum pertains to the IMF's role in funding moral hazard. In order for investors and bankers to behave responsibly and efficiently, they must incorporate all of the relevant risks and returns into their decisions to fund projects. Far too often investors and bankers incorporate all of the possible positive returns into their analysis but disregard many of the relevant risks based on the assumption that their governments, aided by IMF financing, will bail them out if economic conditions deteriorate. In a sense, the IMF provides free insurance to investors and bankers during a crisis, which encourages riskier behavior throughout the financial system.

To deal with this, many on the right have called for disbanding the IMF in order to eliminate this potential source of moral hazard. However, many others feel that the IMF does have an important role in helping governments that are otherwise well-managed survive short-term macroeconomic problems. The argument is similar to the Keynesian arguments made for bailouts and a lender of last resort in a domestic context (and reviewed in Chapters 10 and 11): There is a need during a financial crisis for a lender of last resort in order to prevent bank runs, provide liquidity, reduce risk, and moderate the scale of the economic crisis. The IMF is the only institution that can sufficiently serve as a credible lender of last resort, particularly for smaller countries with weak domestic monetary policy and limited access to financial markets.

There is a large empirical literature that indicates that IMF involvement in a country does, on balance, improve existing conditions and help moderate economic crises. As discussed in Chapter 13, before World War II the world economy had none of the international infrastructure that exists today. The result was that during the Great Depression many countries acted as if they operated in a vacuum with no regard for how their economic policies affected their trading partners. In addition, the absence of a safety net in the form of an international lender of last resort allowed preventable recessions to build into depressions. History has shown us that for a country in crisis, getting the proper outside help, both financially and intellectually, is exceptionally important in avoiding a sustained economic depression.

A preferable approach to dealing with the problem of moral hazard would be to not simply disband the IMF, but for member countries that largely set the boundaries of IMF policy to give it more power, particularly the power to say no more often by making the IMF more independent in its policy decisions. The IMF would continue to provide financing to good governments, but by being more independent the IMF would have more power to say no to investors and bankers who have taken unacceptable risks, to say no to poorly governed countries, and to say no to developed countries that apply pressure on the IMF to conduct bailouts or to place new conditions on bailouts that further their own self-interested political or economic objectives.

However, the IMF rarely says no to any country. Over 70 countries have received "emergency" loans from the IMF for 20 years or more. It is hard for the IMF to say no to poor countries in crisis because the human suffering involved in these economies is real. It is even harder for the IMF to say no when geopolitical and domestic politics mean that many crisis countries have friends among the largest members of the IMF, who ultimately have the power to force the IMF to say yes. Finally, it is hard for the IMF to say no to new loans to countries that already have existing loans from the IMF, because doing so might mean default. As a result, moral hazard will continue to be a significant factor in IMF lending.

Criticisms from the Left

Many on the left have complained that the IMF encroaches on the sovereign rights of nations through the structural adjustment conditions that it places on its loans. In the mid-1980s, there was an average of less than three structural adjustment conditions associated with each IMF loan. During the 1990s, the average loan came attached with more than 12. While many of these conditions are things most economists could agree upon as being beneficial, such as stricter banking standards, many of the conditions were much more controversial. For example, 140 structural adjustment conditions were placed on Indonesia during the East Asian crisis regulating things like the price of gas and the manner of selling plywood. The IMF asked the central bank of Korea to declare price stability as its only goal when choosing its monetary policy and to ignore output stabilization, even though monetary policy and inflation played no role in the East Asian crisis. It also required changes in Korean labor laws to make layoffs easier and mandated more openness to international trade in the Korean auto market (which was, not surprisingly, pushed hard by Japanese and American representatives to the IMF). In addition, the IMF placed requirements on fighting government and financial corruption that the IMF has no history or expertise in administering. Not surprisingly, many of these conditions fostered broad resentment among East Asians, not necessarily because these conditions were harmful but because they were dictated to them by outsiders.

Critics charge that the IMF has suffered from "mission push" as it has tried to expand its authority into areas outside of its original mission, which was to provide macroeconomic advice and short-term financing to countries in economic difficulties. However, much of this mission push is the responsibility of the governments of larger economies that, for economic or political reasons, have prodded the IMF into imposing structural reform conditions that fall outside the scope of traditional macroeconomic policy. Goldstein (2000) reports results from an IMF survey in which IMF staffers themselves consider only 30–40 percent of the structural adjustment conditions imposed during crises critical to a recovery. In addition, as the number of structural adjustment programs has increased, the compliance rate with these programs has decreased as countries either have a hard time meeting all of the conditions or devalue individual conditions as the total number increases.

However, even if the IMF has overstepped, it does not mean that the IMF should not impose structural adjustment conditions in the future. Certain conditions must always be attached to future IMF lending for three reasons. First, the IMF needs to attach conditions that improve the chances that its loans will be repaid. The IMF is not set up to be a grant organization, and it has a right to improve the chances that loans will be repaid. Promises of structural adjustment are the only real source of collateral that the IMF has at its disposal.

Second, the IMF cannot act preemptively within a country. Crises afford the IMF its only opportunity to facilitate change within a country that, while beneficial in the long run, would otherwise be politically unpopular in the short run. It is important to note, however, that the IMF cannot force any country to accept structural adjustment conditions. Because participation with the IMF is entirely voluntary, all loans must be negotiated between the IMF and the crisis country. Often countries agree to structural adjustment conditions with the IMF because they believe in their effectiveness and because the IMF provides convenient political cover and an easy scapegoat on which to lay the responsibility for difficult actions.

Third, there is evidence that structural adjustment programs, if enacted on a temporary and occasional basis, are beneficial. Krueger (1998) and Edwards (1998) find evidence that countries with structural adjustment programs were more likely to improve across a variety of economic measures than countries without them. However, when looking only at only the 20 countries that have been the largest recipients of repeated structural adjustment loans, Easterly (2005) found no evidence that this repeated, almost permanent lending improved policies or economic growth.

Therefore, attaching structural adjustment conditions to loans is important, but the IMF has to make sure that the loans are temporary and has conditions that focus on goals the IMF believes to be absolutely crucial to achieving its most important objectives. IMF policy makers must always ask themselves the following: "If this policy is not enacted, is it important enough to stop the Fund's financing?" Failure to answer "yes" should drop this condition from any future lending. The IMF's priorities should fall within four categories: reform of fiscal policy, reform of monetary policy, reform of the financial sector, and exchange rate management. The IMF will only be able to avoid mission creep and narrow its focus to areas where it is most likely to be successful if its principle financiers and policy makers, namely G7 countries, meddle less and allow the IMF to operate more independently.

Criticisms from the Center

Many critics attack the IMF not from an ideological standpoint but from a more pragmatic view, asserting that the culture and policy approach of the IMF needs to be reformed. For example, Paul Krugman (2008) has referred to the IMF's rationale for its standard program of fixed exchange rates and austerity conditions in response to a crisis as "the confidence game." In order to stem the tide of capital outflows, the IMF asks policy makers to contract monetary and fiscal policy during a crisis. The theory is that higher domestic interest rates will boost the exchange rate and assuage the confidence of foreign investors. However, this comes at the cost of a more severe economic recession in the crisis country. In other words, the confidence game refers to abandoning typical Keynesian policies developed countries follow during economic recessions, which is to stimulate aggregate demand by loosening monetary and fiscal policy. Instead, the IMF asks poorer crisis countries to do the exact opposite of stabilization policy in an effort to maintain foreign capital inflows (this abandonment of Keynesian policies is ironic given that Keynes was the chief architect of the IMF). It is not surprising, then, that financial and economic conditions worsened immediately after the IMF's involvement in East Asia. Most disturbingly, these contractionary policies never did achieve their intended result, which was to restore investors' confidence. This should not be surprising given that deeper depressions are never confidence building.

The impression the IMF leaves with many of the citizens in these crisis countries is that the IMF worries about the prejudices of investors to the exclusion of everything else. Because the IMF tends to focus on restoring capital flows, it often ignores domestic political considerations, failing to build more support for its programs within the crisis country. This reinforces the impression that the IMF is simply a tool of international financiers and not overly concerned about the fate of those who are suffering the most as a result of an economic crisis. It also increases the risk of social and political turmoil, which could truly have devastating long-term effects on politically unstable countries.

Joseph Stiglitz (2002), originator of the theory of credit rationing and former vice president of the World Bank between 1997 and 2000, has been a very harsh critic of the behavior of the IMF. He argues that the IMF is too autocratic, spends too little time debating alternatives, is top-down in its decision making, and does not incorporate outside experts who are familiar with the particulars of the country in crisis. According to Stigliz, this is the reason why IMF programs across countries are often very similar even when the fundamentals in each country are very different. (For example, consider the IMF's almost reflexive request that East Asian countries cut budget deficits and raise interest rates, even when it was clear that fiscal policy was not to blame for the East Asian crisis). It is also the reason, according to Stiglitz, that IMF policies are inherently biased towards the economic interests of the developed nations by whom they are appointed.

The IMF is sensitive to all of these criticisms and has undertaken many recent reforms. For example, the IMF has recently placed much more emphasis on fostering a consistent dialog with countries, not only when a crisis is looming. The IMF has also increasingly reduced the amount of conditionality in its programs. It has reorganized its decision-making structure so that it invites a more diverse set of opinions. While the IMF continues to preach financial liberalization, it has recently changed its directives so that it will push future reforms to take place more gradually and in stages, making sure that the institutional and prudential regulatory structure is in place before the liberalization occurs. During the recent European debt crisis, the IMF has even accepted temporary controls on foreign capital inflows as necessary to limit capital flight and provide time for reform. In addition, the IMF has acknowledged that it must be more sensitive towards building domestic political support for its programs and is developing newer "early warning" techniques aimed at crisis prevention.

These reforms are not just taking place because of the criticisms of economists. These reforms have also been driven by two important changes in the global economy since the East Asian crisis. The first is that less developed economies, which have traditionally been the primary customers of the IMF, have been growing rapidly. As a result of this growth, many countries have been granted more access to international financial markets and to lending from other developing countries trying to further their own economic interests. For example, one of the biggest lenders to governments in Africa and South America is China, which does so with many fewer strings attached than the IMF or World Bank. As a result, the IMF has increasingly found itself with fewer and fewer countries to lend to and looking for ways it can stay relevant. One way that it has done this is to be more accommodating to the needs of potential borrowers.

The other change in the global economy is that today it is not poor countries that have been suffering from excessive debt and balance of payment crises; it is rich countries, such as those in Europe. As we will discuss in more detail in Chapter 17, which examines the Euro-zone debt crisis, the fact that the IMF is now lending to its biggest and most influential contributors means that the IMF has become much more sensitive to many of the complaints made by the countries it lends to.

CONCLUSIONS

While globalization and financial liberalization have made it possible for poor countries to develop at rates that 30 years ago would have been thought to be impossible, they have also brought with them potential costs, especially in countries where governments and financial regulators are not vigilant. One of the unforeseen implications of globalization is that business cycles are likely to increasingly take on an international flavor as countries become more interconnected.

The East Asian crisis has highlighted the importance of strong financial markets in withstanding economic fluctuations. However, this should not be surprising. As discussed in Chapter 13, new research on the Great Depression has led to the conclusion that the Depression was initially a financial crisis precipitated by a naïve but strict adherence to fixed exchange rates under the gold standard. Balance of payment imbalances led to deflation (as opposed to depreciation in the case of East Asia), which had a devastating effect on the labor market but more importantly on a fragile financial system. Recent new Keynesian research has also highlighted the importance of imperfect information, credit rationing, moral hazard, and the financial implications of deflation in generating business cycles, bringing the role of financial institutions to the forefront of business cycle theory.

Given what is now known about depressions and the critical role financial institutions play in them, the relevant question is not "Why in East Asia?" but "Why didn't economists see this crisis coming?" The only excuse is that the modern era of globalization only really began in 1989 with the fall of the Berlin Wall. Many of globalization's implications, for business cycles or international politics, have simply not yet been fully understood given the speed with which they have taken place. The same can be said for financial development in general, as we have seen during the recent global financial crisis (discussed in Chapter 18).

Not only did economists and the IMF not see the East Asian crisis coming, but the policy response both from domestic governments and the IMF was insufficient. While the IMF did not create the crisis, it did not do enough to calm it. The IMF has reorganized its mission around proactively, not reactively, responding to crises when they are building, not just when they occur. The IMF is refocusing its resources on institution building, not just paying for bailouts, and trying to show more flexibility in its thinking, not reflexively imposing punitive austerity conditions. Finally, and most importantly, the IMF wants to say no more often to reckless borrowers in an attempt to limit moral hazard. But the IMF is a political institution that is fighting to stay relevant in a world where the need for its lending has changed significantly. Until its member nations get serious about being tough, the IMF will not be able to get tough either and will increasingly slip into irrelevancy.

Another lesson from the East Asian crisis is that while such crises occur at great costs, they also provide the possibility of creating incentives for much-needed economic reform. Structural adjustment can work, particularly when there is domestic buy-in to reform and not just reform through force. Since the conclusion of the East Asian crisis in 1999, economies throughout East Asia have rebounded dramatically. Growth in East Asia averaged 7 percent in 2000 and has consistently remained above 5 percent across most of the major East Asian economies since. Not surprisingly, the economies that have recovered the most strongly were the economies that took financial reform most seriously. The best example of this is South Korea. Beginning in 1999, South Korea worked with creditors to reschedule its foreign debt. At the same time, South Korea aggressively moved to end its banking crises by setting aside an amount equal to 15 percent of its GDP for a bailout aimed at buying bad loans and closing bad banks. It addition, it merged some stronger banks and sold others to foreigners, opening up South Korean financial markets to international competition. It placed new prudential regulations on connected lending and set higher loan safety standards that limit the amount of hot money and short-term debt in the banking system. South Korea worked to shore up its chaebols while opening domestic markets to international firms in an effort to increase competition. Finally, South Korea abandoned its rigid peg to the dollar and has forced financial markets to account for possible exchange rate risks. As a result, Korea has consistently grown faster than 5 percent since the crisis.

South Korean reforms stand in direct contrast with Indonesia, which has let postcrisis opportunities for reform go to waste. Despite having the weakest banking system in the region, Indonesia has done little to deal with its NPL problems since the crisis ended and has an unevenly regulated banking system dominated by the government and politically-connected lending. Costly credit and credit rationing remain prevalent, and both investment rates and foreign investment in Indonesia have generally remained below their pre-1997 levels. Other East Asian countries fall somewhere between South Korea and Indonesia in terms of both the extent of the reforms enacted and their economic success since the crises ended.

SUGGESTED READINGS

Currencies and Crises, Paul Krugman (1995): A collection of accessible and thought-provoking essays on international finance, exchange rates, currency crises, and financial crises by the Nobel Prize–winning economist.

Globalization and Its Discontents, Joseph Stiglitz (2002): An often scathing indictment of the IMF and its policies from a Nobel Prize winner in economics and one-time chief economist of the World Bank. Chapter 4 of this book provides a review of the East Asian crisis, focusing on a critique of IMF policies adopted during the crisis.

"What Caused the Asian Currency and Financial Crisis?: Parts I and II," Giancarlo Corsetti, Paolo Pesenti, and Nouriel Roubini (1998): A complete review of the data and timeline of the East Asian crisis.

SIXTEEN

The Great Recession in Japan

INTRODUCTION

Since 1991, Japan has suffered through the longest period of below average growth experienced by any developed country since World War II. Figure 16.1 presents GDP growth and unemployment in Japan since 1980. After a decade of very strong growth in the 1980s, the Japanese economy barely grew between 1991 and 2003 and unemployment more than doubled to postwar highs. By 2013, nominal GDP in Japan was still roughly at 1991 levels and had been below its natural rate of output for 17 of the last 20 years. If the Japanese economy had instead grown at a reasonable 2 percent a year since 1991, Japan would be 60 percent richer today than it is. To put this in perspective, by growing at roughly 0 percent instead of 2 percent, Japan has lost what is equivalent to the entire GDP of France.

This "Great Recession" in Japan was actually composed of two closely spaced recessions, the first lasting from 1992 to 1995 and the second beginning in 1997 and lasting until 2003. Both of these recessions were followed by slow growth periods. As illustrated in Figure 16.2, these recessions were accompanied by a significant decrease in inflation beginning in the early 1990s and sustained deflation beginning in 1998 and lasting until 2011—the first sustained deflation experienced in an OECD country since the Great Depression. This deflation had the unprecedented effect of driving nominal interest rates to, and even slightly below, zero. In addition, the Japanese stock market fell by 75 percent and commercial property values fell by 80 percent from their prerecession highs in 1990.

Figure 16.1   Real GDP growth and unemployment rates in Japan.

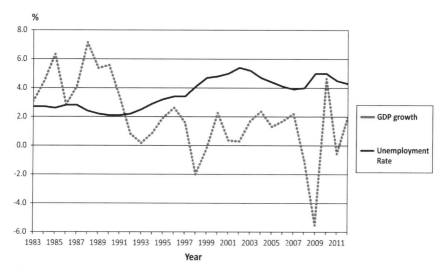

Source: Author's creation based on data from World Bank available at http://data.worldbank.org/indicator/NY.GDP.MKTP.KD.ZG.

More than 20 years after these initial declines, Japanese stocks and property prices remained at one-third of their peak values, despite a strong recent rally in 2013. Most disturbingly, Japanese banks held (and still hold) billions of dollars of bad loans. While their financial industry no longer teeters on the brink of collapse as it did throughout the 1990s, it remains too structurally weak to extend credit to many Japanese firms and households.

It was not always like this. Not too long ago the worry among American and European policy makers was that the Japanese economy was becoming too strong, not too weak. In late 1989, economist Lawrence Summers (future U.S. Treasury secretary and president of Harvard University) said the following: "An Asian economic bloc with Japan at its apex ... is clearly in the making. This all raises the possibility that the majority of American people who now feel that Japan is a greater threat to the United States than the Soviet Union are right" (Summers, 1989). Summers was in no way alone in this opinion. Japan clearly was the single most amazing growth miracle of the twentieth century, averaging 5 percent per capita GDP growth a year and more than quadrupling its standards of living between 1960 and 1990. In a little over two decades, Japan went from a war-ravaged economy with little remaining manufacturing base to the world's largest exporter of steel and automobiles. Based on the assumption that this remarkable economic growth

Figure 16.2   Inflation and interest rates in Japan.

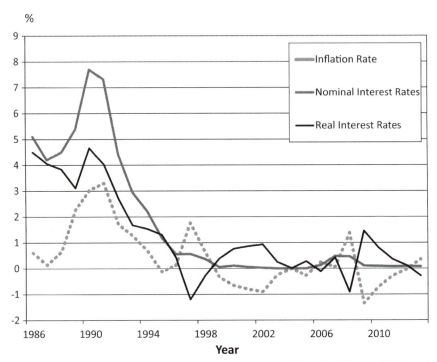

Source: Author's creation based on data from the World Bank available at http://data.worldbank.org/ indicator#topic-7.

would continue indefinitely, many observers anticipated a day when Japan would economically dominate the United States and Europe.

The predicted rise of Japan to the preeminent economic hegemon has not happened. In this chapter, the reasons for the lengthy Japanese slowdown are investigated. This examination begins with a discussion of Japan and the unique institutions that characterize its economy, particularly at the beginning of the 1990s. Included is an explanation of Japan's dual economy with a small export-oriented sector but essentially closed domestic markets, its heavily regulated and concentrated industries, its low consumption and high savings rates, its large but weak banking system, and its slow-moving bureaucratic government. Next, the role that each of these factors played in the Japanese recession is examined. We will see that there are striking similarities between the Great Depression of the 1930s, the East Asian crisis of 1997–1999, and the Great Recession in Japan, specifically regarding the real consequences of deflation on the financial fundamentals of a financial system and how a weak financial system can magnify the size of economic crises. Finally, the failure of stabilization policy in Japan, both monetary and fiscal, to stimulate the Japanese economy and to quickly end the Great Recession is examined. One conclusion of this chapter is that macroeconomic theory, particularly Keynesian and new Keynesian business cycle theory, explains what has happened in Japan quite well. The study of the Great Recession in Japan lends credence to the argument that economists are making advances in their understanding of business cycles but also illustrates that economic theory makes little practical difference if it is ignored by policy makers.

A BRIEF DESCRIPTION OF THE JAPANESE ECONOMY

Japan's economy is structured differently than other developed economies, including other economies in Asia. The key differences fall into three broad categories.

Japan's Dual Economy

Japan has a reputation as an export-oriented economy, but in reality only about 15 percent of its economy is devoted to exports. This export sector is highly efficient because of intense international competition and is composed of the companies that most consumers outside of Japan are familiar with. However, the other 85 percent of the Japanese economy that is primarily devoted to the production of goods and services for domestic consumption is highly protected from international trade. The government closely regulates prices and other market conditions in this domestic sector, and market power is concentrated within a small number of very large firms. As a result, there is a significant productivity difference between Japan's competitive export sector and its inefficient domestic sector.

Because of these inefficient domestic markets, Japanese firms have increasingly moved their operations outside of Japan in order to increase productivity. For example, Japanese car manufacturers now produce more cars abroad than they do at home. Another implication of this market inefficiency is that goods and services are considerably more expensive in Japan than they are anywhere else in the world. The average American household spends 10 percent of its income on food as compared to 20 percent for the average Japanese household. In fact, many goods produced by Japanese companies are sold cheaper in the United States than in Japan itself. The result is that Japan has become one of the most expensive countries in the world in which to live. Tokyo and Osaka, Japan's two largest cities, are two of the most expensive cities in the world, with cost-of-living indicators roughly 35 percent higher than in New York.

Japan's Investment-Driven Economy

The development strategy Japan adopted after World War II focused on building manufacturing industries that could produce goods to be exported abroad. The idea behind this strategy, referred to as *export promotion,* was that it would allow Japan access to larger international markets, which would in turn allow Japan to take advantage of economies of scale and increase its productive efficiency. To do this, however, huge amounts of funds had to be funneled to Japanese corporations in order to finance their capital purchases. The primary economic objective of the Japanese government during the postwar era was to use public policy as a tool to facilitate cheap financing for Japanese industry. The government did this directly by providing subsidies and loans to corporations. It also did this indirectly through two channels. First, Japanese tax policies encouraged household savings by heavily relying on consumption taxes. Second, the dual structure of the economy increased the prices of domestic consumption goods, which in turn discouraged consumption and encouraged savings. Together with Japan's rapidly aging population, these factors explain why Japan consistently saved nearly 15 percent of its GDP until the late 1990s. (The Japanese savings rate has fallen significantly since then, primarily because of falling incomes and the fact that a greater proportion of its rapidly aging population has moved into retirement age). The high level of savings in Japan led to low interest rates and high investment but private consumption that was about 10 percent lower, as a share of GDP, than it was in the United States.

Japan's Banking Conglomerates

Bond and stock markets in Japan are relatively small. Banking in Japan, as it is in most Asian economies, is a much more important source of financial intermediation than in other developed economies. Just like in other areas of the economy, the Japanese government played a major role in the development of the Japanese banking system by using financial regulations and subsidies as a tool to encourage households to hold their savings in banks. In the United States, households hold only about 10 percent of their assets in currency or bank deposits. In Japan, this number was an astounding 54 percent and is the primary reason why Japan had 8 of the 10 largest banks in the world during the early 1990s.

Japanese firms rely heavily on banks for their financing. In Japan, roughly 40 percent of corporate financing comes from bank loans, with only one-third coming in the form of equity financing. This is exactly the opposite of the United States, where banks account for only about 10 percent of corporate financing, but equity accounts for two-thirds of the total. In spite of their size and influence (or maybe because of it), Japanese banks are largely protected from international competition and are relatively inefficient. In addition, because there are few rules separating the operations of banks from the firms they lend money to, most Japanese banks have very close financial ties with large corporations. These corporate/banking conglomerates are referred to as *keiretsu* (these keiretsu are similar to the chaebols in South Korea, which were discussed in Chapter 15). The rationale for these Japanese conglomerates is that, in theory, closer relationships between firms and banks should allow each to make better-informed lending and investment decisions. In other words, connected lending is a way to overcome the problems of asymmetric information. In practice, however, it has often led to "crony capitalism" where loans are made not on the basis of profit but on the basis of relationships. It has also encouraged a "too-big-to-fail" mentality that greatly increased moral hazard and risk in the Japanese banking system, which in turn reduced the financial fundamentals of banks and firms, creating a very shaky financial system.

Further magnifying the problem of moral hazard in Japan was a program of financial deregulation adopted in the 1980s. Just like in the United States and East Asia, weakened lending restrictions in Japan immediately increased the riskiness of bank behavior. Coupled with the excessive optimism of corporate executives and speculators, deregulation fueled the incredible asset bubbles in real estate and stock markets that took place in Japan during the late 1980s. To provide one extreme example of the size of this bubble economy, it was reported that at one point real estate developers in Japan estimated that the square mile surrounding the Emperor's palace in the center of Tokyo was valued at more than all of the land in California (Krugman, 2008). Obviously, bubbles of this size suggest that beliefs, and not just fundamentals, were driving these markets.

WHAT IS RESPONSIBLE FOR THE GREAT RECESSION IN JAPAN?

The similarities between the Great Recession in Japan and the Great Depression of the 1930s are striking. In each case, the first obvious sign of a problem was a large stock market crash, which took place in Japan in December of 1989. Falling inflation, and eventually deflation, subsequently followed. As output began to fall, the bad debts held by banks began to increase and financial fundamentals deteriorated. Credit began to tighten considerably, leading to further falls in aggregate demand and output in a method well described by new Keynesian models of credit. The most significant difference between the Great Recession in Japan and the Great Depression is one of depth and breath. While the Great Depression was absolutely devastating to the world economy, the Great Recession was largely isolated to Japan, and even in Japan the falls in output and the increases in unemployment were much smaller than those that occurred during the Great Depression.

Declines in aggregate supply created by structural inefficiencies in the Japanese economy also played a role in this recession, particularly in explaining why the recession persisted for more than a decade. A number of factors contributed to lower aggregate supply growth in Japan. One was the inflexibility of the Japanese labor market, in large part because of its tradition of lifetime employment that severely limits flexibility in hiring and firing decisions. Coupled with a significant amount of nominal and real wage rigidity in Japan for the reasons suggested by new Keynesian models of wage inflexibility, deflation in Japan led to higher real wages and unemployment levels that were unprecedented in Japanese postwar history. These high unemployment rates existed in spite of the fact that Japanese corporations continued to employ bloated labor forces and resist layoffs. Other factors constraining aggregate supply growth included the high degree of market concentration and lack of international competition that exists within the domestic side of Japan's dual economy, both of which have slowed productivity and growth. Finally, diminishing marginal returns significantly reduced the productivity potential of new capital after decades of very high investment rates.

Despite all of these factors affecting aggregate supply, the existence of sustained deflation clearly indicates that this recession was primarily driven by falling aggregate demand, not by reductions in aggregate supply. These persistent declines in aggregate demand were driven by two primary factors.

Underconsumption

Japan has traditionally heavily relied on investment to generate enough aggregate demand to keep its economy at its natural rate of growth. It was easy to justify and maintain these high investment rates in the early postwar period when the economy was starved for capital and growing at

6 percent a year. However, as the Japanese economy grew larger, diminishing returns to capital began to set in and the productivity of newer investment projects began to fall. A big part of the transition from being a developing country to becoming a developed country involves saving less and consuming more while at the same time shifting demand from investment goods to consumption goods. This transition in the composition of aggregate demand, which also stabilizes aggregate demand because consumption is more stable than investment, has occurred in most Western developed countries. In contrast, Japan (until recently) continued to save roughly 15 percent of its GDP throughout the postwar era. The pressure to find investment projects for all of this savings led to overbuilding, overproduction, falling returns on capital, and a great deal of aggregate demand instability.

If this scenario sounds familiar, think back to the warnings of underconsumptionist theories, which were discussed in Chapter 3. These theories argued that the production of goods within rich economies would outpace the growth rate of consumption. Without adequate aggregate demand to absorb these goods, chronic overproduction would exist that would threaten future economic prosperity. Efforts to stimulate aggregate demand through increasing investment demand might help in the short run but hurt in the long run as higher levels of capital lead to even more excess supply.

A similar underconsumptionist theme is an integral part of Keynesian theory, which argues that higher levels of savings do not guarantee full employment—in fact, just the opposite. In Keynes's model, investment may not be large enough to keep the economy at its potential rate of output because of low expectations. The Keynesian principle of the paradox of thrift suggests that countries can save too much relative to their investment levels, leading to chronic aggregate demand shortfalls and increasingly frequent economic contractions. Because of this, higher savings rates are largely self-defeating because more savings reduces aggregate demand and output, which in turn reduces savings.

The way to avoid lower output and the destabilizing effects of higher savings rates in the Keynesian and underconsumptionist theories is for public policy to encourage consumption by increasing the percent of GDP devoted to government purchases and/or by taxing savings. This is the exact opposite of what the Japanese government chose to do in the 1990s. Instead, their policy makers placed their sole focus throughout the crisis on stimulating investment spending in an effort to maintain full employment. While this might have been the proper policy to follow for a capital-starved economy that had just lost a devastating war, it was not proper stabilization policy for an already prosperous economy. However, Japan seemed to be unable and unwilling to abandon its postwar economic policies. In fact, the desire to sustain high investment rates was one of the primary reasons behind financial deregulation in Japan during the 1980s. The stock market crash of early 1990s signaled the end of a period of economic overconfidence and the beginning of a period of falling expectations, falling investment, falling aggregate demand, and recession.

One final problem with focusing on investment-led growth is raised by the Austrian school, and that is the problem of malinvestment. When investment is excessively subsidized, either through overly expansionary monetary policy or through tax policy, the benefits of this investment are likely to be lower than its real costs to society. Much of this investment is likely to be unprofitable, setting the stage not only for lower future economic growth but also the possibility of financial crises if this unprofitable investment is debt-financed.

Banking Crisis

The second major reason why aggregate demand fell so significantly and so persistently is that a banking crisis threatened to strike Japan soon after the recession started. There are two interrelated factors that precipitated this banking crisis. First, crashes in the stock and real estate bubbles severely reduced the value of assets owned by banks and the collateral that backed many of their loans. As a result, banks immediately found themselves holding large amounts of bad loans, and their financial fundamentals deteriorated. Second, the disinflation and deflation that occurred in the 1990s and 2000s increased the real value of corporations' debt relative to the value of their assets. As explained in the debt-deflation theory, deflation increases the real value of firms' debt because debt contracts have fixed nominal values that do not adjust with the price level. However, the asset values of firms fall during a deflation. As the financial position of firms deteriorate, banks see the number of defaulted or delinquent loans in their portfolio rise, leading to the panic selling of assets. As panic selling spreads, asset prices are further depressed and both firms' and banks' financial fundamentals are further weakened. Many weak banks fail. Those that survive increase the costs of credit intermediation or they ration credit as described in new Keynesian models of credit. Kuttner and Posen (2001) find evidence, similar to that found by Bernanke (1983) in the United States during the Great Depression, that credit rationing was extensive during the Great Recession in Japan. This credit rationing occurred even though, contrary to what happened during the Great

Depression, almost all of the banks in Japan avoided closure. The result of this credit rationing was lower credit, lower investment and consumption, and reduced aggregate demand and output.

If this all sounds familiar, it should. The same scenario that occurred during the Great Depression and during the East Asian crisis occurred within Japan's banking system as well (with the exception that in East Asia it was depreciation of their exchange rates and not deflation that precipitated the crisis). The primary difference is that few Japanese banks actually closed. Some Japanese banks did fail, such as the second and fifth largest credit unions in 1995, followed in 1997 by several mid-sized banks. However, these banks were the exceptions. Most Japanese banks continued to operate in Japan even while they were insolvent. They did this in part with the help of periodic government bailouts that were insufficient (at least until 2003) to make the banks fully solvent. But the primary reason that Japanese banks did not fail was a policy of *regulatory forbearance* by the government: The government permitted insolvent banks to treat bad loans as if they would be paid back. As a result, banks were able to misleadingly inflate the value of their assets so that they appeared to be solvent. Merrill Lynch estimated that if the number of NPLs were accurately reported, 40 percent of Japanese banks were insolvent in 2003. Estimates of NPLs that existed in Japanese banks during the crisis were staggering, ranging between $1.2 trillion to $2.5 trillion dollars, or upwards of 50 percent of Japanese GDP at the time. These insolvent banks were incapable of adequately extending credit at reasonable terms. They were "zombie" banks: dead but not forced to die.

It is the sheer size of these insolvency numbers that explains the inability of Japanese policy makers to quickly put an end to this enduring banking crisis. Briefly consider the problems associated with a government bailout of banks of this magnitude. Where does this money come from? What price should the government pay for bad loans? Who gets bailed out first? Won't a bailout lead to even more moral hazard in the future? Should the government nationalize banks, or bail out banks but allow them to remain private? For banking reform to work, wasn't corporate and structural reform needed first to stabilize the financial position of corporations? These questions are only a small indication of the size and the scope of the banking system problems that left Japan and its policy makers paralyzed with indecision.

STABILIZATION POLICY IN JAPAN

If modern business cycle theory, particularly Keynesian and new Keynesian theory, explains the Great Recession in Japan so well, then why was Keynesian stabilization policy unable to quickly end the contraction? The reasons behind the failure of stabilization policy in Japan are multifaceted and were in many ways the result of the same factors that were responsible for the recession itself.

Monetary Policy in Japan

The Bank of Japan, which is the central bank of Japan, is relatively independent and insulated from political considerations. This is true of many of the powerful ministries that run the Japanese government. These ministries are heavily bureaucratic, and policy is formed in a top-down process directed by life-long government insiders. While this independence from politics can be a good thing in terms of discouraging short-sighted public policies aimed only at advancing special interests, it also makes Japanese decision-making highly conservative and slow to respond to changing economic conditions. As deflation persisted in the Japanese economy, the Bank of Japan was initially very reluctant to abandon its restrictive price level targets. This played a key role in driving prices lower and reducing aggregate demand.

Kuttner and Posen (2001) conducted an extensive review of Japanese monetary policy in the 1990s. They found that the Bank of Japan made only weak efforts to increase the monetary base during most of this period because of, unbelievably, worries about inflation. However, even when the Bank of Japan began to increase the monetary base more aggressively, as it did beginning in 2000, it was not able to generate significant increases in the money supply. For example, between March 2001 and July 2003 the Bank of Japan increased the monetary base by 40 percent, but the money supply only increased by 6 percent. The reason is that the money multiplier fell dramatically compared to where it was when the recession began. The M2 multiplier fell from roughly 13 in 1992 to 10 in 1997 to below 8 in 2002. This drop in the money multiplier was driven by large increases in the currency-to-deposit ratio, which rose from 0.68 in 1992 to 0.85 in 1997 to 1.06 in 2002 (Bank of Japan, 2002). Clearly, Japanese citizens were hoarding more currency as the recession lingered, dampening the money multiplier process and reducing the ability of the Bank of Japan to increase the money supply.

Why did currency holdings rise so dramatically in Japan? The weak positions of Japanese banks definitely played a role. For obvious reasons, Japanese savers were reluctant to place their money in banks that were technically bankrupt, even if deposit insurance was available. However, an even more important reason why currency holdings increased during this recession harkens back to the Keynesian model and its arguments regarding *liquidity traps* and the ineffectiveness of monetary policy during economic contractions. Keynes believed that households and banks tend to increase their holdings of money as a precautionary measure during bad times. This is particularly true when interest rates are low because there is a low opportunity cost of holding money and not placing it in a bank account. Low interest rates also make purchasing bonds unattractive because interest rates are likely to increase, which will reduce the value of any bonds being held. Because of these considerations, Keynes believed that any change in the money supply during recessions is likely to be hoarded, severely reducing the ability of monetary policy to manipulate interest rates, investment, and aggregate demand. As we saw in Figure 16.2, nominal interest rates in Japan were near zero beginning in 1995, indicating that the economy could have been caught in a Keynesian liquidity trap. What is worse, even if the Bank of Japan could have found a way to significantly increase the money supply, nominal interest rates were so close to zero that they could not be driven down any further without eliminating what little incentive there was to hold money in banks. As a result, any increases in the money supply the Bank of Japan created were likely to be hoarded, and the ability of monetary policy to stimulate investment and aggregate demand through further reductions in interest rates was extremely limited.

However, even if monetary policy could not increase the money supply and drive nominal interest rates any lower than they currently were, it does not mean that monetary policy was necessarily powerless to stimulate aggregate demand. Many new Keynesian economists have argued that the Bank of Japan had the ability to stimulate aggregate demand more directly by taking actions to reduce default risk and improve financial fundamentals. In other words, policy makers could have attempted to exploit the balance sheet channels of monetary policy discussed in Chapter 10. For example, one option was for the Bank of Japan to expand the monetary base by buying up long-term government debt. While this might not lead to much of a change in the money supply if the multiplier was low, it might have reduced risk by reducing worries about the size of the public debt in Japan. Lower debt would also have allowed for more expansionary fiscal policy aimed directly at stimulating consumption. Another option would have been to increase the monetary base by lending money directly to firms or by buying corporate financial assets in an effort to stimulate credit directly without relying on banks. Finally, the bank could have bought NPLs, which would not only have provided liquidity to banks but also would have stabilized their financial position so that these new reserves would be lent out. (Note that all of these things were tried by the Federal Reserve during the 2008 global financial crisis, which will be discussed in Chapter 18.)

Regardless of how the monetary base was expanded, however, if it was increased significantly and persistently enough, inflation would eventually begin to rise. If the public came to view the bank's commitment to higher inflation as credible, higher expected inflation would have increased nominal interest rates, encouraged the holding of financial assets, discouraged the hoarding of money, and stabilized banks' balance sheets. Once the health of the financial system improved, traditional monetary policy would once again have become effective. The Bank of Japan, unfortunately, was reluctant to engage in such a radical break from conventional monetary policy and make a real commitment to higher inflation. This has remained true not only during the Great Recession but for at least a decade after the recession was over. The Bank of Japan seemed content to let deflation gradually eat away at the country's financial position.

Fiscal Policy in Japan

Kuttner and Posen (2001) also examined the effects of fiscal policy in Japan since the recession began. They come to the conclusion that while fiscal policy helped stabilize output somewhat, it was too timid to have large benefits. This is primarily because the Japanese government was reluctant to increase government spending and cut taxes simultaneously because of worries about the size of its deficit, which rose to 8 percent of GDP, and the size of its outstanding debt, which rose to more than 150 percent of GDP by 2003 (and stands at roughly 240 percent of GDP in 2013). For example, a 10-year, $500 billion spending package for public works projects (which is small relative to the size of the Japanese economy) was enacted in 1995, but in 1997 an increase in the level of consumption taxes was implemented to cover growing budget deficits (this is just another example of the Japanese government favoring capital projects over consumption). As a result, little net stimulus to aggregate demand was created, and Japan was left with more debt and more capital in an economy that was already overbuilt. Another example of misguided Japanese fiscal policy was the Coupon Issuance Program adopted in 1998. Under this program, roughly $170 of coupons was given to each qualifying Japanese citizen in an effort to stimulate consumption. Of course, just as microeconomic theory would predict, this temporary tax cut simply encouraged consumers to spend their coupons and save more of their income. It had little impact on aggregate demand but significantly increased Japan's budget deficit.

CONCLUSIONS

Two lessons can be learned from the Great Recession in Japan. First, modern macroeconomic theory, particularly Keynesian and new Keynesian theory, can explain many important aspects of the Japanese recession quite well. Specifically, these theories have explained the effects of Japanese policies that encouraged savings and discouraged consumption, the effects of deflation on wages and the financial fundamentals of banks, the causes and effects of asset bubbles and banking crises, the reasons why fragile financial fundamentals led to credit rationing, and how Japan slipped into a low-interest-rate liquidity trap that rendered traditional monetary policy ineffective. If all of these characteristics of the Great Recession in Japan sound familiar, they should. Many of these same factors played important roles in the Great Depression of the 1930s and in the East Asian crisis of 1997–1999, particularly deflation (or depreciation of the exchange rate in the case of the East Asian crisis) and its role in weakening financial fundamentals and creating financial crises that can initiate severe economic contractions. Economists have learned many lessons from these earlier crises, and this has led to a better understanding of the Great Recession in Japan.

The other lesson that can be learned from the Great Recession is that macroeconomic knowledge does not mean a thing if policy makers do not follow sound economic advice. Toshihiko Fukui, the new governor of the Bank of Japan, said that macroeconomic textbooks offered no solution to the problem of ending deflation in Japan. He obviously has not read (or understood) very many macroeconomic textbooks. If bank bailouts, economic stimulus, and structural reforms had been enacted in Japan at the beginning of the recession, it would have helped the Japanese economy begin to grow its way out of its slump much sooner. But by ignoring these reforms, Japan worked its way into a seemingly intractable and unending economic slowdown. In the words of Keynes, "If we do nothing long enough, there will in the end be nothing else that we can do" (Keynes, 1931).

What are the reforms that Japan should have enacted in the 1990s?

1. *Aggressive monetary policy and fiscal policy were needed in Japan, and at the same time.* Japanese policy makers have been reluctant to

significantly loosen monetary policy because of their preoccupation with low inflation. However, a commitment to higher inflation was exactly what was needed in Japan. Even if Japan was in a liquidity trap and future increases in the monetary base would not have led to further reductions in interest rates, this does not mean that monetary policy would have necessarily been ineffective. As new Keynesian models of credit have illustrated, by making a credible commitment to increasing inflation and buying government debt, buying corporate assets, and directly lending money to corporations, the Bank of Japan could have gone a long way toward stabilizing financial fundamentals and reducing risk. Ending deflation sooner would have improved the financial fundamentals of households and banks, loosening credit markets and encouraging consumption and investment. The buying of long-term government debt would also have removed a major constraint on fiscal policy, which is the fear that expansionary fiscal policy would lead to excessive government debt. With this constraint gone, Japanese policy makers would have been freer to aggressively cut taxes and increase government spending (preferably taxes and spending that encourage private consumption) at the same time.

2. *Japan needed to resolve its NPL crisis sooner so that financial intermediation could have begun again.* The threat of a banking collapse hung like a storm cloud over the Japanese economy throughout this recession, leading to protracted credit rationing that severely dampened investment lending, consumer lending, and aggregate demand. In the six years that the crisis was building, the Japanese government was unwilling to tackle most of the difficult issues associated with banking reform. Instead, the government periodically bailed out large banks in a piecemeal process, but never by enough to give life to zombie banks and significantly spur credit. Japan should have aggressively committed itself to a comprehensive bailout program involving buying up bad debts at fair but highly discounted prices (possibly by using new money created by expansionary monetary policy), possibly even nationalizing banks in a process similar to that conducted in Scandinavia during their banking crisis in the 1990s. To avoid future problems with moral hazard incentives created by these bailouts, the Japanese government should have conducted these bailouts in conjunction with imposing new prudential banking regulations that more closely limited the lending practices of banks and also began to sever the close ties that exist between Japanese banks and corporations. The Japanese

government also needed to encourage more direct finance in the form of better and more efficient stock and bond markets, which are under-developed compared to major economies outside the region. Finally, the quickest and maybe the best way to introduce more competition into the system and make these banks more efficient is to allow foreign ownership of Japanese banks and give foreign banks the right to operate within Japan's closed financial markets.

3. *Japan needs to undertake substantial structural reforms aimed at increasing the efficiency of its economy.* Even the Great Recession did not last forever. Japan began to grow, slowly, once again in 2004. However, it suffered another recession when the global financial crisis began in 2008. Japan has left itself vulnerable to future economic contractions unless it engages in significant reform at the microeconomic level aimed at increasing competition and productivity in its economy. This includes opening Japanese domestic markets to international goods. It also includes reducing its reliance on investment and exports to generate aggregate demand and instead switching production towards more consumer goods. The best way to achieve this final objective is to remove the incentives in Japanese fiscal policy that favor savings and investment over consumption.

More than 20 years after the beginning of the Great Recession, Japan is finally attempting these reforms with the election of Shinzo Abe as prime minister. His new economics program, referred to as "Abenomics," is focused on three important policy changes. First, the Bank of Japan will seriously target inflation at a 2 percent level and increase the money supply (and depreciation of the yen) until it gets there. Second, Abe is pushing a set of government spending and tax cut measures aimed at increasing aggregate demand. It will also increase Japan's debt, which already stands at more than 240 percent of GDP. (More on sovereign debt crises in the next chapter.) Third, Abe intends to enact a series of structural reforms aimed at improving competitiveness and efficiency in the domestic sector of the economy. At the time of this writing, these reforms have yet to be pushed through Japan's insulated, inflexible, and bureaucratic political system, which to this point has resisted previous internal and external pressures to reform. The biggest issue facing Japan may not be a liquidity trap but a political trap. Abe seems intent on breaking this political trap, but only time will tell.

For the first time since the Great Recession, the Japanese economy began to grow strongly again in 2013. The return to growth has stabilized the financial fundamentals of banks and firms while boosting the confidence of shaken financial markets, consumers, and investors. However, financial fragility and large levels of bad debt remain in the banking system, while the government's debt has risen to historic levels. In addition, Japan faces a building demographic problem as its low birthrates and limited immigration have led to a rapidly aging population. The days when other countries feared Japan's Great Expansion ended when Japan suffered its Great Recession.

SUGGESTED READINGS

"The Effects of the Great Recession on Central Bank Doctrine and Practice," Ben Bernanke (2011): In a speech given while chairman of the Federal Reserve, Bernanke sketches out how the macroeconomic policy failures of Japan during its Great Recession informed the Federal Reserve's approach when the United States had its own protracted recession in 2008.

"The Great Recession: Lessons for Macroeconomic Policy from Japan," Kenneth Kuttner and Adam Posen (2001): A comprehensive review of the roles played by monetary policy, fiscal policy, and the financial crisis during the Japanese recession

The Holy Grail of Macroeconomics: Lessons from Japan's Great Recession, Richard Koo (2011): A comprehensive review of the Great Recession and an examination of what it tells us about both the Great Depression of the 1920s and the global financial crisis of 2008.

The Return of Depression Economics and the Crisis of 2008, Paul Krugman (2008): Chapter 4 includes an engaging discussion of Japan's boom in the 1980s and slowdown in the 1990s.

SEVENTEEN

Sovereign Debt Crises and the Euro-Zone

INTRODUCTION

Government debt plays an important role in any economy. Sovereign debt provides governments with a means of financing their long-term needs for capital and social welfare programs, which can significantly improve growth and standards of living. Sovereign debt also plays an important role in moderating (and potentially magnifying) the business cycles that threaten the stability of this growth. The ability to issue sovereign bonds allows governments to smooth their spending and tax revenues during a recession via borrowing, helping to stabilize aggregate demand. Also, the buying and selling of sovereign bonds in secondary markets is the primary tool by which central banks change the money supply in order to influence interest rates and stabilize credit. It is no exaggeration to say that the development of sovereign bond markets is one of the greatest economic developments in history. By allowing more governments to gain greater access to credit while at the same time reducing the cost of this credit, increased development in sovereign debt markets has played an important role in the Great Moderation in macroeconomic activity that has occurred in the postwar era.

However, it is always possible to have too much of a good thing. To quote the American founding father Alexander Hamilton, "A national debt, if it is not excessive, will be to us a national blessing." But when it becomes excessive, it then becomes a curse. World sovereign debt more than doubled between 2002 and 2010. Like other forms of debt, sovereign debt has significant financial danger associated with it. The most obvious risk for governments is that sovereign debt requires fixed interest payments that create the possibility of a default in the event that the government becomes unable, or unwilling, to make these payments. As Reinhart and Rogoff (2009) detail in their book *This Time Is Different: Eight Centuries of Financial Folly*, default on sovereign debt is as old as the governments issuing this debt. Almost all countries have experienced at least one sovereign debt default in their history, typically in their early stages of development. Many countries have had multiple defaults and periodic debt crises. For example, France had eight defaults between 1500 and 1800, but zero since. Spain had seven defaults in the 1800s and 13 defaults before 1900, but zero since. More recently, Nigeria has defaulted five times since its independence in 1960, while Argentina has defaulted four times since 1982.

A *sovereign debt crisis (SDC)* is defined as occurring when a government is unable to borrow additional funds or roll over its existing debt in financial markets. Often, this occurs abruptly in a "sudden stop" of credit. While SDCs have been occurring for centuries, something new has occurred over the last two decades in sovereign debt markets. Historically, it is been poorer, developing countries operating within vulnerable political and economic environments that have been most likely to over-borrow and suffer a SDC. Today, however, it is stable, developed countries that have seen their sovereign debt rise to unsustainable levels and are experiencing, or are threatened with, SDCs.

This chapter examines the causes and costs of SDCs as well as the options governments have available to them once a sudden stop in lending occurs. We also discuss the links between sovereign debt crises and other forms of financial crisis, such as banking crises and currency crises. Finally, this chapter takes an extended look at the European Monetary Union (Euro-zone) debt crisis and the severe economic consequences this crisis has had on one of the largest economic regions in the world.

THE GOVERNMENT BUDGET CONSTRAINT AND DEBT CRISES

Governments face a budget constraint like everybody else. However, unlike everybody else, governments have the unique ability to create large levels of financial assets in the form of money and sovereign debt (primarily sovereign bonds) to cover any shortfalls between their spending and its revenue. The government's budget constraint can be summarized as follows:

$$G - T = \Delta MB + \Delta B \qquad (17.1)$$

Any difference between a country's government spending (G) and tax revenue (T)—or the budget deficit (G – T)—must be paid for by issuing new financial assets. These assets can be changes in the monetary base (ΔMB) created by a central bank issuing new currency, creating new bank reserves, or regulating that banks hold more required reserves. The other option is for the government to borrow by issuing new sovereign bonds (ΔB).

Sovereign debt can come in one of two forms. *Domestic debt* is in bonds that are issued under national laws and denominated, typically, in the domestic currency. As a result, they are primarily attractive to domestic residents interested in saving in the same currency in which they receive their income and do most of their spending. Domestic debt is attractive to governments because governments do most of their spending in the domestic currency and because borrowing in the domestic currency allows the government to reduce the exchange rate risk it is exposed to when borrowing in other currencies. The problem with domestic debt for many economies, as discussed in Chapter 15 on the East Asian crisis, is that it is often difficult to sell large amounts of domestic debt in countries that are poorer or have less developed financial markets. However, faster economic growth among emerging market economies has increased the ability of these governments to borrow domestically. While only 40 percent of sovereign debt in emerging countries was domestic in 1900, today over 80 percent of total sovereign debt is domestic.

Sovereign borrowing can also be conducted by issuing *external debt*, or borrowing subject to international financial laws and typically denominated in a foreign currency. External debt can take the form of bonds designed to be sold to private foreign investors or as bilateral or multilateral lending from other governments or from international organizations such as the World Bank or IMF. With the increasing globalization of financial markets, external debt is an increasingly viable option for more economies, and at higher levels, than ever before. The additional risk of external debt, however, is that it must be paid back in a foreign currency. This exposes governments to substantial exchange rate risk that increases the risk of default. In the event of a large depreciation of its currency, a government will find itself in a position where the liabilities it owes in a foreign currency will rise relative to its revenue and assets denominated in the domestic currency, significantly increasing the probability of default on any external debt.

One of the huge disadvantages to savers of purchasing sovereign debt is that it is much easier for governments to default on, or repudiate, their debt than it is for private individuals to default. When it comes to domestic debt, it is the government that makes the laws, giving the government an easy way to "legally" repudiate its debt if it chooses. When it comes to external debt, international bankruptcy laws are notoriously difficult to enforce, particularly when you consider that there can be thousands of different bondholders spread across many different countries. There are also few explicit mechanisms to enforce any legal findings. Historically, lending countries have invaded the debtor country to enforce their claims, as England did in Egypt and Istanbul in 1882 or the United States did in Haiti in 1915. Happily, this no longer is a viable option for modern nation-states.

This being said, governments still have significant incentives to repay their sovereign debt, which in turn creates incentives for investors to purchase this debt. Default can limit the government's future access to borrowing, forcing the government to make difficult and costly fiscal decisions. In the case of domestic debt, default typically means failing to repay the country's own citizens, potentially creating important political consequences. Default on external sovereign bonds can discourage international trade and foreign capital investment because foreigners will likely perceive any default as an increase in the risk of doing business within the country. Finally, there is the possibility, although difficult and time consuming, that assets held abroad by a defaulting country could be seized by foreign creditors.

However, it is occasionally the case that government default is unavoidable. To understand why, consider how the accumulation of debt impacts the government's flows of funds, referred to as the *net transfer equation*:

$$NT = (g - r)D \qquad (17.2)$$

NT is the net transfer (net inflow) of funds to the government, D is the level of sovereign debt, g is the rate of increase in the debt, and r is the average interest rate paid on the debt. Using equation (17.2), we can see that as long as the growth rate of debt accumulation (g) is larger than the interest rate paid on this debt (r), then a government is receiving a net positive inflow of funds from issuing new debt to cover its budget deficits. However, if the growth rate of the debt falls below the level of the interest rate paid on the debt, sovereign debt creates a net outflow of funds that will increase the deficit. In this case, the government must find an alternative way to finance its debt payments or a debt crisis will occur.

One fact is important to note regarding this net transfer equation. Typically, short-term interest rates are lower than long-term interest rates on sovereign debt because short-term debt is exposed to less risk of default and less interest rate risk (changes in the market price of the bond associated with any change in market interest rates). As a result, governments have a significant financial incentive to borrow using short-term debt. However, this also exposes governments to a significant amount of risk. Not only are governments forced to continuously roll over a large fraction of their debt as it expires, but the interest rates that they pay on these bonds are very sensitive to any changes in current market conditions.

Reinhart and Rogoff use historical analysis of past SDCs to identify corollaries with the boom/bust phases of debt crises. The boom phase of a typical SDC is similar to prototypical asset bubbles and credit booms discussed in Chapter 11. During the boom phase, the levels of domestic and external debt increase relative to the size of the economy. This boom phase can be fueled by many factors. For example, belief-based factors such as market psychology or a lack of transparency ("hidden deficits") often play a role. However, fundamentals-based factors such as financial development and financial liberalization also have played a role in many SDCs.

The bust phase of the debt crises occurs after markets lose confidence that the government is either willing or able to meet its debt payments. When perceived risk spikes, a sudden stop in sovereign lending can occur, making the issuance of new debt impossible or prohibitively expensive. As a result, g falls significantly below r, creating a large outflow of funds that cannot be paid given the current level of government spending and tax revenue. The fact that market confidence plays such a large role in triggering debt crises means that debt crises can be self-fulfilling; if markets come to believe that a debt crisis will occur, lending will come to a sudden-stop, interest rates will spike, and a debt crisis will, in fact, occur.

What determines market confidence? Confidence is a function of both the government's ability to pay its debts as well as its perceived willingness to pay its debts. While fundamental indicators such as debt-to-GDP ratios clearly play a role in determining g and r, other less quantifiable factors also play a role, such as the quality of a country's financial institutions, its financial transparency, its future growth prospects, and the government's reputation regarding its commitment to meeting its debt obligations. These factors are often referred to as a government's *debt tolerance*. As a result, it is common to observe governments with relatively low debt-to-GDP levels experiencing SDCs because of a lack of debt tolerance, while some governments with relatively high debt but also high debt tolerance do not.

Debt tolerance differs widely across governments. For example, Reinhart and Rogoff find that only 16 percent of all SDCs occurred at debt-to-GDP levels greater than 100 percent, but 20 percent of SDCs occurred at debt-to-GDP levels of 40 percent or below. The authors find that debt-to-GDP levels above 35 percent appear to significantly increase the probability of default for those governments with histories of default and high inflation. However, this level can be as low as 20 percent for "serial defaulters."

One additional fundamental factor also plays an important role in any SDC, and that is whether markets perceive that the government's primary fiscal problem to be one of illiquidity or insolvency. A government that is insolvent is operating on a path of permanent budget shortfalls that will not change unless the government permanently changes fiscal policy and promotes structural reforms aimed at increasing growth. If judged by markets to be insolvent, a government is much more likely to suffer from a SDC because the policy changes required are much more drastic. On the other hand, a government that is judged to be illiquid has a short-term imbalance in its budget, possibly caused by an economic shock that increases interest rates or a financial crisis that makes it temporarily difficulty to roll over short-term debt. Any government whose basic problem is one of illiquidity is much less likely to suffer from a sudden stop in new lending and a SDC.

POLICY RESPONSES TO DEBT CRISES AND THEIR COSTS

Governments on the precipice of default have several painful policy options that may allow them to avoid default and its consequences. As a first option, governments typically attempt to reschedule their debt, negotiating with their creditors to postpone and/or reduce their debt payments. Debt holders may agree to this because they feel that by accepting something less than full repayment (taking a "haircut") they can maximize their total expected payback. The problem with rescheduling is that there are thousands of different bondholders, each of which has different objectives and each of which has incentives to free-ride off those bondholders who do agree to debt rescheduling (i.e., if you forgive the debts you are owed by a borrower, it increases the chances that the same borrower can pay me back, so I won't forgive).

Regardless of whether rescheduling does or does not take place, any country on the verge of a debt crisis is almost certainly going to have to accept *austerity*: cutting government spending and raising tax revenues. Such austerity measures are certain to provoke a deeper recession by reducing aggregate demand in an environment where the country is already suffering from falling aggregate demand and credit rationing.

As Keynes pointed out, it is not possible for countries to save their way out of crises, particularly during SDCs.

Another painful option for governments to consider is to pay their bills by increasing the monetary base, otherwise known as *seigniorage*. A central bank can purchase bonds issued by the government with increases in the monetary base (through open market operations) and essentially "monetize" any new debt issuances. Of course, a sustained increase in the money supply creates inflation, but this has the positive effect of reducing the real value of any outstanding domestic debt denominated in the local currency. As a result, increasing the monetary base is a particularly effective method of eliminating domestic debt.

Of course, the consequences of the inflation created by monetizing debt are potentially disastrous and can themselves trigger a recession or depression. Inflation increases the cost of using money and, as a result, serves as an implicit tax on most trades within an economy. Inflation also creates confusion and increases risk because it forces prices, which convey important information, to constantly change in often unpredictable ways. This confusion and risk can discourage investment and financial intermediation, reducing output.

When inflation is unanticipated it creates even greater costs. In regards to financial intermediation, unexpected inflation reduces the real value of debt and reduces real interest rates, lowering the net worths of savers and lenders. As a result, as discussed in Chapter 10, inflation increases the costs of credit intermediation and encourages credit rationing. This significantly discourages financial intermediation and also encourages foreign capital flight. By eating away the real value of debt and returns, unexpected inflation also weakens a government's debt tolerance by making it harder for the government to issue additional domestic debt in the local currency.

As an example of how inflation can reduce the net worth of savers, consider Argentina. Between 1960 and 1994, Argentina had an average inflation rate of 127 percent a year. A depositor with $1 billion in an Argentinean bank in 1960 who was forced to keep these deposits in Argentinean pesos would have been left with the real equivalent of 0.0007 American dollars (one-thirteenth of one cent) by the end of 1994!

Not surprisingly, inflations and *hyperinflations* (inflation of greater than 1,000 percent a year) are most likely to occur when countries have issued large amounts of domestic debt denominated in their domestic currency. Reinhart and Rogoff (2009) estimate that inflation rises by an average of 3 percent during defaults on external debt. However, inflation rises by 170 percent during defaults on domestic debt and remains above

100 percent for years following the default. Empirical evidence also suggests that greater central bank independence, which reduces the political pressure to monetize domestic debt during a SDC, is associated with significant reductions in both the level and volatility of inflation across economies (Arnone et al., 2009).

Regardless of the policies adopted to deal with debt crises—default, renegotiation, austerity, or inflation—the economic impact of SDCs is severe. The most obvious reason is that SDCs are often associated with long-lasting effects on a government's ability to borrow and spend. Cruces and Trebesch (2013) find that countries that had a full or partial default are excluded from international financial markets for long periods of time, and even when lending does resume, borrowing costs were an average of 1 percent higher for seven years following the default.

An even more important reason that SDCs are so costly is that they often trigger broader financial crises in currency markets and the banking system. Regarding currency crises, when governments have excessive levels of external debt, SDCs can spark capital flight that can lead to dramatic depreciations of the exchange rate. As discussed in Chapter 15, currency crises reduce wealth, standards of living, and consumer confidence and directly lead to falling aggregate demand and severe recessions.

More importantly, SDCs can directly contribute to banking crises in many different ways. First, as mentioned above, an SDC can cause a currency crisis and capital flight. The resulting depreciation reduces the financial fundamentals of banks that have borrowed in a foreign currency, similar to what occurred during the East Asian banking crisis. Second, SDCs can shake the confidence of the financial system, triggering domestic bank runs. Third, SDCs are often associated with higher inflation that can reduce the real profitability and the asset values of banks. Finally, and most importantly, SDCs directly reduce the financial fundamentals of banks because banks are often the largest holders of government debt. Consistent with these observations, Reinhart and Rogoff (2011) find that booms in external debt levels consistently precede banking crises.

It is important to note that there are many important feedback loops between SDCs and banking crises and that it is also possible for a banking crisis to trigger a SDC. When a country experiences a banking crisis, the resulting spike in interest rates, capital flight, and huge bailouts that occur can directly lead to a SDC.

Taking the direct impact of SDCs in terms of lost wealth and the uncertainty they create, then adding the impacts of the financial crises that typically result, SDCs can be extremely costly. Herndon and colleagues (2013) find that having a debt-to-GDP ratio of greater than 90 percent, even without having a SDC, reduces growth by roughly 1 percent a year. When SDCs do occur, Reinhart and Rogoff (2009) find that, on average, external debt crises lead to 1 percent reduction in GDP. Domestic debt crises are even more costly and reduce GDP by 7 percent on average. However, these average values are somewhat misleading as there is a great deal of variability across countries depending upon the severity of the associated financial crisis and the extent of the default.

THE EURO-ZONE DEBT CRISIS

Between 2008 and 2013, Europe suffered through its slowest growth period since the 1930s. What started as collateral damage from the global financial crisis morphed into a series of SDCs throughout the Euro-zone, but particularly in six crisis countries: Greece, Ireland, Italy, Portugal, Spain, and Cyprus. To casual observers of Europe, the crisis appeared to be easily explainable as just another example of governments living beyond their means. But a closer look at the crisis indicates that the causes and consequences of the Euro-zone crises were different in important ways for each country; understanding these differences provides important insights into the mechanisms behind SDCs and also the costs and benefits of the Euro-zone currency union.

The Euro-Zone Convergence Criteria

The Euro-zone was phased into existence between 1999 and 2002, but the preparations for the Euro began in 1992 with the Maastricht treaty, which required that each member country meet a set of convergence criteria before entering the Euro. These convergence criteria were enhanced in 1997. Each country had to meet five criteria in order to gain membership into the Euro-zone: (1) have long-term interest rates on its sovereign debt within 2 percent of the average of the three European Union (EU) members with the lowest interest rates; (2) keep inflation within 1.5 percent of the average of the three EU members with the lowest inflation rates; (3) join the (EU) fixed exchange rate system already in place, (4) keep its debt-to-GDP ratio at no more than 60 percent; and (5) keep the deficit-to-GDP ratio at no more than 3 percent. While the exact requirements of these criteria are somewhat arbitrary, these convergence criteria were designed to equalize monetary and fiscal policies across member countries so that imbalances would not threaten the stability of the entire zone. The hope was that these convergence criteria would make independent fiscal and monetary policy impossible, because having divergent policies is unsustainable within a monetary union (for the same reasons that a fixed exchange rate system is unsustainable when countries have divergent interest and inflation rates).

These convergence criteria did lead to a great deal of macroeconomic convergence leading up to the Euro's debut. Figure 17.1 presents long-term interest rates within Euro-zone member countries between 1990 and 2000. Clearly, interest rates among member countries were being brought together, and the same could be said for inflation rates as well. Figure 17.2 presents deficit-to-GDP ratios for these same countries. Once again, there was a great deal of convergence. However, note that Greece and Italy barely met the convergence criteria for their deficits by 2000. In fact, neither of these countries was able to meet the debt-to-GDP convergence criteria, which remained above 100 percent in each country. Still, each country was admitted to membership in the Euro-zone.

It was clear to many astute observers at the time that the principles upon which the Euro-zone was built were flawed in a number of important ways. First, and most importantly, while these convergence criteria forced monetary and fiscal discipline on countries before joining the Euro-zone, there were no conditions imposed—and no way to enforce them—after a country was admitted. As a result, there was no way to rein in profligate countries who could now borrow under the auspices of being members

Figure 17.1   Long-term interest rates within the Euro-zone, 1990–2000.

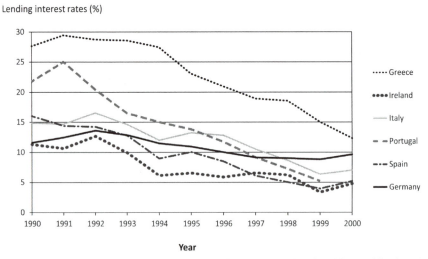

Source: Author's creation based on data from the World Bank available at http://data.worldbank.org/indicator/FR.INR.LEND.

Figure 17.2   Deficit-to-GDP ratios within the Euro-zone, 1990–2000.

Deficit (% of GDP)

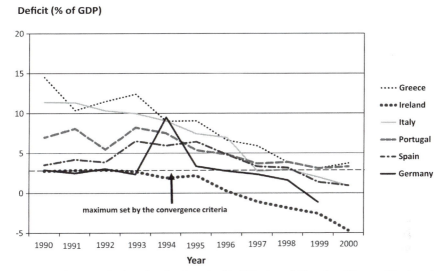

Source: Author's creation based on data from the World Bank available at http://data.worldbank.org/indicator/GC.BAL.CASH.GD.ZS.

of the Euro-zone at much lower interest rates than they could before. In other words, Greece could now borrow like Germany despite the fact that it was not Germany in many important respects.

The second problem is that because the Euro-zone is a monetary union, there are few mechanisms by which each country could respond to a country-specific shock. A member country cannot devalue its currency, it cannot adjust monetary policy, it cannot adjust domestic interest rates, and it has little room to adjust fiscal policy under a monetary union. As a result, almost all of the adjustment to any shock has to take place in output. This means that any recession is likely to be larger for a country in a currency union compared to a country that had the option to devalue and make its exports cheaper or the option to increase monetary policy in an effort to stimulate aggregate demand.

The final problem with the Euro-zone was that there were no mechanisms in place for dealing with any crisis that could result from the misbehavior of member governments. There was no prenuptial agreement for divorce in which a country could be removed from the Euro-zone. There was also no plan in place for dealing with a bailout in the case of a banking crisis or SDC. The European Central Bank (ECB) was initially prohibited from buying the debt of distressed countries, so it was an inadequate lender of last resort. The implication was that if an economic crisis occurred, the policy response would be uncertain and would have to be negotiated at that time among all of the member countries with different objectives and under immense economic and political pressure.

The SDCs in Greece, Italy, Portugal, and Spain

Given these problems with the structure of the Euro-zone, what happened in four of the crisis countries—Greece, Italy, Portugal, and Spain—should have been predictable. As soon as these countries were granted membership into the Euro-zone, their fiscal positions began to deteriorate. In essence, markets began to treat the debt of any country within the Euro-zone as a substitute for any other country within the zone, encouraging cheap and plentiful borrowing among some governments. As can be seen in Figure 17.3, the deficit ratios for Greece, Italy, and Portugal almost immediately jumped above 5 percent upon entry into the Euro-zone.

The Euro-zone also facilitated a domestic credit boom. Because the euro was seen by many investors an attractive currency to save in, banks were able to quickly increase the scale of their operations and move into new financial activities, even when they had little experience in doing so. Bank loans as a percentage of GDP roughly doubled in all four of these

Figure 17.3   Deficit-to-GDP ratios within the Euro-zone, 2000–2012.

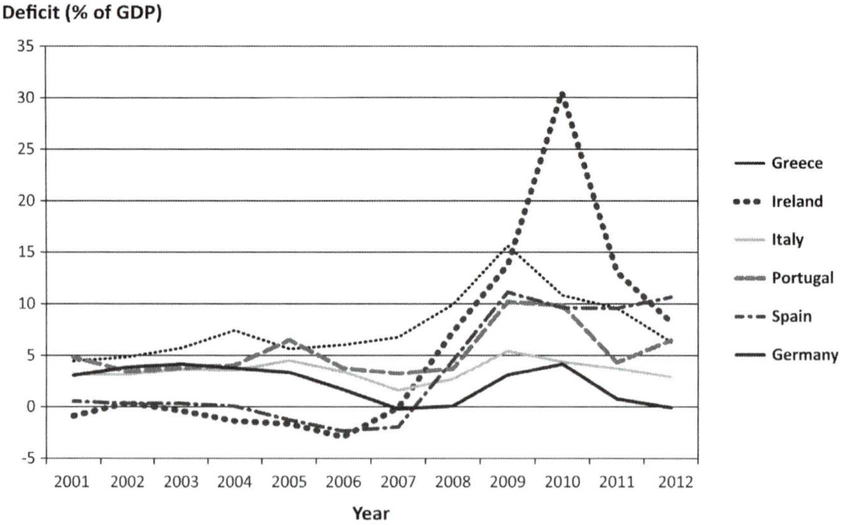

Deficit (% of GDP)

— Greece
••• Ireland
— Italy
— Portugal
—•— Spain
— Germany

Year

Source: Author's creation based on data from the World Bank available at http://data.worldbank.org/indicator/GC.BAL.CASH.GD.ZS.

countries in the decade preceding the Euro-zone crisis. Much of this money fueled asset bubbles, particularly in housing and real estate markets, but also in stock markets and even some durable consumption goods. In other words, risky behavior fueled by moral hazard was running rampant among governments, banks, and asset markets.

The poster child for fiscal irresponsibility was Greece. By 2009, Greece's sovereign debt amounted to more than $1.2 trillion, or roughly $250,000 for every person in the country. Greece's problems were three-fold. First, Greece had a bloated and inefficient public sector. Public workers were paid three times what they were paid in the private sector. Much of Greece's government spending was tied to unprofitable and inefficient state-owned enterprises, particularly in energy and transportation. It also had an unsustainably generous social safety net, where men could retire at 55 years of age (women at 50) and earn a package of benefits greater than what most Greeks earned when they were working.

Second, Greece was generating relatively little tax revenue to pay for all of this generous spending. Roughly 40 percent of income went unreported in Greece, at least twice the rate in other European countries and similar to that of less-developed countries.

Greece's final problem was that it had not been growing as fast as the rest of Europe for an extended period because of the efficiency problems discussed above and the fact that it is a relatively closed economy. In addition, its two largest industries—shipping and tourism—had suffered significantly because of the global financial crisis. Without sufficient economic growth, there was simply not enough income being generated to support the incredible levels of debt that were accumulating throughout the economy.

Taken together, the amount of debt accumulated by the Greek government was clearly unsustainable. Before the crisis Greece's debt-to-GDP ratio was roughly 150 percent and it was paying 6 percent on this debt. As a result, it would then take roughly 9 percent of Greek GDP to just make the payments on the existing debt, setting aside any new debt that it was accumulating. This amounted to nearly one-third of government spending, too large an amount to allow Greek fiscal policy to continue on its precrisis trajectory.

Who was making all of these loans to Greece? In large part, it came from other European banks. European banks were attracted by the slightly higher interest rates Greek debt paid relative to other Euro-zone debt. Many European banks were somehow convinced that Greece could never default as long as it was a member of the Euro-zone. This is despite the fact that, according to Reinhart and Rogoff, Greece has been in partial default of its debt half of the time since its independence in 1821! German banks were particularly large purchasers of Greek debt because Germany was running a large trade surplus with the rest of Europe and was happily assuming the debt of other Euro-zone governments in order to finance the exports it was selling to these countries.

Greece's—and the Euro-zone's—debt problems came to a head in in the summer of 2009 when a new government took power in Greece and began to alert the public that previous governments had been "cooking the books." The new prime minister announced that Greece's actual deficit-to-GDP ratio in 2009 was going to be 12.4 percent instead of the previously estimated 4 percent (it actually turned out to be closer to 14 percent of GDP). Coupled with the fact that global financial markets were already shaken by the global financial crisis, a sovereign debt market panic immediately ensued. Interest rates spiked for Greek debt (rising by more than 35 percent!), capital began to flee the financial system, and it quickly became apparent that Greece would be unable to roll over its short-term debt.

The debt crisis in Greece is an example of how a SDC can trigger a banking crisis. Greek banks, unlike the rest of the Greek economy, were fundamentally sound before the debt crisis. While a credit boom had taken place in Greece (bank loans rose from 31 percent of GDP in 1998 to 84 percent by 2007), Greek banks had not engaged in many of the speculative behaviors (derivatives, credit swaps, etc.) that many global banks had gotten involved in before the global financial crisis. However, Greek banks did make the mistake of holding Greek government bonds, roughly one-fifth of all Greek sovereign bonds outstanding. When it became clear that, regardless of the size of the bailout Greece would receive from the rest of Europe, Greek banks would be taking huge losses on this debt, a banking crisis and a sudden stop in credit took place throughout the country. A sharp recession was inevitable; Greek GDP shrunk by more than 20 percent from its precrisis peak.

Greece did not cause the Euro-zone crisis by itself. Greece is roughly the same proportion of European GDP as Minnesota is of the United States GDP (roughly 1.6 percent). But Greece served as a wake-up call to markets regarding the dangerous levels of sovereign debt in other much larger European countries such as Italy, Spain, and Portugal. As the situation in Greece deteriorated, the banking systems of these countries disintegrated as well and governments began to see their borrowing costs spike, significantly worsening their fiscal positions.

Greece, Italy, and Portugal were all able to receive a series of bailout loans financed by the IMF and other EU (read: German) economies.

These bailouts were attached with standard IMF conditions that imposed austerity, requirements for structural reform, and bank recapitalization to end the banking crises. Negotiating the size and terms of these bailouts was, and continues to be, slow and painful. These bailouts were unpopular in the crisis countries because the austerity conditions imposed were severe and have significantly worsened the recessions in these countries. These bailouts were also unpopular in the noncrisis countries, particularly Germany where these bailouts are seen as financing moral hazard and only justifying the bad behavior of other governments (ignoring the fact that Germany played its own role in facilitating the buildup to the crisis).

The IMF/EU bailouts also required bondholders to renegotiate their payments schedule and accept a "haircut," or a write-off of some of the amounts owed. European banks that were holding Greek bonds were forced to accept a 50 to 75 percent haircut. These haircuts spread the banking crises to other countries in Europe and necessitated bailouts in these countries in order to recapitalize their banking systems. However, even after these write-offs, the sovereign debt levels in Greece remained unsustainably high at 175 percent of GDP.

The ECB has played only a relatively minor role throughout most of the Euro-zone debt crisis. As mentioned before, the ECB was not designed to be a lender of last resort and was specifically prohibited from granting bailouts to governments or banks. The ECB's only mandate was to maintain an inflation target. After two years of negotiation, the ECB became much more aggressive with the ascendency of Mario Draghi to the presidency of the ECB in 2011. The ECB adopted two important programs. First, it began to serve as a lender of last resort through its *longer-term refinancing operations (LTROs)* aimed at allowing European banks to borrow long-term (as long as three years) from the ECB in return for government budgetary reforms. Second, the ECB began to conduct *outright monetary transactions (OMTs)*, which are similar to the program of quantitative easing adopted by the American Federal Reserve in response to its financial crisis (see Chapter 18). The ECB used OMTs to purchase the shorter-term debt (of less than three years) of Euro-zone countries in an attempt to reduce interest rates and stabilize sovereign debt markets. Unfortunately, the size of these OMTs has been much smaller than necessary to sufficiently reduce the costs of borrowing or stabilize aggregate demand in the crisis countries. However, it may be true that by demonstrating its willingness to serve as a lender of last resort and act in order to provide market liquidity, the ECB has stabilized confidence enough to end the most acute phase of the crisis.

The SDCs in Ireland and Cyprus

The SDCs in Ireland and Cyprus differed from those in Greece, Spain, Portugal, and Italy for two reasons. First, the SDCs in Ireland and Cyrus were driven by a banking crisis, not vice versa as in the other European crisis countries. Second, the SDCs were driven primarily by illiquidity concerns, not fundamental insolvency problems that existed before the crisis took place.

Ireland's crisis was surprising to the casual observer because the "Celtic tiger" had been the fastest growing economy in Europe and one of the fastest growing in the world during the previous two decades. Ireland averaged 9.4 percent growth between 1995 and 2000 and nearly 6 percent growth in the 2000s before the crisis. However, to the more careful observer, there were danger signs apparent in this incredible record of growth. Over this same period, Ireland was also experiencing one of the largest credit booms and real estate bubbles in modern history. Bank credit more than tripled in Ireland beginning in 1995, fueling a real estate boom in which prices rose more than 500 percent. By 2006, nearly one-fourth of Irish GDP was related to its booming residential and commercial construction industry.

When the housing bubble burst in the United States, markets immediately looked to Ireland and saw similar circumstances, only worse. By September 2008 (at roughly the same time that Lehman Brothers failed, initiating the financial panic of 2008), housing prices in Ireland had crashed to such an extent that the six largest banks had accumulated losses of roughly 50 percent of their total assets. These losses not only devastated Irish banks but also led to personal financial devastation because of the absence of *nonrecourse mortgages* in Ireland. A nonrecourse mortgage is one in which the owners of a house can walk away from the house and the mortgage if they cannot make the payments (or if the mortgage was worth more than the house) and not place their other personal assets at risk. Ireland's lack of nonrecourse mortgages meant that banks could seize other personal assets in the event of a mortgage default, putting all of a family's wealth at risk and amplifying the impact of the housing bubble on household wealth.

In a panic to prevent a bank run and capital flight, the Irish government guaranteed all of the losses of the six largest banks in Ireland. The Irish government did not just guarantee depositors; it also fully funded the bailouts of all bondholders, foreign and domestic, regardless of the type of bond or activity. No one was asked to take a haircut, regardless of the risk of the financial assets involved. This essentially guaranteed that Ireland's bailout would be one of the costliest in history, eventually accumulating to roughly 90 percent of Irish GDP (the bond guarantees alone cost 40 percent of GDP). Given the size of the collapse in housing prices, the government stood little chance of ever recouping its losses on the bad mortgages it now owned.

As can be seen in Figure 17.3, Ireland's deficit spiked to 32 percent of GDP in 2010 following the bank bailout (a world record), immediately triggering an SDC and another bailout, this time of the government itself, by the IMF and the EU. As a result of the resulting credit crunch, the collapse in confidence, and the severe austerity imposed on Ireland, unemployment rose above 14 percent, the stock market fell by more than 80 percent, and GDP fell by roughly 20 percent between 2010 and 2012.

Cyprus, a small island nation in the Mediterranean, also suffered from a banking crisis driven by a credit boom and real estate bubble. Cyprus has long been an off-shore tax haven for many Europeans, particularly Russians. Waves of foreign capital flowed into the country that were used to finance a real estate boom and large government budget deficits. By 2009, bank deposits had risen to more than 400 percent of GDP, meaning that there was no way the government would ever be able to pay for any bailout in the event of a bank crisis.

When commercial and residential property prices collapsed in 2009 and foreign capital began to leave the country, Cyprus quickly experienced a banking crisis and was exposed to a potential bank bailout that also triggered a SDC. Cyprus appealed for, and eventually received, a bailout from the IMF/EU of more than 50 percent of its GDP. However, the Cyprian bailouts were smaller than the Irish bailout for two reasons. The first is that Cyprus failed to fully guarantee the losses of bondholders and depositors in the Cyprian banking system. Both were forced to take significant haircuts of at least 40 percent. This helped to protect the Cyprian government's finances, but it also increased the possibility of future bank runs given the lack of creditable deposit insurance. These haircuts also imposed huge losses on depositors, both foreign and domestic, that will significantly reduce confidence in the Cyprian financial system and depress future financial and economic development. On the other hand, the fact that someone other than the government incurred losses will certainly reduce future moral hazard behavior in Cyprian banking system.

The second reason this bailout was different from Ireland's is because Cyprus imposed—and the IMF accepted—stringent capital controls that limited the amount of withdrawals that could be made from banks and the capital that could leave the island. The fact that Cyprus was able to adopt these controls but allowed to remain in the Euro-zone was a surprising reversal for both Europe and the IMF. They accepted Cyprus's argument that these controls provided Cyprus time to enact reform, recapitalize banks, and stabilize growth. Once begun, however, such capital controls are difficult to end and often foster corruption and other distorted incentives. The fact that the IMF did not protest certainly signals new thinking from it given that it has traditionally pushed for liberalized capital flows under all circumstances.

CONCLUSIONS

Like all financial assets, sovereign debt provides its holder and its issuer with a risk and a return. For borrowing governments, it provides a way to finance capital and expenditures that have the potential to foster growth and improve standards of living. Of course, it brings with it the temptations of easy money: excessive expenditure, moral hazard, the chance of default, and the possibility of a financial and economic crisis.

Just as Japan faced a lost generation of growth, it is now possible that Europe faces its own lost generation. Like Japan, Europe has faced a financial crisis driven by falling asset prices and insolvency. Europe is also tied to a monetary union that facilitates trade and economic growth in the long run but is not designed to foster stability and manage crises in the short run. Like Japan, although not to the same extent, the Euro-zone has been hamstrung in its inability to enact stabilizing monetary or fiscal policy. Political challenges within the Euro-zone have also delayed bailouts and bank recapitalization, minimizing its effectiveness and magnifying the economic impact of the banking crises.

Given the regularity of SDCs throughout history, Europe will not be the last debt crisis to occur. Where will the next SDC be? Historically, the best bet for the next debt crisis would be an emerging market economy. But today, emerging market economies account for less than 20 percent of all sovereign debt issued and have average debt-to-GDP ratios of less than 40 percent. In developed countries such as the United States, this ratio is at or above 100 percent.

Could the next debt crisis be in the United States? While it is always dangerous to trust the predictions of an economist, there are good reasons to think that a SDC is not imminent in the United States despite its high current deficits driven by the global financial crisis and its projected future deficits driven by higher Social Security and Medicare costs. The United States has many advantages in sovereign debt markets that other countries do not have. First, the dollar is an international currency, meaning that assets denominated in dollars, particularly relatively safe

U.S. government debt, is uniquely attractive to a wide range of investors. And despite its recent dysfunction, the United States has an established democracy and a long record of paying its bills. An additional advantage that the United States possesses is that if a SDC does become imminent, it has also demonstrated the flexibility to adjust its macroeconomic policy, as it did during the global financial crisis. It is to this event that we turn in the next chapter.

SUGGESTED READINGS

Boomerang: Travels in the New Third World, Michael Lewis (2012): A light and, at times, darkly hilarious book chronicling the events and some of the personalities associated with recent debt crises in Iceland and the Euro-zone.

"The European Sovereign Debt Crisis," Philip R. Lane (2012): A detailed economic analysis of the Euro-zone crisis from the perspective of an Irish economist.

This Time Is Different: Eight Centuries of Financial Folly, Carmen Reinhart and Kenneth Rogoff (2009): A historical look at the history and trends in SDCs over the last 500 years across 66 countries on five continents.

EIGHTEEN

The Global Financial Crisis of 2008

INTRODUCTION

If your understanding of macroeconomic events was limited to the two decades between the mid-1980s and the mid-2000s, you would reasonably ask why economists should bother studying business cycles at all. In fact, the academic study of business cycles in macroeconomics did suffer a prolonged slowdown over this time. During the Great Moderation, the United States experienced more than 25 years of growth interrupted by only two mild and short recessions in 1991 and 2001. This was despite the fact that the American economy was subjected to a number of significant shocks: the 1987 stock market crash, the 1991 Gulf War, the 1997 East Asian crisis, the 1997 collapse of the Long Term Capital Management hedge fund, the 9/11 terrorist attacks, the Afghanistan and Iraq wars, and the oil price shock of 2006 to name a few. Throughout this period, however, the U.S. economy remained unsinkable, leading to extended discussions amongst some bullish commentators that a "New Economy" now existed and that business cycles had become obsolete. As we discussed in Chapter 14, empirical evidence from the period suggested that the American economy had become more stable because of its incredibly efficient financial system, its wise and prudent monetary and fiscal policy, its diverse service-based economy, and its ability to create productivity-enhancing technologies. Based on this recent history and this empirical evidence, many economic pundits came to the conclusion that business cycles—in the long run and the short run—were all dead.

How quaint and naïve these discussions seem now. The global financial crisis (GFC) was the worst postwar recession, both in terms of length and depth, in U.S. history. This recession, which began in December 2007 and lasted until the trough in June 2009 (18 months), was associated with a fall in GDP of –4.7 percent and left GDP at 8 percent below where it would have been had it been growing at trend. Making things even worse, the GFC was followed by the worst postrecession GDP growth period and worst postrecession job market performance in American history. Job losses continued to mount after the recession officially ended in mid-2009, and by the end of 2012 roughly 8.8 million jobs had been lost since the start of the recession. This left the American labor market an estimated 12 million jobs below its natural rate of employment; this number of missing jobs is roughly equivalent to the entire population of Ohio, the seventh largest state in the United States. In addition to these losses in income and employment, significant levels of wealth disappeared as a result of the collapse of prices in housing, bond, and stock markets.

Rahm Emanuel, President Obama's chief of staff when he took office during the middle of the crisis, famously said in November 2008 that "You never want a crisis to go to waste." Economists agree, and the GFC has led to the resounding return of the study of recessions and depressions within the profession. It may be that many economists and the American public had forgotten just how much economic contractions hurt. However, when you are in the middle of such a severe recession, it is hard to think about anything else. As we will see in this chapter, modern business cycle theory has a lot to tell us about the causes of this crisis. But this crisis has also identified areas where there is still quite a bit of learning to do, particularly in regards to identifying the most appropriate policies to deal with major financial crises once they begin.

This chapter is organized as follows. It begins with a discussion of the factors that played a role in the buildup to the GFC, primarily focusing on two important changes to the global financial system that occurred in the 1990s and 2000s. The first factor was financial innovation, primarily in the United States but elsewhere as well, that lead to the development of complex new financial assets that could share (and hide) risk in new ways. Foremost among these new financial assets were mortgage-backed securities (MBSs) and financial derivatives such as credit default swaps (CDSs). The second new factor was the growth of global capital flows from poor countries that save, primarily China, to rich countries that consume, primarily the United States. These new capital flows fueled a lending boom in the Unites States that, coupled with financial innovation, set the stage for asset bubbles and a banking crisis that had unexpectedly large consequences across the globe.

The discussion in this chapter then moves to examining the timeline of the GFC, followed by an examination of the wide variety of different fiscal and monetary policies that have been enacted to deal with this crisis. Specifically, we detail the aggressive monetary policy of the Federal Reserve, the bailouts of financial institutions implemented by the U.S. Treasury, fiscal stimulus packages enacted during the crisis, and the financial reforms that were (and are still being) adopted after the crisis. We will discuss why many of these policies worked and why some of them did not live up to expectations.

While this was a global crisis, the focus of this chapter is on the U.S. economy. This is because this is where the crisis began, but also because what happened in the United States is similar to what happened in other countries. However, the impact that the GFC had in tiny Iceland, which suffered the largest depression in world history, and in the Euro-zone debt crisis are examined in some detail towards the end of this chapter. This chapter concludes with a look to the future by asking what we have learned from this crisis and whether it is possible to prevent such economic catastrophes from ever happening again.

WHAT WAS NEW ABOUT THE GLOBAL FINANCIAL SYSTEM OF THE 2000s?

The buildup to the GFC began with two important developments in the global financial system that began to reshape international finance back in the 1980s but did not reach their culmination until the 2000s.

Financial Innovation

The driving force behind the incredible amount of innovation in finance that has taken place over the last three decades has been improvements in IT. Today, savers and investors have better and faster information to make decisions, can make transactions across the globe instantaneously, and have computer programs that can handle the enormous computational requirements of complex financial transactions. Information is the most important input in financial intermediation, and the IT boom has led to a corresponding explosion of financial development.

One of the most important forms of financial innovation has been the securitization of home mortgages. *Securitization* refers to the process of turning assets that are illiquid and difficult to sell into assets that are liquid and easier to sell. Home mortgages are a good example of an illiquid asset because each mortgage is unique, with a different principal amount, different interest rate, different maturity, different default risk, and different probability that the borrower will pay the mortgage off early. As a result, a traditional mortgage was issued by a bank which then held onto this mortgage until the homeowner paid the mortgage off. This was a stable business model, but not particularly profitable or exciting. There was no secondary market for these mortgages because their heterogeneity made them unattractive to small savers or institutional investors.

However, beginning in the 1980s, investment banks (which before this time left mortgage lending to commercial banks) realized that while an individual mortgage is heterogeneous, large pools of mortgages behave in predictable ways. If the pool of mortgages can be made large enough, not only will risk be reduced through diversification, but a financial analyst could quantify the default risk of a pool of loans easier than a single loan. In addition, the other drawbacks of mortgages—their nonstandard amounts, their varying lengths, the fact that they are often paid off early —would disappear if a large enough pool of loans is created where these irregularities would average out. Financial analysts realized that they could issue bonds—referred to as *mortgage-backed securities*—to raise money to buy large portfolios of mortgages and then use the proceeds from the associated mortgage payments to make the interest payments on these bonds (and, of course, make some profit for themselves).

Over time, there has also been an increase in the variety of financial instruments that have been created through securitization. MBSs are often used to create other financial derivatives (which will be discussed later). An addition, many of the MBSs would be broken into different *risk tranches*, or bond groupings based on default risk, in which lower tranches would incur the first default losses, leaving higher tranches to incur losses only if defaults exceeded a specific level. Any MBS could be broken into as many as eight different tranches. Given that many of the loss thresholds for higher tranches were above any historical precedent, many investors considered the highest-tranche MBS to be essentially default-risk free. Home mortgages had recently been very safe: Throughout the 1990s, the default loss rate on mortgages was only 0.15 percent of total mortgage lending.

Mortgage lending and mortgage securitization exploded in the 1990s. By 2007, over 75 percent of all mortgages were securitized. Figure 18.1 presents data on the incredible explosion (and implosion) in the dollar amounts of residential MBSs. Because MBSs were seen as being relatively safe but provided a higher return than many corporate bonds of

Figure 18.1   Residential MBSs issued in the United States.

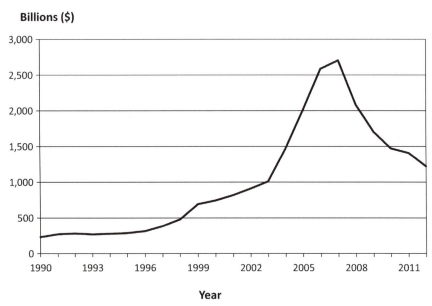

Billions ($)

Year

Source: Author's creation based on data from the Securities Industry and Financial Markets Association available at http://www.sifma.org/uploadedFiles/Research/Statistics/StatisticsFiles/SF-US-Mortgage-Related-SIFMA.xls?n=56256.

similar perceived risk, they were very attractive to savers, both individual and institutional. As more and more savers clamored for these "safe assets," an asset bubble in the MBS bond market grew.

The federal government played a crucial role in facilitating securitization and also enabling the MBS bond bubble. In the United States, one federal government agency has been created to help securitize mortgages, the Government National Mortgage Association (GNMA, or Ginnie Mae), and two other private organizations have been sponsored and subsidized by the government, the Federal National Mortgage Association (FNMA, or Fannie Mae) and the Federal Home Loan Mortgage Corporation (FHLMC, or Freddie Mac). These organizations issue MBSs themselves as well as provide default insurance on mortgages that are securitized by other private financial institutions. By 2008, Fannie Mae and Freddie Mac either held or guaranteed roughly half of all mortgages in the United States, more than $5 trillion. However, the government allowed these organizations to get away with only holding only about 2 percent of this amount as capital to protect against losses. The rationale behind government involvement in the MBS market is to encourage home owner-ship by reducing the risk and costs of mortgage borrowing—primarily by increasing loan maturities and encouraging lower fixed rate mortgage loans—while at the same time increasing the supply of mortgage credit. By increasing information and reducing risk, proponents argued that the government could curtail credit rationing, particularly on the poorest Americans who were most likely to be credit rationed.

The securitization boom, in part facilitated by government policy, was, for a period of time, good for everyone. It was very good for savers and financial institutions, and it was also remarkably good for banks and for homeowners. By selling their mortgages to institutions that engage in securitization (referred to as *loan origination*), banks were able to make their balance sheets more liquid and generate an important new source of revenue without (seemingly) assuming much risk. In addition, securiti-zation increased the supply of funds in the mortgage market, which played a big role in driving down mortgage rates, down payments, and the trans-action costs associated with obtaining mortgages, while at the same time increasing the amount of mortgage lending. Home ownership rates in the United State rose to 70 percent in the 2000s, among the highest rates in the world. Even for those who already had a mortgage, homeowners were now able to refinance their loans at considerably lower rates than were previously possible. Because of all of these factors, mortgage lending boomed in the 2000s.

Securitization also increased the variety of mortgages available to homeowners, including interest-only mortgages and *negative amortiza-tion loans* (in which the buyer pays less than the full interest payment, with the shortfall added to the principal to be repaid at the end of the loan). The best example of a new mortgage market that securitization created is the *subprime mortgage market*, where potential home buyers with low credit ratings could obtain mortgages. Borrowers in the subprime market would never have been able to qualify for a mortgage loan before securi-tization. Some of these borrowers were even able to get loans with little documented income. By early 2007, subprime lending accounted for 20 percent of all new mortgage lending and 10 percent of total mortgage lending ($1.25 trillion in total), up from essentially zero 10 years earlier. On one hand, the aggressive growth in the subprime market had clear social benefits; we know that poorer, newer households are much more likely to be credit rationed than other borrowers. However, the push to minimize credit rationing clearly morphed into moral hazard lending. Many subprime mortgages involved minimal down payments and low ini-tial interest payments that would adjust upward over time. One survey by the National Association of Realtors found that nearly half of all first-time home buyers had zero down payments, and the median first-time home buyer put down only 2 percent of the home's price (Pinto, 2011). As documented by Calomiris and Haber (2014) in their book *Fragile by Design*, the public policy push to expand home ownership was accompanied by a significant weakening of regulated lending standards throughout the 1990s and 2000s. Loan standards were lowered in many ways, but primarily by encouraging the reckless lending of Fannie Mae and Freddie Mac by allowing them to accept limited documentation and maintain little capital to support these loans.

The securitization boom and the MBS bubble in the United States and other countries also played a big role in financing an international housing bubble. Between 1997 and 2006, nominal housing prices increased by more than 100 percent in Australia, Britain, Ireland, Spain, and Sweden. Housing prices rose 85 percent in the United States, the largest real estate gain over any similar period in its history. Mortgage debt rose as housing prices rose. Mortgage debt, which was 20 percent of household income in the United States in 1949, rose to 92 percent of income by 2007 (to a total of nearly $11 trillion).

Securitization was also closely intertwined with other financial innovations, such as financial derivatives. A *financial derivative* is a financial contract whose value is derived from the value of another financial instrument. Many forms of financial derivatives have been developed that allowed people to speculate on or insure themselves against changes in the price of an asset. For example, a *credit default swap* involves creating a contract in which a payment from one party is made to another party in the event of a firm defaulting on a bond or some other financial instrument. A CDS could be purchased from an investment bank or insurance company and used to provide insurance (or a hedge) against default risk if you own such a bond, or it could simply be used as a means of speculating on the failure of a corporation if you do not. A detailed examination of financial derivatives is well beyond the discussion here, but the key point is that financial derivatives can be used to create an almost unlimited number of ways that individuals can swap, share, transfer, speculate, and insure against any form of risk.

Financial innovations such as securitization and financial derivatives increased standards of living by allowing people greater access to cheaper credit, spurring home ownership as well as consumption. However, as stated by Arthur Burns, former chairman of the Federal Reserve, "In a rapidly changing world, the opportunities for making mistakes are legion" (Burns, 1987). Financial innovation increased risk in three ways that, even on the eve of the financial crisis, were not well understood by most financial participants. First, these new financial instruments were risky because of principal/agent problems. In other words, the persons who often issued the assets were not the same people who had to accept the risk associated with them. Consider a securitized mortgage. Because many loan originators (which include commercial banks but also many private companies whose sole purpose was to originate mortgages) sold their mortgages as soon as they were issued, they did not care very much about the default risk of the borrowers. Their only incentive was to create a mortgage that could be sold and leave the risk consequences to others, namely the investment banks and bondholders. In other words, loan originators kept the upside of the loans they made but passed on the potential downside of these loans—conditions under which moral hazard is created. Some loan originators issued "low-doc" loans or "liar loans" in which the borrowers had to provide little real evidence that they had sufficient income or job security to make the payments. These loans were often referred to as NINJA (no income, no job or assets) loans and were made only because the loan originators did not have any "skin in the game" and were not responsible for any losses after the mortgages had been sold (and were allowed to do so given the lax regulatory standards set in place by the federal government). The incentives of loan originators were completely backwards: They had incentives to not conduct due diligence, to not accurately access default risk, and to underprice the mortgage interest rate so that borrowers would appear to be better credit risks and qualify for a mortgage. Stories about the excesses that occurred in the loan origination business are ubiquitous: In one case, a household with only $15,000 in verifiable annual income was able to get a mortgage on a $720,000 house with no money down!

The same principal/agent problem exists in markets for financial derivatives. Derivatives are often sold on unregulated secondary markets (referred to as *over-the-counter derivatives*). In these over-the-counter markets, there is little regulation related to the information that must be provided to the buyer. The seller of a derivative does not have to ensure that the issuer of a derivative has sufficient capital so that it can make a pay-out if required to. The risk that the issuer of a derivative would be unable to meet its financial responsibilities is referred to as *counterparty risk*. Once again, the lack of information coupled with a lack of "skin in the game" creates moral hazard incentives and encourages excessively risky behavior.

The second reason these new instruments were risky was because they were extremely complex. As a result, often the true risk associated with these assets could not be accurately assessed because of "unknown unknowns." For example, the CDS an investor purchases as insurance against a default on a bond may not actually provide any insurance because of counterparty risk in which the issuer of the derivative also defaults. But this counterparty risk is difficult for the holder of any CDS to ascertain without a full knowledge of the issuer's financial fundamentals.

The true risk of an MBS is also notoriously hard to assess for at least two reasons. First, the diversification that exists within a MBS provides insurance against an individual mortgage default, but if a large number of mortgages default at the same time because of some common shock, the advantages of diversification disappear. Calculating the probability that there will be a high correlation between mortgage defaults is an exceedingly complex and highly speculative exercise, one that is subject to a great deal of uncertainty. However, many financial analysts simply assumed that defaults are independent of each other based on the proposition that all real estate markets are local (i.e., the old real estate adage that the three most important things in real estate are location, location, location). As a result, many people significantly underestimated default risk and overestimated the value of diversification. Second, most MBSs were broken into tranches, and calculating the risk of each tranche was incredibly difficult. To understand one reason why this is, consider a high-tranche MBS that would only suffer losses above 10 percent of the pool. This MBS suffers no losses until it hits the seemingly unlikely limit of 10 percent. But once it reaches this point, it incurs 100 percent of all additional losses. In other words, the risk associated with this MBS tranche is discontinuous and goes from extremely low to extremely high the instant it reaches its threshold. In fact, many high-tranche MBSs eventually incurred larger losses than lower tranches. Accurately calculating the risk inherent in any such MBS with tranches is incredibly difficult, particularly because investors had such a small historical record to rely upon.

Finally, the third unique risk of these new financial instruments was that they created risk that did not show up on financial statements, so the true riskiness of financial institutions or in the financial system was largely hidden from investors. For example, a financial institution might issue a CDS that exposes the firm to a huge amount of downside risk in the event of a default. But until that default happens, the impact of this swap on the institution's balance sheet is minimal and the true risk is largely hidden to outside observers, particularly if issued on over-the-counter markets with no capital requirements. For this reason, in 2003 Warren Buffet famously referred to derivatives as "financial weapons of mass destruction."

The same lack of information holds for MBSs in which the bondholders have no way of knowing the true credit risk of all of the borrowers associated with each of the mortgages backing their bonds and each of the tranches the MBS were broken into. A bondholder cannot learn this information simply by looking at the financial statements of the financial institution that issued the MBS.

Finally, many financial institutions were able to hide many of their riskiest activities in *shadow banks*, or seemingly independent banks in which other large financial institutions were the major shareholders. These shadow banks engaged in many of the riskiest MBS and derivative activities. However, the only thing that shows up on the balance sheets of well-known financial institutions was the value of the stock they held in these companies. The true underlying risk was hidden.

To be clear, it was not financial innovation *per se* that caused the financial crisis. But the end result of financial development coupled with a willing lack of prudential regulatory evolution to keep up with this innovation was that financial systems across the globe became more efficient, more profitable, much larger, more interconnected, and much riskier than they had ever been before.

Foreign Capital Flows and the Global Savings Imbalance

Since the dawn of international finance, global capital has primarily flowed between developed countries, with a small amount leaking out to underdeveloped economies. Twenty-five years ago, it would have been hard to fathom a world in which China was lending huge amounts of money to the United States, but that is exactly what came to pass beginning in the 1990s. The huge imbalances between the two countries were in part the outcome of deliberate policy and in part the result of the publics' and policy makers' inability to constrain themselves.

Let's begin by looking at China. China's high rate of savings and current account surpluses are the direct result of their export-orientated development policy. One of the primary aims of China's economic policy has been to encourage the domestic manufacturing of goods that can be sold abroad in order to produce employment for the millions of Chinese that are moving from rural to urban areas every year. One way that China has made its exports competitive is to keep their currency, the RMB, cheap relative to the dollar; this makes Chinese goods less expensive relative to American goods. To keep the RMB cheap, China continually sells RMB for dollar assets, creating what amounts to a huge loan to the United States. In order to afford this massive lending to the United States, as well as all the massive public capital projects China is building, private consumption must purposely be kept low and private savings kept high. As a result, one of the principal aims of Chinese macroeconomic policy is to discourage private consumption and encourage private savings so that exports, particularly to the United States, can thrive. The current account of the United States has been negative since the early 1980s, reflecting the fact that the United States has been running consistent trade deficits since that time. The flip side of running a current account deficit is foreign borrowing: The United States has also been a net foreign borrower since the early 1980s. The United States' persistent trade deficits are largely the result of its low national savings rate. This low savings rate is a function of high federal government budget deficits and the American public's willingness to borrow freely and consume liberally. The United States, among all of the countries in the world, has had the unique advantage of being able to borrow freely from abroad for more than two decades in order to fund its trade deficits. It is able to do this because of its high level of debt tolerance, its (relatively) stable and developed financial markets, the dollar's unique role as an international currency, and China's (and other countries') desire to facilitate this borrowing as part of their export promotion strategy.

This codependent macroeconomic relationship between China and the United States powered growth in both countries beginning in the mid-1990s. But with this codependency came risks, and these risks were identified well before the GFC by many economists. Ben Bernanke (2005), future chairman of the Federal Reserve, warned of the dangers of this codependency in a speech entitled "The Global Savings Glut and the U.S. Current Account Deficit." In this speech, Bernanke discussed how the high savings rate in China created an abundance of "cheap money," much of it ending up in the United States because of the "depth and sophistication of the country's financial markets," the result of the financial innovation and development discussed in the previous section. The problem with all of this cheap money is that it distorted economic decisions. By driving interest rates to historic lows, it encouraged both the American government and its citizens to overconsume, overaccumulate debt, and overinflate their asset prices. On the other hand, Chinese citizens found themselves with lower standards of living, low returns on their savings, and economic growth that was highly dependent upon American consumption. Bernanke's worry, shared by many economists at the time, was that this situation was not sustainable. At what point would debt levels get too high and foreign lenders (including the Chinese government) stop lending to American consumers? If and when this happened, the United States would be forced to immediately make dramatic increases in its savings and drastic reductions in its consumption. This would collapse growth in the United States, China, and across the globe. Before the GFC, few would have predicted how quickly and dramatically such a scenario could actually occur.

A BRIEF TIMELINE OF THE GFC

The crisis began not with a bang, but with a whimper. In July 2007, interest rates ticked upward. Bankruptcies in the subprime market were already up by 40 percent in 2006, and by early 2007 more than 15 percent of all subprime borrowers were behind in their payments. But the interest rate increase in July was a tipping point. Almost immediately, bankruptcies in the subprime market spiked dramatically and housing prices began to tumble as demand for new housing dried up. Quickly, the financial fundamentals of lenders and borrowers began to deteriorate. For borrowers, the acute decline in housing prices in many of the major metropolitan areas was particularly damaging to household net worths. For lenders, financial fundamentals declined because of the rise in defaults and foreclosures. By August 2007, fundamentals in the banking system had deteriorated to the point that there was already talk of a liquidity and credit crisis.

Why did bankruptcies and foreclosures rise so quickly following this increase in interest rates? The reason had to do with the nature of subprime mortgages. Many were adjustable rate mortgages, and many of these had low introductory "teaser" interest rates that ratcheted up significantly over time. In addition, the collateral for all of these mortgages were lower-end properties that were the first and fastest to fall in value when real estate prices began to drop. Also, most of these mortgage borrowers had lower incomes and few reserves to fall back on in response to even slightly higher interest rates (i.e., NINJA loans). Finally, even in the cases where mortgage holders could still make their mortgage payments, many saw that the values of their homes were now *underwater*, meaning that their home's value was significantly less than the amount owed on their mortgage. When this is the case, a homeowner can save thousands of dollars by simply defaulting and turning the home over to the bank, suffering no further financial obligations because most mortgages in the United States are no-recourse loans. In finance parlance, many subprime homeowners found themselves with a valuable *put*, or the option to sell something at a favorable price, and took advantage of it. Default rates were much more responsive to changes in interest rates during this downturn than during previous housing downturns because the low down payments associated with subprime loans increased the likelihood that houses would become underwater and homeowners would exercise their puts.

Problems at two large financial institutions were the first warning signs to the general public that something serious was going on. Northern Rock, the fourth largest bank in England and one which was highly invested in the U.S. subprime market, appealed to the Bank of England for an emergency loan in September 2007. At the time, England did not have fully insured bank deposits. As a result, depositors in Northern Rock immediately panicked, leading to the first bank run in England since 1866. The British government quickly nationalized the bank and acted to fully insure bank deposits, but panic was already beginning to spread. Later that month, Countrywide, an American bank that had specialized in subprime mortgages, had to seek a merger to avoid bankruptcy.

March 2008 brought the next phase of the crisis: The large investment banks that securitized mortgages, held billions in MBSs, and also issued billions of dollars of derivatives associated with these MBSs began to suffer huge losses. Bear Sterns, one of the oldest Wall Street investment banks, was heavily invested in the subprime market. In an effort to stay liquid, it was forced to sell its assets, primarily MBSs, at depressed prices, losing $18 billion during its last week of independence. In an effort to prevent its failure, the Federal Reserve facilitated a "shotgun" merger with JP Morgan by lending Morgan $13 billion and providing guarantees to Morgan that it would compensate it for any losses suffered by Bear's portfolio above a certain threshold.

This was the first time that the Fed had ever lent money to financial institutions—Bear Stearns and JP Morgan—that were not commercial banks. The Fed was widely criticized at the time given that such investment banks were not regulated by the Fed and not insured by the FDIC. While the Fed is generally prohibited from making these kinds of loans, it invoked a little-used emergency authority clause in its charter (the first time since the 1930s) empowering it to make loans to anyone under "unusual and exigent circumstances." The Federal Reserve judged that Bear Stearns was not only "too big to fail" but also "too interconnected to fail." Bear Stearns's collapse would endanger the entire financial system in two specific ways. First, many of the financial transactions Bear and other investment banks were engaged in were highly complex, meaning that very few people fully understood what they were doing. As a result, no one had a clear idea of the risk Bear and other institutions were really exposed to, creating the conditions for panic. Risk was also hidden in the shadow banking system, where the major banks were investors in conjunction with Bear Stearns in an effort to keep risky activities off of their balance sheets.

Second, and maybe most importantly, various financial markets are increasingly connected with every other financial market. This is in part because of herding behavior, where many investment fund managers that followed Bear on its way up quickly fled from Bear when it began to suffer losses, depriving Bear of resources it needed to stay afloat. Markets are also closely correlated because of counterparty risk. A few losses to the system put everyone at risk because every financial institution is dependent upon other institutions to pay their financial obligations. The shadow banking system also exposed banks to losses in other parts of the financial system. Finally, markets are correlated because the supply of credit is contingent upon strong financial fundamentals and stable risk perceptions. As explained in new Keynesian models of credit, when losses occur and financial fundamentals deteriorate, lenders begin to reevaluate the amount of risk they are willing to assume. After significant losses, lenders will increase their costs of credit and tighten credit limits in an attempt to deleverage. This has an impact on everyone, even on those who have not yet suffered any deterioration in their fundamentals. Thus, many corporations and other financial institutions saw their access to credit disappear when Bear was on the verge of failing, just when they needed it most, and this credit rationing would get even worse if Bear actually failed.

Critics charged that Bear was not too big to fail. Instead, critics believed that these loans would greatly exacerbating future moral hazard throughout the financial system by serving as a lasting example of how bad managers can escape the consequences of their actions. When the Fed extended this emergency authority to lend to financial institutions it had never regulated, in their view the Fed was taking unprecedented and extralegal actions that only rewarded the bad behavior of a select few because of the power and privilege they possessed, not for any social good.

During the next phase of the crisis, which took place in July 2008, the federal government turned its implicit guarantees of Fannie Mae and Freddie Mac into explicit guarantees and nationalized their assets in order to prevent their failure. Both institutions heavily invested in MBSs but were allowed to carry little capital; their implicit backing by the government was seen as sufficient protection against losses. This was one of the largest nationalizations in world history: The responsibility for nearly $5 trillion in assets held by these two mortgage lending giants was assumed by the federal government.

For a while, piecemeal bailouts by the federal government, increased lending by the Federal Reserve, and rapid mergers among financial institutions seemed to soothe financial panic. However, the acute stage of the crisis began in September 2008, roughly one year after the crisis first began. On September 14, the investment bank Lehman Brothers failed. Before it failed, the Treasury Department said that no public money was available to Lehman as it was judged to be fundamentally insolvent and not too big to fail. The Federal Reserve said that Lehman did not have sufficient collateral to back any loan from the Fed without a merger partner. Without this public money, potential merger options disappeared and Lehman was forced to close its doors.

It was at this point that unsettled financial markets moved to outright panic. Liquidity dried up in markets, a "flight to quality" took place across international markets, interest rates across assets spiked, asset prices collapsed, and almost every large investment bank in the United States was now in danger of failing. The insurance giant AIG, which before the crisis was one of only six corporations with the highest AAA credit rating but which was also highly involved in derivative markets, also teetered on the brink of collapse. The collapse of AIG would have imposed counterparty losses on almost every major financial institution and further wrecked financial fundamentals.

Maybe the most startling development in September 2008 was the run on the Reserve Primary Fund (RPF), a fund that commercial banks use to hold deposits in money market accounts. The RPF primarily holds low-risk assets: T-bills and *commercial paper* (short-term debt of the highest-rated corporations). But with the failure of Lehman and the resulting panic in the commercial paper market, the RPF suffered heavy losses which, in turn, exposed commercial banks to heavy losses. Commercial banks started a run on RFP, and as the losses built there was a real worry that if this process was allowed to run its course, the failure of RFP would leave many commercial banks without enough resources to repay their depositors and trigger a bank run. It was at this point that the Federal Reserve and the U.S. Treasury realized that they were on the brink of a major banking crisis.

Within one week of Lehman's failure, all of the large, independent investment banks in the United States had disappeared. Many investment banks merged with commercial banks, such as Merrill Lynch. Other investment banks agreed to become a banking holding company and be regulated by the Federal Reserve, such as Goldman Sachs, in exchange for loans. Also, many commercial banks were either forced to merge or failed. This includes Washington Mutual, which was the largest bank failure in American history.

While the recession technically began in December 2007, it was during the peak of the financial crisis in September 2008 that the collapse of the real economy began to pick up pace. GDP growth in the fourth quarter of 2008 was –6.3 percent, the quarterly largest contraction in over 25 years. Unemployment also reached 25-year highs by March 2009. Employment fell by more than 600,000 each month for the first three months of 2009, the first time the U.S. economy had lost so many jobs in such a short period of time since the Great Depression. The stock market fell to 10-year lows, and real estate prices dropped 30 percent below previous highs.

At every step in this rapid decline, the story was the same: Deterioration in the financial fundamentals of borrowers and lenders led to increases in perceived risk and a tightening of credit. As credit became more difficult to obtain, liquidity needs forced panic selling, pushing down the prices of real estate and other assets even further. As the value of assets fell, defaults rose, more losses were incurred, and the financial crisis worsened in a vicious cycle. The macroeconomic models discussed earlier, particularly new Keynesian models of credit such as models of credit rationing, describe this process quiet well. What was so scary to many economists was not what happened but how quickly and overwhelmingly it happened.

THE IMPACT OF GOVERNMENT BAILOUTS AND STABILIZATION POLICY

The U.S. government's response to the crisis was generally reactive, not proactive, and piecemeal, not strategic and comprehensive. The first government entity to enter the fray was the Federal Reserve. Under the guidance of Ben Bernanke, the Fed quickly recognized the dangers posed by crumbling financial fundamentals and skyrocketing risk and how they threatened to bring credit throughout the economy to a sudden stop. The Federal Reserve moved to cut the federal funds interest rate on overnight loans between banks beginning in late 2007, and by late 2008 the target was reduced all the way down to 0.25 percent, the lowest in history. The Fed aggressively expanded loans to commercial banks for longer periods of time and loosened its lending standards. In March 2008, the Fed announced additional plans to purchase more than $1 trillion in MBSs and T-bonds from banks to solidify their balance sheets. It also moved to purchase securities backed with commercial and business loans in order to encourage lending that would support consumption and investment spending. The Federal Reserve also guaranteed lending that facilitated mergers to save struggling financial institutions, such as Bear Stearns.

However, when the acute phase of the crisis began in September 2008, the Federal Reserve was forced to rethink how it was playing its role as lender of last resort. Prior to the failure of Lehman and run on the RPF, the Fed had been focused on lending to individual entities, particularly commercial banks. When the problems with the RPF began, however, the Fed realized that it was not going to be possible to continue to lend to individual institutions with liquidity problems—there were likely to be too many of them if markets continued to collapse. Instead, the best way to protect the system was to stabilize the overall market, not just market participants. The Fed began to purchase commercial paper from both banks and nonbanks in an attempt to provide liquidity and stabilize prices in the commercial paper market. As this market settled down, money started to flow back and the RPF and the overall banking system stabilized. After September 2008, the Fed began similar programs in other markets, particularly the MBS market. It left the bailouts of individual institutions to the U.S. Treasury and the FDIC. (This is an arrangement that is now codified into law in the Dodd–Frank financial reform act, which is discussed later.) As can be seen in Figure 18.2, between 2007 and 2010 the Fed tripled the size of its balance sheet (by roughly $2 trillion!) by making loans to individual institutions early in the crisis and by purchasing financial assets to stabilize entire markets later in the crisis.

Figure 18.2   Federal Reserve assets during the GFC.

Billions ($)

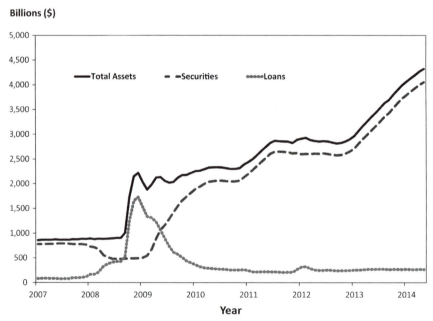

Source: Author's creation based on data from the St. Louis Federal Reserve Bank FRED database available at: http://research.stlouisfed.org/fred2/.

In addition, the Federal Reserve engaged in a number of additional unconventional policies not directly related to the size of its balance sheet. The Fed extended loans to banks for longer periods of time. Given that short-term interest rates were close to zero, the Fed also tried to push longer-term interest rates to zero by changing the composition of its balance sheet through *quantitative easing*: purchasing long-term T-bonds and MBSs issued by Fannie Mae or Freddie Mac (not short-term T-bills as is standard practice in open market operations). Finally, the Fed made a verbal commitment to keep short-term interest rates low for an extended period of time after the recession was over in an effort to ensure that long-term interest rates stayed low.

Despite all of these actions, many of the fears of Keynesians as well as new Keynesians were realized: A central bank's power to influence the economy in a period of high risk and low interest rates has its limits. According to a well-used phrase, the Fed found itself "pushing on a string." When perceived risk is very high, banks will not lend even if interest rates are low and funds from the central bank are easy to obtain (Keynes's liquidity trap). Clearly, this occurred during the GFC. Figure 18.3 presents the level of total reserves, required reserves, and excess reserves in the banking system. As the Fed greatly expanded the money supply and total reserves during the GFC, banks did not lend these new reserves but instead held them as excess reserves. The Fed was able to use unconventional methods—which focused not only on reducing interest rates but also on reducing risk perceptions—to end the full-scale panic and moderate the decline in credit, but it was not able to prevent a decline in credit from occurring. But this is a much better outcome than if the Fed refused to break from convention at all (as the Bank of Japan failed to do during their Great Recession).

The bailout policy response of the U.S. Treasury was much more incoherent, in part because the acute stage of the crisis occurred during the last month of a presidential election. Another problem was that unlike the failure of a traditional commercial bank where the government has a legal responsibility to assume the bank's liabilities and assets, bailing out investment banks and other financial institutions meant buying assets that were clearly private, with no clear rules about what is equitable and what is necessary. For example, in some cases stock and bond holders were forced to take a haircut (e.g., Bear Stearns stockholders), but in many cases no one was forced to take losses. The argument for not imposing haircuts was to limit panic and stabilize markets as quickly as possible. Imposing across-the-board haircuts may have sparked more panic and would have created a number of time-consuming legal complications.

Figure 18.3   Total reserves, required reserves, and excess reserves.

Billions ($)

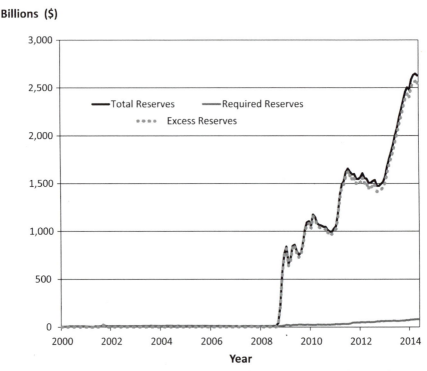

Source: Author's creation based on data from the St. Louis Federal Reserve Bank FRED database available at: http://research.stlouisfed.org/fred2/.

On the other hand, not imposing losses, even in the most egregious examples of mismanagement (e.g., AIG), rewarded risky behavior and encouraged future moral hazard.

After first taking the lead in institutional bailouts, the Federal Reserve made the argument to the Bush administration that it could not continue to do so for two reasons. First, the Fed was obligated by law to require sufficient collateral for its loans, limiting the eligibility of certain candidates who lacked collateral (e.g., Lehman). Second, because it is not a political organization, the Fed believed that future bailouts of such a large scale must take place within the traditional political process in order to be seen as legitimate. In late September 2008, after false starts by the Bush administration and a failed first vote, Congress passed the $700 billion Troubled Asset Relief Program (TARP) in late September 2008. TARP was managed by the U.S. Treasury with the stated aim of improving the financial fundamentals of financial institutions so that they could start lending again.

One problem with TARP was that there were no clear guidelines regarding about how bailouts were to be conducted, and the Bush administration initially lacked a clear vision for implementation. Initially, the Bush administration Treasury wanted to buy "bad" assets from institutions in order to provide them with more "good" assets, so they could resume lending. The rationale for this was largely the political need to avoid looking like the Treasury was nationalizing the banks. Then, after the lobbying efforts of Bernanke and many economists inside and outside of government, the Treasury decided to purchase *preferred equity* in financial institutions, which is stock that has no voting rights, a guaranteed return (in this case, 5 percent), and a higher status than common stock in the case of default. The aim here was to add capital to banks, reduce leverage, and improve financial fundamentals so that banks would no longer fear failure and would begin to lend again. Buying capital also avoided the need to figure out what price bad assets should be purchased at. While in hindsight it is clear to most economists that purchasing capital was the right decision, the lack of a clear plan and also of clear oversight created the dangerous impression that the Treasury did not know what it was doing at the exact time it was supposed to calming fears.

Another problem with the initial TARP is that despite the astronomical price tag, $700 billion, this was only 5 percent of American GDP. This number was essentially picked out of thin air to be sufficiently "overwhelming." But looking back at Table 11.1, 5 percent of GDP is nowhere near the cost of the largest bailouts in history. Regardless of exactly how the bailout was to be conducted, it could have been too little, too late. (Remember that, in comparison, the Fed increased its balance sheet by $2 trillion, nearly three times the size of TARP.)

One final problem with the implementation of TARP was that the Bush Treasury insisted that all banks would be required to purchase preferred capital under the program. The logic for this was to avoid stigmatizing banks that did ask for capital. But it also forced the Treasury to quickly use up a large portion of its fund, leaving it potentially vulnerable should the crisis have worsened. (As it worked out, only $430 billion of the $700 billion available was ever lent out. This includes bailouts for the auto industry and foreclosure mitigation efforts.)

The incoming Obama administration was left $350 billion from the original $700 billion allocated by Congress for financial bailouts under TARP. It continued injecting capital into banks. It also used TARP money for bailouts of General Motors, Ford, and Chrysler. Finally, in an effort to enhance transparency in return for bailout money, the Treasury enacted highly public "stress tests" that were aimed at identifying the capital needs and the potential financial weaknesses of every major financial institution. The positive results from tests—and the data that was shared as a result of them—went a long way toward convincing markets that TARP had stabilized financial fundamentals enough to make more bad surprises from surviving banks unlikely.

By 2010, it was clear to most economists that these bailouts had worked and that the financial crisis had passed its trough. According to one estimate by Blinder and Zandi (2010), the bailouts conducted by the Fed and through TARP increased GDP by roughly 6 percent (roughly $900 billion) compared to its eventual path without the bailouts and saved nearly 4.6 million jobs.

The recipients of bailouts began paying back the government's money soon after markets stabilized, ahead of schedule. By 2014, the net cost to the federal government of the TARP program was only $40 billion. Of these losses, almost all were incurred by Fannie Mae and Freddie Mac; the private sector bailouts were profitable for the government. This $40 billion cost is less than 0.2 percent of GDP. When weighed against the 6 percent of GDP that Blinder and Zandi estimate was saved by the bailouts, the benefits of TARP were 30 times the eventual cost. It can be argued that TARP ended up being the cheapest and most effective bailout program in world history and one of the most effective public policy programs in recent American history.

Despite these successes, TARP suffered from two fundamental and persistent problems. First, while banks now had more capital and better financial fundamentals, banks were still too scared to start lending again and credit rationing continued, serving as a huge drag on the economic recovery. Second, the perception that bad behavior was being rewarded coupled with outrage that the TARP legislation did not limit the huge compensation and bonus packages received by bank executives made TARP a political liability. In the words of Obama's Treasury Secretary Tim Geithner, "We saved the economy, but we kind of lost the public doing it." A Pew research poll in 2012 reported only 39 percent approval for the program. In this same poll, only 15 percent of the population realized that most of TARP's $700 billion fund has been paid back.

The Obama administration also used TARP money to subsidize mortgage restructuring in an effort to help households with underwater mortgages stay in their houses and prevent more defaults and foreclosures. By the beginning of 2009, real estate prices had fallen by 30 percent from their 2006 highs, and nearly 27 percent of the 52 million homeowners in the United States were underwater and owed more on their mortgages than their house was worth. Many other homeowners found themselves paying mortgage rates well above market rates but could not refinance because of the credit crunch. The plan the Obama administration implemented subsidized homeowners who were no more than 5 percent underwater so that they could refinance or modify their existing mortgages in order to reduce their payments. Unfortunately, this plan had three critical problems. First, it did nothing to help those who were underwater by more than 5 percent (to do so would have been too expensive). Second, the reworking of many first mortgages was blocked by the holders of second mortgages, making many banks reluctant to work with the program. Third, largely because of these legal issues, the process was so complicated and slow that many underwater homeowners failed to see it through to the end. Only 1.3 million homeowners of the estimated 5 million eligible for the plan actually were able to refinance their mortgages.

There was a huge difference between the Obama and the Bush administrations' approach in the area of fiscal policy. The Economic Stimulus Act of 2008 passed under Bush focused on tax incentives for investment and tax rebates of $300 per taxpayer (total cost: $152 billion, or a little more than 1 percent of GDP). By focusing on tax cuts that were small and temporary, this act did little to stimulate aggregate demand and stabilize output. The Obama administration proposed and passed a much more ambitious $787 billion stimulus package of tax cuts and government spending aimed at increasing aggregate demand and restoring consumer confidence. This package was a return to Keynesian-style fiscal policy on a scale not seen since the Great Depression, although still relatively modest (5.5 percent of GDP) relative to the size of the economy. While the stimulus package undoubtedly helped to stabilize growth, its performance was disappointing relative to the overly optimistic forecasts that the Obama administration initially touted. These initial forecasts were flawed because they were based on overly optimistic baseline projections of postcrisis growth regardless of whether the stimulus was passed or not.

Another significant problem with the Obama stimulus package was that it contributed to the burgeoning federal debt. The federal deficit rose to $1.3 trillion, or 9 percent of GDP, in 2011. This is a level that would have triggered a sovereign debt crisis in most other countries and is unsustainable even for the United States. While less than one-sixth of this deficit was attributable to the Obama stimulus package (most was attributable to automatic stabilizers such as falling tax receipts and an increase in social safety net payments), fears about the consequences of such large deficits directly reduced consumer confidence. It also led to protracted political squabbling and postrecession contractionary fiscal policy that contributed to the very slow postrecession recovery.

THE GFC ACROSS THE GLOBE

As global income fell during 2008, no economy escaped the pain associated with the GFC. Japan and most of Europe suffered recessions between 2008 and 2009, but less developed countries contracted as well. Growth in sub-Saharan Africa fell by 5 percent in 2008 and 2 percent in 2009, pushing nearly 7 million people into poverty.

Why were other countries impacted by the events in the United States? Because the United States is the hub of a complex network of financial and trade linkages across countries, other countries found themselves linked to the United States in ways that they may not have imagined before the crisis. The first linkage was through exposure to the American subprime market. Many foreign banks purchased American MBSs based on the assumption that these bonds were "safe as houses." Banking crises in England and Ireland were directly linked to problems in the American subprime market.

A second linkage was through global financial institutions, many of which have operations centered in the United States. When these institutions began to crumble, they were forced to contract their business everywhere. This reduced foreign capital flows and increased credit rationing across the globe.

A third linkage was through "hidden" financial linkages between the United States and the rest of the world. For example, remittances from immigrants working in the United States back to their home countries fell dramatically during the GFC. Also, *trade credit*, or loans between firms to facilitate trade, shrank significantly as the companies that were credit rationed by American banks were forced to credit ration their foreign customers as well.

A fourth linkage was through contagion. When investors in the United States began to panic, they re-evaluated the risk in their global positions as well. As a result, many foreigners found it increasingly difficult and more expensive to borrow as savers fled to the safest assets possible. This was particularly true in sovereign debt markets, where interest rates peaked across the globe.

One final linkage was through international trade. World trade flows fell by an incredible 30 percent in the second half of 2008 and fell by 14 percent in 2009. Given the export promotion strategies followed by many less developed and emerging market economies, this collapse in world trade devastated economic growth outside of the developed world.

Of course, linkages work both ways: The contraction in world output growth also weakened the United States' recovery from the GFC. This was especially true regarding the Euro-zone debt crisis, which negatively impacted trade, finance, and growth in the United States in the same way that the financial crisis in the United States impacted Europe. Some estimates suggest that the Euro-zone crisis may have reduced GDP growth in the United States by 1 percent in 2011, explaining a large portion of the weak recovery from the GFC.

However, the country that suffered the most, bar none, during the GFC was Iceland. Iceland encapsulates the dangers of relying too heavily on finance to fuel economic growth. Iceland was a microcosm of what happened in the United States and other countries, only on a proportionally grander scale. Total losses in Iceland's banking system accumulated to more than 75 percent of precrisis GDP, making it the largest banking crisis relative to the size of its economy in history.

The Icelandic crisis began in 2000. After a history of government-owned banking, the three large banks that comprise most of Iceland's financial system were privatized. These banks went from being tightly regulated to lightly regulated, and bank managers were light on experience in operating within a highly competitive and global financial system. Immediately, these banks began aggressively lending domestically and borrowing from abroad. Bank assets rose from 100 percent of GDP in 2003 to an unbelievable 850 percent of GDP by 2007! Much of this foreign debt was denominated in foreign currencies. Foreign debt increased by 500 percent during this same time. As long as Iceland's currency, the krone, remained strong, these debts could be serviced. But in the event of devaluation, such as what happened during the currency crises that precipitated the East Asian crisis, these debts would skyrocket in value and lead to the insolvency of the entire financial system.

The massive leverage taken on by Iceland's three banks fueled asset bubbles and an economic boom for most of the 2000s. Iceland's stock market increased 40 percent a year between 2001 and 2007 (900 percent in total), housing prices rose by 300 percent, and its GDP rose 50 percent in 5 years. At the same time, private debt rose to more than 200 percent of disposable income—unsustainable for any economy, but particularly for an economy whose principal export is fish.

When the GFC began, Iceland was in an exceedingly vulnerable position. As the crisis in the United States grew, the foreign lenders that Iceland relied upon to support its house of cards began to re-evaluate their risk exposure and examine the fragile financial fundamentals of Icelandic banks more closely. These investors realized that there was no way that Iceland's government had sufficient resources to bail out banks and protect bank depositors in the event of a currency crisis. Capital flight from Iceland took place quickly, and the krone depreciated by 43 percent in the first 10 months of 2008. The real value of foreign-denominated debt rose as the krone fell, destroying wealth and weakening financial fundamentals. By September 2008, Iceland's total debt, private and sovereign, was 10 times its GDP. Iceland's banks suffered $100 billion in losses— roughly $330,000 per Icelandic citizen. The financial system as a whole was insolvent and collapsed: Stock prices fell by 90 percent, government bond markets ceased to trade, banks closed their doors, and currency markets dried up as demand for the krone disappeared.

Iceland immediately appealed to the IMF and Nordic countries, who provided a $5.1 billion loan to finance the renationalization of banks and refund depositors whose assets had been frozen to prevent a bank run. Bondholders were forced to take a significant haircut, limiting the size of the bailout, which still amounted to over 30 percent of GDP. But the IMF bailout only stopped the leaking, it didn't refloat the boat. Unemployment in Iceland tripled and GDP shrank by 12 percent between 2008 and 2010. Iceland is left with much lower wealth and sovereign debt levels of nearly 100 percent of GDP, both likely to serve as huge drags on growth for the foreseeable future.

CONCLUSIONS

It has been said that the most expensive words in finance are "This time it is different." Bordo and colleagues (2001) find that financial crises have been almost twice as common between 1973 and 1997 as they were between 1945 and 1971. They identified 139 financial crises that took place between 1973 and 1997. Yet, despite the increasing number of financial crises across the globe since the 1970s, somehow many thought that the United States and other developed economies were immune and that something like the Great Depression could never happen again. Not only have those in the financial industry been humbled by this crisis, but policy makers, homeowners, and economists have been humbled as well.

To say that this crisis and other crises that came before it were largely unanticipated is not to say that we do not have the capabilities to learn from the mistakes that fostered them. In fact, there are some quite clear lessons from this crisis that need to be taken to head and to heart.

Microeconomic Indicators Such as Measures of Perceived Risk and Financial Fundamentals Matter Just as Much as Macroeconomic Fundamentals Such as Growth, Unemployment, and Credit

Why didn't more economists see this coming? Keynes, Fisher, Minsky, and proponents of behavioral economics would argue that the reason is the typical boom/bust psychology that dominates all cycles. When the boom is occurring, people (including economists) are too optimistic, and when it turns bad they become overly pessimistic. Psychology certainly played a role in the GFC, in large part because it was easy for many observers to fool themselves given the strong macroeconomic fundamentals before and even during the early stages of the crisis. Consumption and investment growth were strong and unemployment low. But like the buildup to the East Asian crisis, there is often too much preoccupation with macroeconomic fundamentals and not enough with microeconomic fundamentals, particularly regarding balance sheets, leverage ratios, debt levels, and other indicators of the financial risk of firms, households, and governments. These financial fundamentals were out of line with historical averages before the crisis and should have been a clearer warning signal that something dangerous was building, particularly to those who understand modern macroeconomic theory and new Keynesian models of credit. The fact that American financial markets had become so efficient during the boom only magnified the speed of the crash in these financial fundamentals when they began to crumble.

The financial reforms implemented in the United States after the GFC, primarily through the Dodd–Frank Wall Street Reform and Consumer Protection Act passed in 2010, attempt to better regulate financial fundamentals in two ways. First, the U.S. system of multiple prudential regulatory agencies has been subsumed under one systematic regulator, the Federal Reserve, which is now responsible for the entire system, including banks and nonbanks. Second, capital requirements on all financial institutions have been increased, making these institutions less risky (but also less profitable).

Financial Bailouts Should Be Immediate, Overwhelming, Indiscriminate, and Very Costly to the Recipients

The importance of risk perceptions cannot be underestimated, and psychology certainly plays a role in the assessment of risk. The longer the financial system is allowed to crumble and the more piecemeal bailouts are, the less likely bailouts are to actually work. In hindsight, the indecision and reluctance of the federal government during the early stages of the crisis to face up to its true size and costs likely made the crisis even larger.

Bailouts also need to be indiscriminate, meaning that they have to apply to all institutions whose failure could threaten the stability of the entire financial system. In hindsight, the biggest mistake the U.S. government made during this crisis was to bail out numerous financial institutions but to let Lehman Brothers fail. It undermined the whole strategy of bailouts, significantly increasing risk and uncertainty in the system just when the government should have been trying to promote calm. Also, many of the terms of specific bailout packages have been considerably different across firms—sometimes haircuts were imposed, sometimes not—leading to a perception of favoritism that has also contributed to uncertainty.

One of the biggest insights gained during this crisis, however, is that the best means of providing indiscriminate lending is to focus on stabilizing markets and not just directly lending to individual institutions. Conducting purchasing programs in specific markets allowed the Fed to broadly increase liquidity and enhance stability without having to determine which individual institution is deserving of a loan and which is not.

Moral hazard is one of the biggest concerns associated with indiscriminate bailouts. Financial institutions might be even less likely to behave responsibly in the future based on the bailouts they received during this crisis (either directly or through government intervention in markets). Worry about moral hazard was one of the primary reasons the Bush Treasury refused to bail out Lehman, which it viewed as behaving less responsibly than other institutions that did receive bailouts. But you cannot prevent moral hazard by bailing out some "too big to fail" firms and not bailing out others. There is no middle way, and to attempt to find one will lead to incurring all of the costs of a bailout without any of its benefits. In for a penny, in for a pound: Either you should let every insolvent institution fail, or you should bail them all out (barring outright fraud). History has shown that the first option is even more expensive than the second.

While the impulse to punish financial institutions for their mistakes is understandable, immediate retribution is inconsistent with recovery. You would not ask someone who crashed their car while driving recklessly to first go to jail, then later to the hospital. The difference between this example and what occurs during a financial crisis is that by denying the financial system the resources for a quick recovery, we are hurting not just financial institutions but ourselves by deepening and prolonging the economic downturn. The time for punishment is after the crisis is over.

Consistent with this, the best way of dealing with future moral hazard is to increase the penalties associated with accepting a bailout after the crisis is over. The Dodd–Frank Act attempts to do this in two ways. First, it explicitly prohibits the Federal Reserve or the treasury from bailing out individual insolvent banks in the future. Instead, the government will be given *resolution authority*, meaning that systematically important banks that receive future bailouts will be nationalized and then methodically "wound down" by the FDIC over time in a way that will not destabilize the entire system (in a process somewhat similar to an organized bankruptcy). Any losses the FDIC incurs are to be paid by the financial sector (in an unspecified way). This makes bailouts much more costly to recipients than they have been in the past. Second, executive compensation of failing firms will be regulated by the government in the event of a bailout. Both of these provisions are intriguing but untested.

Mortgage and Securitization Rules Need to Be Re-evaluated

While securitization has been a huge wealth creator, like many good things it can be dangerous if taken to extremes. By separating the originators and the securitizers of loans from those who bought MBSs and assumed the risk associated with them, too much information was lost and excessive risk from moral hazard was buried in these MBS. The Dodd–Frank Act deals with the principal/agent incentive problems in two ways. First, securitizers (but not originators) of loans will have to retain 5 percent of the mortgage pool on their balance sheets, increasing their incentive to pay attention to loan quality. Second, the Consumer Financial Protection Bureau has been established to provide oversight and ensure that homeowners are not unscrupulously sold mortgages that they cannot afford or understand. While these prudential regulations are necessary, they will also be costly: Fewer people will be homeowners in the foreseeable future, and those that are will have to pay more.

Dealing with Unknown Unknowns

Too often, financial analysts (and economists) assume that financial risk can be quantified and that mathematical models can calculate the exact probability of certain events. The events associated with this crisis suggest otherwise. One problem with mathematical models that assume quantifiable uncertainty is that financial innovation means that the next crisis will be caused by a much different set of factors than the last one, even if it shares many of the same broad similarities. Mathematical models cannot anticipate innovation, and so they cannot anticipate the next big shock.

The other problem with assuming that uncertainty can be fully quantified is that shocks are not independent but are correlated in ways that cannot be anticipated. During the GFC, the decline in real estate markets across the country contributed to a national spike in defaults in the subprime mortgage market. This then led to rising unemployment and a big drop in the stock market which, in turn, reduced the fundamentals of millions of borrowers and lenders. At the same time, losses in financial derivatives tied to assets in other markets increased counterparty risk in ways that were previously thought to be almost impossible by most market observers. Likewise, the collapse of the real estate market in the United States eventually led to an unprecedented economic crisis in Iceland, contributed to the Euro-zone crisis, and led to slower growth across the globe. This last sentence even now seems improbable, but it happened, and recessions will continue to be globalized given the increasing interconnectedness of economies through growing financial linkages and trade.

Dealing with unknown unknowns is obviously difficult. The Dodd–Frank Act does attempt to deal with the most dangerous unknown unknowns—derivatives and speculative trading—in three ways. First, over-the-counter derivatives are to be regulated by moving these trades into organized markets where collateral is required and better price data and information is available. Second, commercial banks will be limited in the types of derivatives they can issue in the future. Third, the Dodd–Frank Act imposes the Volker Rule (named after the former chairman of the Federal Reserve). The Volker Rule prohibits commercial banks that receive deposit insurance from *proprietary trading*, or trading on their own account and not for their customers. The aim here is to prevent commercial banks from engaging in excessive speculation in volatile financial market. But the Volker Rule is one of the most controversial aspects of the Dodd–Frank act. In the real world, it is very difficult to distinguish a trade for the banks' own benefit from a trade that a bank might be conducting for a customer. In addition, banks often engage in many trading activities that hedge risk in other parts of the bank, reducing overall risk. As a result, it is not clear at the time of this writing how this rule will actually be enforced.

Will the implementation of financial reform prevent financial and economic crises from ever happening again? Unfortunately, history teaches us that finance is like a locomotive: a powerful engine of propulsion, but dangerous when it veers off track. For a while, the humility learned from this crisis coupled with much needed financial reforms will make the U.S. financial system a safer place. But this will only last until prudential regulatory law falls behind financial innovation and the lessons of this crisis have been forgotten.

SUGGESTED READINGS

After the Music Stopped: The Financial Crisis, the Response, and the Work Ahead, Alan Blinder (2013): The best, most complete review of the buildup to the GFC, its impact on the world economy, and the postcrisis aftershocks by a former member of the Federal Reserve Board of Governors. The title comes from a quote by Chuck Prince, CEO of Citigroup, weeks before the subprime crisis struck: "When the music stops … things will be complicated. But as long as the music is playing, you've got to get up and dance. We're still dancing."

The Federal Reserve and the Banking Crisis, Ben Bernanke (2013): A series of lectures in which Bernanke provides his perspective on the GFC, focusing on the thinking that drove the Fed's policies during these dramatic events.

When Genius Failed: The Rise and Fall of Long-Term Capital Management, Roger Lowenstein (2000): This book is an entertaining look at the spectacular rise and dramatic failure of Long-Term Capital Management, a hedge fund founded by two Nobel Prize–winning economists. Its collapse in 1998 is, in hindsight, a precursor to the GFC 10 years later.

NINETEEN

Conclusions—What We Know and Do Not Know about Business Cycles

A QUICK TRIP THROUGH BUSINESS CYCLE THEORY

Just like the subject itself, the study of business cycles has undergone periods of remarkable progress and unexpected retrenchment, of irrational confidence in our knowledge and unjustified skepticism in the ability of economists to formulate economic policies that improve our quality of life. Despite the ups and downs, the best way to judge our understanding of recessions and depressions, just like the best way to judge economies themselves, is to evaluate their long-run record of growth. By this measure there has been real and significant progress in the field of business cycle research. All one has to do is look back at the first models of business cycles, which focused on things such as sunspots and weather fluctuations, to understand just how far we have come. These early models were simple (comfortingly so) and focused on a single cause of business cycles. Experience has taught us, however, that there is nothing simple about recessions and depressions. Their characteristics are variable, their fundamentals complex, and their transmission multifaceted.

When the first modern theories of business cycles were developed in the 1920s and 1930s, the primary focus of debate surrounded this question: Are economies inherently stable and business cycles caused by misguided government policy, or are economies inherently volatile and government policy able to be used to moderate business cycles? (This continues to be the question around much of the modern debate regarding business cycles.) Keynes and Keynesian models argue that fluctuations in aggregate demand are the source of business cycles caused by unstable expectations that lead to investment and consumption volatility. In Keynes's words, "the tendency to transform doing well into a speculative investment boom is the basic instability in a capitalist system." Coupled with wage and price inflexibility, these fluctuations in investment and consumption lead to large swings in aggregate output. Because of this inherent instability, macroeconomic management in the form of countercyclical monetary and fiscal policy is needed in order to stabilize aggregate demand and avoid frequent and persistent business cycles.

Keynesian arguments are so persuasive that a huge portion of economic research over the last 80 years has been devoted to challenging and modifying them. While monetarists agree with Keynesians that aggregate demand fluctuations are the source of business cycles, they assert that it is monetary policy that is responsible for this volatility because central bankers insist on conducting just the kind of stabilization policy that Keynesians advocate. Monetarists believe that wages and prices are perfectly flexible, and they believe in the natural rate hypothesis, or the principle that aggregate supply determines output in the long run and changes in aggregate demand only affect output in the short run. Because policy makers have limited information, especially about what the natural rate of the economy actually is, central bankers often aim too high in an effort to stimulate output in the short run, creating excessive inflation in the long run. When faced with the fact that higher and higher levels of inflation are necessary to keep output at or above the natural rate, the central bank is eventually forced to reverse course and create a recession in order to reduce inflation. This means that monetary policy becomes a destabilizing, not stabilizing, factor in the economy. Monetarist theory played a crucial role in convincing most mainstream economists that some limits on the use of active macroeconomic policy is prudent.

This monetarist skepticism about government intervention in the economy is entirely consistent with Austrian economics. In the words of Hayek, "The curious task of economics is to demonstrate to men how little they really know about what they imagine they can design." The Austrians' skepticism of government also leads them to blame government for business cycles because policy makers distort investment decisions through their manipulation of monetary policy and interest rates. According to the Austrians, government policies that distort the price system serve to incentivize malinvestment, setting the stage for the familiar boom/bust cycles that are commonly associated with business cycles.

The rational expectations model, with its assertion that only unexpected changes in policy can have real effects on output, agrees with the monetarist/Austrian assertion that stabilization policy cannot play a positive role in the economy. However, by asserting that only unexpected changes in monetary policy have real effects, the rational expectations model raises significant questions about the monetarist and Austrian theories of business cycles and about how monetary policy can be the primary source of recessions and depressions in a world where economic information is widely available. In the end, the rational expectations model's largest contribution to business cycle theory is twofold. First, the rational expectations hypothesis has forced economists to focus on the importance of information and the implications of rational expectations when it exists and, just as importantly, when it does not. Second, by showing that rational expectations coupled with perfect competition implies policy irrelevance, it has forced many economists to rethink how imperfect competition plays a role in business cycles with or without rational expectations (setting the stage for new Keynesian models).

The 1970s illustrated that aggregate demand shocks are not the only potential source of business cycles. A series of oil price spikes during the decade led to significant declines in aggregate supply. Likewise, the 1980s and 1990s were two decades generally characterized by robust growth and falling inflation, which was consistent with strong growth in aggregate supply. These events fed a neoclassical resurgence in business cycle theory that emphasized perfectly flexible prices and aggregate supply-driven business cycles. This is best exemplified by real business cycle models, which argue that changes in productivity create fluctuations in aggregate supply that are the primary determinant of fluctuations in output. Because business cycles are optimal responses to changes in the real fundamentals of an economy, real business cycle economists preach laissez-faire policies. While real business cycle models have the appealing feature of being built upon microeconomic foundations, they have no plausible explanation for the cause of major economic contractions such as the Great Depression or the global financial crisis of 2008.

The term *new Keynesian* has been used to refer to a group of models that incorporate the microeconomic foundations of imperfect competition, either in the form of wage inflexibility, price inflexibility, or imperfect information and risk. New Keynesian models attempt to synthesize the most appealing characteristics of business cycle models that came before them: adopting both rational expectations and the natural rate hypothesis, developing models based on microfoundations, and incorporating both aggregate demand and aggregate supply shocks. As a result, they are consistent with a broad range of business cycle behaviors and illustrate how market failure at the microeconomic level can lead to economic contractions. They also attempt to characterize the benefits and limitations of stabilization policy in a more nuanced way than either Keynesian or neoclassical models.

This new Keynesian focus on microfoundations and imperfect competition is particularly insightful in explaining the role that finance plays in economic performance and how the fragile financial fundamentals of borrowers and lenders can destabilize economies and create business cycles. In these models, the strength or weakness of financial fundamentals at the microeconomic level plays a large role in determining perceived risk, which in turn determines the cost of credit intermediation and the supply of credit through credit rationing. Risk is also created through moral hazard and adverse selection, which reduces both the quantity and quality of credit. Recessions are triggered by reductions in financial fundamentals that increase perceived risk, leading to reductions in financial intermediation that reduce consumption and investment and increase the costs of production. This reduces both aggregate demand and aggregate supply and can trigger an economic contraction.

The most extreme instances of financial collapse occur during asset bubbles, banking crises, and currency crises. During these financial crises, risk perceptions spike and financial fundamentals decline so precipitously that financial intermediation comes to a sudden stop and a dramatic economic contraction is likely. Our understanding of financial crises has been greatly deepened by new research in behavioral economics, which has striven to identify the conditions under which people exhibit biased decision-making and the impact of these biases on economic outcomes. While shocks to economic fundamentals certainly play a role in many financial crises, it is also true that beliefs are important. Behavioral economics and new Keynesian research has shown how changes in beliefs contribute to the boom/bust cycles associated with financial crises and explain exactly why belief-based financial crises are likely to occur whenever one person's optimal behavior is a function of what they believe other people believe.

These new Keynesian models represent the best and most insightful descriptions of how business cycles work and the mechanisms by which they have real and persistent effects on an economy. They provide crucial understanding into the role of financial systems in economic contractions, which has been crucial to our understanding of modern economic crises. However, their biggest drawback is that they are still more of a collection of related models than a single, coherent, and comprehensive model of business cycles. As a result, new Keynesian models provide multidimensional explanations of recessions and depressions that appear to be close to the complex reality of business cycles but do not provide any simple explanations or prescriptions. For example, new Keynesian models recognize the potential dangers of the excessive use of stabilization policy, such as inflation and debt crises, and are sympathetic to the use of policy rules. However, these models also recognize that in many cases macroeconomic policy has an important and potentially effective role to play, particularly in moderating risk and stabilizing financial fundamentals. As a result, new Keynesian models provide insight but no easy policy making recipes.

WHAT WE KNOW ABOUT BUSINESS CYCLES

Quite a bit of ground, both theoretical and empirical, has been covered in this book. Clearly, significant progress has been made in our understanding of recessions and depressions. It is worth the time and effort to briefly review conclusions on which economists have reached some consensus. These key findings can be summarized in six statements.

1. *Both aggregate demand and aggregate supply shocks are important sources of business cycle fluctuations.* The first empirical fact about business cycles covered in this book was that business cycles are not cyclical, meaning that they do not exhibit a regular pattern. This suggests that recessions have multiple causes. The case studies covered in this book support this idiosyncratic view of business cycles. As emphasized by Keynesians and monetarists, fluctuations in aggregate demand are clearly important sources of fluctuations in output. The cyclical behaviors observed during the Great Depression, postwar business cycles in the United States before the 1970s, the 2001 recession in the United States, the East Asian crisis, the Great Recession in Japan, and the 2008 global financial crisis are all consistent with aggregate demand-driven business cycles, with prices moving procyclically and real wages moving countercyclically. On the other hand, the 1970s, 1980s, and 1990s in the United States were periods of countercyclical price and procyclical real wage movements that are consistent with shifts in aggregate supply, such as the productivity shocks emphasized by real business cycle models.

   Thus, a comprehensive model of business cycles must incorporate both demand and supply shocks. New Keynesian models show how a negative shock, such as to firms' financial fundamentals, can not only negatively impact aggregate demand by increasing risk and reducing credit but can also reduce investment and increase the riskiness of production, reducing aggregate supply. Thus, business cycles may not be exclusively driven by either demand or supply but by both simultaneously.

2. *Imperfectly competitive labor markets play a key role in propagating business cycles.* Two types of market failure play a prominent role in generating business cycles. The first is that labor markets do not clear, particularly during business cycles. Unemployment has long been one of the most reliable and sensitive indicators of business cycle trends. It is obvious that most cyclical unemployment is involuntary because unemployment moves too much relative to the acyclical behavior of real wages for it to be entirely voluntary.

There is considerable evidence that both nominal wage and real wage inflexibility exists in labor markets because of efficiency wages, implicit and explicit contracts, coordination failure, and other imperfections highlighted by new Keynesian models. What is interesting about these models is that wage inflexibility does not necessarily mean that real wages have to be consistently countercyclical, as argued by Keynes. Instead, different market imperfections within labor markets and between labor and goods markets can interact to generate procyclical or even the acyclical real wage behavior we observe in the data.

3. *Imperfect information and beliefs play a key role in propagating business cycles.* Imperfect information is the second important form of market failure that plays a prominent role in generating business cycles. Imperfect information implies uncertainty, and it also means that people will have different expectations of the future based upon differences in information. Even the very first business cycle theories recognized the importance of beliefs, and expectations of the future have played a significant role in every modern business cycle theory developed since. However, these modern theories argue that beliefs are important for very different reasons.

The idea that expectations could be self-fulfilling was first proposed by the sunspot theory in the 1800s. This idea later was incorporated into Keynes's concept of animal spirits, where he argued that fundamental uncertainty and unstable expectations lead to volatile investment and aggregate demand. In Keynes's mind, expectations are largely irrational, and the volatility they create necessitates a role for government in offsetting fluctuations in aggregate demand using countercyclical monetary and fiscal policy. This idea of irrational expectations was also adopted in early business cycle theories that focused on financial volatility: Fischer's debt-deflation theory and

Minsky's financial instability hypothesis. In these models, financial manias and panics drive asset bubbles and market crashes which then impact the rest of the economy through fluctuations in financial intermediation and its impact on consumption and investment.

Other theories have focused on the how mistaken price expectations can lead to market disequilibria. The early cobweb theory, which postulated that business cycles are the result of backward-looking price expectations, was largely adopted by the monetarist model, which asserts that price expectations are slow to adjust to changes in the price level created by changes in monetary policy. This implies that changes in monetary policy have real effects on output. In contrast, the rational expectations model argued that if agents use the rational choice model and balance marginal benefits and marginal costs when making their decisions to consume, work, or invest, they must do the same thing when forming their expectations. As a result, expectations should be forward-looking, meaning that people will anticipate and act to offset any changes in policy that are observable. This rational expectations model highlighted two important ways that expectations affect fiscal and monetary policy. The first is policy irrelevance, which states that predictable policy, such as stabilization policy, cannot have real effects on an economy if markets are perfectly competitive. The second is the Lucas critique, which states that the impact of any policy is unpredictable unless policy makers know exactly how expectations will change in response to this change in policy. Both of these concepts raise serious questions about the effectiveness of using government policy to stabilize output.

Finally, new Keynesian models also emphasize the role of expectations and beliefs, particularly as it pertains to peoples' perceptions of financial risk. Even if people are perfectly rational, imperfect and asymmetric information can lead to rational actions such as banks and firms engaging in riskier behavior during economic expansions (moral hazard) or banks restricting lending during recessions (rationing credit and increasing the costs of credit intermediation), both of which can magnify the size of business cycle fluctuations. Even when expectations are rational, beliefs can play an important role in generating large fluctuations. As emphasized in belief-based theories of financial crises, when people's optimal behavior is a function of their subjective opinions of what other people believe, it is often optimal for them to behave in ways that are individually rational but lead to outcomes that appear irrational in the aggregate. This is even more likely to be true if there are psychological biases in economic decision-making as described by behavioral economics, such as overconfidence bias, confirmation bias, and contamination bias. It is this potential combination of imperfect information, intertwined incentives, and decision biases that make manias, panics, greater fool investing, herding, and self-fulfilling behaviors common in financial markets and so central to propagating business cycles.

4. *Understanding the natural rate hypothesis is crucial to understanding business cycles, stabilization policy, and the Great Moderation.* The primary concept that defines modern thinking about stabilization policy is the natural rate hypothesis, which states that changes in the money supply and aggregate demand only influence output in the short run and not in the long run. As a result, a tradeoff is inherent in monetary policy between stimulating growth in the short run and the inflationary effects of such a policy in the long run.

The postwar history of monetary policy in the United States can be viewed as a tug of war between these two competing objectives of increasing output and maintaining low inflation. On numerous occasions the Federal Reserve has used timely monetary policy to prevent or minimize recessions, such as after the 1987 stock market crash and during 2001 when the Federal Reserve prevented a significant recession after the 9/11 terrorist attacks occurred. In fact, improved stabilization policy (in addition to other structural changes in the economy) is a significant factor in explaining the Great Moderation of postwar business cycles in the United States. During this period, output volatility has been reduced by more than one-third relative to what it was before World War II, while inflation volatility has fallen by roughly 80 percent. In addition, recessions have occurred less frequently because expansions have been longer-lasting.

On the other hand, the Fed has also fallen into the trap of excessively relying on monetary policy to sustain growth, even when the natural rate of output growth has fallen. The result of this, as seen during the 1970s, was accelerating inflation that eventually forced the Fed to contract money growth and the economy in the early 1980s in order to bring inflation back in line. Inflationary fears have preceded numerous economic contractions in the United States, including the Great Depression, the severe 1981 recession, and the 1990–1991 recession that took place during the Gulf War.

Thus, while countercyclical monetary policy prevented some recessions and contributed to the Great Moderation, the gains have not been as large as they could have been. In fact, the active use of monetary policy has led to an era in which many business cycles have been policy driven.

5. *When deflation, currency depreciation, or debt crises occur (from macroeconomic policy mistakes) within countries with weak financial systems (from a lack of prudential regulation of microeconomic fundamentals), recessions turn into depressions.* Each of the major depressions of the twentieth century has had two distinguishing characteristics. First, each was initiated by major macroeconomic policy mistakes that led to either deflation or depreciation. During the Great Depression, the primary policy mistake was the naïve adherence of central banks to a flawed gold standard, which led to lower money growth even as prices and GDPs began to fall worldwide. During the Great Recession in Japan it was adherence to low inflation targets, even in the face of a recession and contractionary fiscal policy, which led to deflation. In East Asia, the critical macroeconomic policy mistakes were inflexible commitments to fixed exchange rates with the dollar, even in the face of an unsustainable appreciation of their currency. Eventually this led to currency crises and steep depreciations of their currencies.

While the Euro-zone and 2008 global financial crises each fell short of a depression, they both had their own forms of deflation when asset bubbles in sovereign debt, housing, and bond market popped. These asset bubbles were fueled by macroeconomic policy mistakes leading up to the crisis in the form of overly expansionary monetary policy (in the United States) and fiscal policy (in both Europe and the United States) that encouraged excessive debt accumulation by both private individuals (in the form of mortgages and consumer debt) and governments (in the form of sovereign debt).

However, macroeconomic policy mistakes alone do not make depressions. Each of the major twentieth-century economic crises also occurred within countries with financial systems—particularly banks—that were vulnerable to financial crises even before the economic contractions began. This is primarily because of a lack of bank regulation at the microeconomic level, particularly the absence of prudential regulations aimed at limiting moral hazard lending and excessive credit expansion. This includes a lack of limits on connected lending, minimal capital adequacy requirements, few loan safety standards, and a history of freely available government bail-outs. Because of this lack of regulatory oversight, banks expose themselves to the kind of risk that you usually only see only at a casino table. This was true in the United States during the Great Depression, when it had a large number of small, undiversified banks with little or no protection from bank panics in the form of deposit insurance or lending from the Federal Reserve. This was also true in East Asia and Japan, where financial deregulation led to huge expansions in credit driven by moral hazard. It was true in the Euro-zone, where banks faced no restrictions on the amount of government debt they could hold and recklessly bought sovereign debt based on the belief that the EMU ensured that the probability of Greece defaulting on its debt was the same as that of Germany default-ing on its debt. Finally, it was true in the United States and other coun-tries during the global financial crisis, where banks were able to excessively pursue a belief that securitization ensured that fundamen-tally risky subprime mortgages could be pooled and magically turned into almost risk-free bonds, like spinning straw into gold.

It is when these events—deflation or depreciation and weak finan-cial fundamentals—occur simultaneously that depressions take place. Keynes recognized that deflation could lead to higher real wages and involuntary unemployment when nominal wage rigidity exists. However, economists have increasingly begun to emphasize the role of nominal debt rigidity as being even more important in generating financial crises and depressions. Deflation (in either the price level or in asset prices) and/or depreciation increases the real value of debt (because its nominal value is fixed) relative to the value of assets (whose nominal value is not fixed). Because of this, firms see their financial fundamentals deteriorate, and they begin to default on their bank loans. These higher default rates lead many banks to become insolvent and stop lending altogether, especially if they were in a weak financial position to begin with. As banks close, panic and herding behavior among depositors spreads that becomes self-fulfilling and can weaken banks that were fundamentally sound. Those banks that manage to stay open in the midst of a banking cri-sis protect against additional deposit outflows and bad loans by sell-ing their assets, placing further downward pressure on prices and further weakening the financial system. Those banks that remain open also credit ration, or restrict the amount of new lending they undertake. As all of these things occur, financial intermediation grinds to a halt, investment and durable consumption spending collapse, and a downturn that could have remained a recession becomes a depression.

Depressions end only after two changes take place. First, countries have to reverse their policy mistakes and end the deflation and depreciation. During the Great Depression, deflation ended in the United States when it abandoned the gold standard and Roosevelt expanded fiscal policy under the New Deal. In East Asia, the IMF initially asked crisis countries to restrict their monetary and fiscal policies even further in an effort to re-attract the foreign investment that fled their countries once the contraction began. This made the economic situation even worse and failed to end the depreciations of their exchange rates. It was not until the IMF saw the error of its ways and reduced the austerity conditions in its bailout programs that these countries' exchange rates stabilized. Japan was extremely slow to take significant action to stimulate aggregate demand and stop their deflation, which is the primary reason why its economy remained in recession for 12 years. During the Euro-zone and global financial crises, the severe contractions ended with expansionary monetary policy that solidified asset prices and stopped the economic bleeding. In the United States, the monetary policies adopted were unconventional and focused not only on lowering short-term interest rates, which led to the dead-end of a liquidity trap, but primarily focused on policies aimed at stabilizing risk and financial fundamentals by reducing long-term interest rates and increasing liquidity in markets.

The second part of the solution is to resolve the banking crises and restore lending by quickly and broadly providing government bailouts in conjunction with implementing better prudential bank regulation aimed at improving the soundness of the financial system. This took place in Korea after the East Asian crisis, in Scandinavia after their banking crisis in the early 1990s, and in the United States in 2008. However, in other countries such as Japan and the Euro-zone, bailouts and financial reform have been slow to take place. This is one of the principle reasons why lending and investment remained low and economic slowdowns lingered in these countries.

In most of the business cycle theories developed in during the last half of the twentieth century, financial collapse was a symptom, not the cause, of recessions and depressions. However, new Keynesian theories have placed the spotlight directly on the role of financial systems in generating contractions, and economists have increasingly come to realize that banks play an integral role in explaining why the supply (not just the demand) of credit contracts during a recession and the role that this plays in magnifying business cycles. These insights have led to dramatic improvements in our theory and have been the most important advances in our understanding of recessions and depressions over the last 20 years.

6. *Business cycles have become more globalized.* Increasingly, all economic crises are global economic crises because of the greater interconnectedness of modern economies that are linked together in a complex network of trade and financial linkages. Trade flows between countries have become increasingly important as many emerging market economies, which are the world's fastest growing economies, follow export promotion strategies that leave them highly dependent on the import demand of their trade partners. Financial linkages across countries reflect the fact that governments and individuals increasingly own foreign assets. Global financial institutions operate in many countries, and when they suffer losses in one country they are often forced to contract their credit everywhere. This reduces foreign capital flows and increases credit rationing across the globe during recessions. There are also "hidden" financial linkages between countries, such as remittances and trade credit between businesses that conduct business internationally. Finally, there is contagion. When investors in one country begin to panic, they re-evaluate their risk perceptions and change their global financial positions as well. The full extent of all these changes brought about by globalization is still not fully understood because they are still occurring. But there can be no doubt that closed-economy thinking about business cycles is increasingly antiquated and going the way of the sunspot and cobweb theories.

WHAT WE DO NOT KNOW ABOUT BUSINESS CYCLES

Here are four questions about business cycles that economists are still grappling with, questions that serve as a roadmap to future progress in our understanding of recessions and depressions.

1. *When does stabilization policy become destabilizing?* The debate over the proper policy response to business cycles is a lightly veiled debate over the proper role of government within an economy. This debate has always been at the forefront of business cycle research; it continues to dominate our thinking about business cycles today, and it will do so in the future.

On one hand, you have Keynesians and, to a lesser extent, new Keynesians who argue that the economy is inherently unstable and that stabilization policy, if used judiciously, can moderate some of this volatility. But even between these groups there are disagreements. While Keynesians argue for active stabilization policy with little worry about the impact of inflation, new Keynesians have taken a more nuanced view of discretionary policy and worry about its potential to generate high and uncertain inflation that is costly to an economy. Inflation targeting rules are appealing to new Keynesians because they appear to offer the best of both worlds: A rule that can help reduce uncertainty and create stable inflation expectations, but one that is adaptable enough to allow for some flexibility to respond to shocks.

In other ways, new Keynesians are even more ambitious than traditional Keynesians when it comes to thinking about the kinds of monetary policy that can prove beneficial to an economy. While Keynesians worried about the liquidity trap, new Keynesians have advocated many different unconventional monetary policies aimed at reducing risk and solidifying financial fundamentals. They have done this by focusing on long-term interest rates, not just short-term rates, and by trying to increase liquidity in markets to reduce risk and stabilize asset prices. These new channels of monetary policy, while no panacea, proved to be effective at preventing a complete collapse in credit and a depression during the global financial crisis. In regards to fiscal policy, however, new Keynesians are more circumspect than traditional Keynesians and worry more about the impact of large deficits and their potential to trigger a damaging sovereign debt crisis.

The debates between Keynesians and new Keynesians are minor compared to the debates between these groups and other economists that believe that economies are inherently stable and that it is government policy itself that is destabilizing. The critics of stabilization policy and the active role that governments have played in responding to business cycles are many and their criticisms are varied. You have the Austrians and real business cycle proponents, who believe that creative destruction is natural and necessary to economic growth. Business cycles are, in their view, efficient, and trying to prevent them reduces productivity. It can also incentivize malinvestment that slows long-run growth and makes future business cycles more likely. You also have monetarists and rational expectations proponents that argue that unstable monetary and fiscal policy are the primary sources of uncertainty within an economy. In their view, central banks' proclivity towards stimulating output during recessions then fighting inflation afterwards creates costs that more than outweigh any benefits of countercyclical monetary policy. Finally, you have agreement among all of these groups with Hyman Minsky's claim that "stability breeds instability." By trying to mitigate risk, stabilization policy often creates moral hazard and encourages individuals to make riskier decisions, leading to the opposite of its intended effect.

These debates over stabilization policy are clearest when it comes to arguments over how governments should respond to banking crises. The Keynesian wing argues that bailouts of banks should be immediate and indiscriminate. The primary objective must be to stabilize aggregate demand before pessimism reaches the point of no return. In Keynes's words: "If we do nothing long enough, there will in the end be nothing else that we can do." This Keynesian view has largely been validated, with caveats, by history that has taught us that successful bank bailouts have three components. First, viable financial institutions have to be quickly and aggressively recapitalized in order to increase their net worth and reduce their risk of failure. This means that governments have to promptly purchase the capital of crumbling financial institutions (and possibly some of their "distressed" assets). But bailouts should not be made to institutions that have no reasonable chance of recovery; these institutions should be liquidated as soon as possible with the government assuming any losses to depositors (but not necessarily the losses to bondholders). Second, recapitalization should be costly to banks (at a penalty rate) and should be done in a way in which the government has a reasonable chance to not only recoup its money but to make a profit. Third, transparency must be ensured throughout the process. The public must feel that the process is open, and investors must have enough information to be convinced to reinvest their private resources in the financial system. When these three components are done reasonably well, as they were in the United States during the global financial crisis, a full-scale financial collapse and depression can be avoided. When they are done less well, such as during the Great Recession in Japan, the East Asian crisis, and the Euro-zone crisis, a prolonged financial and economic calamity is the likely result.

But critics of bailouts have legitimate criticisms of this process. First and foremost, there is the problem of moral hazard. While a bailout might help end the current financial crisis, what about the next financial crisis? Bailouts, critics charge, are a form of short-term thinking that prioritizes today over tomorrow. By rewarding failure, bailouts also encourage malinvestment that reduces productivity and can also contribute to future crises. In addition, given the economic and political chaos that always surrounds crises, bailouts are always going to be implemented in ways that favor the powerful over what is fair or efficient. These are not minor or easily dismissible criticisms. Should stabilization policy be used to focus on short-run output because, as argued by Keynes, in the long run we are all dead? Or should stabilization policy prioritize long-run, sustainable growth over moderating short-term pain? When posed this way, debates over stabilization policy are often as much about value judgments as about economics.

2. *Why the jobless recoveries?* A disturbing phenomenon has taken place over the last two decades in developed economies: The recovery in output following recessions has not been associated with a correspondingly strong recovery in employment. This was true in the United States following the 2001 and 2008 recessions, and it is currently true in the Euro-zone. These jobless recoveries are inconsistent with past business cycles—where employment was strongly procyclical—and have greatly increased the social costs of recessions, creating personal misery as well as economic pain as the long-term unemployed see their marketable skills fade away the longer they are unable to rejoin the labor market.

Explaining these jobless recoveries should now become one of the top priorities of macroeconomic research. However, at this point there is much more speculation than actual understanding of its fundamental causes. Supply-side (neoclassical theories) theories argue that the fundamental problem is one of skills mismatch: Many workers do not have the skills necessary to be consistently employable in a modern and constantly evolving economy. Over the last two decades, job and wage growth has largely occurred in jobs that require a college education; lower-skilled sectors such as manufacturing have lost jobs and experienced little wage growth. Until the labor force that exists can evolve into the labor force that is needed for full employment, persistent unemployment will be the new normal. Obviously, a big part of doing this would be to provide better educational opportunities for all workers, but how to do this effectively is a deeply contentious issue.

Demand-side (Keynesian theories) theories argue that more needs to be done to stimulate aggregate demand and output growth in the macroeconomy before labor demand is strong enough to clear the market. However, it is not clear that stimulating aggregate demand alone is sufficient to increase labor demand. In the aftermath of the global financial crisis, the unconventional monetary policies followed by the Fed, the fiscal stimulus package, and the TARP bailout all served to stabilize output. But their impact on employment is less observable, and there appears to be a dearth of new ideas about exactly what new monetary or fiscal policies could be adopted that would specifically stimulate labor demand.

This lack of a clear policy direction regarding how to deal with jobless recoveries has fueled the perception that economists have no clear ideas about how to deal with business cycles at the level that many people experience them: as a threat to their employment security. Until economists can better understand jobless recoveries, it is difficult for us to argue that we understand how modern business cycles work.

3. *How can we more accurately forecast business cycles?* Forecasting is absolutely critical to mitigating the effects of business cycles because stabilization policies are subject to implementation and response lags. Economic policy must be forward looking, but if we cannot see where we are going, it is hard to say how we can correct course to stay on our desired path. As discussed in detail in Chapter 12, there are two fundamental problems with macroeconomic forecasting. First, to get the right forecast, you need the right model. Right now there is no consensus model in macroeconomics that incorporates everything that matters to future macroeconomic performance. As a result, there are is no ability to consistently forecast with the accuracy we need.

The second fundamental problem with macroeconomic forecasting has to do with unknown unknowns. The complexity of macroeconomics coupled with the fact that macroeconomic activity is an evolutionary process means that our models will always lag behind and fall short of reality. In addition, the fact that people are involved—incorporating all of the biases and intertwined incentives that we have—means that market psychology and beliefs are often not quantifiable and shocks to one sector of the economy may impact other sectors in ways that cannot be mathematically modeled. Macroeconomics can never be a predictive science in the same way as mechanical physics. Instead, macroeconomic forecasting might be better thought of as a form of punditry: informed speculation, but subject to the errors inherent in any form of conjecture.

All of this is not to say that macroeconomic forecasting cannot be improved. Using more market-based indicators in forecasting, such as prediction markets, hold a great deal of promise. One additional area for improvement is to incorporate more microeconomic data on financial fundamentals into macroeconomic forecasting models. Theory has made great advances in understanding the microeconomics behind macroeconomic failures. But macroeconomic forecasting focuses too much on macroeconomic data and not enough on microeconomic fundamentals, particularly regarding balance sheets, leverage ratios, debt levels, and other indicators of the financial risk of firms, households, and governments. This is one area where practice needs to catch up with theory.

4. *Where will the next major economic crisis occur?* Having raised serious questions about our ability to forecast, it is not surprising that there is no consensus about where and when the next large economic calamity will occur. One obvious candidate is any of a number of developed countries with excessively high levels of private and sovereign debt. A repeat of the Euro-zone sovereign debt crisis could happen in Japan or the United States (although, as argued in Chapter 17, this is less likely), or it could occur again in Europe.

No country has ever transformed from a less developed to developed economy without suffering a financial crisis and a recession. As a result, fast-growing emerging market economies are also good candidates for the next crisis. First among these is China. Despite its strong macroeconomic fundamentals, the microeconomic fundamentals of China's growth miracle are frightening, particularly in its massive banking system. A complex system of financial repression, connected lending, corruption, price controls, hidden debts, credit booms, malinvestment, housing bubbles, and moral hazard has made China's big four banks, which are among the largest in the world, also among the most opaque and risky. Any crisis in the Chinese financial system would almost assuredly put every country in the world at risk for a recession given China's large share of world exports and its role as the largest financier of the rising debt levels in developed countries. If China, or other emerging economies that follow similar policies, are forced by a future crisis to rebalance their economies, the consequences for the increasingly globalized world economy will be momentous. If the global volatility experienced since 2007 is any indication, the period of the Great Moderation may be replaced with a period of the Great Hangover, where countries such as China struggle to find macroeconomic balance in this changing environment and every other country in the world has to adjust as a result.

CONCLUSIONS

If failure is a necessary part of learning, then it is little wonder that our understanding of business cycles has progressed as far as it has. Again and again, economists have developed theories, have had these theories contradicted by the facts, and have then developed new theories based on these new facts. When a critic once charged Keynes with being inconsistent and always changing his mind, Keynes pointedly responded, "When the facts change, I change my mind. What do you do, sir?" This mindset of hypothesis and revision is at the heart of the scientific method of study and is clearly evident in business cycle research.

Chances are that some of the things that we hold true today will be proven wrong in the future. But after a careful reading of this book, it should be clear that our knowledge of business cycles is improving. Just like falling down is part of the process of a child learning to walk, economists' failures, both in the past and in the future, indicate that we are converging towards a fuller understanding, however complicated, of why economies experience costly recessions and depressions.

Bibliography

Allen, Franklin, and Douglas Gale. 1999. "Bubbles, Crises, and Policy." *Oxford Review of Economic Policy* 15: 9–18.

Allen, Franklin, and Douglas Gale. 2000. "Bubbles and Crises." *The Economic Journal* 53: 236–255.

Anderson, Richard G., Marcelle Chauvet, and Barry Jones. 2012. "Nonlinear Relationship between Permanent and Transitory Components of Monetary Aggregates and the Economy." St. Louis Federal Reserve Working Paper No. 2013-018A.

Arnone, Marco, Bernard J. Laurens, Jean François Segalotto, and Martin Sommer. 2009. "Central Bank Autonomy: Lessons from Global Trends." IMF Staff Papers No. 56.

Artis, Michael J., Zenon F. Kontolemis, and Denise R. Osborn. 1997. "Business Cycles for G7 and European Countries." *Journal of Business* 70: 249–279.

Asea, Patrick K., and Brock Blomberg. 1998. "Lending Cycles." *Journal of Econometrics* 83: 89–128.

Ashraf, Mohammad, and Khan A. Mohabbat. 2011. "A Panel Data Analysis of the Lucas Hypothesis." *Journal of Business and Economics Research* 1: 33–42.

Baghot, Walter. 1873 [1991]. *Lombard Street: A Description of the Money Market.* Philadelphia, PA: Orion Editions.

Bailey, Martin Neil. 2002. "The New Economy: Post Mortem or Second Wind?" *Journal of Economic Perspectives* 16: 3–22.

Ball, Laurence, N. Gregory Mankiw, and David Romer. 1988. "The New Keynesian Economics and the Output–Inflation Tradeoff." *Brookings Papers on Economic Activity* 1: 1–82.

Bank of Japan. 2002. "How Should the Recent Increase in Japan's Monetary Base Be Understood?" Research Paper. Accessed March 7, 2014. http://www.boj.or.jp/en/research/brp/ron_2002/data/ron0209a.pdf.

Barattieri, Alessandro, Susanto Basu, and Peter Gottschalk. 2014. "Some Evidence on the Importance of Sticky Wages." *American Economic Journal: Macroeconomics* 6: 70–101.

Basu, Susanto, and Alan M. Taylor. 1999. "Business Cycles in International Historical Perspective." *Journal of Economic Perspectives* 13: 45–68.

Beck, Thorsen, Asli Demirgüç-Kunt, and Vojislav Maksimovic. 2008. "Financing Patterns around the World: Are Small Firms Different?" *Journal of Financial Economics* 89: 467–487.

Bernanke, Ben. 1983. "Nonmonetary Effects of the Financial Crisis in the Propagation of the Great Depression." *American Economic Review* 73: 257–276.

Bernanke, Ben. 1995. "The Macroeconomics of the Great Depression: A Comparative Approach." *Journal of Money, Credit, and Banking* 27: 1–28.

Bernanke, Ben. 2002. "Asset Price 'Bubbles' and Monetary Policy." Speech given to the New York chapter of the National Association for Business Economics, New York, October 15, accessed March 17, 2014, http://www.federalreserve.gov/boarddocs/speeches/2002/20021015/default.htm.

Bernanke, Ben. 2005. "The Global Savings Glut and the U.S. Current Account Deficit." Speech given on March 10, accessed March 17, 2014, http://www.federalreserve.gov/boarddocs/speeches/2005/200503102/.

Bernanke, Ben. 2011. "The Effects of the Great Recession on Central Bank Doctrine and Practice." Speech given on October 18, accessed March 17, 2014, http://www.federalreserve.gov/newsevents/speech/bernanke20111018a.htm.

Bernanke, Ben. 2013. *The Federal Reserve and the Banking Crisis.* Princeton, NJ: Princeton University Press.

Bernanke, Ben, and Mark Gertler. 1987. "Banking and Macroeconomic Equilibrium." In *New Approaches to Monetary Economics*, edited by William A. Barnett and Kenneth J. Singleton. Cambridge, MA: Cambridge University Press.

Bernanke, Ben, and Mark Gertler. 1989. "Agency Costs, Net Worth, and Business Fluctuations." *American Economic Review* 79: 14–31.

Bernanke, Ben, and Mark Gertler. 1990. "Financial Fragility and Economic Performance." *Quarterly Journal of Economics* 105: 87–114.

Bernanke, Ben, and Mark Gertler. 1995. "Inside the Black Box: The Credit Channel of Monetary Policy." *Journal of Economic Perspectives* 9: 27–48.

Bernanke, Ben, Mark Gertler, and Simon Gilchrist. 1996. "The Financial Accelerator and the Flight to Quality." *The Review of Economics and Statistics* 78: 1–15.

Bernanke, Ben, and Harold James. 1991. "The Gold Standard, Deflation, and Financial Crises in the Great Depression: An International Comparison." In *Financial Markets and Financial Crises*, edited by Glenn Hubbard. Chicago, IL: University of Chicago Press.

Black, David, and Michael Dowd. 2009. "The Changing Composition of Output and the Great Moderation." *Applied Economics Letters* 16: 1265–1270.

Blanchard, Oliver, and John Simon. 2001. "The Long and Large Decline in U.S. Output Volatility." *Brookings Papers on Economic Activity* 32: 135–174.

Blinder, Alan. 1988. "The Fall and Rise of Keynesian Economics." *Economic Record* 64: 278–294.

Blinder, Alan. 1991. "Why Are Prices Sticky? Preliminary Results from an Interview Study." *American Economic Review* 91: 89–96.

Blinder, Alan. 2013. *After the Music Stopped: The Financial Crisis, the Response, and the Work Ahead.* New York, NY: The Penguin Press.

Blinder, Alan, and Mark Zandi. 2010. "How the Great Recession Was Brought to an End." *Moody's Analytics*, July 27.

Bordo, Michael, Barry Eichengreen, Daniela Kingebiel, and Maria Soledad Martinez. 2001. "Is the Crisis Problem Growing More Severe?" *Economic Policy* 24: 51–82.

Boyd, John H., Sungkyu Kwak, and Bruce Smith. 2005. "Real Output Losses Associated with Modern Banking Crises." *Journal of Money, Credit, and Banking* 37: 977–999.

Brunnermeier, Markus K. 2009. "Deciphering the Liquidity and Credit Crunch 2007–2008." *Journal of Economic Perspectives* 23: 77–100.

Burns, Aurthur F. 1987. "The Anguish of Central Banking." *Federal Reserve Bulletin* 73: 687—698.

Calderón, César, and Rodrigo Fuentes. 2010. "Characterizing the Business Cycles of Emerging Economies." World Bank Policy Research Working Paper No. 5343.

Calomiris, Charles W., and Stephen H. Haber. 2014. *Fragile by Design: The Political Origins of Banking Crises.* Princeton, NJ: Princeton University Press.

Carroll, Christopher, Misuzu Otsuka, and Jirka Slacalek. 2010. "How Large Is the Housing Wealth Effect? A New Approach." European Central Bank Working Paper No. 1283.

Cecchetti, Stephen C. 2006. *Money, Banking, and Financial Markets.* New York, NY: McGraw-Hill.

Chauvet, Marcelle, and Chengxuan Yu. 2006. "International Business Cycles: G7 and OECD Countries." *Federal Reserve of Atlanta Economic Review*, first quarter, 43–54.

Christiano, Lawrence J., Roberto Motto, and Massimo Rostagno. 2014. "Risk Shocks." *American Economic Review* 104: 27–65.

Cipriani, Marco, and Antonio Guarino. 2014. "Estimating a Structural Model of Herd Behavior in Financial Markets." *American Economic Review* 104: 224–251.

Clarida, Richard, Jordi Gali, and Mark Gertler. 2000. "Monetary Policy Rules and Macroeconomic Stability: Evidence and Some Theory." *Quarterly Journal of Economics* 115: 147–180.

Clark, John M. 1917. "Business Acceleration and the Law of Demand: A Technical Factor in Economic Cycles." *Journal of Political Economy* 25: 217–235.

Clements, Michael P. 2002. "An Evaluation of the Survey of Professional Forecasters Probability Distributions of Expected Inflation and Output Growth." University of Warwick Working Paper.

Corsetti, Giancarlo, Paolo Pesenti, and Nouriel Roubini. 1998. "What Caused the Asian Currency and Financial Crisis? Parts I and II." National Bureau of Economic Research Working Papers No. 6833 and 6834.

Cruces, Juan J., and Christoph Trebesch. 2013. "Sovereign Defaults: The Price of Haircuts." *American Economic Review* 5: 85–117.

Davis, Steven J., and James A. Kahn. 2008. "Interpreting the Great Moderation: Changes in the Volatility of Economic Activity at the Macro and Micro Levels." *Journal of Economic Perspectives* 22: 155–180.

Del Negro, Marco, and Frank Schorfheide. 2012. "DSGE Model-Based Forecasting." Federal Reserve Bank of New York Staff Report No. 554.

De Long, Bradford. 2000. "The Triumph of Monetarism." *Journal of Economic Perspectives* 14: 83–94.

De Long, Bradford, and Lawrence H. Summers. 2001. "The 'New Economy': Background, Historical Perspective, Questions, and

Speculations." *Economic Review, The Federal Reserve Bank of Kansas City*, fourth quarter, 29–59.

Diamond, Douglas W., and Philip H. Dybvig. 1983. "Bank Runs, Deposit Insurance, and Liquidity." *The Journal of Political Economy* 91: 401–419.

Diebold, Francis X. 1998. "The Past, Present, and Future of Macroeconomic Forecasting." *Journal of Economic Perspectives* 12: 175–192.

Diebold, Francis X., and Glenn D. Rudebusch. 1999. *Business Cycles: Durations, Dynamics, and Forecasting*. Princeton, NJ: Princeton University Press.

Dornbusch, Rudiger. 1997. "How Real Is U.S. Prosperity?" Column reprinted in *World Economic Laboratory Columns*, Massachusetts Institute of Technology, December.

Dynan, Karen E., Douglas W. Elmendorf, and Daniel E. Sichel. 2006. "Can Financial Innovation Help to Explain the Reduced Volatility of Economic Activity?" *Journal of Monetary Economics* 53: 123–150.

Easterly, William. 2005. "What Did Structural Adjustment Adjust? The Association of Policies and Growth with Repeated IMF and World Bank Adjustment Loans." *Journal of Development Economics* 76: 1–22.

Ebenstein, Alan. 2001. *Friedrich Hayek: A Biography*. New York, NY: St. Martin's Press.

Edwards, Sebastian. 1998. "Capital Flows, Real Exchange Rates, and Capital Controls: Some Latin American Examples." National Bureau of Economic Research Working Paper No. W6800.

Eichengreen, Barry, and Carlos Arteta. 2002. "Banking Crises in Emerging Markets: Presumptions and Evidence." In *Financial Policies in Emerging Markets*, edited by Mario I. Blejer and Marko Skreb. Cambridge, MA: The MIT Press.

Enders, Walter, and Jun Ma. 2011. "Sources of the Great Moderation: A Time-Series Analysis of GDP Subsectors." *Journal of Economic Dynamics and Control* 35: 67–79.

Estrella, Arturo, and Frederic S. Mishkin. 1998. "Predicting U.S. Recessions: Financial Variables as Leading Indicators." *The Review of Economics and Statistics* 80: 45–61.

Ezekial, Mordecai. 1938. "The Cobweb Theorem." *Quarterly Journal of Economics* 52: 255–280.

Fischer, Irving. 1933. "The Debt-Deflation Theory of Great Depressions." *Econometrica* 1: 337–357.

Fischer, Stanley. 1977. "Long-Term Contracts, Rational Expectations, and the Optimal Money Supply Rule." *Journal of Political Economy* 85: 191–205.

Fraser, Steve. 2005. *Wall Street: A Cultural History*. London: Faber & Faber.

Friedman, Milton. 1968. "The Role of Monetary Policy." *American Economic Review* 58: 1–17.

Friedman, Milton, and Anna Schwartz. 1963. *A Monetary History of the United States, 1867–1960*. Princeton, NJ: Princeton University Press.

Froot, Kenneth A., Paul G. J. O'Connell, and Mark S. Seasholes. 1999. "The Portfolio Flows of International Investors." Harvard Business School Working Paper.

Gertler, Mark, and Simon Gilchrist. 1993. "The Role of Credit Market Imperfections in the Monetary Transmission Mechanism: Arguments and Evidence." *Scandinavian Journal of Economics* 95: 43–64.

Gilchrist, Simon, and Egon Zakrajsek. 2012. "Credit Spreads and Business Cycle Fluctuations." *American Economic Review* 102: 1692–1720.

Goldstein, Morris. 2000. "IMF Structural Conditionality: How Much Is Too Much?" National Bureau of Economic Research Working Paper No. 01-4.

Gordon, Robert J. 1976. "Recent Developments in the Theory of Inflation and Unemployment." *Journal of Monetary Economics* 2: 185–220.

Gordon, Robert J. 2000. "Does the 'New Economy' Measure Up to the Great Inventions of the Past?" *Journal of Economic Perspectives* 14: 49–74.

Gorton, Gary B. 2012. *Misunderstanding Financial Crises: Why We Don't See Them Coming*. Oxford, UK: Oxford University Press.

Greenspan, Alan. 1998. Testimony before the Subcommittee on Foreign Operations of the Committee on Appropriations, U.S. Senate, March 3.

Greenspan, Alan. 2008. *The Age of Turbulence: Adventures in a New World*. New York, NY: Penguin Books.

Greenwald, Bruce, and Joseph Stiglitz. 1993. "New and Old Keynesians." *Journal of Economic Perspectives* 7: 23–44.

Guerard, John B. Jr., and Eli Schwartz. 2007. "Time Series Modeling and the Forecasting Effectiveness of the U.S. Leading Economic Indicators." In *Quantitative Corporate Finance*, edited by John B. Guerard Jr. and Eli Swartz, 303–336. New York, NY: Springer.

Hanes, Christopher. 2000. "Nominal Wage Rigidity and Industry Characteristics in the Downturns of 1893, 1929, and 1981." *American Economic Review* 90: 1432–1446.

Haubrich, Joseph G., and Ann M. Dombrosky. 1996. "Predicting Real Growth Using the Yield Curve." *Economic Review* 32: 26–35.

Hawtrey, Robert George. 1913. *Good and Bad Trade*. London: Constable & Co.

Hayek, Friedrich A. 1935 [1967]. *Prices and Production*. New York, NY: Augustus M. Kelly Publishing.

Hayek, Friedrich A. 1944 [1994]. *The Road to Serfdom*. Chicago, IL: University of Chicago Press.

Hayek, Friedrich A. 1991. *The Fatal Conceit: The Errors of Socialism*. Chicago, IL: University of Chicago Press.

Heilbroner, Robert L. 1986. *The Worldly Philosophers*. New York, NY: Simon and Schuster.

Heisenberg, W. 1971. *Physics and Beyond*. London: George Allen & Unwin Ltd.

Herndon, Thomas, Michael Ash, and Robert Pollin. 2013. "Does High Public Debt Consistently Stifle Economic Growth? A Critique of Reinhart and Rogoff." Political Economy Research Institute (University of Massachusetts) Working Paper.

Hicks, John R. 1937. "Mr. Keynes and the 'Classics': A Suggested Interpretation." *Econometrica* 5: 147–159.

Hobson, John A. 1922. *The Economics of Unemployment*. London: G. Allen & Unwin Ltd.

Holmes, Mark J. 2000. "The Output–Inflation Trade-off in African Less Developed Countries." *Journal of Economic Development* 25: 41–55.

Hoover, Herbert. 1952. *Memoirs*. New York, NY: Macmillan.

IMF. 1996. *World Economic Outlook*. Washington, D.C.: IMF.

Jevons, William Stanley. 1884. *Investigations in Currency and Finance*. London: Macmillan.

Jiménez, Gabriel, Steven Ongena, José-Luis Peydró, and Jesús Saurina. 2012. "Credit Supply and Monetary Policy: Identifying the Bank Balance-Sheet Channel with Loan Applications." *American Economic Review* 102: 2301–2326.

Kahneman, Daniel. 2011. *Thinking, Fast and Slow*. New York, NY: Farrar, Straus, and Giroux.

Kaminsky, Graciela L., and Carmen M. Reinhart. 1999. "The Twin Crises: The Causes of Banking and Balance-of-Payments Problems." *American Economic Review* 89: 473–500.

Kaminsky, Graciela L., Carmen M. Reinhart, and Carlos A. Vegh. 2003. "The Unholy Trinity of Financial Contagion." *Journal of Economic Perspectives* 17: 51–74.

Kandil, Magda. 2010. "Demand Shocks and the Cyclical Behavior of the Real Wage: Some International Evidence." *Journal of Applied Economics* 13: 135–158.

Kashyap, Anil K., and Jeremy C. Stein. 2000. "What Do a Million Observations on Banks Say about the Transmission of Monetary Policy?" *American Economic Review* 90: 407–428.

Keating, John W., and Victor J. Valcarcel. 2012. "What's So Great about the Great Moderation? A Multi-Country Investigation of Time-Varying Volatilities of Output Growth and Inflation." University of Kansas Working Paper Series in Theoretical and Applied Economics No. 201204.

Keynes, John Maynard. 1920. *The Economic Consequences of Peace.* New York, NY: Harcourt, Brace.

Keynes, John Maynard. 1923. *A Tract on Monetary Reform.* London: Macmillan.

Keynes, John Maynard. 1931. *Essays in Persuasion.* London: Macmillan.

Keynes, John Maynard. 1936. *The General Theory of Employment, Interest, and Money.* London: Macmillan.

Kiley, Michael. 2000. "Endogenous Price Stickiness and Business Cycle Persistence." *Journal of Money, Credit, and Banking* 32: 28–53.

Kindleberger, Charles. 1978. *Mania, Panics, and Crashes: A History of Financial Crises.* New York, NY: Basic Books, Inc.

Kiyotaki, Nobuhiro, and John Moore. 1997. "Credit Cycles." *Journal of Political Economy* 105: 211–248.

Klenow, Peter J., and Benjamin A. Malin. 2010. "Microeconomic Evidence on Price-Setting." NBER Working Paper No. 15826.

Klieser, Kevin L. 2003. "The 2001 Recession: How Was It Different and What Developments May Have Caused It?" *Review, Federal Reserve Bank of St. Louis* 85: 23–37.

Knoop, Todd A. 2013. "Business Cycles and the Cyclical Behavior of Profits." Working Paper.

Kondratiev, Nikolai D. 1935. "The Long Waves in Economic Life." *Review of Economics and Statistics* 27: 105–115.

Koo, Richard C. 2011. *The Holy Grail of Macroeconomics: Lessons from Japan's Great Recession.* New York, NY: Wiley.

Krueger, Anne O. 1998. "Whither the World Bank and the IMF?" *Journal of Economic Literature* 36: 1983–2020.

Krueger, Anne O. 2003. "IMF Stabilization Programs." In *Economic and Financial Crises in Emerging Market Economies*, edited by Martin Feldstein, 297–346. Chicago, IL: University of Chicago Press.

Krugman, Paul. 1995. *Currencies and Crises*. Cambridge, MA: The MIT Press.

Krugman, Paul. 2008. *The Return of Depression Economics and the Crisis of 2008*. New York, NY: W.W. Norton.

Kuttner, Kenneth N., and Adam S. Posen. 2001. "The Great Recession: Lessons for Macroeconomic Policy from Japan." *Brookings Papers on Economic Activity* 2: 93–160.

Kydland, Finn E., and Edward C. Prescott. 1982. "Time to Build and Aggregate Fluctuations." *Econometrica* 50: 1345–1370.

Laeven, Luc, and Fabián Valencia. 2013. "Systematic Banking Crises Database." *IMF Economic Review* 61: 225–270.

Lane, Philip R. 2012. "The European Debt Crisis." *Journal of Economic Perspectives* 26: 49–68.

Levy, Daniel, Mark Bergen, Shantanu Dutta, and Robert Venable. 1997. "The Magnitude of Menu Costs: Direct Evidence from Large U.S. Supermarket Chains." *Quarterly Journal of Economics* 112: 791–825.

Lewis, Michael. 2012. *Boomerang: Travels in the New Third World*. New York, NY: W.W. Norton.

Liu, Zheng, and Pengfei Wang. 2014. "Credit Constraints and Self-Fulfilling Business Cycles." *American Economic Journal: Macroeconomics* 6: 32–69.

Long, John B. Jr., and Charles I. Plosser. 1983. "Real Business Cycles." *Journal of Political Economy* 91: 39–69.

Lowenstein, Roger. 2000. *When Genius Failed: The Rise and Fall of Long-Term Capital Management*. New York, NY: Random House.

Lown, Cara, and Donald P. Morgan. 2006. "The Credit Cycle and the Business Cycle: New Findings Using the Loan Officer Opinion Survey." *Journal of Money, Credit, and Banking* 38: 1575–1597.

Lucas, Robert E. 1972. "Expectations and the Neutrality of Money." *Journal of Economic Theory* 4: 103–124.

Lucas, Robert E. 1973. "Some International Evidence on Output–Inflation Tradeoffs." *American Economic Review* 63: 326–334.

Lucas, Robert E. 1978. "Unemployment Policy." *American Economic Review: Papers and Proceedings* 68: 353–357.

Lucas, Robert E. 1980. "Rules, Discretion, and the Role of the Economic Advisor." In *Rational Expectations and Economic Policy*, edited by Stanley Fischer. Chicago, IL: University of Chicago Press.

Lucas, Robert E., and Thomas J. Sargent. 1978. "After Keynesian Economics." In *After the Phillips Curve: Persistence of High Inflation and High Unemployment.* Boston, MA: Federal Reserve Bank of Boston.

Lugauer, Steven. 2012. "Demographic Change and the Great Moderation in an Overlapping Generations Model with Matching Frictions." *Macroeconomic Dynamics* 16: 706–731.

Maddock, Rodney, and Michael Carter. 1982. "A Child's Guide to Rational Expectations." *Journal of Economic Literature* 20: 39–51.

Malthus, Thomas R. 1798. *An Essay on the Principle of Population.* London: W. Pickering.

Mankiw, N. Gregory. 1985. "Small Menu Costs and Large Business Cycles." *Quarterly Journal of Economics* 100: 529–537.

Mankiw, N. Gregory. 1989. "Real Business Cycles: A New Keynesian Perspective." *Journal of Economic Perspectives* 3: 79–90.

Mankiw, N. Gregory. 1990. "A Quick Refresher Course in Macroeconomics." *Journal of Economic Literature* 28: 1645–1660.

Mankiw, N. Gregory. 1992. "The Reincarnation of Keynesian Economics." *European Economic Review* 36: 559–565.

Mankiw, N. Gregory, and Ricardo Reis. 2002. "Sticky Information versus Sticky Prices: A Proposal to Replace the New Keynesian Phillips Curve." *Quarterly Journal of Economics* 117: 1295–1328.

Mankiw, N. Gregory, Ricardo Reis, and Justin Wolfers. 2004. "Disagreement about Inflation Expectations." *NBER Macroeconomics Annual* 18: 209–258.

Mann, Horace. 1855. *Lectures on Education.* Boston, MA: Ide & Duncan.

Mayer, Thomas. 1975. "The Structure of Monetarism." *Kredit and Kapital* 8: 292–313.

McKinsey Global Institute. 2001. "U.S. Productivity Growth 1995–2000." *McKinsey Global Institute,* October.

McNees, Steven K. 1990. "The Role of Judgment in Macroeconomic Forecasting Accuracy." *International Journal of Forecasting* 6: 287–299.

Meltzer, Alan H. 2010. *A History of the Federal Reserve, Volume 2, Book 2, 1970–1986.* Chicago, IL: University of Chicago Press.

Mertens, Karel, and Morten Overgaard Ravn. 2011. "Understand the Aggregate Effects of Anticipated and Unanticipated Tax Policy Shocks." *Journal of Economic Dynamics* 14: 27–54.

Messina, Julian, Chiara Strozzi, and Jarkko Turunen. 2009. "Real Wages over the Business Cycle: OECD Evidence from the Time and Frequency Domains." *Journal of Economic Dynamics and Control* 33: 1183–1200.

Minsky, Hyman P. 1982. *Can "It" Happen Again? Essays on Instability and Finance.* Armonk, NY: M.E. Sharpe.

Mitchell, Wesley. 1927. *Business Cycles: The Problem and Its Setting.* New York, NY: National Bureau of Economic Research.

Muth, John. 1961. "Rational Expectations and the Theory of Price Movements." *Econometrica* 29: 37–43.

Nakov, Anton, and Andrea Pescatori. 2010. "Oil and the Great Moderation." *Economic Journal* 120: 131–156.

Nasar, Sylvia. 2011. *Grand Pursuit: The Story of Economic Genius.* New York, NY: Simon & Schuster.

Nilsen, Jeffrey H. 2002. "Trade Credit and the Bank Lending Channel." *Journal of Money, Credit, and Banking* 34: 226–253.

Oliner, Stephen D., and Daniel E. Sichel. 2000. "The Resurgence of Growth in the Late 1990s: Is Information Technology the Story?" *Journal of Economic Perspectives* 14: 3–22.

Oray, Paul. 2008. "The Making of an Investment Banker: Stock Market Shocks, Career Choice, and Lifetime Income." *The Journal of Finance* 63: 2601–2628.

Peregrine. 1997. "Peregrine Sees Asian Ex-Japanese Bad Debts at $500B." *Bloomberg*, November 11–12.

Perez, Stephen J. 1998. "Testing for Credit Rationing: An Application of Disequilibrium Econometrics." *Journal of Macroeconomics* 20: 721–739.

Phillips, Arthur W. 1958. "The Relation between Unemployment and the Rate of Change in Money Wage Rates in the United Kingdom, 1862–1957." *Economica* 25: 283–299.

Pinto, Edward J. 2011. "Government Housing Policies in the Lead-up to the Financial Crisis." Accessed April 3, 2014. http://www.aei.org/papers/economics/financial-services/housing-finance/government-housing-policies-in-the-lead-up-to-the-financial-crisis-a-forensic-study/.

Plosser, Charles. 1989. "Understanding Real Business Cycles." *Journal of Economic Perspectives* 3: 51–78.

Pomerleano, Michael. 1998. "The East Asian Crisis and Corporate Finances: The Untold Micro Story." World Bank Policy Research Working Paper #1990.

Rebelo, Sergio. 2005. "Real Business Cycle Models: Past, Present, and Future." *Scandinavian Journal of Economics* 107: 217–238.

Reinhart, Carmen M., and Kenneth S. Rogoff. 2009. *This Time Is Different: Eight Centuries of Financial Folly.* Princeton, NJ: Princeton University Press.

Reinhart, Carmen M., and Kenneth S. Rogoff. 2011. "From Financial Crash to Debt Crisis." *American Economic Review* 101: 1676–1706.

Romer, Christina D. 1993. "The Nation in Depression." *Journal of Economic Perspectives* 7: 19–39.

Romer, Christina D. 1999. "Changes in Business Cycles: Evidence and Explanations." *Journal of Economic Perspectives* 13: 23–44.

Romer, Christina D., and David H. Romer. 1994. "What Ends Recessions?" *NBER Macroeconomics Annual* 9: 13–57.

Rosen, Sherwin. 1997. "Austrian and Neoclassical Economics: Any Gains from Trade?" *Journal of Economic Perspectives* 11: 139–152.

Rotemberg, Julio J., and Michael Woodford. 1996. "Real-Business-Cycle Models and the Forecastable Movements in Output, Hours, and Consumption." *American Economic Review* 86: 71–89.

Samuleson, Paul. 1964. "The General Theory: 1946." In *Keynes' General Theory: Reports of Three Decades*, edited by Robert Lekachman. New York, NY: St. Martin's Press.

Sargent, Thomas. 1986. "The End of Four Big Inflations." In *Rational Expectations and Inflation*, edited by Thomas Sargent. New York, NY: Harper Collins.

Sargent, Thomas. 2013. *Rational Expectations and Inflation*. Third edition. Princeton, NJ: Princeton University Press.

Schrimpf, Andreas, and Qingwei Wang. 2010. "A Reappraisal of the Leading Indicator Properties of the Yield Curve under Structural Instability." *International Journal of Forecasting* 26: 836–857.

Schumpeter, Joseph. 1939. *Business Cycles*. New York, NY: McGraw Hill Book Co.

Schumpeter, Joseph. 1942 [2008]. *Capitalism, Socialism, and Democracy*. London: Routledge.

Silver, Nate. 2012. *The Signal and the Noise: Why So Many Predictions Fail—but Some Don't*. New York, NY: The Penguin Press.

Skidelsky, Robert. 2010. *Keynes: The Return of the Master*. New York, NY: Public Affairs.

Smith, Adam. 1776 [1981]. *An Inquiry into the Nature and the Causes of the Wealth of Nations*. Indianapolis, IN: Liberty Press.

Snowberg, Erik, Justin Wolfers, and Eric Zitzewitz. 2012. "Prediction Markets for Economic Forecasting." CESinfo Working Paper No. 3884.

Solow, Robert. 1956. "A Contribution to the Theory of Economic Growth." *Quarterly Journal of Economics* 70: 65–94.

Solow, Robert. 1957. "Technical Change and the Aggregate Production Function." *Review of Economics and Statistics* 39: 312–320.

Stanca, Luca Matteo. 2002. *The Role of Financial Markets in Generating Business Cycles*. Lewiston, NY: The Edwin Mellen Press.

Stiglitz, Joseph E. 1990. "Symposium on Bubbles." *Journal of Economic Perspectives* 4: 13–18.

Stiglitz, Joseph E. 1997. "Reflections on the Natural Rate Hypothesis." *Journal of Economic Perspectives* 11: 3–10.

Stiglitz, Joseph E. 2002. *Globalization and Its Discontents*. New York, NY: W.W. Norton.

Stiglitz, Joseph E., and Andrew Weiss. 1981. "Credit Rationing in Markets with Imperfect Information." *American Economic Review* 71: 333–421.

Stock, James H., and Mark W. Watson. 2003. "Has the Business Cycle Changed and Why?" *NBER Macroeconomics Annual 2002* 17: 159–230.

Summers, Lawrence. 1989. "The Ishihara-Morita Brouhaha." *International Economy* 52: 1–15.

Summers, Peter M. 2005. "What Caused the Great Moderation? Some Cross-Country Evidence." *Economic Review* 90: 5–32.

Sumner, Scott, and Stephen Silver. 1989. "Real Wages, Employment, and the Phillips Curve." *Journal of Political Economy* 97: 706–720.

Temin, Peter. 1989. *Lessons from the Great Depression*. Cambridge, MA: The MIT Press.

Temin, Peter. 1993. "Transmission of the Great Depression." *Journal of Economic Perspectives* 7: 87—102.

Tobin, James. 1993. "Price Flexibility and Output Stability: An Old Keynesian View." *Journal of Economic Perspectives* 7: 45–65.

Uribe, Martín. 2013. "Open Economy Macroeconomics." Accessed March 17, 2014. http://www.columbia.edu/~mu2166/book/oem.pdf.

Wicksell, Knut. 1936. *Interest and Prices: A Study of the Causes Regulating the Value of Money*. London: Macmillan.

Williamson, John, and Molly Mahar. 1998. "A Survey of Financial Liberalization." Princeton Essays in International Finance No. 211.

Woitek, Ulrich. 2004. "Real Wages and Business Cycle Asymmetries." CESifo Working Paper No. 1206.

Woodford, Michael. 2007. "Forecast Targeting as a Monetary Policy Strategy: Policy Rules in Practice." NBER Working Paper No. 13716.

Yaeger, Leland B. 1997. "Austrian Economics, Neoclassicism, and the Market Test." *Journal of Economic Perspectives* 11: 153–165.

Index

About the Author

Todd A. Knoop is the David Joyce Professor of Economics and Business at Cornell College in Mount Vernon, Iowa. He is the author of multiple articles as well as the books *Global Finance in Emerging Market Economies* and *Modern Financial Macroeconomics: Panics, Crashes and Crises.*